SECRET INCOMES OF THE SOVIET STATE BUDGET

Secret Incomes of the Soviet State Budget

IGOR BIRMAN

1981

MARTINUS NIJHOFF PUBLISHERS

THE HAGUE / BOSTON / LONDON

Distributors:

for the United States and Canada

Kluwer Boston, Inc.
190 Old Derby Street
Hingham, MA 02043
USA

for all other countries

Kluwer Academic Publishers Group
Distribution Center
P.O. Box 322
3300 AH Dordrecht
The Netherlands

Library of Congress Catalog Card Number: 81-50369

ISBN 978-94-011-8642-1 ISBN 978-94-011-9427-3 (eBook)
DOI 10.1007/978-94-011-9427-3

In Memory of
Rush V. Greenslade

Table of Contents

Preface

As far as I know, relatively little attention has been devoted in the West to the study of various financial problems in the USSR. Among the works I have seen are Gallik et al., *The Soviet*, 1968[1]—evidently the most important work on this theme; Powell, "Monetary," 1972, in which the statistics of monetary circulation in the USSR are examined; Laulan, *Banking*, 1973, in which some of the questions I examine are also addressed; and CIA, *The Soviet*, 1977, which is about an analysis of the budget. Moreover, many specialists have turned to the analysis of the expenditures of the budget in an attempt to determine the amount of financing of military expenditures—for example, Holzman, *Financial*, 1975.

Due to the scarcity of data a large number of important problems have remained unstudied in all these works. One of these is the following. If we believe official Soviet statistics, the state budget of the USSR regularly comes out with an excess of revenues over expenditures; each year a "budget profit" is formed. This in itself already seems quite strange. We all know that the Soviet economy, although it developed quite rapidly (especially in the past), has experienced constant and serious difficulties; we know that the plans are rarely fulfilled and that there were years of great crop failures. In spite of all these things, we are assured that with the exception of only three years (that is, not even every year during World War II) the Soviet budget has not had a deficit.

Also directly connected with this is a mystery to which attention was turned long ago in the West. In the attempt to figure out the sources of all budget revenues, a considerable and ever increasing gap comes to light, and it is simply impossible to explain it.[2]

In the summer of 1976 I advanced the hypothesis that a part of this gap is covered by the emission of cash, and then together with Rush V. Greenslade we suggested the existence of emission, so to speak, into noncash money circulation *(beznalichnoye denezhnoye obrashcheniye)*. This led to an effort to determine how much emission in both the cash and noncash spheres of circulation can be considered "normal" for the Soviet economy and to identify all other revenues which might account for this gap. This book is an attempt to prove that the Soviet budget is in fact of a deficit nature and the regular "budget profits" are just a financial-statistical trick. Moreover, I do not limit my task only to proving this fact, but I also attempt to make the appropriate calculations in order to quantitatively evaluate this phenomenon.

The study of this problem is closely connected with a number of other very important questions which have also, in my opinion, been inadequately studied. Among them are: the budget revenues from foreign trade, the monetary savings of the population (and in connection with this the balance of the monetary income and expenditures of the population) and bank credits to enterprises and organizations. These questions are examined here most of all in connection with the main subject, but at the same time an attempt is made to show their importance for the overall financial and, consequently, economic situation in the country.

What is the logic of this research and the presentation of its results in the book which is in front of you?

In chapter I, regularly published data about the annual amounts of budget revenues and various items on the income side of the budget are considered. A large and rapidly growing gap between the total figure and the sum of separate items is demonstrated here. Thus, the chapter raises the question which is in fact the central topic of the book.

Further, in the following chapters, I try to consider all revenues of the budget, attempting to do so as scrupulously as I can, and make all the necessary computations.

The analysis begins in chapter II, where the official classification of revenues of the budget is presented. Such a classification has never been published in the Soviet literature and I had to collect bits of relevant information from numerous sources.

On the basis of this classification all the revenues are considered item by item in chapter III. I try here to establish which particular revenues are included in the published data and which are not and to determine the concrete amounts of the revenues. As a result we are able to reduce the gap, mainly by taking into consideration some revenues of republic budgets.

However, for some items of the classification this is not possible—those particular revenues are rather, or even very, ambiguous. Chapter IV is devoted to just these revenues, especially those from foreign trade. All hypothetical revenues of the budget are also considered here. Lacking reliable data, I make some estimates in this chapter, and once again, we are able to reduce the gap substantially.

The "profit" of the budget was already mentioned above. I consider this phenomenon in chapter V and conclude that the profits are left-overs of money appropriated but not completely spent during the budget year. It is important that the existence of these "profits" does not explain the rest of the gap and, on the other hand, does not contradict the fact of the deficit nature of the budget.

In chapter VI, using data from appendix B and some other appendices, I consider the balance of monetary incomes and expenditures of the population and conclude (in spite of some evidence to the contrary) that the incomes are annually higher than the expenditures. I make some, of necessity, rough estimates and demonstrate that these amounts (with some adjustments) are covered partially by emission of money into cash circulation. Thus, the gap is reduced again, but not eliminated.

Chapter VII analyzes the astronomically rapid growth of the savings of the population. Strictly speaking this chapter does not belong directly to our topic, but the very fact that the Soviet population has accumulated such savings is extremely interesting and in my deep conviction this has many, and very important, economic and political consequences.

Chapter VIII is about noncash circulation, including bank credits to enterprises and organizations. It is shown here that budget funding and bank credits are interconnected and in many cases substitute for each other.

Sources of bank credits are considered in chapter IX. The main conclusion is that, quite on the contrary to Soviet theory, the total amount of bank credits in the country is not limited and is not in reality coordinated with the corresponding material and labor resources. In other words, even given the limitations of the Soviet theoretical conception of credit resources, the Soviets could extend more bank credits than published data show.

In chapter X, on the basis of the entire foregoing analysis I reach the conclusion about the constant deficit of the Soviet State budget. This means that expenditures of the budget are covered by (in addition to real revenues) emitting cash into circulation and by something like emission in noncash circulation. The latter is most likely technically done as bank credits to the budget, which are never paid back. I also analyze here various consequences of the budget deficit.

In the conclusion some unanswered questions are listed, and I consider the very complicated one of how the result of this research may affect computations of the well-known model of Soviet GNP accounts.

Several appendices to the book provide various statistical calculations needed for the analysis of topics treated in the book.

In my opinion the most important results of this work are the following:

(a) On the basis of a detailed analysis a certain clarity is brought to the published data on the budget revenues. I show that it is possible to trust the published figures on the revenues from the public, the turnover tax, the payments out of profits, and so on. An analysis of other revenues of the budget is made, and in many instances sources characterizing their amount either are found or they are estimated;

(b) In particular, I analyse the revenues from foreign trade, a question which has not been previously studied, and estimate their magnitude. Of principal importance is the conclusion about the extreme significance of the revenues from foreign trade for covering budget expenditures, which should be taken into account in various trade negotiations with the USSR;

(c) The monetary income and expenditures of the public are analyzed. Unfortunately, I cannot consider my estimate of the monetary income of the public completely satisfactory, and therefore I advance hypotheses on the possible errors. As to the estimates of the monetary expenditure of the public obtained, I think that these indicators on the whole can be trusted;

(d) The important conclusion is reached that one of the constant sources of budget revenues is the continuous emission of cash. This fact can be considered proven beyond a doubt; as to the estimates of the extent of this phenomenon, they are perhaps slightly in error;

(e) The monetary savings of the public are analyzed and, in particular, an estimate of the magnitude of the accumulations of cash is given. An attempt is made to show that the extremely rapid increase and the achieved level of monetary savings of the public (at savings banks, in cash and so on) are one of the most serious and difficult problems of the Soviet rulers. It is my firm conviction that the significance of this problem is incomparably more serious than, for example, the problem of oil production;

(f) It can be considered proven that the Soviet budget has a rapidly increasing deficit, which is covered not only by the emission of cash but also by something like loans to the budget from the bank. The indicators I derive of the amounts of the deficit, to all appearances, reflect their minimum magnitude;

(g) The data on credits to enterprises and organizations are analyzed and it is shown that the substantially faster growth of credits, together with the budget deficit, over production has led to something like inflation in the noncash sphere of circulation;

(*h*) Together, these facts make it possible to describe the entire financial situation of the country as a crisis. On the one hand, the financial crisis reflects the fundamental, structural failures of the Soviet economic system. On the other hand, the financial crisis is intensifying the overall crisis of the Soviet economy;
(*i*) Of great importance, in my opinion, is the following hypothesis. In the attempts made to date to determine the true magnitude of Soviet military expenditures, the expenditures of the budget have been carefully analyzed, but at the same time serious difficulties have arisen due to the fact that there was not sufficient "room" in the budget for large military expenditures. It seems to me that the proven fact of the deficit nature of the budget makes it possible to assume that substantial amounts are being spent for military purposes in excess of the overall amounts of the budget. This financing can be carried out at the expense of an even greater budget deficit and/or at the expense of additional bank credits[3].

This book is completely based on the Soviet literature. Using these sources I managed to reveal what may be the most guarded secret of Soviet economics. The code of Bolshevik morals requires one to be modest, and having been a member of the Party, I try my best to be as modest as possible. So, modestly, very modestly, I hope the book is of methodological interest. Indeed, the secret is revealed, I repeat, on the basis of Soviet literature. Thus, the book is one more example of what can be extracted from the Soviet literature and how.

The reader will see that I refer to my personal experience very rarely and only in not very significant cases. I don't expose any secrets which were trusted to me and which I brought to the West in hidden places of my memory. It happens that the topic of this book is rather distant from what I was doing in the USSR as an economist. So, on the one hand, this work could have been done by anybody else who knows Russian and who understands Soviet economic theory. But, on the other hand, I must say that all notorious Soviet economic secrets are first of all secrets from the Soviet people.

This book turned out to be difficult reading; at least such is the opinion of some readers of the manuscript. The basic results of the research are formulated above[4] and the rest of the text is for those who wish to go through this labyrinth together with me, stumbling and clambering, trying numerous parallel paths, including cul-de-sacs. I hope that for the specialist, to whom the book is addressed, all these details, unhappy attempts, doubts, and questions which I haven't managed to answer are even more valuable than the final results. And if this is so, you are welcome to join our voyage.

My work on this topic was begun and then continued at the initiative of R. Greenslade and G. Schroeder. I received some extremely valuable advice and comments from the former, who died in the spring of 1978, and I am dedicating the book to his memory.

The research for this book was done for the Foreign Demographic Analysis Division of the U.S. Department of Commerce, where I worked as a consultant from 1976–78. In carrying out my research, I discussed various questions with M. Feshbach, Dm. Gallik, B. Kostinsky, L. Kurtzweg and S. Rapawy.

The initial translation from Russian was done by S. Cadmus. The manuscript was read and commented on by L. Aliyevskaya, T. Brewster, E. Domar, B. Rumer, V. Shlapentokh, V. Treml, and by A. Tretyakova; the latter also helped me greatly in the preparation of the book for publication. My very special thanks to J. Gillula who edited the translation from Russian, found and corrected many errors, made excellent suggestions, and helped prepare the manuscript for publication.

I am also very grateful to Yu. Luryi who brought me into contact with Sijthoff and Noordhoff and, of course, to my editor Robert Lyng.

I should say that never in my not so short life have I done such a difficult job. On the one hand, the topic itself is extremely complicated and it was easier to advance ideas and hypothesis than to document them or, especially, make concrete calculations: there are 579 footnotes and 56 tables in the book; the bibliography lists more than 200 sources actually quoted in the text. On the other hand, after the initial research for the U.S. Department of Commerce was done, no organization or fund supported me financially. Almost nobody supported me in finishing the research and publishing its results (including most of those listed above who had read the manuscript). I had to overcome enormous difficulties in the community of American sovietologists. I heard that I am wrong, that my calculations go too far, that my style is too personal, that I too often ignore modern theory, that I should not be surprised if I receive severe criticism or . . . silence. Still I take full responsibility for both the errors which may still remain in the text and for my opinions, judgements and conclusions. And I will be really very grateful for fair, constructive criticism.

All the indicators in the book for years prior to the 1961 change in the scale of prices are given in post-1961 rubles.

My comments in the text of quotations are inserted in brackets.

December 1980
Silver Spring,
Maryland, USA

Notes

1. Here and in the rest of this book references to the literature are made in the following way. All works are cited by short titles, and there is a complete bibliography at the end of the book. For the sake of simplicity, two frequently used series of handbooks are referred to as follows: The handbook—Tsentral'noye statisticheskoye upravleniye SSSR, *Narodnoye khozyaystvo SSSR v* 1978 g., Statisticheskyy yezhegodnik, Moscow, "Statiska," 1979—is cited as *Narkhoz 78* and all other yearbooks in the series are referred to accordingly. Similarly, the handbook—Ministerstvo Finansov SSSR, *Gosudarstvennyy byudzhet SSSR i byudzhety soyuznykh respublik*, 1971–75, Statisticheskyy sbornik, Moscow, "Finansy," 1976—is referred to as *Byudzhet 76*, and all other budget handbooks are cited accordingly.

2. My attention was attracted to this gap by the work CIA, *USSR*, 1975, in which its existence was mentioned and several explanations were offered. Thus, the authors of this work stimulated my research (though unwittingly), and I cannot but be grateful to them for this.

3. I am now finishing a book on Soviet military expenditures where this hypothesis is examined. See also my article "The Way to Slow the Arms Race", the Washington Post, 27 October 1980, p. A-15.

4. An extended variant of the description of the basic results is published in *Soviet Studies*, Volume XXII, No. 1, January of 1980. See also a reply to the article and my answer to the reply in *Soviet Studies*, Volume XXII, No. 4, October 1980.

Some other publications by me on the topic are: "Dokatilis", *Novoye Russkoye Slovo*, New York, 6 and 7 December 1979; "Ugroza", *Vremya i my*, Jerusalem, No. 53, 1980 and "Ekonomicheskiy Detektiv", *Kontinent*, Paris, No. 22, 1980 (translation in German published in: *Kontinent Magazin*, Forum für Ost-West-Fragen, No. 15, October 1980).

Some theoretical issues of the topic are considered in "Too much Money—Soviet Variant of the Problem"—my paper to the Second World Congress on Soviet and East European Studies, Garmish, Germany, October 1980.

Chapter I

Secret Revenues of the Budget

Let us examine the revenues of the budget in the form in which the budget is accessible to the broad public, including us. In table I-1, I reproduce the data for 1970 and 1975 as they are published in the *Narkhoz* yearbooks. Previously the yearbooks published these data somewhat differently, but basically this form has remained unchanged for decades. In table I-2 data are cited for the same years in the form in which they are published in the *Byudzhet* handbooks.[1] This table is slightly more detailed, but only slightly: it does not give a breakdown of all the revenues.

Table I-1. Budget Revenues According to the *Narkhoz* Yearbooks
(in billions of rubles)

	1970	1975
Total revenues	156.7	218.8
Including		
Turnover tax	49.4	66.6
Payments of state enterprises and organizations from profits	54.2	69.7
Of them:		
Fee for fixed productive capital and for normed working capital	13.7	22.6
Payments of the free remainder of profits	24.8	33.0
Fixed (rent) payments	2.5	2.4
Deductions from profits and other payments	13.2	11.7
Income tax from cooperatives, kolkhozes and enterprises of public organizations	1.2	1.5
State loans	0.5	0.6
State taxes from the population	12.7	18.4
State social insurance funds	8.3	11.3
Amount of total revenues received from state and cooperative enterprises and organizations	142.9	199.1

Source: *Narkhoz 75*, p. 742.

Table I-2. Budget Revenues According to *Byudzhet* Handbooks (in millions of rubles)

	1970	1975
Total	156,702.7	218,768.9
Including		
I. Receipts from the socialist economy	142,858.7	199,088.5
Of them:		
1. Turnover tax	49,379.8	66,606.9
2. Payments of state enterprises and organizations from profits	54,156.8	69,712.8
a) by sectors of the national economy:		
industry and construction[1]	37,502.6	46,297.3
agriculture	2,328.6	2,491.1
transportation	6,988.3	9,595.0
communications	594.5	876.3
housing and municipal services	1,568.6	2,524.8
trade	1,348.2	1,934.1
b) by types of payments		
fee for fixed productive capital and for normed working capital	13,659.7	22,542.4
payments of amounts of free remainder of profits	24,777.6	33,023.6
fixed payments	2,534.8	2,438.5
deductions from profits and other payments	13,184.7	11,708.3
3. Income tax from cooperative and public enterprises and organizations	1,234.4	1,464.9
Including:		
from kolkhozes	665.7	704.0
from cooperative enterprises and organizations and enterprises of public organizations	568.7	760.9
4. State social insurance revenue	8,203.4[2]	11,064.2[3]
5. Forestry revenue	492.4	509.1
II. Receipts from the population	13,844.0	19,680.4
Of them:		
1. State taxes from the population	12,736.8	18,357.6
Including:		
personal income tax from the population	11,606.7	16,993.5
agricultural tax	326.9	286.2
tax on unmarried citizens and small family tax	803.2	1,077.9
2. Receipts from the sale of the state 3-percent loan	470.2	561.5
3. Lottery revenue	253.8	258.7

Source: *Byudzhet 76*, pp. 8–9.

1. For incomprehensible reasons (perhaps a misprint) in *Byudzhet 72*, pp. 11 and 13, this line is called simply "industry."

2. According to *Narkhoz 76*, p. 652, these expenditures are 8.3 billion rubles.

3. According to *Narkhoz 76*, p. 652—11.3 billion rubles.

As we see already from table I-1 (though only in table I-2 is this distinction made consistently) all the budget revenues are broken down into two groups—the revenues from the socialist economy (*sotsialisticheskoye khozyaystvo*), i.e. from state and cooperative enterprises and organizations, and the revenues from the population. These very names deserve criticism, but this is not our business.[2] In sum, these two types of revenues give the total amount of the budget revenues; that is, apart from them there are no other revenues.[3] At any rate the Soviet literature has never mentioned anything about any other revenues.

The breakdowns for each of these two groups reveal incomprehensible gaps. As to the revenues from the population, table I-2 cites, in addition to the data in table I-1, the revenues from cash-commodity lotteries. But here, taking into account all the revenues from the population indicated (the income tax, the agricultural tax, bachelors and small families tax, receipts from loans and lotteries), a gap of 383.2 million rubles remains in the total amount for 1970 and 508.6 million rubles for 1975. What is behind this gap? If all the riddles of Soviet statistics were so "difficult," sovietologists would soon have nothing to do. It is not even the point that the amounts of this gap are quite small as compared with the total amount of budget revenues. As we will see in chapter III, this gap is quite easily explained, and perhaps the most mysterious thing about it is the fact that these amounts are not published.

In table I-3, I calculate the gap for the revenues of the population. This table was compiled in part to assemble some data we will need later on. In column 8, for comparison, I present data on loans to the budget from savings banks—a practice which existed until 1963 and is quite interesting methodologically. We will return to this question in chapter VI. Right here I should say that the very definition of these loans as revenues "from the population" is at least debatable.

In spite of the apparent simplicity of assembling table I-3, I should say that there are difficulties here. First of all, due to rounding, some data for 1970 and 1975 do not agree either with table I-2 or with some of the indicators which are calculated below in table I-4. This, of course, is a trivial point.

It is considerably more significant, at least methodologically, that in the sources used some very strange inconsistencies of totals are found. And not only do gaps arise, which can be understood, but often, on the contrary, the sum of the parts exceeds the value of the total. Since I cannot explain this phenomenon, I am forced to leave it to future researchers.[4]

However, in spite of these oddities, on the whole the indicators

Table I-3. Gaps in the Budget Revenues from the Population
(in billions of rubles)

Year	Total revenues from the population	Including					Difference (gap)	For comparison—loans from savings banks
		Taxes	Loans	Lotteries	Payments for education	Total		
	1	2	3	4	5	6	7	8
1940	2.0	0.9	1.1	—	—	2.0	0	0.02
1950	6.9	3.6	3.1	—	0.05	6.7	0.2	0.3
1951	8.2	4.3	3.7	—	0.1	8.1	0.1	0.3
1952	9.3	4.7	4.2	—	0.1	9.0	0.3	0.4
1953	8.0	4.6	3.0	—	0.1	7.7	0.3	1.2
1954	7.5	4.5	2.7	—	0.1	7.3	0.2	1.0
1955	8.8	4.8	3.7	—	0.1	8.6	0.2	0.5
1956	9.8	5.1	4.4	—		9.5	0.3	1.0
1957	9.0	5.2	3.5	—		8.7	0.3	1.7
1958	6.8	5.2	1.1	0.3		6.6	0.2	0.7
1959	7.4	5.5	1.5	0.1		7.1	0.3	1.3
1960	6.9	5.6	0.9	0.1		6.6	0.3	0.9
1961	7.1	5.8	0.8	0.1		6.7	0.4	0.8
1962	7.6	6.0	1.2	0.1		7.3	0.3	1.1
1963	8.1	6.3	1.3	0.1		7.7	0.4	1.2
1964	7.4	6.8	0.1	0.2		7.1	0.3	—
1965	8.4	7.7	0.2	0.2		8.1	0.3	—
1966	9.3	8.4	0.2	0.2		8.8	0.5	—
1967	10.1	9.3	0.1	0.2		9.6	0.5	—
1968	11.4	10.5	0.3	0.2		11.0	0.4	—
1969	12.6	11.6	0.4	0.2		12.2	0.4	—

Table I-3 continued

1970	13.8	12.7	0.5	0.3		13.5	0.3	—
1971	14.7	13.7	0.3	0.2		14.2	0.5	—
1972	15.8	14.8	0.3	0.3		15.4	0.4	—
1973	16.9	15.8	0.4	0.3		16.5	0.4	—
1974	18.3	17.1	0.4	0.3		17.8	0.5	—
1975	19.7	18.4	0.6	0.3		19.3	0.4	—
1976	20.9	19.6	0.6	0.3		20.5	0.4	—
1977	22.1	20.8	0.6	0.3		21.7	0.4	—
1978	23.5	22.1	0.6	0.3		23.0	0.5	—

Sources: Columns 1–5, 8:
1976–78 (columns 1–3)—*Narkhoz 78,* p. 533
(column 4)—extrapolation
1970–75—*Byudzhet 76,* p. 9
1965–69—*Byudzhet 72,* p. 12
1950, 1955, 1960–64—*Byudzhet 66,* p. 11
(column 5—*Byudzhet 57,* p. 15)
1940, 1956–59—*Byudzhet 62,* pp. 8–9
1951–54 (column 1)—calculated according to table I-4
(columns 2–3)—*Byudzhet 57,* p. 5
(column 5)—*Byudzhet 57,* p. 15

Column 6:
total of columns 2–5
Column 7:
column 1 less column 6
Column 8:
1940, 1950—*Byudzhet 62,* p. 9
the rest—table VII-1, column 4.

calculated in column 7 of table I-3 should be trusted; the accuracy of our calculations is confirmed, if only by the fact that these indicators do not jump.[5]

The situation with revenues from the "socialist economy" is incomparably worse. In table I-2 the amounts of this gap are somewhat less than in table I-1 because of the forestry revenue. However, even taking into account the forestry revenue, we find that the overall gap for the "socialist economy" was 29.4 billion rubles for 1970, while for 1975 it was 49.7 billion rubles.[6] These are colossal amounts.

For the other totals in table I-2 there is only one other gap. If we add up the payments of state enterprises and organizations from profits for the sectors of the national economy shown here, a gap is found in the amount of 3.8 and 6 billion rubles respectively for 1970 and 1975.[7] We will deal with this gap in chapter III.

It is also worthwhile to say a few words on the breakdown in table I-2 of the payments from profits of state enterprises and organizations "by types of payments." Here there is no obvious gap, but there is an implicit one. The point is that the last line in this breakdown is called "deductions from profits and other payments," and the obvious question arises—what are these "other payments"? Examining this question especially in chapter III, we will see that "other payments from profits" in fact have nothing to do with profits.

Returning to the gap revealed in table I-2 in the total amount of the revenues from the socialist economy, I should immediately say that some quite small portion of it is quite easily explained, and we will determine it in subsequent chapters. However, the remaining bulk of this gap does not yield to such an easy explanation and, all the more so, to calculations of its components. We have already obtained a rough idea of the magnitude of this gap when examining tables I-1 and I-2. Table I-4 shows the movement of the amounts of this gap in the past 40 years. Here I indicate first the total amount of revenues of the budget and the amount of revenues from the socialist economy,[8] and then the amount of those revenues for which data are regularly published. I call this amount the "conglomerate" and include in it the turnover tax, deductions from profits, the income tax from kolkhozes, cooperative and public organizations, as well as the deductions for social insurance. For several years the so-called tax on noncommodity operations is also included in this amount.

Moreover, using available sources (primarily the *Byudzhet* handbooks) three additional types of revenues are quite easily explained: the revenues from machine and tractor stations,[9] forestry revenue and the revenues of local soviets from the leasing of buildings. There are no other reasons to include them in our calculations for table I-4 except for the fact that the data on them are easily found for all years. Other budget revenues of approximately the same nature will be examined and taken into account in our calculations in chapter III.

Thus, in column 8 of table I-4 we have obtained a more or less rough estimate of the magnitude of the gap. We see that the total amount of the gap is increasing rapidly, although it is interrupted at times by slowdowns (the last time was in 1966), and in spite of great fluctuations, the share of the gap in the total amount of budget revenues and in the amount of budget revenues from the socialist economy—column 9—is increasing.

Note the immenseness of these amounts. Not only has the gap already achieved a fourth of all the revenues of the budget, but if we compare the indicators of column 8 of table I-4 with those of column 1 of table I-6, we see that beginning already in 1955 this gap exceeded the amount of the official expenditures on defense, while now it exceeds it by more than four times. In other words, such a large part of budget revenues is not broken down that it is four times greater than such a major article of expenditure as defense.

This gap is the main secret of the revenue part of the USSR State budget, and this book primarily describes the results of research which, I hope, exposes this secret.

A secret is a secret, and Soviet literature not only does not expose it, but even does not mention at all the existence of this gap. In Western literature the gap was noticed,[10] but the secret was not solved. In a comparatively recent CIA publication[11] the existence of this gap is noted. This question is also briefly discussed in another recent CIA publication.[12]

Let us now examine table I-5, which characterizes another very strange and also thus far unexplained mystery—in nearly every year, except for three war years, the budget revenues exceed its expenditures; the budget always, so to speak, runs a profit. During the entire period under review the profit of the budget fluctuates over a relatively narrow range, and therefore its proportion relative to the total amount of revenues reveals an obvious downward trend with some fluctuations.

Why do I say this is a mystery? For the simple reason that this contradicts all our notions of the Soviet economy. At least the following points are significant here.

Firstly, it is unclear why this profit is necessary at all. The ruble is inconvertible and is "paper currency," i.e., it is not backed by reserves of gold,[13] so, the accumulation of this profit leads to nothing.

Secondly, it is striking that this profit always exists regardless of the real state of affairs in the Soviet economy. We could make a

Table I-4. Rough Estimate of the Gap in Budget Revenues From the Socialist Economy (in billions of rubles)

			Including					Gap	
Year	Total revenues	Of them "from socialist economy"	Conglomerate[1]	Revenue from machine-tractor stations	Forestry revenue	Rental income	Total	Absolute	Percent
	1	2	3	4	5	6	7	8	9
1940	18.0	16.0	13.9	0.2	0.1	0.1	14.3	1.7	11
1950	42.3	35.4	30.2	0.4	0.1	0.1	30.8	4.6	13
1951	47.0	38.8	32.5	0.4	0.1	0.1	33.1	5.7	15
1952	49.8	40.5	33.6	0.5	0.1	0.1	34.3	6.2	15
1953	54.0	46.0	34.7	0.5	0.1	0.1	35.4	10.6	23
1954	55.9	48.4	34.4	0.5	0.1	0.1	35.1	13.3	27
1955	56.4	47.6	38.4	0.6	0.1	0.2	39.3	8.3	17
1956	58.6[2]	48.8	40.4	1.1	0.2	0.2	41.9	6.9	14
1957	62.7	53.7	44.1	1.1	0.2	0.1	45.5	8.2	15
1958	67.2	60.4	48.9	1.0	0.2	0.1	50.2	10.2	17
1959	74.0	66.6	52.5	0.2	0.2	0.1	53.0	13.6	20
1960	77.1	70.1	55.6	—	0.2	0.1	55.9	14.2	20
1961	78.0	71.0	57.0	—	0.3	0.1	57.4	13.6	19
1962	84.3	76.7	62.6	—	0.3	0.1	63.0	13.7	18
1963	89.5	81.4	66.3	—	0.3	0.1	66.7	14.7	18
1964	94.4	87.0	71.7	—	0.3	0.1	72.1	14.9	17
1965	102.3	93.9	76.7	—	0.2	0.1	77.0	16.9	18
1966	106.3	97.0	82.2	—	0.2	0.1	82.5	14.5	15
1967	117.2	107.1	89.7	—	0.4	0.1	90.2	16.9	16
1968	130.8	119.4	97.1	—	0.5	0.1	97.7	21.7	18

Table I-4 continued

1969	140.0	127.4	101.5	—	0.5	0.1	102.1	25.3	20
1970	156.7	142.9	113.1	—	0.5	0.1	113.7	29.2	20
1971	166.0	151.2	120.3	—	0.5	0.1	120.9	30.3	20
1972	175.1	159.3	126.2	—	0.5	0.1	126.8	32.5	20
1973	187.8	170.9	130.5	—	0.5	0.1	131.1	39.8	23
1974	201.3	183.0	140.0	—	0.5	0.1	140.6	42.4	23
1975	218.8	199.1	149.1	—	0.5	0.1	149.7	49.4	25
1976	232.2	211.3	155.0	—	0.5	0.1	155.6	55.7	26
1977	247.8	225.7	167.0	—	0.5	0.1	167.6	58.1	26
1978	265.8	242.3	177.4	—	0.5	0.1	178.0	64.3	27

Sources[3]: Columns 1, 2 and 3:
1965, 1970, 1975–78—*Narkhoz 78*, p. 533
1971–74—*Narkhoz 75*, p. 742
1968–69—*Narkhoz 69*, p. 769
1966–67—*Narkhoz 67*, p. 886
1963–64—*Narkhoz 64*, p. 770
1952, 1961–62—*Narkhoz 62*, p. 635
1955–60—*Byudzhet 62*, pp. 7–8
1940, 1950, 1953—*Narkhoz 59*, p. 800
1951, 1954—*Byudzhet 57*, p. 5, (Column 2, according to the trend)

Column 4:
1940, 1955–59—*Byudzhet 62*, p. 8
1950–54—*Byudzhet 57*, p. 5

Columns 5 and 6:
1976–78—estimate according to the trend
1970–75—*Byudzhet 76*, p. 75
1965–69—*Byudzhet 72*, p. 78
1960–64—*Byudzhet 66*, p. 71
1940, 1950, 1955–59—*Byudzhet 62*, pp. 8, 69
1951–54—*Byudzhet 57*, p. 14

Column 7:
total of columns 3–6

Column 8:
column 2 less column 7

Column 9:
column 8 as a percentage of column 2.

Notes:
1. "Conglomerate" includes the turnover tax, deductions from profits, deductions for social insurance, the income tax from kolkhozes, cooperatives and enterprises of public organizations, as well as the tax on noncommodity operations.
2. According to *Narkhoz 56*, p. 279, and *Narkhoz 58*, p. 899, the total amount of revenues was 0.6 billion rubles more (see chapter IV).
3. Here and below wherever possible I prefer to give as the source the *Narkhoz* yearbooks and not the *Byudzhet* handbooks, since the former are considerably more accessible.

detailed analysis of the year-to-year values in this table with allowance made for the various facts of Soviet economic life that we know—changes in wholesale and retail prices, the growth of production, changes in the pattern of capital investments, crop failures and so forth—but even without such an analysis it is quite clear that the sort of ties which should certainly have been evident are not there. The main thing is that the profit exists always, under all circumstances. For example, as I well remember, following the crop failure of 1972, many plans, including the capital investment plans, were quickly revised. Some of the funds allocated to all ministries and departments by the plan were taken away in order to channel them into agriculture.[14] But, as table I-5 shows, in 1972 the budget profit was approximately the same as in preceding years, while in 1973 it doubled. Let us remember this fact; as will be shown in chapter V, precisely the revision of plans and the reduction of previously allocated assets, as paradoxical as this might seem, caused large budget "profits." But this becomes clear only when we understand just what these profits are.

Thirdly, a fact already mentioned above is very bewildering—only during three of the five war years was there a budget deficit. And in the worst year, 1942, the deficit was amazingly small—less than 11 percent of the total amount of revenues—while during the last two war years, when the war was still being waged on the territory of the country, when the economy had not yet been restored, when monetary circulation was so ruined that soon after the end of the war it was necessary to carry out monetary reform (chapter VI), in spite of all this both in 1944 and 1945 a budget profit was obtained. As is stated in Soviet literature,[15] the shortage of assets during the war was covered by emission and the mobilization of material resources. As to emission, this is actually so—in chapter VI it is shown that even after the war emission has been an important source of budget revenue. As to the mobilization of material resources, this is obviously not true since the shortage of resources from the very beginning of the war is a widely-known fact. Numerous Soviet authors note with pride the lack of a deficit in the budget in the last war years as evidence of some particular advantages of the Soviet financial system. This fact seems so improbable to me that I simply do not believe it—not once in recent history has a country had a nondeficit state budget during wartime.

Fourthly, the following is also curious. As we all are well aware, very rarely are the annual plan assignments actually fulfilled, and the plan assignments are practically never fulfilled in physical indicators. But the plan for the "profit" of the budget is always, and by a very large amount, over-fulfilled. It is sufficient to compare the values of the excess of budget revenues over expenditures for the plan budget with

Table I-5. Excess of Budget Revenues Over Expenditures—"Budget Profit" (in billions of rubles)

	Budget revenues	Budget expenditures	Excess of revenues over expenditures	
			Absolute	Percent
Year	1	2	3	4
1940	18.0	17.4	0.6	0.3
1941	17.7	19.1	−1.4	−7.9
1942	16.5	18.3	−1.8	−10.9
1943	20.4	21.0	−0.6	−2.9
1944	26.9	26.4	0.5	1.9
1945	30.2	29.9	0.3	0.1
1946	32.5	30.8	1.7	5.2
1947	38.6	36.2	2.4	6.2
1948	41.1	37.1	4.0	9.7
1949	43.7	41.2	2.5	5.7
1950	42.3	41.3	1.0	2.4
1951	47.0	44.3	2.7	5.7
1952	49.8	46.0	3.8	7.6
1953	54.0	51.5	2.5	4.6
1954	55.9	55.4	0.5	0.9
1955	56.4	54.0	2.4	4.3
1956	58.6	56.4	2.2	3.8
1957	62.7	60.7	2.0	3.2
1958	67.2	64.3	2.9	4.3
1959	74.0	70.4	3.6	4.9
1960	77.1	73.1	4.0	5.2
1961	78.0	76.3	1.7	2.2
1962	84.3	82.2	2.1	2.5
1963	89.5	87.0	2.5	2.8
1964	94.4	92.2	2.2	2.3
1965	102.3	101.6	0.7	0.7
1966	106.3	105.6	0.7	0.7
1967	117.2	115.2	2.0	1.7
1968	130.8	128.6	2.2	1.7
1969	140.0	138.5	1.5	1.1
1970	156.7	154.6	2.1	1.3
1971	166.0	164.2	1.8	1.1
1972	175.1	173.2	1.9	1.1
1973	187.8	184.0	3.8	2.0
1974	201.3	197.4	3.9	1.9
1975	218.8	214.5	4.3	2.0
1976	232.2	226.7	5.5	2.4
1977	247.8	242.8	5.0	2.0
1978	265.8	260.2	5.6	2.1

Sources to table I-5: Columns 1 and 2:

1940, 1965, 1970, 1975–78—*Narkhoz 78*, p. 533.
1971–74—*Narkhoz 75*, p. 742
1950, 1960, 1968–69—*Narkhoz 69*, p. 769
1966–67—*Narkhoz 67*, p. 886
1958, 1963–64—*Narkhoz 64*, p. 770
1952, 1959, 1961–62—*Narkhoz 62*, p. 635
1957—*Byudzhet 62*, p. 5
1956—*Narkhoz 58*, pp. 899–900
1955—*Narkhoz 60*, p. 844
1951, 1954—*Byudzhet 57*, pp. 5, 7
1953—*Narkhoz 59*, pp. 800–01
1947–49—Dymshits, *Financy*, 1956, p. 129
1946—TsSU, *Strana*, 1967, p. 40
1941–45—*Financy*, 1957, p. 276

Column 3:
column 1 less column 2

Column 4:
column 3 as a percentage of column 1.

the *ex post* budget results for any year in order to see this. This in no way fits into any logical framework. The shortage of every kind of asset in the USSR is a fact of everyday life, but each year the budget expenditures are apparently lower than it would seem possible.

Fifthly, as we will see in chapter IX, there are some confusing and even strange things with respect to the actual use of the budget profit obtained.

So, there are more than enough oddities with the budget profit, and I am relating all this here by no means just to pose new riddles. As will be shown below, the existence of a constant budget profit and the fact that it yields poorly to logical explanation indirectly provide one of the keys to the solution of the secret of the revenues of the Soviet budget. We will examine this very phenomenon—the budget profit—in chapter V.

It is also appropriate here to discuss at least briefly another secret of the Soviet budget—the inconceivably low official indicators of expenditures on defense. It is appropriate because, as will be shown later, this question has a quite definite relation to the question of the secret revenues of the budget.

The fact that the official indicators of defense spending are, to say the least, suspect is sufficiently well known. Let us examine in this connection table I-6, in which the expenditures on defense as shown in official Soviet publications are compared with national income[16] and with total budget expenditures. All the indicators are taken "in prices of the corresponding years."

One is immediately struck by the fact that over the entire period in question both national income and total budget expenditures increased approximately four times faster than expenditures on defense. As a result, the share of military expenditures has now reached an inconceivably low level, and it is impossible to understand how with such comparatively small expenditures the USSR has been able to achieve at least equality in military strength with the United States.

We will not make a comparison with 1940; after all, that was too long ago. Let us look at the dynamics of the indicators since 1955 or even since 1960. During these 20 years military technology has become completely different; qualitatively new weapons have appeared, which should be substantially more expensive. During this period new and unbelievably expensive defense systems began to be developed and the USSR became a major naval power. But according to official data, during all this time the annual military expenditures of the USSR increased only approximately 1.5-fold. If we take into account that at the same time wholesale prices increased substantially,[17] this unbelievably low indicator would be even less.

The following point is also directly related to our topic. The indicators in column 1 of table I-6 say that from 1960 through 1969 military expenditures gradually increased (with a slowdown in 1964–66), while since 1969 they have stabilized, and in most recent years have begun even to decrease slightly. But as is known, during these years several cycles of rearmament took place, and precisely rearmament, and not the current maintenance of armed forces, costs the most. How can this be explained? If we do not think that the published indicators of military expenditures simply mean nothing,[18] then the situation may be as follows. The published indicators in fact are not all military expenditures of the USSR, but show only the expenditures of the Ministry of Defense itself.[19] In addition to these expenditures, considerable outlays are also made on the development of new types of weapons and these expenditures are taken into account somewhere separately. Where?

I completely agree with the opinion of many that a very large portion of the budget expenditures for science goes for military research.[20] I do not agree with the opinion[21] that military expenditures are contained in the two gaps of the expenditures of the budget well known to specialists. When examining the expenditures of the

Table I-6. Defense Spending (in billions of rubles)

Year	Defense spending	Produced national income	Total budget expenditures	Defense spending as a percent of: National income	Total budget expenditures
	1	2	3	4	5
1940	5.7	31.8	17.4	17.9	32.8
1950	8.3	52.1	41.3	15.9	20.1
1955	10.7	89.4	54.0	12.0	19.8
1960	9.3	145.0	73.1	6.4	12.7
1961	11.6	152.9	76.3	7.6	15.2
1962	12.7	164.6	82.2	7.7	15.5
1963	13.9	168.8	87.0	8.2	16.0
1964	13.3	181.3	92.2	7.3	14.4
1965	12.8	193.5	101.6	6.6	12.6
1966	13.4	207.4	105.6	6.5	12.7
1967	14.5	225.5	115.2	6.4	12.6
1968	16.7	244.1	128.6	6.8	13.0
1969	17.7	261.9	138.5	6.8	12.8
1970	17.9	289.9	154.6	6.2	11.6
1971	17.9	305.0	164.2	5.9	10.9
1972	17.9	313.6	173.2	5.7	10.3
1973	17.9	337.8	184.0	5.3	9.7
1974	17.7	354.0	197.4	5.0	9.0
1975	17.4	363.3	214.5	4.8	8.1
1976	17.4	385.7	226.7	4.5	7.7
1977	17.2	405.6	242.8	4.2	7.1
1978	17.2	422.5	260.2	4.1	6.6

Sources:

Columns 1 and 3:
- 1940, 1965, 1970, 1975–78—*Narkhoz 78,* p. 533
- 1971–74—*Narkhoz 75,* p. 742
- 1950, 1960, 1968–69—*Narkhoz 69,* p. 769
- 1966–67—*Narkhoz 67,* p. 886
- 1963–64—*Narkhoz 64,* p. 770
- 1961–62—*Narkhoz 62,* p. 635
- 1955—*Narkhoz 60,* p. 844

Column 2:
- 1965–78—*Narkhoz 78,* p. 385
- 1960–64—*Narkhoz 69,* p. 557
- 1940, 1950, 1955—calculated according to *Narkhoz 75,* p. 563

Column 4:
- column 1 as a percentage of column 2

Column 5:
- column 1 as a percentage of column 3.

budget I discovered that there is no room for military expenditures in these gaps. I agree with the opinion[22] that considerable spending for military purposes is included in the expenditures of the budget on the national economy, particularly in the expenditures on industry.[23] Nevertheless, it seems to me that these amounts are insufficient to explain all the military expenditures. I should also direct the reader's attention to the fact that these amounts, so to speak, do not jump around, i.e., they change more or less smoothly, without great drops or peaks. But this does not fit in with the fact that there are cycles of rearmament.

Why am I talking here about all these more or less well-known things? The point is that even such a superficial analysis suggests the idea of the existence of some regulating source for covering military expenditures—a source which is constantly resorted to for quite large amounts; and the amounts of these funds must to all appearances sometimes increase and sometimes decrease. Since in the other articles of the expenditures of the budget it is possible to identify only amounts which on the one hand are not very great and, on the other, do not "jump," we must consider the existence of this source outside the budget. Unfortunately, this seemingly quite logical conclusion runs into the following circumstance. In accepting such a hypothesis we should explain at what expense these expenditures are being made, what is their source? It is quite possible to presume that in the revenue part of the budget some revenues in excess of the published indicators are not shown, and it is they that serve as this source. However, this is not very likely since it is even difficult to explain all sources of the published total of revenues, which is why we can speak about a budget deficit.

When we draw and substantiate the conclusion about the deficit nature of the budget at the end of the book we will return to this question and I will attempt to show precisely what the solution of this riddle might be.

* * *

To conclude this chapter, I would like to explain some things and define some terms.

(1) The USSR State budget (*Gosudarstvennyy Byudzhet SSSR*) has a very complicated structure. It consists of (figure 1) the union budget (*soyuznyy byudzhet*) and the state republic budget for each of the 15 union republics. In turn each state republic budget, which is also called the state budget of a union republic (*gosudarstvennyy byudzhet*

soyuznoy respubliki), consists of the republic budget itself and various local budgets (*mestnyye byudzhety*).

It should be remembered that in addition to union republics there are so-called autonomous republics in the USSR. Budgets of these republics are treated as local budgets.

Figure 1. USSR State Budget Structure

State Budget of the USSR		
Fifteen state budgets of union republics		Union budget
Fifteen republic budgets	All local budgets	

In this book I use these terms:
—USSR State budget (or the state budget)—the sum of all budgets: union, republic, and local;
—republic budgets—the sum of the budgets of all 15 republics, including all local budgets. Although the proper term here is "state republic budget" for brevity I refer throughout simply to "republic budgets." In the few cases where we are talking about republic budgets without the local ones, this is specifically stipulated;
—union budget—the USSR State budget less the sum of all republic (including local) budgets.

(2) There is no simple answer to the question—which expenditures are made by each budget (and how?) and especially, which budget collects (receives) which revenues? Generally speaking, the appropriations of each budget follow the administrative subordination of organizations and enterprises, but there are many exceptions to this guideline. As to revenues, just this question is one of the basic ones discussed in this book; we will address it mainly in chapter III.

(3) It is commonly thought that everything in the USSR belongs to the state, at least that which does not belong directly to private citizens. This is not quite true.

Collective farms (kolkhozes) belong (in any case formally) to collective farmers, and there are cooperatives, which operate mainly in retail trade. There are also nonstate organizations which belong to their members: the Communist Party, trade unions (there is a special association of them), Komsomol (Young Communist Party League) and some others.

I am not referring here to who is in real control in the country and how; what I am saying is that all Soviet statistics are based on a distinction between state, cooperative, and public enterprises and organizations and collective farms. In particular, Soviet statistics about "state and cooperative enterprizes and organizations" include only those cooperatives which are in special trade-cooperative associations (*Tsentrosoyuz*), and they do not include collective farms and housing cooperatives.

(4) There are many plan indicators in the Soviet literature, but with very few exceptions (which are explicitly noted) I use *ex post* indicators.

Notes

1. For a reason incomprehensible to me, in the source from which I reproduce table I-2 the amount of the deductions for social insurance 1975 is at least 0.1 billion rubles less than in the *Narkhoz* yearbooks. Perhaps there is simply a misprint here.

2. Nevertheless, it is worth noting that the "population economy" (*khozyaystva naseleniya*) is thus not socialist. On the other hand, the revenues from the "socialist economy" include the turnover tax, which is almost entirely an indirect tax on the population.

3. It is amusing that the budget deficit is thus a revenue from the "socialist economy."

4. Here are some of the oddities:

(a) According to *Byudzhet 62*, pp. 8–9, it turns out that the sum of the revenues from the population and loans in 1940 was 3,176.3 million rubles. This is 1 billion rubles more (!) than the total cited here;

(b) The gap for 1940 in taxes is explained by the fact that at the time the so-called cultural levy (*kul'tsbor*) existed, but I do not know how to explain the gaps in taxes of 2 million rubles in 1955, 3.8 million rubles in 1960, 8.6 million rubles for 1961–65 and so on. The regularity of this gap suggests the existence of some special tax, which obviously should not be the case. It is possible that this is the influence of some recalculation for past years;

(c) The gaps for loans are completely incomprehensible—206 million rubles for 1940, 92 million rubles for 1950 and so on.

5. Nevertheless, I cannot explain one thing here—why the gap "jumps up" very slightly as compared with the preceding year at the beginning of each five-year plan. (Data for 1976 do not indicate this since they are calculated from a *Narkhoz* yearbook, where values are rounded.)

6. Due to the discrepancies with other sources, which were mentioned in the notes to table I-2, the corresponding amounts calculated further in table I-4 are somewhat different.

7. The amounts of this gap for individual years are shown in appendix A.

8. Generally speaking, the revenues from the socialist economy should be equal to the difference between the total amount of the revenues of the budget and the revenues from the population, which are indicated in table I-3. However, in order to

avoid errors due to rounding, in table I-4, I cite the data on the revenues from the socialist economy directly according to the primary sources.

9. They were eliminated in 1958–59 and since 1960 the budget has no longer received them.

10. Becker, *Soviet,* 1969, p. 31.

11. CIA, *USSR,* 1975, p. 14.

12. CIA, *The Soviet,* 1977.

13. True, officially, the Soviet ruble is backed by "gold, precious stones and other assets of the State Bank (Gosbank)," but this has never been verified, and the numerous changes in the domestic retail prices for gold are the best indication of the absence of such a connection.

14. I was told this at the time by workers of ministries and Gosplan, and this is also evident from the Soviet press at that time, which called even more persistently than usual for strict economy.

15. For example, Ikonnikov, *Denezhnoye,* 1962, p. 161.

16. Of course, in this case it is necessary to use values of "produced national income" and not "national income used for consumption and accumulation," although the difference between them is not great.

17. True, according to official data the wholesale price indexes for all industry and for branches of heavy industry relative, in particular, to 1955 and 1966 practically did not change (*Narkhoz 72,* p. 197 and *Narkhoz 78,* p. 138), but these data should not be believed. See also chapter X.

18. There is some possibility for this. As A. Tretyakova showed me, the overall indicators of defense spending, which are cited in tables on the amounts of national income used for consumption and accumulation (for example, *Narkhoz 74,* p. 576 and *Narkhoz 75,* p. 566—this table disappeared from later yearbooks) coincide exactly (with allowance made for rounding) with the corresponding indicators of the budgets. But this should on no account be so, since the indicators of national income in these tables are given in comparable prices of 1965, while all the budget indicators are given in the actual prices of the corresponding years. Apparently the published indicators of the budget expenditures differ so much from the actual figures that no attempt is even made to convert them into comparable prices.

19. In some sources (for example, Lavrov and Plotnikov, *Gosudarstvennyy,* 1968, p. 341) it is asserted that these expenditures are "estimates of the expenditures of the Ministry of Defense."

20. But it is difficult to calculate because only a portion of the budget expenditures on science pass through the corresponding section of the budget.

21. See, for example, Holzman, *Financial,* 1975.

22. See, for example, CIA, *The Soviet,* 1977.

23. In particular, it is completely beyond doubt, so beyond doubt that I do not see a need to prove this, that capital investments on the creation and development of the military industry are made at the expense of expenditures on the national economy (not necessarily only budget expenditures).

Chapter II

Classification of the Budget Revenues

The breakdown of budget revenues by type shown in tables I-1 and I-2 is extremely aggregated; actually, a much more detailed classification of revenues is used in budget practice.

> The budget classifications are established by the USSR Ministry of Finance to ensure its uniform construction and accounting as well as the necessary analysis of the implementation of the state budget.... In order to ensure the comparability of data of the state budget, the classification of revenues and expenditures should, as a rule, be stable and should not be subjected to frequent, and even more so, fundamental changes. But this does not mean that partial changes and additions may not be made to it. Two budget classifications are currently in use: one for the union budget and the republic budgets of union republics, and the other for republic budgets of autonomous republics and local budgets.[1]

A book published in 1970 states:

> At present, a classification approved by an order of the USSR Ministry of Finance of 29 April 1967, No. 133, 'On the classification of revenues and expenditures of the union budget and the republic budgets of union republics' is in force.[2]

About three years ago, articles appeared in which a coming change in the classification was discussed. However, it seems that there have been no changes to date in the 1967 classification.

The question might be asked: why on earth is this classification needed? Why is a separate, though short, chapter devoted to this? I hasten to agree. This is a very technical matter, and the classification itself should, in principle, only be of interest to those in various Soviet administrations who in practice enter a certain income in the appropriate blank of numerous bureaucratic forms. What is important for us is not in which blank a revenue will be placed, but its amount or, more precisely, the total amount of all budget revenues. However, unlike Soviet bureaucrats, we do not know this total amount of *actual* budget revenues. We must, using various direct or indirect data or even estimates, try to determine this amount. And for this a knowledge of the classification is quite important. As the reader will see in the next two chapters, it will help us to clarify a number of issues and make many calculations and estimates.

So the aim of this chapter is to list all elements of the classification, and in the next chapter we will examine in detail just what each item really means.

I did not find a complete description of the classification in the literature, so it must be reconstructed from various sources. In doing this it is necessary to use publications from different periods of time, and there is, therefore, no certainty that some of them are not obsolete.

All budget revenues are classified by sections, and these sections are what we must identify. The sections are, in turn, divided into paragraphs and articles,[3] but for the purposes of this work such detail is not necessary.

For the entire classification of the union budget and the republic budgets of union republics, 60 numbers of various sections of the revenue part of the budget are given, and in 1974 there were 31 existing specified sections.[4] This means that 29 numbers are not used.

The most complete list of sections names a total of 24.[5] The names of three other sections are found in other Soviet sources,[6] and four more are identified in a Western study of the Soviet financial system.[7]

The list of sections of the revenue part of the budget that could be compiled from the sources cited is given below, including the section number for each actually used in the classification. This list leaves a number of instances (more precisely, 28) in which a particular number is skipped.

1. Turnover tax
2. Deductions from profits of state enterprises and economic (*khozyaystvennyye*) organizations
3. Income taxes on cooperative and public enterprises and organizations[8]
4. State taxes on the population
5. State loans
6. Revenues from machine-tractor stations
7. State social insurance funds
8. Customs revenues
9. Reimbursement *(vozmeschcheniye)* for budget expenditures
10. Forestry revenue
11. State duties *(poshliny)*, entertainment tax, local taxes and levies *(sbory)*

12. Levies and various nontax revenues
13. Payments of state enterprises and economic organizations for fixed productive capital and normed working capital[9]
14. Rental income
15. Excess of own current assets and the planned free balances of amortization allowances earmarked for capital investment
16. Return of funds received but not spent by institutes and organizations during the preceding year
17. Free remainder of profits of state enterprises and organizations
18. Fixed payments
19. Receipts from revaluation of inventories of goods
20. Receipts in connection with a change in retail prices
21. Deductions of funds by enterprises in connection with the approval of temporary prices for new goods of improved quality and variety[10]

*

*

*

25. Payments to the state-wide fund of financial resources

*

27. Payments to the union budget to cover expenditures on geological prospecting and exploration operations
28. Receipts of excess revenues of local budgets
29. Receipts of fines for discharging untreated sewage water
30. Funds received from the union budget
31. Receipts from cash-commodity lotteries

*

33. Receipts from the 3-percent loan

*

*

*

41. Receipts of 95 percent of the difference between fines collected and paid.

*

43. Receipts from economizing on administrative expenditures

*

*

*

59. Balances of budget funds at the beginning of the year that are allocated to cover expenditures
60. Receipts of specifically earmarked funds *(tselevyye sredstva).*

Thus, we have counted 32 sections in all, that is, one section seems to be extra. However, in fact, sections 5 and 6 are not among those in effect.[11] Thus we do not know the name of at least one of the currently used sections. Moreover, since all the revenues of section 11 belong to local budgets (see chapter III), it is possible that it does not belong to this classification. If this is so, we are missing two sections. Furthermore, there are doubts concerning section 14—it also should apparently belong only to the classification of local budgets.

As we will see in the next chapter, this classification will help us, but not completely; we will not be able to answer all questions confidently.

One work under the heading "Classification of the Main Articles of the Revenues and Expenditures of the State Budget"[12] cites the names of 27 types of revenues, which are combined into 5 groups. There are no section numbers here, some sections are combined, and there is no mention of sections 25 and 29, to say nothing of sections 5 and 6. Section 27 is also missing, but it is quite possible that the corresponding funds are assumed under "Receipts of Specifically Earmarked Funds."

Of most interest for us in this source is that it refers to types of budget revenues about which nothing is said in other sources:

—revenues from exports (they are separated from customs revenues here)
—deductions from insurance payments allocated to cover expenditures
—receipts of revenue from vocational-technical schools.

If these types of revenues are individual sections, then it is quite likely that we have an almost complete classification of the revenue part of the budget by section.

Why in spite of the abundance of Soviet literature on finance has a complete classification never been published? It would seem necessary at least for the teaching of future specialists in finance; one would not think that there are any real secrets there. All the same, a fact is a fact, and we are forced to assume that something not intended to be public knowledge is being hidden in the very names of several sections of the classification of budget revenues. Therefore, the fact that I was able to compile this relatively detailed list does not guarantee that it is complete; it is quite possible that there are some other sections.

Notes

1. Darkov and Maksimov, *Finansovaya,* 1975, pp. 9–10.

2. Zlobin, *Gosudarstvennyy,* 1970, p. 44. The classification of local budgets was ratified in a separate order.

3. Paragraphs indicate the ministries and agencies from which revenues come and articles identify branches within them. Zlobin, *Gosudarststvennyy,* 1970, pp. 45–46.

4. Yevdokimov, *Kontrol',* 1974, p. 12 and also the note on p. 10.

5. Darkov and Maksimov, *Finansovaya,* 1975, p. 10.

6. Sections 11 and 14 are named in Aleksandrov, *Gosudarstvennyy,* 1965, p. 46, and section 21 is named in Yevdokimov, *Kontrol',* 1974, p. 13.

7. Sections 5, 6, 15 and 16 are taken from Gallik, et al., *The Soviet,* 1968, pp. 57–58. So, finally, my list of the sections is based on only four sources. But, in fact, to check these sources and especially to be sure that there is no other section, I looked through literally hundreds of books and articles.

8. According to Yevdokimov, "0 klassifikatsii," 1976, p. 32, the complete name of this section is "Income tax from kolkhozes, cooperative enterprises, and economic organs of social organizations."

9. Working capital is divided into two parts—"normed" and "unnormed." Very roughly speaking, normed working capital is what is needed by an enterprise during the entire year, and unnormed capital is what is needed additionally in certain periods of the year (for example, stocks of fuels for winter).

10. According to Yevdokimov, "0 klassifikatsii," 1976, p. 32, this section is called "Receipts in connection with a change in wholesale prices."

11. Section 5 has not been used since 1959 when the obligatory subscription to loans was abolished—see *Narkhoz* 59, p. 800. In connection with the liquidation of the machine-tractor stations section 6 was eliminated from publications beginning with *Narkhoz* 60, p. 844 (see also *Byudzhet* 62, p. 8).

12. Kurchenko, *Balansovyy,* 1973, pp. 108–109. The book was published by the Scientific Research Institute of Finance of the USSR Ministry of Finance.

Chapter III

Budget Revenues by Articles of the Classification

The existence of a budget classification is, of course, very useful, but this in no way solves all our problems:

(a) there is no certainty that our classification is complete;
(b) not in all cases is it possible to know exactly which revenues are contained in a particular section—we have their names, but not descriptions;
(c) by no means can we determine for all sections of the classification the corresponding values of revenues.

This chapter describes my attempts to overcome these difficulties. We will examine in order all the sections of the classification which were named in chapter II, and we will attempt to determine both the list of concrete revenues, which are taken into account in each section, and their magnitude.

In a number of instances the comparison of the classification with published indicators will help us, but unfortunately, as we will soon see, in available sources many revenues are grouped differently than in the budget classification. The obvious reason for this is that in these sources, revenues from the population are singled out, while the classification by sections does not provide for such a subdivision; it is composed of paragraphs and articles.

I will note from the very start that we will not succeed in establishing the amount of revenues for a large number of sections. At the same time we will be able to clarify the extent of coverage of some published figures using the overall indicators for a number of the most important sections of the classification. It is also very important that in our analysis we will be able to establish, for many cases, whether the given revenue belongs completely or partially to the union budget. The point is that the revenues of the republic budgets are published completely; as is evident from the *Byudzhet* handbooks, there are no gaps there (we will return to this question). But the revenues of the union budget are not fully identified and the entire riddle pertains to it. Therefore, if (when) we see that some types of revenues relate to republic and/or local budgets, we don't have to be concerned with determining their actual values, and, just the opposite, if a certain revenue relates to the union budget it is quite important to determine its magnitude.

In a few cases the magnitude remains unclear, and we will deal especially in the following chapter with just those revenues of the union budget for which only estimates are possible.

Let me emphasize that our task in this chapter is limited—we have to find secret (unpublished) revenues of the union budget. Therefore we will not deal in detail with revenues which are defined in the literature clearly—for example, turnover tax. As was already said in chapter I, a truly hard-to-explain gap in the revenues exists only for the revenues "from the socialist economy." Therefore we will also not deal in detail with the revenues from the population.

The remainder of this chapter consists of a purely technical analysis of the Soviet literature and, in my own opinion, is extremely dull and difficult reading. If the reader believes my conclusions he/she may simply skip over this material.

Thus, let us examine in order the revenues of the budget for all the sections of the classification which are known to us and are listed in chapter II.

Section 1. Turnover Tax

We have no grounds to doubt the accuracy of the published amount of this tax. Nevertheless, it is in order to mention some points.

Budget revenues do not include the entire calculated amount of the turnover tax. A part of it goes directly to cover some expenditures, so to speak, outside the budget. The corresponding amounts are shown in the *Byudzhet* handbooks.[1] Numerous calculations that were made at the Foreign Demographic Analysis Division of the U.S. Department of Commerce show that the published amounts of the turnover tax (both those collected and those paid to the budget) are quite realistic, that is, there should not be any other amounts of the turnover tax which enter the budget in excess of the published amounts.

It might be thought that there are separate, and considerable, amounts of turnover tax on imported goods in the budget which are included in the revenues from foreign trade; however, first of all, it is the buyer, i.e., the organizations (enterprises) which receive the goods and not the foreign trade organizations that pay the turnover tax,[2] and it would be strange, to say the least, if they somehow separated the turnover tax on imported goods from the tax on domestically produced goods,[3] and, secondly, the receipts from industry nearly exhaust the total amounts of the turnover tax.[4]

There is also no turnover tax on goods being exported (except on the exports of trade cooperatives—*Tsentrosoyuz*).[5]

Section 2. Deductions from Profits of State Enterprises and Economic Organizations[6]

In examining this section we will encounter a number of complicated questions and perforce we will have to deal with them at length. The section pertains to those state enterprises and organizations which "have not been converted to the new system of management."[7] The corresponding amounts (though there is no precise coincidence here) for enterprises which have already been converted to this new system fall in sections 13 and 17. Precisely for this reason the amount of the revenues in section 2 in the postreform period have been decreasing from year to year and the amounts in sections 13 and 17 have increased sharply.

The estimation of the amounts for section 2 (as well as for section 17) is somewhat complicated by a circumstance which is also significant for some of our other arguments. The point is that whereas the so-called cost accounting *(khozraschetnyye)* organizations cover their expenditures with their own revenues, and their financial relations with the budget are based only on the net results of their activity—payments to the budget from profits or a budget subsidy to cover losses[8]—the non-cost accounting organizations and some enterprises, which are otherwise called "budget-carried," have another type of interrelation with the budget. They are completely financed by the budget, which covers all their expenditures, but in return they pay to the budget all their revenues. In particular, the machine-tractor stations were financed in precisely this manner until their elimination.[9]

The next question that we must discuss is—what precisely do the published figures on payments out of profits mean? In the following pages I try to answer this extremely important and very complicated question, analyzing all available data from different sources. (I would advise the reader to look at the tables in the sources to which I refer.)

The first point to consider here was already mentioned in chapter I—the breakdown of the amount of payments from profit by sector of the economy in table I-2 does not add up to the overall total. What can this gap mean? The most natural explanation is that some sector or even sectors have been omitted in the list in table I-2. Indeed, in comparing the list of sectors in table I-2 with the list of sectors in the tables "Profit of Enterprises and Economic Organizations" in *Narkhoz* yearbooks,[10] we find quite obvious confirmation of this—in the latter table procurements, as well as supply and sales, are also indicated. However, a closer look shows that it is far from that simple. Even the total amount of profits for these sectors is substantially less than our gap, and only a part of the profit should be paid to the budget. It is also alarming that according to table I-2 in 1975 agriculture gave nearly 2.5 billion rubles of profit to the budget, while according to *Narkhoz* 76, p. 635, sovkhozes and other state agricultural organizations had a loss during that year of nearly 0.5 billion rubles. Something is obviously wrong here.

There are two explanations. The first pertains only to part of the discrepancy being discussed in the breakdown of the amounts of payments from profits in table I-2. In the tables "Profit of Enterprises and Economic Organizations" from the *Narkhoz* yearbooks, some "other sectors" are shown, and the profit for them is quite significant—1.8 billion rubles in 1970 and 3.4 billion rubles in 1975.[11] It seems to me that these sectors include not only the collection of mushrooms and berries, re-use of scrap material and certain forms of entertainment (primarily movies), but also banks and Gosstrakh (the Main Administration of State Insurance). In principle it would be possible to calculate the approximate amounts of the revenues of banks and Gosstrakh, but it is more or less clear that they are very significant and are increasing rapidly.[12]

In the literature there are indications that the banks and Gosstrakh pay deductions from profits to the budget[13] but, this is insufficient. We need to ascertain where precisely—which section of the classification of the budget revenues—these profits enter. This question is very important for us, since if these profits enter any other section of the budget, i.e., if they do not belong to the published value of deductions from profits, this can seriously influence the results of our further calculations. It seems to me that such a supposition is incorrect for the following reasons:

—the very name of section 2, which is being examined, speaks of deductions from profits not only of "enterprises," but also of "organizations";
—there are no reasons whatever to think that this should not be so, i.e., that the profits of Gosstrakh and banks should be paid to some other section of the budget;
-in the classification we do not find such an "other" section;[14]
—without the profits of Gosstrakh and the banks it is impossible to

explain the very large amounts of the deductions from profits of "other" sectors.

In appendix A, I present a breakdown of the gap in the deductions from profits by sector and compare these indicators with the amounts of the profit obtained in different sectors. It seems that it would be worthwhile to study these figures further.

Before speaking about the second explanation of the gap in the payments from profits by a sector of the economy, let us consider another riddle. According to *Narkhoz 76,* p. 635, the entire profit of state enterprises and economic organizations in 1970 was 85.7 billion rubles, while in 1975 it was 102.8 billion rubles. Let us turn the page of the same yearbook and we will find that in these two years the shares of profits paid to the budget were 59 and 56 percent respectively, that is, as is easy to calculate, 50.5 and 57.6 billion rubles. At the same time, as we saw in table I-2, the payments from profits to the budget were 54.2 and 69.7 billion rubles, i.e., 3.7 and 12.1 billion rubles more. Where did these additional billions come from?

Unfortunately, the *Narkhoz* yearbooks put one on the wrong path here (perhaps not on purpose) and at first I followed it. In the notes to the corresponding tables[15] it is indicated that they pertain only to enterprises and economic organizations which have profits. Hence it seems to follow directly that payments to the budget are also made by organizations which did not have a profit. And this is indeed so—they pay the fee for capital and fixed (rent) payments. Since both the fee for capital and the fixed payments are a part of the total amounts of payments from profits,"[16] and since some manipulations with the indicators of these fees and payments, at first glance, do not contradict this, we would seem to have found the explanation.

However, this example only shows that it is necessary to be careful with such suggestive suppositions. That this cannot be so is evident from the following. If we follow this supposition, then unprofitable enterprises turned over approximately 3.5 million rubles to the budget each year in the first half of the 1970s and three times more in 1975, as was indicated above. At the same time we know that in 1972 and 1973 all the losses of industry were respectively 3.1 and 3.4 billion rubles.[17] This amount is comparatively small, which indicates that a relatively small number of enterprises had losses. But if this is so, it is difficult to believe that just these enterprises turned over so much money to the budget in the form of fees for capital and rent payments.[18]

This view in no way refutes the fact that some payments to the budget are made by unprofitable enterprises, but it is clear that these amounts cannot be great enough to explain the gap obtained. What is going on?

In examining table I-2, I noted that the classification of payments contains in particular the line "deductions from profits and other payments." Note that in this breakdown the fee for capital and fixed payments have already been listed. It turns out that the words "other payments" are by no means accidental. We will now see that they refer to amounts that have nothing to do with profit. Since this is a matter of large amounts, it is worthwhile to deal with this question in detail and to cite a number of quotations.

As a matter of fact, the *Narkhoz* yearbooks have always given a quite definite hint about this.[19] We find a more precise indication in a recent reliable textbook:

> The payment to the budget of the surpluses of their own working capital and planned excess depreciation payments that are intended for capital investments are reflected in section 17 of the budget classification for enterprises and organizations converted to the new system of planning and economic stimulation, and in section 2 for enterprises and organizations that have not been converted to the new system.[20]

It is quite clearly and unambiguously stated here that sections 2 and 17 of the classification of the budget revenues include, in addition to profits, the withdrawal of an enterprise's own excess working capital and those amounts of amortization that are not intended by the plan for use at the given organization for capital investments. These amounts, of course, have nothing to do with profit, and I am not the one who should be asked why they are included here.

The same thing is discussed even more clearly and specifically in such a serious source as a recent article by the Minister of Finance:

> Financial organs are faced with a large task in handling the payments from profits. In 1975 their total amount will reach 69.1 billion rubles, including payments from profits of the current year of 65.2 billion rubles, payments for the past year of 0.5 billion rubles, the withdrawal of the unused amounts of depreciation of 1.2 billion rubles, deductions for geological work of 1.6 billion rubles, and the withdrawal of excess working capital of 0.4 billion rubles.[21]

Thus, the minister of finance himself confirms that the excess of working capital and the unused amounts of amortization—section 15 of the classification of revenues—belong to the payments from profits, and furthermore, he indicates that the deductions for geological prospecting operations—section 27 of the classification of revenues—also belong here.

Let us also turn our attention to the following. According to table

I-2, in 1970 and 1975 the payments from profits from housing and municipal services were 1.6 and 2.5 billion rubles respectively. Meanwhile the entire profits of municipal services during the same years were 1.0 and 1.3 billion rubles.[22] If we even suppose unbelievably that the entire profit of municipal services is paid to the budget,[23] then enormous amounts will fall to the share of housing services, although, as is well known, they are basically unprofitable. We find the explanation for this in the textbook cited above:

> All the interrelations of housing services with the budget are reflected in the consolidated financial plan.... Among the payments to the budget that are singled out are deductions from profits, the withdrawal of the freed amortization, which is paid by repair and construction (*remontno–stroitel'nyye*) organizations, the rent for nonresidential buildings (95 percent) and the gross revenues of housing services, which are financed on an estimate basis.[24]

Thus, it is quite clear that very considerable amounts in addition to profits themselves and the "freed" amortization are received by the budget from housing services. Although in the quotation cited this is not directly asserted, the entire context as well as the indicators given clearly attest that these amounts belong to payments from profits. True, I do not have other examples of the same phenomenon (I think they can be found),[25] but in principle, the question seems clear, and on the whole it is quite unquestionable that this section of the classification of revenues is so to speak a collective section. Here, *various* payments to the budget are taken into account, which (this is very important for us) narrows the possibilities of the payment of funds to other sections of the budget. At the same time at least the following questions remain.

Firstly, the simple adding up of the data cited by the minister reveals a gap of 200 million rubles. I have not found any data which explain this amount. In examining further all the sections of the budget we will see that there is quite a large number of different revenues from enterprises and organizations, and some of them enter the union budget. It is quite likely that these 200 million rubles reflect the plan for these payments for 1975.

Secondly, the minister speaks separately about the payment from profits of "the current year" and about the profit "for the past year." In itself this is quite normal, but it creates certain difficulties for us in making comparisons of the profit obtained by enterprises and organizations with the payments to the budget; a lag arises here, and it is not quite clear how to take it into account.

Thirdly, as G. Schroeder pointed out to me, the following point requires explanation. According to the data given by the minister, it

Table III-1. Comparison of the Indicators of the Payment of Profits to the Budget of State Enterprises and Economic Organizations with the Corresponding Amounts in the Budget (in billions of rubles)

Year	Amount of profit	Percent paid to budget	Total paid to budget	Amount of payments	Difference: column 4 – column 3
	1	2	3	4	5
1960	24.4	62.0	15.1	18.6	3.5
1961	26.1	64.1	16.7	20.7	4.0
1962	29.8	65.5	19.5	23.9	4.4
1963	29.8	68.5	20.4	28.7	8.3
1964	34.0	69.4	23.6	28.7	5.1
1965	36.1	69.0	24.9	30.9	6.0
1966	43.1	69.0	29.7	35.7	6.0
1967	54.8	67.0	36.7	41.8	5.1
1968	66.4	64.0	42.5	48.0	5.5
1969	71.5	59.0	42.2	48.0	5.8
1970	85.7	58.0	49.7	54.2	4.5
1971	88.5	56.0	49.6	55.6	6.0
1972	91.7	57.0	52.3	60.0	7.7
1973	96.2	55.0	52.9	60.0	7.1
1974	101.0	55.0	55.6	64.4	8.8
1975	102.8	56.0	57.6	69.7	12.1
1976	104.7	55.0	57.6	70.6	13.0
1977	108.6	58.0	63.0	78.4	15.4
1978	112.6	56.0	63.1	78.6	15.5

Sources: Columns 1 and 2:
1965, 1970, 1975–78—*Narkhoz 78,* pp. 515–516
1971–74—*Narkhoz 75,* pp. 725–726
1960, 1969—*Narkhoz 70,* pp. 703–704
1968—*Narkhoz 69,* pp. 741–742
1966–67—*Narkhoz 68,* pp. 743–744
1964—*Narkhoz 65,* pp. 757–758
1963—*Narkhoz 64,* pp. 747–750
1962—*Narkhoz 63,* pp. 637–639
1961—*Narkhoz 62,* pp. 627–628
Column 3:
Column 1 multiplied by column 2 divided by 100
Column 4:
1965, 1970, 1975–78—*Narkhoz 78,* p. 533
1971–74—*Narkhoz 75,* p. 742
1960, 1969—*Narkhoz 70,* p. 730
1968—*Narkhoz 69,* p. 769
1966–67—*Narkhoz 68,* p. 777
1964—*Narkhoz 65,* p. 781
1963—*Narkhoz 64,* p. 771
1962—*Narkhoz 63,* p. 654
1961—*Narkhoz 62,* p. 635.

turns out that for 1975 the total amount of payments anticipated other than those directly from profits were 69.1 billion rubles less 65.5 billion rubles, or 3.6 billion rubles. But a few pages above we calculated that in fact according to the report for the same 1975 these payments were 12 billion rubles, that is, nearly 4 times more. The discrepancy is too significant to believe that this is a matter only of the overfulfillment of the plan.[26]

In this connection let us examine table III-1.[27] The values given there lead to the following notion. Since a permanent, regular and rather steadily increasing gap exists between the values we obtained and the values in the publications on the budget, it is clear that these are not some accidental errors. Unquestionably, this gap can be explained by a number of factors. Among them are the payments of unprofitable enterprises and the withdrawal of the freed amounts of amortization and working capital. Incidentally, it is quite possible that the amounts of these types of payments to the budget in 1975 and 1976 were considerably greater than anticipated by the plan.[28]

It is also unquestionable that the values in column 5 are affected by the fact that part of the payments of profits into the budget are the result of recalculations for the previous year.

For all this, the differences obtained are so great that these explanations are probably insufficient and I would like to see what their real source is.

Let us summarize our examination of this section of the budget:

(*a*) the most important result is that this section (and also section 17) includes not only the payments from profit per se, but also a number of other payments such as the "freed" amortization, deductions for geological prospecting, and the withdrawal of the excesses of working capital. The significance of this is that we need not explain the corresponding amounts in further calculations;

(*b*) in spite of a number of discrepancies and puzzles noted above, the quite definite impression is formed that on the whole the indicators of this section more or less agree with the values of profit that we know. More precisely, we have no grounds to believe that there are any substantial additional amounts of profit that could be paid to the budget. Rather it may be to the contrary, i.e., it is possible that there are still some other budget revenues, not from profits, that are shown in this section. This means that profits cannot be the source of budget revenues in other sections;

(*c*) in the course of events we analyzed a number of well-known indicators of profits and their payments to the budget.

Section 3. Income Taxes on Cooperative and Public Enterprises and Organizations

I have little to say about this section. The so-called tax on noncommodity operations was included here.[29] This tax is a variant of the turnover tax, but it was included precisely in this section, and not in section 1, since it was *not* levied on *state* organizations.

Noncommodity operations include the production of goods from material supplied by the buyer, repair services, shipments, and nonproductive services.[30] After *Norkhoz 62*, references to them disappear, and in a book published in 1972 it is stated:[31] "Noncommodity operations are not subject to imposition of the turnover tax."

The tax from kolkhozes is shown in table I-2. As to the tax from the business organs of public organizations, we know that enterprises of the Party and Komsomol organizations are exempt from it.[32] At the same time

> . . . the number of public enterprises and organizations that pay the income tax has increased by nearly 30 percent in the last five years and by 1 January 1977 had reached 4,580. Today they pay to the union and republic (local) budgets about 220 million rubles a year in income tax.

There are no grounds whatever to think that the amounts of the payments to the budget according to this section are greater than is officially published.

Section 4. State Taxes on the Population

We also do not have to discuss this section at length. All the types of taxes enumerated in table I-2 belong here, and, again, we have no grounds to think that the published values are understated. Not only would such an understatement make no sense, but also by quite simple calculations the overall correctness of the indicators cited in table I-2 can be confirmed.[34]

Moreover, as shown in appendix B, we have quite considerable difficulties in determining the monetary income of the population; additional taxes would contradict the results of our calculations of the balance of the monetary income and expenditure of the population.

It is worth noting that this section includes taxes not only from workers and employees, but also from a very few artisans, craftsmen and other payers (in particular, people of the "free" professions). The corresponding amounts are extremely small.

As stated in chapter II, section 5—state loans—and section

6—revenues from machine-tractor stations—are not used now, and we will not consider them.

Section 7. State Social Insurance Funds

The largest part of the payments recorded in this section consists of withholdings for social insurance from enterprises and organizations, and approximate calcultions show that the numbers here should be reliable.[35] Precise calculations are not possible since the data on total wage payments are given by "economic" *(khozyaystvennyye)* sectors,[36] and the established rates for social insurance payments differ by ministry.

The second reason for the difficulty of making precise calculations is that, in addition to these withholdings, state social insurance funds include "... amounts received [by enterprises, institutions and organizations] from workers and employees, according to established procedures, for accommodations in sanatoria, rest homes, tourist camps, and mountain resorts provided by trade union organizations."[37] The corresponding amounts and also several other relatively small payments (which, incidentally, include the funds of kolkhozes)[38] amount to several hundred million rubles a year.[39]

In this connection, I will note that in the literature the question of the assets of the so-called centralized funds of state insurance and social security of kolkhoz members is not made very clear. It is so unclear that, in particular, the suspicion arises that the amounts contributed to this fund by kolkhoz members go into the budget as revenue and then payments are made from the budget. Surprisingly, nothing is said about this in the literature, but simple reasoning, and, more important, an examination of the expenditure part of the budget show that this should not be the case, since the corresponding expenditures cannot be found in the expenditure part of the budget. So, these funds must not enter the budget (see also chapter IV).

In conclusion, there is one more interesting point to consider. As already indicated in chapter I, the state budget of the USSR is the sum of the union budget and the republic budgets (the state budgets of union republics). From this it follows that in no case should the sum of a particular type of revenue for all republic budgets be greater than that shown for the state budget of the USSR. However, as V. Treml demonstrated to me, a very strange thing occurs with the social insurance funds. For almost all years, beginning with 1958, the revenues of all state budgets of union republics for "social insurance funds" turn out to be more (and often quite a bit more) than the revenue entry of the same name in the state budget of the USSR.

From this it unquestionably follows that the same name is being given to different things in these budgets. This question is examined in appendix L, but no reliable answer to it is found.

Section 8. Customs Revenues

This is the first section of the budget in our analysis for which we have little material for discussion and especially for calculations. Customs revenues consist of customs duties, customs levies (for storage in warehouses), the receipts from the sale of confiscated goods, and fines. They belong entirely to the revenues of the union budget.[40]

Let us immediately set aside the customs levies, the receipts, and the fines—the corresponding amounts can in no way be significant to any extent on the scale of the budget. Thus, only the customs duties remain. For our analysis it makes sense to divide them into (1) those paid by both Soviet citizens and by foreigners who cross the border in both directions and send packages, and (2) the duties paid by state organizations which carry out foreign trade.

By elementary reasoning and relying on personal experience, I can show that the customs duties from citizens are very small.[41] Moreover, conceptually they should be a part of the total amount of revenues from the population, and consequently we have no need to deal with them at all.

The situation is quite different with customs duties from organizations; this question is of exceptionally great importance to us. What do we actually know about them? We know that customs duties are collected on imports,[42] but I did not find anything in the literature with respect to exports, and I believe that under the conditions of a state monopoly there should be no such duties on foreign trade.[43] We have absolutely no information about the total amount of customs revenues.[44]

Our task is made somewhat simpler by the fact that in addition to the customs revenues themselves there also exist so-called revenues from foreign trade. Some 20 years ago they were identified with each other,[45] but now most sources treat them separately. Nevertheless, it seems to me that it is quite possible to examine the customs revenues and the revenues from foreign trade jointly, and we will deal with this in detail in chapter IV.

In our discussion we need not be concerned with the customs duties which are levied on foreign organizations. They are levied in convertible foreign currency, and not in rubles, and for this reason should not have anything to do with the budget revenues.

Section 9. Reimbursement for Budget Expenditures

I have not found any indications of the content of this section in the literature. Judging only by the name, I think that revenues of budget-carried organizations which partially cover their expenditures are gathered here. As I have already noted, these organizations are not financed on a "balance" basis.[46]

If this is indeed so, this section should include the amounts collected from parents for the care of their children at state children's nurseries, kindergartens and boarding schools. It is also possible that the rent for housing services which have not been converted to cost accounting is gathered precisely here.[47] Perhaps the so-called revenues from state properties, references to which abound in all the sources, are also taken into account precisely here. All these revenues should relate primarily to local and republic budgets and partly to the union budget.[48]

It is appropriate to ask why are such institutions financed by the budget in full, and not on a balance basis? The formal reason is that complete financial control over the activity of these institutions can only be assured with such a procedure. The real reason probably is that financial organs insist on such a procedure out of quite understandable bureaucratic pretensions and out of a desire to boost the amounts of the budget.

Two more remarks: first, if my interpretation of the content of this section is correct, it is necessary to separate the revenues which enter this section from those which enter section 60, "Receipts of specifically earmarked funds." In principle the existence of section 60 does not contradict my interpretation.

The second is that it is possible that I am completely incorrect here and it is precisely in this section where the assets which cover the budget deficit enter—we will return to this question in chapter X.

Section 10. Forestry Revenue

The forestry revenue is paid to the republic and local budgets; data on it are available and we have already taken its amount into account in table I-4.

Section 11. State Duties, Entertainment Tax, Local Taxes and Levies

This section presents certain difficulties. The most important of them is that both revenues from the population and revenues from the "socialist sector" belong here. Precisely for this reason in the *Byudzhet* handbooks they are not shown in breakdowns of the USSR state budget, but only in tables on the republic budgets, since the division of revenues into those received from the population and those received from the "socialist sector" is not made in the latter. Just for this reason I was not able to use the data on these revenues in table I-4.

In table III-2 the values of revenues from the *Byudzhet* handbooks for different periods are gathered.

As for the tax on buildings and ground rent,[49] this is a tax which is collected not only from the population, but also from cooperative enterprises and organizations.[50] Why it has fallen so sharply since 1960, I do not know.

The entertainment tax[51] is economically a turnover tax, and it is hard for me to say exactly why it is included in this group. I also cannot say why data on it have not been published since 1969.

State duties are collected both from the population and from institutions and organizations. They include court costs, the payments to the arbitration board, to notary organs, for registration, for services of the Civil Registry Office, for hunting permits, and for the issuing of foreign passports.[52]

The one-time levy, as I understand it, includes the levies on kolkhoz markets. For a reason I do not understand, beginning in 1970 the publication of the amounts of the one-time levy was halted, and in examining the appropriate table in *Byudzhet 72*, (p. 77), you are led to the conclusion that the separate accounting of this type of revenue was also stopped. What is happening here, I do not know.

In table III-2 there is a gap between the sum of all the revenues listed and their published total amount.[53] Apparently, the gap should be explained by the levy from the owners of livestock and means of transportation and by some other levies from the population. The amounts of the gaps are relatively small.

Two things are of particular interest to us about the group of revenues being examined. On the one hand, there are numerous different budget revenues here, which, not knowing the precise figures, might be thought to be considerable. Precisely for this reason I have presented some fairly detailed data in table III-2 in order to have a basis for comparison with other, more or less similar revenues. On the other hand, it is very important for us that all these revenues are included in the local budgets,[54] which are a component of the republic budgets, but not of the union budget.

One last point on this section: I noted in chapter I the existence of a gap in the revenues from the population and stated there that this gap is easily explained. Indeed, using the numbers in table III-2 we

Table III-2. Local Taxes and Levies (in millions of rubles)

Year	Total	Including: tax on buildings and ground rent	entertainment tax	state duties	one-time levy	Gap
	1	2	3	4	5	6
1940	192.5	79.1	42.0	25.9	37.8	7.7
1950	673.5	259.5	187.9	69.5	79.5	77.1
1951	701.1	282.4	194.2	68.6	76.4	79.5
1952	772.6	314.4	232.2	69.3	74.3	82.4
1953	798.9	340.3	242.7	75.8	65.0	75.1
1954	819.9	379.0	259.4	75.1	46.3	60.1
1955	809.4	330.5	292.2	73.8	48.6	64.3
1956	867.4	359.1	323.2	76.1	48.0	61.0
1957	916.3	387.5	337.9	81.4	47.9	61.6
1958	962.3	422.5	369.2	86.9	48.7	35.0
1959	1,004.6	477.2	381.4	88.5	47.2	10.3
1960	660.7	140.9	374.1	89.8	45.9	10.0
1961	681.2	148.2	391.2	87.0	44.3	10.5
1962	697.6	158.4	391.5	92.4	44.3	11.0
1963	724.5	166.6	383.8	94.7	43.5	35.9
1964	740.0	175.5	406.7	94.4	42.9	20.5
1965	754.8	181.2	418.7	99.5	42.4	13.0
1966	763.8	186.0	399.8	120.8	43.6	13.6
1967	815.9	191.5	441.3	123.0	45.7	14.4
1968	850.0	197.6	457.9	133.2	46.4	14.9
1969	860.2	204.3	n.a.	140.6	45.2	470.1
1970	842.0	211.4	n.a.	149.9	n.a.	480.7
1971	876.6	219.9	n.a.	171.8	n.a.	484.9
1972	923.0	225.0	n.a.	223.7	n.a.	474.3
1973	949.1	234.3	n.a.	236.5	n.a.	478.3
1974	972.3	244.1	n.a.	236.1	n.a.	492.1
1975	988.7	253.3	n.a.	239.1	n.a.	496.3

Sources: Columns 1–5:
1970–75—*Byudzhet 76*, p. 74
1966–69—*Byudzhet 72*, p. 77
(Column 3—Pavlov, *Mestnyye*, 1970, p. 11)
1950, 1955, 1960–65—*Byudzhet 66*, p. 70
1940, 1956–59—*Byudzhet 62*, p. 67–68
1951–54—*Byudzhet 57*, p. 14

Column 6:
Column 1 less sum of columns 2–5.

can quite easily explain why the gaps in the budget revenues from the population shown in column 7 of table I-3 occur. However, some additional information is needed in order to make precise calculations.

Section 12. Levies and Various Nontax Revenues

It seems to me that the existence of this section in addition to section 11 is due to the fact that section 11 takes into account only revenues paid into local budgets, and section 12 includes those revenues which go into republic and union budgets.

This section includes the so-called coin revenue and its revenues enter the union budget.[55] Also included here are the amounts of some fines,[56] and I think that part of these fines are paid into the union budget.

Further, the following revenues also belong here: "If a good is sold at too high a price . . . the difference resulting from this increase is withdrawn into the revenue of the budget in section 12."[57] These amounts go into the union budget. The reference here is to an illegal exceeding of prices.[58] If prices are raised in the normal manner, the corresponding revenues are taken into account in sections 19 and 20.

Also taken into account here—and again entering the union budget—are the levies collected in connection with the use of motor transport by the population.[59] It is not quite clear to me where exactly to assign these revenues—to the revenues from the population or from the "socialist economy." However, the amounts here are very small.

Finally, this section includes payments associated with surpluses of goods held by enterprises and the excess of accounts receivable over accounts payable.[60]

Even with the boldest of assumptions it is impossible to presume that all these amounts can be significant to any extent on the scale of our discussion. Generally speaking, it is quite possible that these amounts should be, if only in part, included in the gap in the revenues we are examining, but because they are insignificant we may completely disregard them.

Section 13. Payments of State Enterprises and Economic Organizations for Fixed Productive Capital and Normed Working Capital

The name of this section is so long that it explains everything by itself. Moreover, the corresponding amounts are published—we saw this in both table I-1 and table I-2—and there are no grounds to assume that these amounts are understated.

Perhaps the only remark of importance is that both this very section and the corresponding payments appeared relatively recently—in the second half of the 1960s—after the so-called economic reform.

Section 14. Rental Income

These revenues pertain only to local budgets,[61] but are included in the list of revenues of the republic budgets.

The amounts of these revenues are published and were given in table I-4.

Section 15. Excess of Own Current Assets and the Planned Free Balances of Amortization Allowances Earmarked for Capital Investment

When examining section 2, we already saw that in the published data the corresponding amounts enter in the deductions from profits. Therefore, generally speaking, it would be possible to limit ourselves to this. However, we had specific indicators for only one year, and then only the plan indicators. But as the reader, perhaps, recalls, it was noted there that the actual values for this year were substantially different from the plan indicators. And in general it seems that several remarks concerning this type of revenue would not hurt.

As to the "excess of own current assets," i.e., working capital, at the end of the 1940s there was a very boisterous campaign to accelerate its turnover and at the time some enterprises indeed did pay relatively large amounts to the budget. However, with the exception of this period, the general trend is diametrically opposed—working capital is increasing much more rapidly than output, especially as a result of bank credit (we will examine this in detail in chapter X).

Let us also take into account that in a large number of instances the excesses of working capital are redistributed by superior organizations and are not paid to the budget. Furthermore, the circumstances under which the plan for the payment to the budget of excess working capital could be substantially overfulfilled are very atypical.

Therefore, it seems extremely unlikely to me that the withdrawal to the budget of excess working capital can be an appreciable source of budget revenues.

As for amortization, according to all canons it should be used by the enterprises themselves or be redistributed by superior organizations. Therefore, the withdrawal of amortization to the budget can occur only under exceptional circumstances.[62] Nevertheless, this is done and here is why:

> . . . in 1972 . . . in the national economy . . . 4.8 percent of the total renovation fund was paid to the budget . . . amortization is transferred to the budget by enterprises for which capital investments are less than the amortization investments in renovation, as well as in instances when the administrative subordination of the enterprises changes.[63]

The amount of the amortization for renovation for the entire economy in 1972 was 17.5 billion rubles,[64] and 4.8 percent of this amount equals 840 million rubles.[65]

As we saw above, the plan for 1975 stipulated that 1.2 billion rubles of amortization would be paid to the budget, i.e., 1.5 times more than were actually paid in 1972. The rapid increase is unquestionable. Nevertheless, it does not seem to me that the actual amount of amortization paid into the budget in 1975 could have been very much more than stipulated in the plan. In other words, the strange fact, which was noted when examining section 2, of the sharp "overfulfillment of the plan" in 1975 for the components of the budget revenue, other than the profit, included in "deductions from profits" cannot be satisfactorily explained either by the withdrawal of working capital or by the withdrawal of amortization.

As was already noted above, these revenues are included in section 2 and/or section 17. Therefore, generally speaking, it is not very clear why a special section 15 is needed. It is possible that initially these revenues are gathered precisely in this section, and then are redistributed to sections 2 and 17. Another possibility is that this section is not even currently used in practice, but all these and other possibilities are not of importance; the main thing is that we have no grounds to believe that the corresponding amounts are not included in the published data.

Section 16. Return of Funds Received But not Spent by Institutes and Organizations During the Preceding Year

As follows from the title, this section relates to budget-carried organizations. By comparing the title with the title of section 59, it may be concluded that the difference is that funds which have actually already been received by the organizations are shown here, while funds which have been allocated but not received are shown in that section.

As I understand the practice of the financing of budget-carried organizations, the receipt of money usually takes place in conformity with needs, and the financial organs pay attention to how money was used during the preceding quarter. As in America, at the end of the fiscal year the organizations try in every possible way to spend all the funds they received. In short, it is very unlikely that really substantial amounts can be formed here.

Let us also take into account that a considerable portion of these amounts should be attributed to republic and local budgets.

For all these reasons I think that we can disregard these amounts in our analysis (see also chapter V).

Section 17. Free Remainder of Profits of State Enterprises and Organizations
and
Section 18. Fixed Payments

I have nothing to add to what was said about these two sections when examining sections 2 and 15.

Section 19. Receipts from Revaluation of Inventories of Goods
and
Section 20. Receipts in Connection with a Change in Retail Prices

I am examining these two sections together because in essence they are one and the same.[66] The logic here is as follows. When prices are revised *before* the approval of the plan for the following period, all the plan indicators are changed correspondingly. But if prices are revised *after* the plan is already approved, the results of such a change in prices, which are not dependent on the enterprise, should not affect the results of its economic activity. Consequently any additional (above-plan) profits which are obtained as a result of the increase in prices for the goods being produced are subject to withdrawal into the budget and, on the contrary, the budget should reimburse enterprises for losses due to the increase of prices.

These budget revenues also cannot be significant in practice. The main thing is that unplanned increases of both retail and wholesale prices occur very rarely, and planned changes, by the way, also are not too frequent. Furthermore, it is significant that, as I just noted, when there is a reduction of prices the budget should offset the additional expenditures, which it does. Therefore, it is quite possible that in such cases settlements with the budget are made on a "balance" basis. True, there are data on the amounts which the budget has allocated for a number of years to trade in order to offset increases in the procurement prices for vegetables[67] and, judging from this, balancing might not have taken place. However, it is typical that in the same table there are no other references to the budget financing of changes in prices.

In a special work on the finances of trade[68] there are no references to payments to the budget of amounts connected with changes in prices.

Finally, let us once again take into account that practically all retail trade is under republic, and not union, subordination.

To sum up, I believe, first, that the corresponding budget revenues can be only of a sporadic nature; secondly, they can be amounts of several hundreds of millions, but not billions of rubles; and thirdly, all these amounts or the largest part of them should go into republic budgets.

Section 21. Deductions of Funds by Enterprises in Connection with the Approval of Temporary Prices for New Goods of Improved Quality and Variety

The following quotation explains what this is, and at the same time we learn that this section has nothing to do with revenues of the union budget:

> In accordance with established procedure, both fixed and temporary . . . prices are simultaneously approved for new knit goods, shoes, fabrics, furniture and sewn articles of improved quality and variety. In order to cover the losses from markdowns on the inventories of these goods in the trade network, deductions for the budget have been established. . . . These deductions are subject to payment to the revenue of the budget of the appropriate union republic. . . .[69]

Section 25. Payments to the State-wide Fund of Financial Resources

The name of this section tells me nothing. In the literature I found only two references to it, and in one case it is mentioned in a discussion of the interrelations of trade organizations with the budget,[70] while in the other an example is cited in which the enterprise transfers small amounts from its profits to this fund.[71]

It is very difficult to prove, but nevertheless I have the feeling that there should not be any substantial amounts here, except for those about which we already know. Firstly, it is difficult to name any significant special source of funds of this type, and secondly, it is not clear why, if this section indeed has any substantial importance, practically nothing is said about it in the literature.

More on intuition than knowledge I will venture the following assumption. In the practice of economic operations, various campaigns for economizing on funds are quite frequent. I have already mentioned one such campaign—the reduction of working capital. We will speak of another when examining section 43, but there it is a question of an established practice, and therefore a special section was introduced. It is quite possible that section 25 was introduced for some "irregular" campaigns. Here is an example. After the well-known crop failure of 1972, as I already stated above, the strictest economy was introduced; allocations already earmarked for practically all ministries were taken away. The enterprises could have paid the funds thus unspent (in cases when they had already managed to receive them) precisely to this section.

The most difficult questions for us here are: what might the actual amounts be, in which budget are they included, and where are they reflected in the published data, that is, are they included, say, in the published indicators of payments from profits or do they form a part of the gap we are studying?

According to the only example we know (cited above) this section involves amounts paid from profits. Hence these amounts should fall in the published values of "deductions from profits and other payments." It is quite possible that these amounts belong precisely to that enormous gap in the reported values of these payments, which we discussed when examining section 2. I understand that all this does not sound very convincing, but I wish to repeat that another appreciable source of payments of funds to this section is not evident.

From the title of the section it would seem to follow quite indisputably that it pertains to the union budget. However, in the same sole example known to us, it is stated that the funds enter the republic budget.

On the whole I believe that the amounts in this section cannot help us to explain the gap in budget revenues.

Section 27. Payments to the Union Budget to Cover Expenditures on Geological Prospecting and Geological Exploration Operations

This type of revenue is comparatively new; it was introducted in the middle of 1967,[72] and the corresponding amounts are increasing rapidly. According to the plan for 1969 the amount of these payments should have been 40 million rubles in all,[73] while for the five-year period of 1971–75 the annual payments should already have been 800 million rubles.[74]

Economically this type of revenue is completely identical to the forestry revenue, but, unlike it, it is paid to the union budget.[75] The most important thing for us is that, as we saw above, according to an authoritative statement of the minister of finance himself,[76] the corresponding payments are included in the published data on payments from profits and therefore should not particularly interest us.

Section 28. Receipts of Excess Revenues of Local Budgets

One source asserts that this section appears only in local budgets,[77] while according to our main source it turns out that this is not so.[78] In still another source, which lists quite a number of sections of the classification of the union and republic budgets, it is absent.[79] Because of all these circumstances I think that, first, these amounts cannot be very substantial, and, second, they should not be in the union budget, the only budget which concerns us.

Section 29. Receipts of Fines for Discharging Untreated Sewage Water

I found only one reference to this section.[80] Even if this section actually does still exist—it is hard to understand why no recent publications would mention it—the amounts for it could not be substantial, and it is practically certain that these amounts should be included in the revenues of local budgets.

Section 30. Funds Received from the Union Budget

The very title of this section clearly attests that it should not interest us, i.e., concerns funds *received* by republic budgets from the union budget.

Section 31. Receipts from Cash-Commodity Lotteries
and
Section 33. Receipts from the 3-Percent Loan

We do not have to speak at length about these two sections. They pertain to revenues from the population and therefore should not interest us.[81]

It would nevertheless be interesting to determine whether these sections show the balance of receipts and expenditures or only the corresponding receipts, with expenditures for these purposes shown in the expenditures part of the budget. It seems that precisely the balance is shown here, but this needs to be proven.

Section 41. Receipts of 95 Percent of the Difference Between Fines Collected and Paid

This title refers to the excess of fine payments received over fines paid by wholesale trade organizations, railroads, steamship lines, ports, and main administrations of trade.

> During the year these organizations pay to the budget not the entire amount of the excess, but only 95 percent of it (hence the name of the payment). The remaining 5 percent, which is determined according to the annual report, is combined with the amount paid out of profits according to the annual recalculation and is entered in the budget as deductions from profits.
>
> ". . . enterprises and organizations, subordinated to union ministries, committees, main administrations and administrations, make the payments to the union budget, while those subordinate to republic organizations of the union republics make them to the republic budgets of the appropriate union republics.[82]

As I understand this, the basic amounts which might interest us here are the fines which are received by the Ministry of Railroads for the above-norm lay-over of cars. How much can these fines be? I do not believe that it is more than, say, 100–200 million rubles a year.[83] However, the point is not that these amounts can in no way reach into the billions, which interest us. The main thing was said in the quotation cited. If 5 percent "enters the budget as deductions from profit," we have every reason to believe that the other 95 percent also goes into the amounts which are shown as payments from profits.

Section 43. Receipts from Economizing on Administrative Expenditures

This section title must be explained since, to put it lightly, this phenomenon is quite unique. The amount of the so-called administrative and managerial expenses of all enterprises and organizations without exception is approved by their superior organizations. It is very strictly limited and controlled and in no case can be exceeded. Until approximately the second half of the 1950s the amount was also specially verified by financial organs; this was called "registration." I stress that we are talking about the administrative and managerial expenses of *all* enterprises and organizations, that is, both budget-carried and cost accounting.

The planning and approval of these expenses takes place in conformity with special norms, and usually they cannot on any account be greater than during the preceding year. But even this is recognized as inadequate—each year the government approves a special target, in percent, for their reduction, and the corresponding amounts are to be paid to the budget as special revenue.

We will examine this type of revenue in chapter IV, since the amounts are significant but we do not have complete data and must resort to estimates.

Section 59. Balances of Budget Funds at the Beginning of the Year That Are Allocated to Cover Expenditures

Above, when examining section 16, we spoke of amounts received but not spent by enterprises and organizations. Here it is a matter of budget allocations which were stipulated but for some reason were not paid out. Because of its complexity and importance, we will examine this question separately in chapter V.

Here, however, it is worth noting that this section pertains only to local budgets.[84]

Section 60. Receipts of Specifically Earmarked Funds

The title of this section clearly shows that the funds which enter here are of "a special nature," i.e., they are paid to the budget as its revenue in order to be spent for quite definite purposes. Among them are:

(a) special payments of enterprises and organizations for the construction and repair of roads. Since "the procedure, dates, and forms of involvement in road work . . . are established by the presidiums of the Supreme Soviets of the union republics,"[85] we can conclude with confidence that the corresponding amounts enter the revenues of the republic and/or local budgets;
(b) the revenues from the markups to retail prices of radios and televisions, which were introduced in 1962. These revenues enter the republic budgets.[86]
(c) the content of the following type of receipts is evident from its name: "Amounts of Budget Receipts From the Profits of Consumer Service Enterprises which Produce Industrial Products, as well as Local Industry for Expenditures on Housing, Cultural and General Construction and Civic Improvement."[87] These funds enter the local budgets.
(d) "deductions from insurance payments for obligatory and all types of voluntary insurance of property, which are allocated for special measures." These funds also enter the republic budgets.[88]

It is also worth noting that in one reliable source these "earmarked" receipts also include "the levies for the state inspection of standards and measuring instruments, for the registration of trademarks, and the levies which are collected in connection with the use of motor transport,"[89] but then in the same source it is indicated that all these revenues enter section 12 of the classification of revenues.

It is possible that some amounts, about which I spoke when examining section 9, in fact belong precisely here.

All the revenues that we know for certain belong here enter the revenue of republic budgets. If, nevertheless, some other revenues, about which we do not know for sure, belong to the union budget, the amounts cannot be very significant on the scale of our calculations. Therefore in further calculations we will not take them into account.

* * *

Thus, using the classification we have specifically examined many types of revenues and, it seems to me, have clarified a number of questions. Let us try to evaluate all of this.

First of all, we have no grounds to believe that the published values of the revenues could be understated. More specifically:

(a) there is no reason to doubt the correctness of the data on the turnover tax;
(b) apparently everything is also in order with the values of payments to the budget from profits. The budget data agree quite well (with allowance for our additional calculations) with the published indicators for profits. Moreover, as we saw, the published values of the payments from profits include some amounts above profits themselves;
(c) we did not deal with this in detail, but there are no grounds to doubt the correctness of the data on taxes from cooperative and public organizations, as well as the taxes from the population.

Stating the same thing in different words, our analysis confirmed that it is quite possible to trust the values of the "conglomerate," which were used in the calculations in table I-4. We also have no doubts about the correctness of the other indicators in the table. Thus, we may take the next step. I have already mentioned that the revenues of the republic budgets are published without gaps. In calculating the gap in table I-4 I did not take into account a number of revenues of the republic budgets. Now is the very time to do this. The corresponding calculations are made in table III-3.

In chapter V we will speak specifically about the surpluses of budget funds. Here, for the time being, let us take into account that part of these surpluses for republic budgets which is allocated to the revenues of the budget.

In column 4 of table III-3, the revenues about which we did not speak above are shown. They are given in some *Byudzhet* handbooks and are called "Receipts of the Difference in Prices for Agricultural Machinery and Spare Parts." What this is, I do not know. I have not found any other references to this in the literature. It is widely known that *Sel'khoztekhnika* sells machinery to kolkhozes at subsidized prices, but why and how this is connected with the revenue of the budget remains unclear. However, the fact that we do not know why and from what source these amounts enter the budget does not prevent us in any way from taking them into account. The corresponding amounts are published for 1958 through 1965, and then these revenues are combined with "others."[90]

As we saw in this chapter, revenues shown in table III-3 also include revenues from the population. We were not able to separate the revenues from the population from the revenues from the socialist sector in the republic budgets. At the same time, it is quite clear that the majority of the revenues from the population do go into the republic budgets. Therefore, let us proceed as follows. Column 6 of table III-3 shows the values of the gap in the revenues from the population from table I-3. Assuming, with a very small error, that this entire gap pertains to the republic budgets, let us subtract it from the amounts taken into account in table III-3. As a result we obtain new indicators of the gap in the revenues from the socialist sector—column 7.

In table III-3, "other revenues" are shown about which nothing was said above—there is no such section in the classification of revenues. I took them from the *Byudzhet* handbooks. It is clear that these "other revenues" are the amount of revenues in a number of sections. Examining the classification once again and taking into account that there is no gap in the revenues of the republic budgets, we come to the clear-cut conclusion that these "other revenues" should include the amounts in sections 9, 11, 16, 19, 20, 21, 29, 41 and 60. Apparently a portion of the amounts for section 43, which are to be examined in the next chapter, also belong here. It seems to me that, in addition to section 43, the amounts of sections 9 and 60 should be of the greatest importance here.

In speaking about "other revenues" it is also necessary to discuss some revenues not examined in our analysis that are endlessly being referred to in Soviet sources. Precisely because these revenues are mentioned so often in Soviet literature, a great importance is mistakenly ascribed to them in some Western publications. It is not quite

Table III–3. First Refinement of the Gap in the Revenues from the Socialist Economy (in billions of rubles)

Year	Previous gap	Revenues of republic budgets				Gap in revenues from the population	New amount of gap
		Local taxes and levies	Other revenues	Difference in prices	Surpluses of budget assets		
	1	2	3	4	5	6	7
1940	1.7	0.2	0.2	—	0.1	0	1.2
1950	4.6	0.7	0.2	—	0.2	0.2	3.7
1951	5.7	0.7	0.2	—	0.2	0.1	4.7
1952	6.2	0.8	0.2	—	0.3	0.3	5.2
1953	10.6	0.8	0.2	—	0.1	0.3	9.8
1954	13.3	0.8	0.3	—	0.01	0.2	12.4
1955	8.3	0.8	0.4	—	0.1	0.2	7.2
1956	6.9	0.9	0.4	—	0.1	0.3	5.8
1957	8.2	0.9	0.8	—	0	0.3	6.8
1958	10.2	1.0	1.0	0.04	0.2	0.2	8.2
1959	13.6	1.0	1.1	1.6	0.3	0.3	9.9
1960	14.2	0.7	1.2	1.9	0.4	0.3	10.3
1961	13.6	0.7	1.2	1.1	0.4	0.4	10.6
1962	13.7	0.7	1.2	1.0	0.4	0.3	10.7
1963	14.7	0.7	2.1	1.1	0.5	0.4	10.7
1964	14.9	0.7	1.5	1.3	0.8	0.3	10.9
1965	16.9	0.8	1.5	1.3	0.9	0.3	12.7
1966	14.5	0.8	1.9	—	0.6	0.5	11.7
1967	16.9	0.8	2.0	—	0.6	0.5	14.0

Table III-3 continued.

1968	21.7	0.9	1.7	—	1.2	0.4	18.3
1969	25.3	0.9	2.0	—	1.7	0.4	21.1
1970	29.2	0.8	3.0	—	1.3	0.3	24.4
1971	30.3	0.9	2.8	—	1.6	0.5	25.5
1972	32.5	0.9	2.4	—	1.3	0.4	28.3
1973	39.8	0.9	4.8	—	1.4	0.4	33.1
1974	42.4	1.0	5.9	—	2.1	0.5	33.9
1975	49.4	1.0	6.0	—	2.2	0.4	40.6
1976	55.7	1.0	6.4	—	2.3	0.4	46.4
1977	58.1	1.1	6.8	—	2.4	0.4	48.2
1978	64.3	1.1	7.2	—	2.5	0.5	54.0

Sources: Column 1:
Table I–4, column 8
Column 2:
1940–1975—Table III-2, column 1
1976–78—extrapolation
Columns 3, 4 and 5:
1976–78—extrapolation
1970–76—*Byudzhet 76*, p. 75
1966–69—*Byudzhet 72*, p. 78
1950, 1955, 1960–65—*Byudzhet 66*, p. 71–72
1940, 1956–59—*Byudzhet 62*, p. 69
1951–54—*Byudzhet 57*, p. 15
Column 6:
Table I–3, column 7
Column 7:
sum of columns 1 and 6 less columns 2, 3, 4 and 5.

clear to me to which sections of the classification these revenues belong, but this is not all that important.

First of all, there are the so-called "Revenues from State Property and Other Sources":[91]

—revenues from the sale of property which has come to the state: confiscated property, ownerless property and property which has been transferred to the state by inheritance;
—revenues from the sale of unclaimed freight;
—revenues from undelivered mail;
—the amounts from the sale of the products and instruments of illegal fishing;[92]
—the amounts from the sale of the confiscated products of poaching;
—the recovery of accounts payable and depositor debts;
—amounts on deposit;
—amounts recovered for cases of thefts and deficits of goods.

In one of our main sources[93] we find in addition:

—receipts from the sale of the property of budget-carried institutions;
—fishing levy from kolkhozes;
—treasures (less 25 percent, which is paid to whoever found them), but, as I have already noted above, it is possible that precisely these amounts constitute the coin levy which is taken into account in section 12 of the classification;
—the fee for the working and mining of peat for fuel.

With respect to all these revenues, I repeat, it is not completely clear to which sections they belong, although it seems that for the most part they should be attributed to section 12. Similarly, for the majority of them it is not clear whether they pertain to the republic budgets or the union budget. For some of them we have evidence that this question is resolved on the basis of the subordination of the corresponding organizations:[94] "The revenues from the sale of property confiscated by organs of the USSR are transferred to the union budget, and that confiscated in accordance with decisions of organs of the union republics is transferred to the republic budgets." The same thing also pertains to amounts on deposit, which are transformed into the revenue of the budget, and to the amounts obtained as a result of the violation of prices.[95]

Thus, from these two examples it is already evident that some things in the list given pertain to the union budget. However, even without any evidence it is clear that these revenues of the union budget cannot be significant to any extent, and we can completely disregard them in the further analysis. Moreover, it is quite possible that at least some of them are included in that part of the revenues from profits which we were not able to break down.

Let us summarize our results. The significance of the values given in column 7 of table III-3 is that our accurate calculations end with them. Up to this moment our calculations were based entirely on official Soviet publications, and it is not advisable to doubt them. However, further we have to enter the domain of estimates, suppositions, logical inferences and the use of fragmentary data. I do not wish in any way to belittle the importance of all this, but nevertheless later we will have to take into account the fact that certain inaccuracies in our constructions quite possibly exist, and what we will obtain will be estimates, not exact figures.

Thus, what exactly do we know with respect to the figures shown in column 7 of table III-3, which characterize the gap of the revenues of the union budget?

Firstly, in the course of our discussion we saw a number of revenues which surely exist in the union budget, but which are also surely too small in order to further deal with them seriously.

Secondly, some revenues were named for which we were not able to find precise data:

—the revenues of section 43—economizing on administrative expenditures;
—the revenues from foreign trade and/or customs revenues;
—the revenues from the surpluses of budget funds which were not used at the end of the year.

We will examine these revenues in the next two chapters.

Thirdly, it is quite possible that there are some revenues which are not indicated in the classification. We will examine these possibilities in the next chapter.

Notes

1. For example, *Byudzhet 66*, p. 15; *Byudzhet 72*, p. 17; *Byudzhet 76*, p. 14. It is not very clear why these particular amounts do not pass through the budget. Although this simplifies the procedures, it contradicts the general practice of the Ministry of Finance of boosting the amount of the budget (see chapter X).

2. Feonova, et al., *Organizatsiya*, 1974, p. 78.

3. This does not contradict the fact that usually prices of imported consumer goods are higher than those domestically produced.

4. They are more than 99 percent of all receipts (Popadyuk, *Finansy*, 1973, p. 106).

5. Feonova, et al., *Organizatsiya*, 1974, p. 61.

6. It is worth mentioning that only a part of profits are paid into the budget. A considerable share of them remains at the disposal of enterprises and organizations.

7. Rusin and Eydinova, *Gosudarstvennyy*, 1975, p. 35, and also Yevdokimov, *Kontrol'*, 1974, p. 65.

8. At the same time everything that has been said must not be understood too narrowly. The financial relations of the budget and enterprises are very complicated and are practically never limited to only settlements based on a balance. Many enterprises, which pay part of their profits into the budget, at the same time receive from the budget allocations for capital investments, the training of personnel, scientific research, so-called operating expenses and so on. Therefore, it is more correct to say that the interrelations of cost-accounting organizations with the budget are such that the "bulk" of their economic expenditures are covered by their own revenues, while budget financing is aimed at covering only some special expenditures.

9. The railroads were financed in exactly this way until 1930, and some Soviet authors carelessly write about payments to the budget of funds from rail transport along with payments from profit (for example, Tsapkin, *Finansy*, 1972, p. 43). In fact it has been necessary for more than 45 years now to speak about ordinary deductions from profits by the railroads (Yevdokimov, *Kontrol'*, 1974, p. 67, as well as Aleksandrov, *Gosudarstvennyy*, 1965, p. 276). The same thing pertains to other types of transport (ibid., chapter XVIII).

10. For example, *Narkhoz 75*, p. 725.

11. Ibid.

12. "The revenues of Gosbank consist primarily of interest and fees for the collection of receipts. Expenditures include the interest paid by the bank on the balances of funds in the accounts of kolkhoz and cooperative organizations; the interest paid on the deposits of the population in institutions of the bank; administrative and managerial expenses; expenditures connected with the production of bank notes and coins; the making of capital investments by the bank itself and others" (Poskonov, *Kreditno*, 1967, p. 152). There are sufficient guidelines here for making the corresponding estimates.

It is also worth considering that "Gosbank pays interest on the funds deposited in accounts of savings banks in the amount of 2.7 percent per annum" (Gnutov, "Sberkassa", 1974, p. 21). "From enterprises, institutions and organizations the savings banks receive remuneration for the receipt in their favor of monetary payments and other services—7 kopecks for each transaction" (Ibid). The corresponding amounts are quite significant. In particular, savings banks receive hundreds of millions of housing and municipal services payments annually. "The excess of revenues over expenditures [of savings banks] forms the profits of the savings banks. Half of the total amount of the profit is transferred to the union budget. . . ." (Ibid). In 1976, as is easy to calculate from table VII-1, savings banks should have received 388 million rubles for the difference between the interest received and paid (taking the latter as 2.3 percent).

One more thing. In Sverdlik, "Mezhotraslevoy", 1976, p. 338, it is calculated that in 1970 industrial enterprises, which had been converted to the new system of planning (83 percent of all enterprises), paid the bank from profit 0.9 billion rubles. The author attributes this amount to the revenues of the budget.

Garbuzov, in "Byudzhet", 1978, p. 5, indicates that the plan for 1978 stipulated that enterprises will allocate 6 billion rubles from their profits "for the repayment of bank loans and interest on the use of credit."

13. For example: "Some enterprises and organizations make settlements with the

budget on deductions from profits according to a special procedure. . . . Among them are, for example, credit institutions—Gosbank, Stroybank, the republic organs of state insurance, the Main Administration for State Savings Banks and State Credit, and the Foreign Insurance Administration of the Ministry of Finance. These organizations pay to the budget 50 percent of the amount of their actual profit" (Massarygin, *Finansovaya*, 1968, p. 95).

14. There is a theoretical possibility that profits of Gosstrakh and the banks go to section 25, but it seems to me very unlikely.

15. For example, *Narkhoz 75*, p. 726.

16. There is at least a terminological inaccuracy here—I would not attribute either fixed payments or the fee for capital to "payments from profits," but, after all, this is a matter for Soviet economists themselves. A little further we will see that it is not accidental.

17. Zhevtyak and Kolesnikov, *Pribyl'*, 1976, p. 48. As far as I know, this is the first instance in the Soviet literature when indicators of the losses for industry as a whole have appeared. In this connection it is also worth noting that in themselves these indicators look reliable, but perhaps some military sectors are being financed directly, and as a result their losses are not included here.

18. Indeed, for example, in 1970 the total amount of the funds paid to the budget for fixed payments and the fee for capital was approximately 16 billion rubles (*Narkhoz 75*, p. 742), and approximately 20 percent of these payments would have to have been from unprofitable enterprises. It is clear that during these years only a small part, and by no means a fifth, of all these enterprises were unprofitable.

19. Earlier in a note to the corresponding line it was indicated—for example, in *Narkhoz 72*, p. 724—"Payments from profit include: the fee for fixed productive capital and working capital, rent (fixed) payments, remission of the free remainder of profits, deductions from profits and others." Beginning with *Narkhoz 73*, p. 778, the data on "deductions from profits and other payments" are cited separately. In the comments to the yearbooks it is stated—for example, *Narkhoz 74*, p. 828—"The data on all the monetary accumulations of industrial enterprises include (in addition to profits) turnover tax, special markups which are levied in excess of the basic price, as well as other amounts which enter the revenue of the state budget directly, but are a part of the net income of industry." Here all these "others," "other payments" and "other amounts" are the revenues of the budget, about which we are speaking here.

20. Rusin and Eydinova, *Gosudarstvennyy*, 1975, p. 35.

21. Garbuzov, "Byudzhet," 1975, p. 8. The fact that this procedure is not new is evident from the note to the table in Kosyachenko, *50let*, 1967, p. 346.

22. *Narkhoz 75*, p. 725.

23. It is well known that a considerable portion of the profit of municipal services (they are now basically cost accounting) remains at the disposal of the municipal enterprises themselves.

24. Aleksandrov, *Gosudarstvennyy*, 1965, p. 267.

25. This is also indirectly supported by the following. In Bobrovnikov, *O Gosudarstvennom*, 1974, p. 6, it is stated that in 1974 payments to the RSFSR budget from housing and municipal services in the amount of 1,458.2 million rubles were anticipated. At the same time, all profits of municipal services for the USSR as a whole in 1974 were 1,432 million rubles (*Narkhoz 74*, p. 739). It is clear that a quite substantial part of the payments from housing and municipal services must have no relation to profits.

26. As is evident from Garbuzov, "Byudzhet Pervogo," 1976, pp. 4–5, the plan for 1976 also stipulated only 4.3 billion rubles for "other payments." But according to *Narkhoz 76*, pp. 635–36, it is easy to calculate that these other payments in fact were

almost 10 billion rubles. Hence, 1975 is not just an exception. It is also significant that the total amount of all payments to the budget from profits in 1976 actually exceeded the plan indicators by only 0.7 billion rubles.

27. In Zhevtyak and Kolesnikov, *Pribyl'*, 1976, p. 98, a table is presented in which the amounts of the payments of profits to the budget are calculated. The table was compiled according to the data of *Narkhoz* yearbooks but an obvious mistake was made—cooperatives were grouped with state enterprises and organizations. In fact, the payments of cooperatives consist of a tax, but not of deductions from profits.

28. It is possible that I am incorrectly interpreting the percentage distribution of profits published in the *Narkhoz* yearbooks. I use (for column 2 of table III-1) the value "payments to the budget from profits," while, apparently the value "payments to the budget" should be used; the difference is usually 1 percent.

29. See, for example, *Narkhoz 62*, p. 636.

30. Larionov, et al., *Dokhody*, 1954, p. 15.

31. Azarkh, *Spravochnik*, 1972, p. 91.

32. Aleksandrov, *Gosudarstvennyy*, 1965, p. 127.

33. Marachevskaya, "O kontrole," 1978, p. 80.

34. We must, of course, take into account in such calculations that as the average wage increases the share of income tax grows since it reaches a maximum—13 percent—only when wages are 100 rubles a month or more. At the same time, changes in the payments of taxes on being single and on having small families have occurred as a result of sharp demographic shifts.

35. For example, for 1975 the average annual number of workers and empolyees was 102.2 million, while the average monthly wage was 146 rubles (*Narkhoz 75*, pp. 532, 545). Thus, the annual wage fund was 179 billion rubles. The deductions for social insurance during this year were 11.3 billion rubles (*Narkhoz 75*, p. 742), that is, 6.3 percent. This looks quite realistic, although I have doubts about the correctness of the indicators of employment—see chapter VI. But even if my doubts are correct, it is very difficult to take this into account in calculating the value of the deductions for social insurance.

36. I believe that the data on employment and the average wage in construction—for example, *Narkhoz 75*, pp. 532, 533, 546, 547—are given for the "pure" sectors. I show this in my work on the statistics of construction which I hope to complete in a year or two.

37. Simonenko, *Sotsial'noe*, 1976, p. 203.

38. Ibid., pp. 203–4.

39. According to Makarenko, *Sbornik*, 1976, p. 15, the payments of enterprises and organizations for social insurance according to the 1976 plan were to be 11,356.5 million rubles, and the "receipts for accommodations and other revenues" were to be 345 million rubles.

40. Tsapkin, *Finansy*, 1972, p. 60.

41. Duties for some goods are rather high, up to 200 percent of the price itself, but because of the relatively small amount of goods which cross the border as personal belongings (and/or by mail), the total sum of these duties is negligible.

42. Aleksandrov, *Gosudarstvennyy*, 1965, p. 154.

43. Just on the contrary, as is asserted in Ladygin and Zotova, *Sotsialisticheskaya*, 1977, p. 309, there is a subsidy from the state budget for exports—see chapter IV.

44. Rates of customs duties are published (see, in particular, Ministerstvo, *Tamozhennyye*, 1971) but it is practically impossible to calculate the total value of customs revenues from them since these rates, like the data on exports and imports, are not complete.

45. Larionov, et al., *Dokhody*, 1954, p. 14.

46. An example: "For small-scale municipal enterprises which have not been converted to cost accounting, the gross amounts of their revenues and expenditures are included in the budget" (Aleksandrov, *Gosudarstvennyy*, 1965, p. 255).

47. Above I said that the payment of some revenues from housing services to section 2 is quite probable. We do not know anything for certain here, but the payment of different revenues of housing services to different sections of the classification of the budget revenues does not contradict anything.

48. In part kindergartens and boarding schools (but not nurseries) are financed from the union budget (see *Byudzhet 76*, pp. 37, 43, 47 and 66).

49. In *Byudzhet 57*, p. 14, there are data on the tax on buildings and on the ground rent separately. However, in all other handbooks these data are combined.

50. Aleksandrov, *Gosudarstvennyy*, 1965, pp. 185–86.

51. For quite a long time now this has been a tax not "on entertainment," but only on movies. All other performances are exempt from this tax—Aleksandrov, *Gosudarstvennyy*, 1965, p. 108.

52. Ibid., pp. 154 ff.

53. This overall gap has included the entertainment tax since 1969 and the one-time levy since 1970.

54. The fact that this entire section is only revenues of local budgets is best seen from a comparison of the indicators in Pavlov, *Mestnyye*, 1970, p. 11, with those for the same years given in *Byudzhet 72*, p. 77.

55. Rusin and Eydinova, *Gosudarstvennyy*, 1975, p. 36; Gerashchenko, *Operatsionnaya*, 1975, p. 217.

56. Rusin and Eydinova, *Gosudarstvennyy*, 1975, p. 36.

57. Yevdokimov, *Kontrol'*, 1974, p. 30.

58. Millionshchikov, *Nenalogovyye*, 1967, pp. 25–26. In describing this budget revenue here, the author adheres to a very epic tone. The impression is formed that such a practice—a deliberate deviation from the standards—is recognized almost as normal.

59. Ibid., pp. 39–40.

60. Ibid., p. 17ff; Yevdokimov, *Kontrol'*, 1974, p. 195. In this section other revenues are also taken into account, such as the levy for state verification of standards and measuring instruments, the levy for the registration of trademarks and others (Millionshchikov, *Nenalogovyye*, 1967). Although the list of such taxes is quite long, as a whole the amounts are trivial.

Zhilyakov, "Poryadok", 1979, p. 59, indicates that the amounts of "illegal and overstated planned allocations for administrative expenses" enter in this section. These sorts of collections amounted to 65 million rubles in 1967 and almost 80 million in 1977 (ibid., p. 60). Since these collections are directed to the union, republic, or local budgets depending on the subordination of the particular organization or enterprise, it is obvious that only several million rubles could have been paid into the union budget.

61. This is clearly seen from a comparison of the amounts for republic and local budgets—see, for example, *Byudzhet 72*, pp. 78 and 102.

62. A. Birman, *Ocherki*, 1968, p. 119.

63. Senchagov, et al., *Amortizatsionnyy*, 1975, p. 27; see also pp. 30 and 34.

64. *Narkhoz 74*, p. 755.

65. In 1971 220 million rubles of amortization in industry were paid to the budget (Senchagov, *Finansy*, 1973, p. 78).

66. I have already indicated in chapter II that in Yevdokimov, "O klassifikatsii," 1976. p. 32 (and also in Yevdokimov, *Kontrol'*, 1974, p. 13) section 19 is called "receipts in connection with changes in wholesale prices."

67. G. Schroeder brought these data to my attention—see *Narkhoz 74,* p. 651.
68. A. Birman, *Finansy,* 1975.
69. Azarkh, *Spravochnik,* 1972, p. 94.
70. A. Birman, *Finansy,* 1975, p. 325.
71. Yevdokimov, *Kontrol',* 1974, p. 78.
72. True, Aleksandrov, *Gosudarstvennyy,* 1965, p. 147, speaks about budget revenues from the deductions for these operations for petroleum and gas. If this is indeed so, that is, if even then there were already such deductions, they went directly to "payments from profits."
73. Zlobin, *Gosudarstvennyy,* 1970, p. 103.
74. Yevdokimov, *Kontrol',* 1974, p. 84.
75. Azarkh, *Spravochnik,* 1972, p. 120.
76. Garbuzov, "Byudzhet," 1975, p. 8.
77. Zlobin, *Gosudarstvennyy,* 1970, p. 48. Here the section is called "Payments of Surplus Revenues from Lower Budgets."
78. Darkov and Maksimov, *Finansovaya,* 1975, p. 10.
79. Yevdokimov, *Kontrol',* 1974, p. 13.
80. Gallik, et al., *The Soviet,* 1968, p. 61.
81. The following is worth noting: As is apparent, for example, in *Narkhoz 70,* p. 730, and also in the *Byudzhet* handbooks, there is a gap for 1940 between the overall sum of "state loans" (1.1 billion rubles) and its breakdown into "loans to the population" (0.9 billion rubles) and "loans acquired by savings banks" (0.02 billion rubles), i.e., 180 million rubles. There is a smaller gap for 1950, and then the gap disappears. It seems that these gaps must be explained by loans acquired by cooperatives; however, it is quite possible that these are loans of Gosstrakh. The latter loans are discussed in Zlobin, *Finansy,* 1967, p. 251. At the same time, if this were the case, it would be necessary to explain why these loans later ceased.

Unfortunately, in an article on loans, Millar, "History," 1975, this question is not examined.

82. Millionshchikov, *Nenalogovyye,* 1967, pp. 5–6.
83. It is possible that I am not entirely correct in this estimate. "Each year as many as 400,000 claims for an overall sum of as much as 800 million rubles are received by the organs of the State Bureau of Arbitration of the Council of Ministers of the RSFSR alone; more than 300 million rubles in levies and fines are exacted from the guilty economic organizations (Orlov V.M., "Ukrepleniye," 1977, p. 67). However, it is also written here that "The most widespread violations include: not observing delivery dates and agreed assortments, shipping inferior quality goods, spoilage and shortages of valuable articles." Therefore, a relatively smaller part of this overall sum should be made up of fines for above-norm layover of cars. However, it is possible that the latter fines are collected without being submitted to arbitration.
84. Rusin and Eydinova, *Gosudarstvennyy,* 1965, p. 53.
85. Aleksandrov, *Gosudarstvennyy,* 1965, p. 287.
86. Azarkh, *Spravochnik,* 1972, pp. 86, 87. However, according to Millionshchikov, *Nenalogoyye,* 1967, p. 15, these revenues do not belong here but to section 12 of the republic budgets.
87. Maslennikov and Kheyfets, *Vzaimootnosheniya,* 1971, p. 68, as well as Kheyfets and Zlatkis, *Sostavleniye,* 1976, pp. 54–55.
88. Aleksandrov, *Gosudarstvennyy,* 1965, p. 28.
89. Millionshchikov, *Nenalogovyye,* 1967, p. 4.
90. This follows quite precisely from a comparison of the values in *Byudzhet 66,* pp. 71–72, and *Byudzhet 72,* p. 78.

91. Rusin and Eydinova, *Gosudarstvennyy,* 1975, p. 75.

92. A portion of these revenues go to the union budget. Azarkh, *Spravochnik,* 1972, p. 48.

93. Ibid., pp. 25, 50, 61, 144.

94. Zlobin, *Finansy,* 1971, p. 234.

95. Ibid., p. 237. As already noted above, the so to speak "legal" increasing of prices is taken into account in sections 19 and 20. Here it is a matter of revenues obtained illegally, when goods are sold at prices higher than the established prices.

Chapter IV

Other Budget Revenues

This chapter is about those budget revenues on which we do not have precise data. We will begin with those which we know definitely exist, and then we will address those the very existence of which is questionable. In all cases we will be forced to make assumptions and estimates (sometimes guesstimates).

Revenues from Foreign Trade

As was already shown in chapter III, there is no question that revenues from foreign trade enter the union budget—this is stated in a number of sources—but nearly everything else is very far from being clear. We do not even know whether there are other revenues from foreign trade separate from customs revenues. As to the amount of the revenues, there is only one rather recent statement in the Soviet literature and, as we will soon see, it is rather ambiguous. Nevertheless we should and will try our best.[1]

In chapter III it has already been indicated that it makes no sense to complicate the question by examining the customs revenues from the population; they cannot be at all significant on the scale of the budget. As to the customs revenues paid by state (and cooperative) enterprises and organizations, since we cannot separate them, we will speak about them together with the revenues from foreign trade (this will be clarified below).

The volume of foreign trade is increasing rapidly and has achieved a very large scale, which is evident from the data on exports and imports in physical terms,[2] as well as from the data in value terms in so-called "transferable" rubles (the latter are shown in table IV-1). However, the data in physical terms are published only in part and are not broken down by types, grades and other parameters, which makes estimating their total incredibly difficult,[3] while the data in "transferable" rubles are a very peculiar measure[4] and it is not clear how one might shift from them to values in "normal" domestic rubles. At the same time there are some data on exports and imports in domestic rubles for the economy as a whole and for major branches for 1959, 1966 and 1972, i.e., for the years for which input-output tables were constructed.

Foreign trade is only a part of so-called foreign economic activity which additionally includes the "noncommercial operations." We see this in the following citations:[5] "The import and export of goods for rendering uncompensated aid and other noncommercial operations (parcels, baggage and others) are not included in the foreign trade turnover."

The fact that these operations are not included in the "foreign trade turnover" does not at all mean that their financial results are not reflected in some form in the budget. But it is hardly worth talking about postal packages, baggage, and other things of this sort. Concerning "uncompensated aid," the situation is as follows. Its amounts, including the free delivery of arms, may be quite significant, but certainly not extremely significant. According to B. Kostinsky, many arms deliveries are included in the published amounts of foreign trade (this follows from the gaps revealed by his calculations using published data on the structure of exports.) A number of indirect indications lead him to conclude that in many cases "aid" is given in the form of advantageous credit conditions or relatively low prices.[6] At the same time, we definitely know that the USSR gave considerable aid to Viet Nam and Cuba, and while we do not know the economic conditions of that aid, it is quite probable (more so with respect to Viet Nam) that this aid was in fact free.

There are two possibilities. Either this aid is reflected in the expenditure part of the budget or it is taken from the overall amount of the revenue from foreign trade (we will discuss what this is shortly) prior to its being recorded in the budget. There may well be a, so to speak, mixed variant of the two. For example, payments to the UN may go through the expenditure part of the budget, and some other expenditures may be charged against revenues from foreign trade.[7] All the same, I do not think that the overall amount of aid could seriously affect our calculations, and we will ignore it in the future.

Thus, we have more or less dealt with the noncommercial operations, but there are also commercial operations that are not included in the foreign trade turnover. They are the operations of Soviet banks abroad, various insurance operations, tourism, credit, and freight and passenger transportation. We do not have sufficient information about most of these operations, so we must resort to discussing them.

The activities of the banks operated by the USSR abroad[8] and the insurance operations do not involve revenues of any significance in the scale of our discussion.

As for tourism, we have only some data on the number of trips to and from the USSR for 1975.[9] According to these data, 3.7 million foreign tourists entered the USSR, and 2.5 million Soviet tourists went abroad. With respect to the so-called capitalist countries, there were three times as many foreign visitors to the USSR as there were Soviet citizens visiting these countries. From these data it unquestionably follows that on the whole the USSR gains from tourism. How much? Let us make some elementary calculations. 1.5 million people went from the USSR to the so-called socialist countries. A vacation there cost about 250 rubles; hence the total is about 400 million rubles. Let us take 500 rubles as the average cost of vacations to other countries. One million people visited there, hence we have another 500 million rubles.

It is more difficult to make a calculation for the 3.7 million foreigners who visited the country in 1975, but let us take into account two considerations. Firstly, both the receipts from foreign tourists and the expenditures of those visiting outside the country are made in foreign currency and it seems that the balance of foreign currency payments is not included in the budget.[10] Secondly, we calculated the *total* expenditures on trips of Soviet citizens above, and they must at least be comparable with the expenditures of foreign tourists. The overall amount turns out to be quite impressive, but, I repeat, this is the *overall* amount, and the "gains" from tourism, i.e., revenues less expenditures, must be substantially less.

On the whole, it seems that a part of the earnings from tourism is taken into account as a budget revenue. However, it is more likely that this revenue is included in the budget in the total amount of receipts from profits. If I am mistaken, that is, if the revenues from tourism enter the budget in the revenues from foreign trade, the corresponding error in our calculations considering the overall scale of these operations noted above can not be more than 100–300 million rubles for 1975 and a substantially smaller amount (tourism is growing rapidly) for preceding years.

A few words about credit operations. In trade with capitalist countries the USSR is persistently receiving credits and now has an enormous (enormous compared with its possibilities to repay it back) debt on the order of 16 billion rubles.[11] This does not necessarily mean that the budget has never had some temporary revenues from credits, but they cannot be substantial. It is more complicated with the socialist countries and the countries of the Third World. Here credits have been granted, and it is theoretically quite possible that the repayment of credits and interest payments could create a revenue. However, it could not be of great significance relative to the amounts we are concerned with.[12] The following must also be borne in mind. If in the trade with some "socialist" country a steady favorable balance arises or credits are repayed, the funds obtained according to the logic of things should be channelled into covering the overall unfavorable balance of payments of the country. If we all the same assume that these funds are taken into account as budget revenues, then the assumption is inevitable that the issue of credits as well as their repayment and interest payments should be reflected in the budget. However, there is not enough room for large amounts of credits in the budget; the only place where they could be—the gap between the total amount of the budget expenditures and the amount of all the parts—is "occupied," so to speak, by other expenses.

A similar argument can be made with respect to the activity of the merchant fleet (airlines and, even more so, rail and auto transport are insignificant for our calculations). Shipping of the merchant fleet has grown greatly, particularly during the past 10-15 years, and much foreign currency is undoubtedly earned (it is well known that more than 90 percent of all the shipments are for foreign trade).[13] One textbook asserts:

> The basic indicator of foreign shipping is the net foreign currency earnings (the difference between revenues and expenditures of the fleet in foreign currency).[14]

It must be taken into account that the merchant fleet receives practically no allocations from the budget for its economic activity,[15] which means that its expenditures are covered by its own incomes. But it is not clear exactly how payments for shipments of Soviet freight are handled. There is some possibility that these shipments are paid for with budget allocations for trade (see below). It seems (I found no direct information on this in the literature) that the situation is apparently as follows.

Foreign currency revenues of the merchant fleet must go to cover in part the overall negative foreign currency balance of the country. It is quite probable that the profits of the merchant fleet in "ordinary" rubles enter the budget in the normal manner, that is, they are included in the payments from profits. In any case I do not think that the profits from the merchant fleet in either rubles or foreign currency are entered as revenue from foreign trade. However, if I am not correct, the corresponding revenues from the merchant fleet should, it seems, amount to about 100–200 million rubles, i.e., they are not of real significance for our calculations.

Summarizing the examination of these various types of foreign economic activity that are not a part of the foreign trade turnover, I repeat that it is most expedient to limit ourselves in this study only to the amounts of revenues from foreign trade as such. We will have to make quite rough assumptions all the same, and therefore the results of our calculations cannot be precise in any case.

Let us turn now directly to the revenues from foreign trade themselves. Very little light is thrown on this question in the Soviet literature, and in the Western literature it has practically not been touched upon. True, in studies of Soviet input-output tables the question of how foreign trade is taken into account in these tables and in national income accounts has been analyzed, and we base our calculations on some of the results of these findings. However, I repeat, as far as I know no one has yet dealt with the question of how foreign trade is reflected in the budget itself. The few Soviet works on this point often serve just to confuse things.

What must we keep in mind in examining this quite difficult (as the reader will soon see) and important (since these revenues amount to billions of rubles) question? First of all we must note that since 1918 there has been a state monopoly on foreign trade in the country. This should not be understood too literally; in particular, the Tsentrosoyuz, which formally is not a state but a cooperative organization, trades with foreign firms. Many organizations and enterprises participate in negotiations and even have the right to determine what they will buy within the limits of a given foreign currency constraint.[16] All the same, the basic fact for us here is that all commercial operations for foreign trade are carried out through a special Ministry of Foreign Trade (MFT), which signs all contracts and agreements, and payments are also made through a special Foreign Trade Bank (*Vneshtorgbank*).

This should be explained. Soviet currency—the ruble—is used only and exclusively within the country; the transactions of all Soviet organizations and enterprises with the MFT and Vneshtorgbank are also made in rubles. And on the contrary all transactions with any other country are carried out not in rubles but in either international (hard) currency or in the currency of that country. True, transactions within CEMA are carried out in units which are called transferable rubles, but they have no relation to the "real," "normal" ruble. What exactly are they?

Transferable rubles are determined by special coefficients for converting foreign currencies at their current international exchange rates, and these coefficients are regularly published by Gosbank on the basis of the so-called "gold content of the ruble" established in 1960.[17] It must also be said that the transferable ruble physically does not exist; it is a bookkeeping fiction. However, as I just said, it is used as an accounting unit in transactions with CEMA countries and for determining the overall volume of imports and exports (in particular, all figures below on volumes of exports and imports are given precisely in transferable rubles; foreign trade in other units, e.g., in "normal" internal rubles, is not published). Furthermore, of particular importance to us, the transferable ruble is used in transactions within the country for foreign trade operations, and we will turn to this shortly. Technically, things are as follows.

All receipts and payments in foreign currency are handled by Vneshtorgbank, and it handles all its receipts and payments in rubles separately. Real transactions in rubles and in foreign currency are not mixed; they are connected with each other, but only in a bookkeeping, accounting sense. The connection is made through the transferable ruble as we will soon see.

The fact that there is no real connection between foreign currencies and the ruble leads to many consequences, in particular to the extreme difficulty of all international comparisons with the USSR.[18] This also frustrates the attempts of Soviet economists to determine the effectiveness of foreign trade. While all these problems are in themselves quite interesting, we are discussing only the economic results of foreign trade and, more narrowly, the reflection of these results in the budget. Here a fundamental fact must be explained: because the ruble is not connected with foreign currencies, there is not a single financial result of foreign trade but two different results—one in foreign currency and the other in rubles. In practice this means the following. Total imports and exports must be valued both in international prices and in rubles. The difference between total exports and imports in international prices is the financial result of foreign trade in foreign currency, and the difference between imports and exports in internal prices is the financial result of foreign trade in rubles. This statement seems trivial, but in fact not everything is that simple and it requires elucidation.

With respect to transactions in *foreign currency*, it would seem that a comparison of the volumes of exports and imports in transferable rubles would give a crude impression of them, since, to repeat, these values are amounts converted from real world prices at certain exchange rates. At the same time, in order to characterize the financial position of the USSR in the world, a number of additional factors must be considered—results of noncommercial operations (in particular, tourism), Soviet expenditures on their diplomatic and foreign trade missions abroad, the sale of gold (which for the most part is not included in the volume of foreign trade), credit operations including in particular the payment of interest on bank and commercial credit, activities of special Soviet banks abroad, etc. In spite of all this, the overall result is determined primarily by foreign trade, and we know basically what this result is—data were presented above which showed that the USSR has a substantial external debt. In other words, in terms of foreign currency the USSR has spent more than it has received in recent years.

I already noted above that a special foreign currency plan is compiled and that there is no mention in the literature of its connections with the budget. However, even if there is a connection, it must be with the expenditure part of the budget and not with its revenues. So, it seems to me that the foreign currency results of foreign trade are in no way connected with the results of foreign trade in rubles (we will elaborate on this below). We will now talk about these *ruble* results, because it is precisely these results that form the revenue from foreign trade.

It seems logically indisputable that the net financial result of foreign trade for the budget must be the difference between the total value of imports and exports in rubles. But this requires some elaboration, and in fact the entire remaining discussion of budget revenues from foreign trade here is devoted to this and to some calculations.

First of all, why do I think this is so? For the simple reason that anything else would be incorrect. True, no one forces the Soviets to follow logic; they might do this otherwise for some other than logical reasons. Then two variants are possible. The first: the method actually used leads to smaller budget revenues than the indicated difference. Then our calculations exceed the real amount of the revenues and, to skip ahead, it will lead to our overstating the true budget deficit. But our final figures (chapter X) are so big especially for the last few years, that the fact of the existance of the deficit is nevertheless undeniable. The second variant is that the method used results in showing larger revenues from foreign trade in the budget than the difference defined above. This possibility cannot be excluded, but it also does not contradict the basic line of our argument. In this case the amount of the excess is not a real but a "paper" revenue and amounts to nothing more than an additional source for covering up the budget deficit.

The next question is: why must this entire difference be a budget revenue and why precisely in the foreign trade section? Theoretically it could be that enterprises and organizations producing goods for export receive part of this discrepancy as their own income or, on the contrary, bear losses. This is not so for a reason already mentioned: all transactions involving exports and imports within the country are carried out in internal prices.[19] An enterprise can profit from the production of export goods in the usual manner—by reducing production cost—and part of these earnings will go to the budget in the form of the corresponding deductions from profits. However, no enterprise earns (or loses) anything out of the amount which forms the revenues under consideration—the overall difference between the amounts of exported and imported goods. These earnings are accumulated by the MFT (and Vneshtorgbank) and are transferred to the budget, separately from all other revenues.

One more thing. As we saw above, the USSR has been losing foreign currency in foreign trade, but in internal prices, as we will see, it earns tremendous amounts of money—many billions of rubles. We could discuss the theoretical significance of this situation, but that would take us far aside from our basic theme. Also, a seemingly simple question—can we say that overall the country benefits from foreign trade?—is not simple. It turns out to be complex because of difficulties in determining the real economic effect of imported technology and because the simultaneous unprofitability of some production and subsidies to others confuses everything greatly. I mention all of this only to point out the further path of investigation of the problem—this also is not relevant to our theme: we are not studying the economic effectiveness of the Soviet economic system here; this question is beyond the scope of this book.

Let us now address the more technical question of how in fact all this takes place. We find some answers in the following long quotations from a relatively recent book.

> Suppliers are paid for export deliveries by foreign trade associations in internal wholesale prices excluding turnover tax, but including the markup for the special quality of export goods. This markup compensates the producer for the additional expenditures in connection with the demands of the world market and foreign customers.[20]

Further it is stated here that foreign trade associations pay suppliers for exports using credits of the Vneshtorgbank and then:

> Foreign currency earnings in transferable rubles from the export of goods are paid to the Vneshtorgbank to repay the loan that had been issued to the foreign trade association. In doing this, the foreign currency earnings are recalculated in internal rubles at a ratio of 1:1, since the gold content of the transferable and the internal ruble is the same. The difference between the amount of the payment to the supplier of an export good and the earnings received for it from a foreign buyer are entered in the accounts of foreign trade associations either as a negative amount (in which case it is entered as a subsidy from the state budget) or as a positive amount (a revenue paid to the budget).

And a little further:

> Foreign trade organizations pay foreign suppliers the value of imported goods in foreign currency prices (transferable rubles) with credit (loans) from the Vneshtorgbank . . . Payment [for imported goods by internal buyers] is made for most goods in internal wholesale prices (as a rule, the prices of similar domestically produced goods, taking into account differences in their quality) excluding turnover tax, although for some consumer goods in prices including turnover tax. Some goods (fabrics, leather shoes, etc.) are paid for by the internal buyer (import bureaus of the USSR Ministry of Trade) in retail prices. . . .
>
> The difference between the amounts paid to the foreign supplier in foreign currency and received from the buyer (the recalculation of foreign currency amounts into internal amounts is made at a ratio of 1 : 1) are paid to the budget by foreign trade associations in the form of customs revenues. At the same time there may be subsidies for exports. The overall difference for all goods between the customs revenues and subsidies for exports constitute the amount of income from foreign trade in the state budget.

Not everything here is so simple, and we must overcome a number of difficulties before making calculations.

The main difficulty, as these quotations imply, is that there is no direct comparison of the amounts of exports and imports in internal prices. Instead internal prices for both imports and exports are compared with world market prices in transferable rubles, and the differences thus obtained form the budget revenues and subsidies from the budget. We will examine the question of subsidies a little below, but first more on this comparison.

I cannot say why it is done this way or what is the point of such a comparison to determine this difference for each individual good. Apparently this practice developed historically and reflects an entirely understandable striving to connect two unrelated things—world market prices and the internal prices of the USSR. The difference in prices is quickly made clear by such comparisons, although it is not easy to use this difference as a guide. Indeed, let the price of good A in transferable rubles be greater than in normal rubles. What does that mean—sell it, or buy it? From the standpoint of spending foreign currency it would be more expedient to sell it, while from the standpoint of creating an internal financial revenue it would be better to buy it. (The reader may in this connection think over whether it would be more profitable for the USSR to buy or sell oil and grain if everything were determined only by the relation of prices.)

All the same, formally things are done just this way[21] and it would seem that this completely refutes my basic thesis that the amount of budget revenues from foreign trade are determined as the difference between imports and exports in internal prices. In fact both of these seemingly mutually exclusive situations are simultaneously correct

Table IV-1. Volume of Exports and Imports in Transferable Rubles (in millions of rubles)

	Export	Import	Percentage
	1	2	3
1940	240	245	102
1950	1,615	1,310	81
1951	2,061	1,792	87
1952	2,511	2,255	90
1953	2,653	2,492	94
1954	2,900	2,864	99
1955	3,084	2,754	89
1956	3,250	3,252	100
1957	3,943	3,544	90
1958	3,868	3,915	101
1959	4,897	4,566	93
1960	5,007	5,066	101
1961	5,399	5,245	97
1962	6,327	5,810	92
1963	6,545	6,353	97
1964	6,915	6,963	101
1965	7,359	7,252	99
1966	7,957	7,122	90
1967	8,687	7,683	88
1968	9,571	8,469	88
1969	10,490	9,294	89
1970	11,520	10,559	92
1971	12,425	11,232	90
1972	12,734	13,310	105
1973	15,802	15,544	98
1974	20,738	18,829	91
1975	24,034	26,670	111
1976	28,022	28,733	103
1977	33,255	30,093	90
1978	35,668	34,556	97
Total			
1950–1978	299,237	287,827	96
1961–1978	263,448	254,017	96

Sources: Columns 1 and 2:
1940, 1950, 1955, 1960, 1965, 1970, 1975–78—*Narkhoz 78,* p. 547
1966–69, 1971–74—*Narkhoz 75,* p. 753
1961–64—*Narkhoz 72,* p. 737
1959—*Narkhoz 62,* p. 544
1950–58—*Narkhoz 60,* p. 744
Column 3:
column 2 divided by column 1 multiplied by 100.

because of the following simple fact—in all years the total amount of imports in transferable rubles is very close to the total amount of exports in transferable rubles; they almost coincide. This is shown in table IV-1, where we see that after 1951 the difference between exports and imports in transferable rubles did not exceed 12 percent in any year and was in general significantly less. Overall for the last 29 years this difference amounted to only 4 percent, and the difference was the same—4 percent—for 1961–78, i.e., after the change in the "gold content of the ruble." What does this mean in practice? It means that since the amounts of imports and exports in transferable rubles practically coincide, their participation in transactions changes nothing; in fact total exports and imports are compared precisely in internal prices, in "normal" rubles. I will illustrate this with an elementary example. Assume we have the following figures:

	in transferable rubles	in internal prices
exports	120	75
imports	120	100

According to what I have asserted, the overall financial result of foreign trade should be 25, i.e., 100 minus 75. But we also obtain the same result if we follow the procedure actually used—20 is lost on imports but 45 is earned in exports, so the sum is the same 25.

Thus we can get by without complicated calculations and base our further estimates on available figures on the difference in internal prices. Unfortunately, we have such data for only three years (see below), but this is infinitely better than nothing at all.

It was already evident from the example given that knowing this difference is in itself insufficient: we must also know the amounts that the budget spends on subsidies for foreign trade. This difference shows the "net" final result, however the budget not only receives revenues from foreign trade but has expenditures on foreign trade as well. In principle, there are three possibilities: One—the revenues and expenditures are balanced, and the budget shows the final result. This is obviously not so. On the one hand, we have a number of citations which say that the relations of the budget with foreign trade are not based on a balance,[22] and on the other hand we know with near certainty that the budget includes expenditures on foreign trade, and below we even calculate them. Two—only the difference between the values of imports in transferable rubles and in internal prices enters the budget. Theoretically this is a possibility, but only hypothetically; this would mean that the budget reduces its revenues, which is logically inconsistent with everything that we know. If this were so then in our subsequent calculations the size of the budget deficit would be substantially—by several billions of rubles—larger in each year. Therefore, the most probable is the third possibility, which I use further as a working hypothesis—precisely because the budget has expenditures on foreign trade, in order to determine the budget revenues the amount of budget expenditures on foreign trade must be added to the difference between total imports and exports in internal prices.[23] To repeat what I have just said, if we are mistaken here it is in the direction which favors the entire line of our argument.

The remaining things which follow from the citations or from an examination of other circumstances are not all that significant, but we will discuss them nevertheless.

The citations say that foreign trade organizations sell some imported goods to domestic buyers at prices including turnover tax. This does not create any complications since, as we saw in chapter III (note 4), 99 percent of all turnover tax comes from industry. Therefore, if the price at which a foreign trade organization delivers a good to a domestic buyer includes an amount corresponding to turnover tax, it is not singled out and it enters the budget as part of the total amount of receipts from foreign trade. Or, to simplify, foreign trade itself does not collect turnover tax.[24]

A more serious question is the treatment of various expenditures connected with foreign trade operations, in particular the maintenance of the staff of various foreign trade organizations and the cost of transporting foreign trade freight. With respect to the personnel, a part of them—the employees of the MFT itself—must be paid, as are employees of all other ministries, from special budget allocations for administration. However, many other people are employed in foreign trade.[25]

It should be mentioned that we are concerned here only with those expenditures on personnel that are made in rubles since the amounts that some of these people receive in foreign currency are paid out of general foreign currency resources.

It is very difficult to say anything at all about expenditures on transportation. A significant part of shipments are paid for by foreign contractors in foreign currency, and these do not concern us. We have almost no data to even approximately estimate expenditures on shipping foreign trade freight by railroad, by sea, or by truck.

Both the expenditures on foreign trade personnel and on shipping must grow in some relation to the overall volume of exports and imports. Let us assume that they amount to 5 percent of total foreign trade turnover. Then the corresponding amounts must be (in millions of rubles, see table IV-1):

1950 — 145	1970 — 1105
1955 — 290	1975 — 2535
1960 — 505	1978 — 3510
1965 — 730	

What is the source of these expenditures? The natural assumption is that they are paid by the budget. However, as we will see below, in several years the total amount of budget expenditures for this purpose is insufficient to explain both these expenditures and the subsidies for the differences in prices for exports. Therefore, it is quite possible that the amount of revenues paid into the budget is reduced by the amount of these expenditures. It is no less probable that there were changes in this procedure in various years, which should explain the jumps in these budget expenditures (see table IV-2). Not having a definite answer to this question and also being far from certain about the reliability of these amounts, I will simply ignore them in our further calculations. In effect this means that the budget revenues from foreign trade determined below are clearly overstated.

Now about the budget expenditures on foreign trade: what are the corresponding amounts? In examining the expenditures of the budget I noticed that the total expenditures on trade for the state budget of the USSR are published regularly in the *Byudzhet* handbooks, as are the trade expenditures for local budgets (though not for all years), but the expenditures on trade for the republic budgets are not published. In spite of this, I succeeded in finding some fragmentary data on expenditures on trade for individual republics, and they turned out to be very close to the corresponding data for local budgets. In the *Narkhoz* yearbooks, there are also some data on budget expenditures on raising the wages of workers in trade and on the repricing of some goods. Considering that the overwhelming majority of trade organizations are of local subordination, we can with confidence take the total amount of expenditures on internal trade to be quite close to the expenditures of local budgets plus the expenditures just mentioned (we may assume that the latter expenditures are made from the union budget). If we now subtract this sum from the total amount of expenditures on trade in the USSR State budget, we are left with an extremely large difference amounting to billions of rubles. It is significant and also puzzling that the latter amounts jump around strangely—they get larger, then significantly, by billions of rubles, smaller. What are these expenditures?

Table IV-2. Expenditures for Trade in Various Budgets (in millions of rubles)

	Total—The state budget of the USSR	Including—internal trade			
		Local budgets	All—union and republic budgets	Various expenditures[1]	Difference
Year	1	2	3	4	5
1950	705	77	40	0	588
1955	1,073	150	75	—	848
1956	1,220	180	90	—	950
1957	1,731	220	110	—	1,401
1958	2,035	260	130	0	1,645
1959	3,206	300	150	—	2,756
1960	3,591	337	169	0	3,085
1961	1,767	193	97	—	1,477
1962	1,745	208	104	—	1,433
1963	2,158	227	114	—	1,817
1964	1,788	187	94	0	1,507
1965	2,272	402	201	430	1,239
1966	2,842	296	148	0	2,398
1967	4,921	281	141	0	4,499
1968	6,094	375	188	215	5,316
1969	6,430	298	149	0	5,983
1970	6,258	220	110	0	5,928
1971	6,394	254	127	0	6,013
1972	6,553	576	288	411	5,278
1973	6,803	541	271	428	5,563
1974	3,714	728	364	511	2,111
1975	4,427	786	393	575	2,673

Sources:

Column 1:
1970–75—*Byudzhet 76,* p. 22
1965–69—*Byudzhet 72,* p. 25
1950, 1955, 1960–64—*Byudzhet 66,* p. 20
1956–59—*Byudzhet 62,* p. 18

Column 2:
1970-75—*Byudzhet 76,* p. 100
1969—*Byudzhet 72,* p. 103
1950, 1960–68—Pavlov, *Mestnyye,* 1970, p. 242

Column 3:
50 percent of column 2

Column 4:
1950, 1955, 1970–75—*Narkhoz 75,* p. 642
1960, 1968–69—*Narkhoz 70,* p. 601
1958, 1964,—*Narkhoz 65,* p. 652
1966–67—*Narkhoz 67,* p. 739

Column 5:
column 1 less columns 2, 3 and 4.

Note: 1. Budget expenditures on increasing the pay of trade workers, reducing prices, etc. "0" means that there was no such expenditure in the corresponding year, "—" means that there are no data.

G. Schroeder proposed the explanation that at least part of this money goes for the growth of state material reserves. In principle, this possibility—and in particular that these amounts are somehow connected with material reserves—cannot be dismissed. At the same time, it is impossible to think that all of this money from year to year goes to further increase reserves.

Therefore, the most natural assumption is that this money goes precisely for foreign trade. The possibility cannot be excluded that in assuming this we are overstating these expenditures, but this will only further strengthen our final conclusions.

In table IV-2 I have reproduced all data that we have on expenditures of the state budget on trade, the expenditures of local budgets, and the expenditures on the measures mentioned above. Values for those years for which we do not have data were extrapolated or interpolated. Then I assume that expenditures on internal trade in all republic budgets and the union budget together amount to 50 percent of the expenditures in local budgets for each year. This almost certainly overstates the latter amounts. The remaining difference (column 5) is the amount which according to my hypothesis is the budget expenditures on foreign trade.[26]

After all these speculations, hypothesizing and so on, let us now turn to the final calculations. For them we have:

(a) data on exports and imports in transferable rubles;
(b) data on expenditures of the budget for foreign trade;
(c) data on the difference between exports and imports in domestic prices for 1959, 1966 and 1972,[27]
(d) the following statement by the Minister of Finance:[28]

> In the financial resources of the Soviet Union the receipts from foreign trade are occupying a more and more appreciable position. The revenues from it during the years of the Tenth Five-Year Plan will increase 1.2-fold. During the first two years of the five-year plan they will increase by 10–12 percent and will be more than 10 percent of the entire budget.

Actually this is the only statement we know on the amounts of the budget revenues from foreign trade. It is from a more than authoritative author, and it certainly must be examined.

In 1976 the budget revenues were 232 billion rubles, and in 1977—248 billion rubles (table I-5). In other words, the revenues from foreign trade during these years should be something on the order of 24 billion rubles. We are told that they "will increase by 10–12 percent," that is, in 1975 they should have been on the order of 21.5 billion rubles.

Columns 1 and 2 of table IV-3 show imports and exports in transferable rubles and column 3—the total foreign trade turnover, i.e., the sum of exports and imports in the same transferable rubles. We have these values for all years.

Column 4 is the difference between imports and exports in domestic prices—we have data only for 1959, 1966 and 1972; other years are estimated (see below). Then, in column 5, expenditures of the budget of foreign trade are shown and in column 6 these expenditures are expressed as a percentage of exports in transferable rubles. I see no evident correlation between the numbers of column 5 and 2, but interestingly enough "jumps" in the expenditures follow more or less the changes in wholesale prices in 1955, 1967 and 1973. We know that prices were changed once more in 1975, but our data on expenditures of the budget for years after 1975 are not reliable.

The most likely reason for the jumps in the percentages shown in column 6 of the expenditures in the budget is, very likely, changes in wholesale prices in 1955 (but we do not observe a jump here), 1967, 1973, and 1975. I cannot say how the last change will affect the expenditures in 1976–78 and took for these years the same percentage which I had calculated for 1975.

For years for which I did not have numbers in column 5, I calculated them on the basis of corresponding numbers in column 6.

Of most importance for us, certainly, is column 7. Figures for 1959, 1966 and 1972 were calculated as sums of columns 4 and 5. Figures for 1975–77 were derived from the article by Garbuzov cited above. For all other years, I calculated the values on the basis of the percentages in column 8.

Here, in column 8, the figures for 1959, 1966, 1972 and 1975–77 were calculated on the basis of data from columns 1 and 7. For all other years I interpolated and extrapolated. The question might be asked—why did I base my calculations on the estimated ratios in column 8 rather than using similar estimated ratios of revenues to total trade turnover? The reason is that revenues of the budget are calculated on the basis of a comparison precisely of imports in transferable and domestic rubles. Of course, this reason is not valid enough and I justify myself by the fact that our other choice—interpolating and extrapolating the figures in column 9—is not more reasonable. Therefore, the calculations in column 9—revenues of the budget as a percentage of total trade turnover—which were calculated after I had estimated the figures in column 7, are meaningful only for comparisons and analysis.

The crucial question is, of course, the reliability of the results of all these calculations. As to the first three of them, the only possibility is that my figures are too large. Indeed, we are quite sure that the amounts of the difference between imports and exports for these

Table IV-3. Revenues from Foreign Trade (in billions of rubles)

Year	Volumes of foreign trade in transferable rubles			Imports less exports in domestic prices	Expenditures of the budget		Revenues of the budget		
	Exports	Imports	Total trade turnover		Sum in domestic prices	as % of exports	Sum in domestic prices	as % of imports	as % of trade turnover
	1	2	3	4	5	6	7	8	9
1940	0.2	0.2	0.4	—	—	—	0.3	143	75
1950	1.6	1.3	2.9	1.3	0.6	38	1.9	143	66
1951	2.1	1.8	3.9	2.0	0.6	29	2.6	143	67
1952	2.5	2.3	4.8	2.6	0.7	28	3.3	143	69
1953	2.7	2.5	5.2	2.9	0.7	26	3.6	143	69
1954	2.9	2.9	5.8	3.3	0.8	28	4.1	143	71
1955	3.1	2.8	5.9	3.2	0.8	26	4.0	143	68
1956	3.3	3.3	6.6	3.7	1.0	30	4.7	143	71
1957	3.9	3.5	7.4	3.6	1.4	36	5.0	143	68
1958	3.9	3.9	7.8	4.0	1.6	41	5.6	143	72
1959	4.9	4.6	9.5	3.8	2.8	57	6.6	143	69
1960	5.0	5.1	10.1	4.0	3.1	62	7.1	139	76
1961	5.4	5.2	10.6	5.5	1.5	28	7.0	135	66
1962	6.3	5.8	12.1	6.3	1.4	22	7.7	132	64
1963	6.5	6.4	12.9	6.4	1.8	28	8.2	128	64
1964	6.9	7.0	13.9	7.2	1.5	22	8.7	124	63
1965	7.4	7.3	14.7	7.6	1.2	16	8.8	121	60
1966	8.0	7.1	15.1	6.0	2.4	30	8.4	118	56
1967	8.7	7.7	16.4	4.9	4.5	52	9.4	122	57
1968	9.6	8.5	18.1	5.4	5.3	55	10.7	126	59

Table IV-3 continued.

1969	10.5	9.3	19.8	6.1	6.0	57	12.1	130	61
1970	11.5	10.6	22.1	8.3	5.9	51	14.2	134	64
1971	12.4	11.2	23.6	9.5	6.0	48	15.5	138	66
1972	12.7	13.3	26.0	13.6	5.3	42	18.9	142	73
1973	15.8	15.5	31.3	13.4	5.6	35	19.0	122	61
1974	20.7	18.8	39.5	16.8	2.1	10	18.9	101	48
1975	24.0	26.7	50.7	19.8	2.7	11	21.5	81	42
1976	28.0	28.7	56.7	20.9	3.1	11	24.0	84	42
1977	33.3	30.1	63.4	21.6	3.7	11	25.3	84	40
1978	35.7	34.6	70.3	25.9	3.9	11	29.1	84	41

Sources: Columns 1 and 2:
table IV-1
Column 3:
sum of columns 1 and 2
Column 4:
1959, 1966—Kostinsky, *Foreign*, 1976, p. 7
1972—Kostinsky, personal communication all other years column 7 less column 5
Column 5:
1950, 1955–75—table IV-2
1951–54—interpolation
1976–78—from columns 1 and 6
Column 6:
1950–75—as a percentage of column 5 to column 1
1976–78 estimation
Column 7:
1959, 1966, 1972—sum of columns 4 and 5
1975–77—estimated from Garbuzov, "Finansovaya," 1977, p. 10
1950–58, 1960–65, 1967–71, 1973–74, 1978—according to columns 2 and 8
Column 8:
1959, 1966, 1972, 1975–77—as a percentage of column 7 to column 2
1940–58, 1960–65, 1967–71, 1973–74, 1978—interpolation and extrapolation
Column 9:
as a percentage of column 7 to column 3.

years in domestic prices are right, and the figures for budget expenditures for the same years are based on official publications.

As to 1975–77 I rely on the statement of the highest Soviet official in finance. True, it is possible that he was talking here about *net* results, which means that I underestimated the revenues by about 3 billion rubles for each this year. But, first, this possibility does not seem to be likely; secondly, the resulting mistake would be relatively small; and thirdly, as the reader can see in table X-1, it would not dramatically change our conclusions.

As to all other years, I can only say that the results obtained in table IV-3 are much better than nothing, and I would not insist on their absolute correctness. However, I did what I could and my intuition is that they must be basically of the right order of magnitude. I ask my future critics to suggest a better method.

The question might be asked why the values of the difference between imports and exports in domestic prices and the expenditures of the budget sometimes go down, but the revenues are steadily going up (except in 1975 and 1978). As to the jumps of the expenditures, we can only guess about particular changes in bookkeeping procedures which led to this. We should also remember that the revenues depend not only on the growth of foreign trade but on the price situation on world markets and within the USSR and the structure of trade as well. Frankly speaking, just this fact—the steady increase of the revenues—is to me the most strange of all our results.

And finally: as we remember the Minister of Finance stated that the revenues will increase during the Tenth Five-Year Plan 1.2-fold. So, to be only 1.2-fold bigger in 1980 than in 1975, they should increase less in 1978–80, and I took this into consideration in calculating the figures for 1978.[29]

So, our calculations of the revenues of the budget from foreign trade are finished and I will use them further, being quite sure that the revenues might be overstated but not understated. But it is not out of place to make some additional comments:

(1) It is not quite clear how the conversion into transferable rubles is made in trade with CEMA countries. This trade differs not only in that it is carried out in rubles (as opposed to hard currency) but also in that there is widespread use of clearing accounts. The point is that there is a possibility that the revenues from the trade with CEMA countries could be less because of such different procedures;
(2) The question about expenditures for the foreign trade apparatus and for transportation of foreign trade cargo needs additional work. Quite possibly my estimates of the revenues should be significantly reduced because of this factor;

(3) Quotations from Ladygin and Zotova cited above lead to the conclusion that the total revenues, as well as expenditures, of the budget depend essentially on the organizational structure of foreign trade. In fact, if, for example, two foreign trade associations merged, and one of them had earned a profit while the other had received a budget subsidy, then as a result either a corresponding amount of revenues or subsidies would disappear; they would offset each other.

Moreover, if a certain product was being sold (bought) by one foreign trade association until a certain point in time, and then the same product began to be sold (bought) by another, then this alone could change the amount of budget revenues from foreign trade or its subsidies;

On the one hand, this once again demonstrates the artificial nature of the figures on budget revenues from foreign trade (see also below). But on the other hand, it is possible that just these circumstances partially explain the jumps in budget revenues for trade shown above.

(4) A very difficult question is how exactly the revenues from foreign trade differ from the customs revenues. Judging from a statement by the Minister of Finance, "customs revenues and other receipts from foreign trade occupy a significant place among budget revenues,"[30] it is clear that there are revenues from foreign trade distinct from the customs revenues. But in the basic citation we are examining here it is stated that[31] precisely the difference between the transferable ruble and internal prices for imports noted above is "paid by foreign trade associations to the budget in the form of customs revenues," and if this is the case there should be no revenues from foreign trade other than customs. On this point, I don't even have a hypothesis;

(5) It would be useful to consider the question about gold trade. Lacking the data I did not address the issue at all. We know that the country earns hard currency by selling gold, but we do not know how these sales influence the financial results of foreign trade in domestic rubles.[32] More precisely it is clear that the sales should increase the revenues from foreign trade in domestic rubles (in spite of the high cost of gold mining), but I do not know how to estimate these amounts.[33]

Finishing our discussion of the revenues from foreign trade let me once more note that the problem is very far from being exhausted by our analysis.

On the one hand, I was forced to make a lot of adjustments and estimates (including very rough ones), so my final figures can by no means be precise.[34] To illustrate this point I ask the reader to look at appendix J—there on the basis of some calculations I obtain much smaller amounts of the revenues and, frankly, cannot explain why the combined results of both these calculations are so puzzling.

On the other hand, I think that the issue of the revenues should be addressed in the context of national economic indicators. Let us look at table IV-4. It turns out that for the last 20 years the revenues from foreign trade have remained approximately the same percentage of all revenues of the budget. But, interestingly enough, the total amount of imports in domestic prices is growing two times faster than national income, and by now imported goods are about 15 percent of national income. Of course, all these comparisons are conditional (in particular, my way of estimating the volume of imports in domestic prices is questionable), but nevertheless these numbers and this topic deserve further attention.

The very fact that the Soviet Union earns tremendous amounts of money from foreign trade should be taken into account in various trade (and nontrade) negotiations. Till now it was believed correctly that the country is dependent on imports for a number of goods (for example, grain) and imports of technology. But as far as I know no attention has yet been paid to the possibility that the USSR also needs foreign trade to plug a gaping hole in its budget. In order to get some

Table IV-4. Comparisons of Foreign Trade with Other Economic Indicators (in billions of rubles)

Year	All budget revenues	Budget revenues from foreign trade	%	National income	Imports in domestic prices	%
	1	2	3	4	5	6
1960	77.1	7.1	9	145.0	9.1	6
1965	102.3	8.8	9	193.5	14.9	8
1970	156.7	14.2	9	289.9	18.9	7
1975	218.8	21.5	10	363.3	45.5	13
1978	265.8	29.1	11	422.5	59.8	14

Sources: Column 1—table I-4
Column 2—table IV-3, column 7
Column 3—column 2 divided by column 1 multiplied by 100
Column 4—1960—*Narkhoz 70*, p. 533; all other years—*Narkhoz 78*, p. 385
Column 5—table IV-3: column 1 plus column 7 less column 5
Column 6—column 5 divided by column 4 multiplied by 100.

practical use out of the knowledge of this fact it would be necessary to make a comparison of international market prices and internal Soviet prices for all goods that the country imports.

Almost automatically I thought that Soviet earnings from foreign trade should come primarily from the imports of consumer goods. Not quite so. In a rather serious work, the authors of which display a concrete knowledge of their subject, it is asserted.

> At present about 40 percent of all imports are consumer goods and raw materials for their production as well as food products. During the Ninth Five-Year Plan, 34.8 billion rubles were spent in payment for these goods. The annual delivery of imported goods to the internal market of the country amounts to 9-10 billion rubles in retail prices or 6-7 percent of the total volume of commodity resources.[35]

It directly follows from this that during the Ninth Five-Year Plan (1971-75) the budget could have earned from consumer goods and food products no more than 3 billion rubles per year, even if we do not take into account trade costs. What is going on; why is the total revenue from foreign trade so much more?

First of all, the USSR imports primarily not finished consumer goods but raw materials for the production and semifabricates. According to B. Kostinsky, the total amount of imports in 1972 of the products of light industry (both for direct consumption and raw materials and semifabricates) and agriculture in internal prices amounted to 18.9 billion rubles (of which, the latter were 3.2).

Secondly, we should understand that the Soviets gain a lot even financially when buying machinery and technology.

And, thirdly, this is still more evidence of the fact that the amounts of budget revenues from foreign trade that we arrived at are almost certainly overestimated.

Revenues from the Reduction of Administrative and Managerial Expenses

In chapter III, when examining section 43, we already spoke briefly about what this is. Recall that each year a special assignment on the reduction of the administrative and managerial staff and related expenditures is established and the amounts saved are to be paid into the budget. These assignments are established not only for cost accounting but also for budget-carried organizations.

The practice of establishing obligatory assignments on the reduction of administrative and managerial expenses has existed for a long time.[36] However, these amounts began to be regarded as budget revenues only starting in 1966:[37] "The budget for 1966 stipulates a saving from the improvement and reduction of the cost of the administrative staff of 527 million rubles. *In contrast to past years* [my emphasis] enterprises and organizations should transfer the freed assets directly to the budget."

The sole source of data on these particular payments to the budget is the reports of the Minister of Finance. I have gathered these data in table IV-5, and they refer to the plan assignment, not the amounts actually paid. It seems that in this case it is quite possible to use precisely the plan data. The point is that it makes no sense for enterprises and organizations to overfulfill this plan target, but it is impossible not to fulfill the plan; the budget extracts these amounts with no recourse for enterprises. We have, in addition, two quite direct indications in the literature.[38]

Table IV-5. The Economy from Reduction of Expenditures on Management and Payments to the Union Budget

Year	Planned amount of economy (millions of rubles)	50 percent payment to the union budget (billions of rubles)	Year, number and page of *Finansy SSSR* where planned amount (column 1) is published
	1	2	3
1954–59 (average per year)	340	—	1961, no. 1, p. 20
1960	350	—	no data; taken according to trend
1961	350	—	
1962	350	—	
1963	346	—	1963, no. 1, p. 6
1964	503	—	1964, no. 1, p. 13
1965	520*	—	1965, no. 1, p. 18
1966	527	0.3	1966, no. 1, p. 16
1967	868	0.4	1967, no. 1, p. 19
1968	1,300	0.7	1967, no. 12, p. 17
1969	1,400	0.7	1969, no. 1, p. 17
1970	1,700	0.9	1971, no. 1, p. 15
1971	1,500	0.8	1971, no. 1, p. 16
1972	700	0.4	1972, no. 1, p. 16
1973	600	0.3	1973, no. 1, p. 16
1974	846	0.4	1974, no. 1, p. 15
1975	730	0.4	1975, no. 1, p. 15
1976	1,300	0.7	1976, no. 1, p. 15
1977	800	0.4	1976, no. 12, p. 16
1978	964	0.5	1978, no. 1, p. 15

*According to Garbuzov, "Uspeshnoye", 1964, p. 13, earlier this amount was planned at 352 million rubles.

The planned amounts of the economy are given in table IV-5, and I cite them beginning in 1954, although they began to be paid to the budget only in 1966.[39] We know that the amounts of the economy are paid to different budgets depending on the subordination of the enterprises.[40] How do we divide these amounts among the budgets or, more precisely, how do we distinguish the amounts which go to the union budget? In a book which examines a consolidated financial plan for the RSFSR for 1974, which was compiled by the author, the amount of the economy from reducing expenditures on management is given as 209 million rubles.[41] As is evident from table IV-5, 846 million rubles of these revenues should have been paid in all during this year. In principle it would be possible to find the percentage of payment of these revenues to the union budget if it were possible to calculate the share of the expenditures on management of organizations and enterprises of union subordination in the total amount of the expenditures for all organizations, but I do not have such data. Therefore I take the share of the revenues of the RSFSR State budget in the total amount of the expenditures of all republic budgets, and the share of the latter in the USSR State budget. In 1974 the revenues of the USSR State budget were 201 billion rubles, and those of the state budgets of all union republics (without direct payments from the union budget) were 93 billion rubles, including 50 billion rubles for the RSFSR State budget.[42] It turns out that the amount of this economy paid to the RSFSR budget in 1974 was, roughly speaking, in proportion to the share of its expenditures in the total amount of all revenues of the USSR State budget.[43] If we take this correlation as a constant one (and on the whole nothing contradicts this),[44] the payments to the union budget should be something near half of the amounts indicated in column 1 of table IV-5. The corresponding amounts are calculated in column 2 of this table.

Of course, our calculation is rather arbitrary. However, I not only do not see how to improve it, but I also do not believe that this is necessary. In spite of all the assumptions made, we hardly could be grossly mistaken.

State Insurance

It must be said that to date the question of state (not to be confused with social, which is also "state") insurance has been insufficiently studied, and in spite of the abundance of Soviet literature not everything here is completely clear.[45] Nevertheless, it seems to me, in this case we can come to a quite definite conclusion.

Much evidence indicates that the budget has revenues from Gosstrakh,[46] and our problem is to determine precisely where—which budgets and which sections—these revenues enter.

Let us immediately put aside as unlikely the possibility that all the receipts from insurance are included in the budget revenues and, correspondingly, all insurance claim payments pass through the budget expenditures. This cannot be if only because there is no room in the expenditures of the budget for payments of several billion rubles a year of insurance claims.

We know that quite considerable amounts are received by local budgets for implementing various preventive measures.

> .... Since 1963 the urban budgets (cities of *kray* and *oblast'* subordination) and *rayon* budgets have included deductions from the receipts of funds for state insurance: for voluntary and obligatory payments of kolkhozes, cooperative and public organizations in the amount of 10 percent and payments of the population (except for long-term life insurance) in the amount of 50 percent....
>
> Since 1963 deductions in the amount of 5 percent of the receipts of funds for obligatory wage insurance have been allocated to rural and settlement budgets and to the budgets of towns of *rayon* subordination.
>
> In addition to the enumerated revenues, the local (primarily *kray* and *oblast'*) budgets include special deductions in the amount of 8-10 percent from the payments for obligatory and all types of voluntary property insurance. These amounts are spent on measures for fire prevention and battling fires and for the prevention of the loss and damage of agricultural crops.[47]

Here is another recent bit of evidence:

> In the Belorussian SSR 50 percent of the receipts for the voluntary property insurance of cooperative and public organizations, the obligatory insurance on passenger transportation and other types, as well as the insurance payments of the population, except for long-term life insurance and accident insurance, are deducted for local budgets.[48]

Thus, there are a number of types of insurance, for which deductions are made for local and republic budgets; and these amounts should not interest us.

However, there are, in addition, the deductions from the profits of Gosstrakh.

> State insurance organs carry out their activity on the basis of cost accounting. From the performance of insurance operations (except for operations on the insurance of the property of kolkhozes) they receive a profit, which is turned over to the revenues of the state budget....[49]

Two points are significant here. Firstly, this profit is allocated in conformity with the subordination of the organs of Gosstrakh: "The deductions from profits from the operations of the USSR Gosstrakh are allocated to the union budget. The profit from insurance carried out in a union republic enters ... the corresponding republic budget."[50] Let us take into account here that USSR Gosstrakh itself carries out operations only on the obligatory passenger insurance on rail transport and the insurance of workers paid for with the funds of enterprises of union subordination, and it is clear that a considerable profit is hardly formed from these two operations. All the remaining operations are performed by the republic Gosstrakhs; they receive the corresponding profit and, as we just saw, pay it to the republic budgets.

Secondly, the funds which USSR Gosstrakh turns over to the union budget are a part of the deductions from profits. The basis for such a conclusion is the following quotation:[51] "The payments of the population for state property and personal insurance should not be taken into account in the funds drawn from the population, since the end results of the operations of Gosstrakh are reflected in the article 'Profit'." True, in this context the author is speaking not about the actual state of affairs with the budget, but about the scheme of the structure of the financial balance that he is proposing. However, I do not see any reason why he should propose here something different from the practice which already exists and which he knows. Moreover, if we do not take into account the profit of Gosstrakh, it is rather difficult to explain the profits of "other sectors." (We discussed this question in considering payments from profit in chapter III.)

Thus, we have no grounds to calculate the revenues of the union budget separately from the funds of state insurance.[52]

The Economy of Expenditures on Construction and Capital Repair

Above in this chapter we examined budget revenues that we know for certain exist, and our task was primarily to determine their amounts. Now we turn to those that we can only assume exist. More specifically, just with respect to the economy of expenditures on construction and capital repair it may be thought that there are some budget revenues. Thus, in a list of the various payments to the budget in one textbook, we read:[53] "the economy from the reduction of the prices for equipment and materials for noncentralized capital investments." Another source speaks about[54] "the economy in connection with the reduction of the prices for equipment in construction."

It must be said that the entire problem of financing capital investments is extremely complicated, and it is greatly confused by the fact that the terminology is not the best.[55] What, actually, is the first of the two quotations in question referring to? Until 1976 enterprises and organizations could make some capital investments using "their own" assets, in addition to the centrally-approved plan. These capital investments were thus called "noncentralized" unlike those stipulated in the national economic plan which were called "centralized." In Soviet construction the amount of assets needed is determined by calculating the so-called estimated cost (*smetnaya stoimost'*) and the latter does not take into account the changes in the prices for materials and equipment after the time of the approval of the estimated norms in effect at each moment. When financing centralized capital investments, the corresponding deviations from the estimated cost are determined by using specially calculated coefficients or by direct calculation, and these deviations are taken into account when determining the very amounts of financing. With respect to noncentralized capital investments, to all appearances a different procedure was used (since 1976, there are no noncentralized capital investments): if, due to higher prices, an enterprise needed more assets than provided for by the estimated cost, this was the affair of the enterprise; but if, on the contrary, fewer assets were needed, as we see, the enterprise had to pay the difference to the budget. It should be noted, though, that noncentralized capital investment is carried out in part with budget funds.

What could the corresponding amounts be? The noncentralized capital investments themselves amounted to billions of rubles,[56] and, roughly speaking, a third of all capital investments are spent for equipment, while half of the cost of construction and installation operations is for materials. Therefore, generally speaking, this economy could have been something on the order of several hundred million rubles a year, although here I am overstating rather than understating.

I will not take these amounts into account further, since:

(*a*) there are direct statements that these amounts enter the budget in only two sources, and this is not mentioned anywhere else;
(*b*) it is quite possible that only that part of the economy which was formed from noncentralized capital investments financed by the budget was withdrawn to the budget; in that case only very small amounts would be involved;
(*c*) it is not clear how these amounts were distributed between the republic and union budgets. It is quite possible that they were distributed on the basis of the type of subordination of the construction project, and noncentralized capital investment was carried out primarily by enterprises and organizations not of union subordination;
(*d*) as I have already noted, even with the maximum assumptions the

corresponding amounts should be relatively small on the scale of our calculations.

Concerning the savings from reducing the cost of capital repair made "in house," it should be noted first of all that there are not even data on the overall volume of this capital repair in the literature. According to my calculations based on several estimates, the amount of this repair was quite significant; in 1960, 1965, 1970, 1975, and 1977 respectively, it was 2.0, 3.4, 5.2, 8.6, and 9.5 billion rubles (in 1969 estimate prices). We do not have at our disposal any data on the amounts of savings from cost reduction. However, as I understand this entire process, they should not be very great. It is of principal importance to distinguish between the "estimated savings, i.e., that which is automatically included in the cost estimates in the case of noncentralized capital investments, and the fundamentally different phenomenon here—the savings that is actually realized in comparison with the original estimated cost. Enterprises and organizations are not at all interested in achieving such savings just to pay the entire sum into the budget.

Concerning the savings from the reduction of prices on equipment in construction, in principle there are large amounts involved here. When newly-revised estimate prices are put into effect (for example, the 1969 estimate prices), they incorporate fixed prices for equipment, and if (when) these prices are reduced some savings result. After such reexaminations of the prices of equipment, the plans incorporate large amounts for these savings due to cost reductions; in 1978 they were to be 1.1 billion rubles.[57] However, first, the actually planned amounts of these savings are not achieved, [58] and, secondly, and even more important, these amounts are treated as an additional source of funds for capital investment. For example, in the report by Garbuzov just mentioned the savings from the reduction of equipment prices are considered a source of paying for capital investment *additional* to budget allocations, which in principle excludes the possibility that the corresponding amounts of these savings enter the budget as one of its revenues.

I will also note that the so-called "mobilization of internal assets in construction" (this is primarily the reduction of the working capital of construction organizations, especially assets in uncompleted construction) is also an additional source of financing capital investment[59] and just for this reason should not be treated as a budget revenue.

In short, we will not consider all these funds in our further discussions and calculations.

Deductions of Kolkhozes for Social Insurance and Social Security

I mention this because statements are encountered in the literature which can be interpreted in such a way that these amounts are paid by kolkhozes to the budget and are spent from the budget along with the budget allocations for these purposes. For some time I myself thought just this. However, a careful reading of one source[60] shows that this cannot be; these amounts do not pass through the budget.

Revaluations

In a note to table I-4 I indicated that a different amount of budget revenues for 1965 is reported in different *Narkhoz* yearbooks. In one of them[61] we find out what was going on. The balances of grain products as of 1 January 1956 were revalued (obviously upward), and at first the amount of the upward price adjustment—0.6 billion rubles—was not included in the budget, but then it was taken precisely as a budget revenue.

I did not encounter any other references to such upward price adjustments and revaluations in the literature,[62] but in principle it is impossible to rule out the possibility that with price revisions such cases might have occurred. Let us take into account here that, first, price revisions occur rarely. Secondly, such an upward price adjustment will be carried out and its amounts taken into account only for goods which are directly at the disposal of the state—for example, state reserves.

For these reasons, as well as because we have no data whatever concerning this, we will again not take this into account.

Revenues from Vocational and Technical Schools

In chapter II I noted that according to one work[63] there is even a special section of the classification of budget revenues with this name, but this section is not referred to in any other source. If such a section exists at all and, if these revenues enter the budget, the corresponding amounts can only be very small; moreover, they should be attributed to the republic budgets in conformity with the subordination of the schools.

Revenues from the Labor of Prisoners

The fact that Soviet prisoners work is widely known, and we have an appropriate quotation which S. Rapawy pointed out to me:

> The majority of corrective labor colonies have their own production plant (as a rule, of industrial specialization). There are also agricultural colonies and logging colonies. There are also colonies which under contractual conditions supply manpower to various enterprises and departments which have the status of a legal entity.[64]

It follows indirectly from this quotation that these production plants are cost accounting. This also indirectly follows from the fact that the "educational" labor colonies and reception and distribution centers of the USSR MVD are exempt from payment of the turnover tax.[65] This means that the adult (not educational) labor colonies, and more simply speaking the camps, are not exempt from the turnover tax, and it is difficult to imagine that non-cost accounting organizations pay the turnover tax. But if the camps are on a cost accounting basis, this inevitably means that they should cover their own expenses with their own revenues, that is, they can pay to the budget only their own profit (part of it).

In appendix B it is shown that even given bold assumptions, the wages of prisoners can be only on the order of 300-500 million rubles a year. Prisoners are as a rule used for unskilled labor, which is not very productive, so substantial amounts of profits and revenues of the budget cannot be obtained here.

Moreover, the MVD is a union-republic ministry and it is likely that the camps are under republic subordination.

In short, I again think that we should not take the revenues from camps into account as an individual type of revenue of the union budget.

* * *

In the next chapter we will examine separately the question of surpluses of funds as a source of budget revenues and will calculate (table V-6) the adjusted amount of the gap. I will say here that the amounts of the gap, although decreasing (primarily due to the revenues from foreign trade) remain extremely great. It is appropriate, therefore, already here to stress that the most detailed examination of the classification of the budget and of statements in textbooks, monographs and articles, as well as logical deductions permit us to conclude quite certainly that with the exception of the budget revenues that we have already examined, there are not and cannot be any other substantial budget revenues except emission. In fact precisely this conclusion predetermines the logic of our further reasoning and the conclusion which we will finally draw and substantiate in chapter X.

In this connection two other factors are significant. First, there is extensive literature on control and audits; in the journal *Finansy SSSR* instructional articles are regularly published about the work of financial organs on improving the payment of revenues to the budget. And in all these materials there is not even a hint of any other types of revenues. Moreover, it is quite characteristic that, for example, in one article of the deputy minister of finance the state of affairs regarding the payment to the budget of the turnover tax, deductions from profits, and other taxes is examined in detail, and then "other revenues" are discussed, including "some other types of payments," and it is stated that:[66] "This group of payments . . . takes up a small share [!] in the revenues of the state budget." In a special and, incidentally, very thorough book devoted to the monitoring of the fulfillment of the budget which I have already repeatedly quoted, once again there is not even a hint of any other types of revenues.[67]

And at the same time practically everywhere in the discussion of budget revenues the problem of credit resources is always mentioned. Their growth is given special and increasing attention in all instructional materials.

Secondly, it is difficult to explain why the Soviets have to hide their revenues. The most fantastic suppositions concerning this do not lead to any logical explanation of this strange phenomenon. Indeed, the reasons for the exaggeration of the real amounts of revenues for some articles are not evident and it is not clear why it would be necessary to conceal, and amazingly carefully, some special types of revenues.

It is clear that Soviet authorities are concealing expenditures (and quite successfully—so far, for example, there is no clarity on military expenditures); but revenues?

The only logically possible answer is that indeed there are no other *real* budget revenues. But before I substantiate this conclusion finally and try to show what important consequences stem from it, we will have to examine another set of quite difficult questions, each of which, while connected with my theme, is of independent importance.

Notes

1. J. Gillula and B. Kostinsky helped me in dealing with this problem.

2. They are regularly published in annual statistical yearbooks of foreign trade, for example, Ministerstvo, *Vneshnyaya*, 1976.

3. The most difficult thing is to estimate the exports and imports of the products of machine building, but for other goods this is also not easy.

4. These indicators are regularly published in statistical yearbooks on foreign trade, Ministerstvo, *Vneshnyaya*, as well as in *Narkhoz* yearbooks.

Values of "transferable" rubles are determined by converting the volume of foreign trade in foreign currency to rubles at the rate of exchange established by Gosbank based on the gold content of the ruble (see, for example, *Narkhoz 78*, p. 547).

As I understand it, both the "transferable ruble" and the estimate of the international rate of exchange arose historically and are maintained mostly as a statistical propaganda device. The question is quite complex and deserves further analysis. One quite practical use of the "the gold content of the ruble" is to force foreign tourists visiting the country to exchange foreign currency for rubles at an extreme disadvantage. The rate is something like 70 kopecks for a dollar, and on the black market, it is something like 5 rubles for a dollar.

5. Ministerstvo, *Vneshnyaya*, 1976, p. 311 or *Narkhoz 78*, p. 603. There is one thing I do not understand here. I sent an English-Hebrew dictionary by registered mail to a city near Moscow. The addressee did not receive the package and I was paid $15.00 as compensation, apparently from the Postal Department of the USSR. Under precisely what expenditure heading is this money included?

6. Kostinsky, *Description*, pp. 55–73. During the latest Cuban crisis President Carter said that Soviet aid to Cuba is 6 million dollars a day but he did not say how it was determined.

7. It is quite possible that in delivering some types of weapons, especially those that are not very new, all financial operations amount to just "writing off" the weapons, all the more so since weapons are not included in fixed capital.

8. See, in particular, CIA, *Soviet Commercial*, 1977.

9. Nikitin, "Inostrannyy," 1976, pp. 2, 3, 4.

There are additional data in *Izvestiya*, No. 18843 of 8 April 1978, p. 4. It is indicated here that "in 1977, 2,704,202 Soviet citizens went abroad." It is also stated that in the same year 1.2 million people from Poland visited the USSR, and in all "about two-thirds of the tourist exchange of the USSR falls to the socialist countries."

Also of interest here is the statement that the construction of hotels, motels, and campgrounds in the country is done ". . . not at the expense of the local budgets of cities, but using the assets of Inturist."

10. A special so-called "foreign-currency plan (balance of payments of the USSR)" is made as a part of the foreign trade plan (Gosplan, *Metodicheskiye*, 1974, p. 590) but there are no indications in the literature that this is somehow connected with the budget.

11. *The Washington Post*, 10 December 1978. In Karr, *CMEA*, 1978, p. 3, it is stated that this debt exceeds 17 billion rubles.

12. ". . . during 1945–75 the USSR granted to the fraternal socialist countries long-term credits in excess of 15 billion rubles, including more than 12 billion rubles to CEMA member countries" (M. Atlas, *Natsional'nyy*, 1977, p. 327). It is also said here that "international socialist credit is granted on easy terms (usually 1–2 percent per annum), and in some cases without the collection of interest." Still it is not clear precisely what kind of rubles are being referred to here.

13. Zhevtyak, *Finansy*, 1974, p. 249.

14. A. Birman, *Finansy*, 1970, p. 273.

15. Koryakin, *Ekonomika*, 1971, p. 375.

16. A description of which organizations plan foreign trade and which participate in it is given, in particular, in Ladygin and Zotova, *Sotsialisticheskaya*, 1977, pp. 290ff.

17. V. Treml pointed this out to me. The "gold content of the ruble" existed before 1960, but it changed radically just at this time. There was a monetary reform then

under which all prices were reduced by a factor of ten (see chapter VI), but the "gold content of the ruble" was changed by a different proportion.

18. Because of this, for example, it is so difficult to compare the military expenditures of the USA in dollars with those of the USSR in rubles, and it is also difficult to make comparisons of GNP (see my article in The Washington Post, 27 October, 1980, p. A-15). One attempt to determine the real relation between the ruble and the dollar is CIA, *Ruble*, 1976.

19. As will be shown below, this is not so obvious; formally the transactions of enterprises with the MFT are carried out on the basis of a comparison of internal prices and world market prices. However, as will also be shown below *in the final analysis* everything is determined by a comparison of internal prices only.

20. Ladygin and Zotova, *Sotsialisticheskaya*, 1977, pp. 308-10.

21. The fact that this is the procedure used follows from other citations. For example, in A. Birman, *Ocherki*, 1972, p. 58, we read that imported goods are valued at the purchase prices in foreign currency and then the amount is multiplied by parity in rubles (the "parity" pertains only to transferable rubles), and compared with the internal price. When the internal price is higher the difference is customs revenue.

Another citation: "The excess of the value of imports in internal prices over their value in foreign currency prices is entered into the income part of the financial balance" (Belkin and Ivanter, "Finansovyye," 1977, p. 67). Of course, this refers to the "financial plan" and not to the budget itself, but it does not change the essence of the statement.

22. In Yevdokimov, *Kontrol'*, 1974, p. 160, it is stated that provision is made in the expenditure part of the budget for "carrying out foreign trade operations involving the export and import of goods." In Shekhovtsev, *Svodnoye*, 1976, pp. 9 and 48, it is stated that the results of foreign trade are reflected in the budget "*razvernuto*," i.e., on both the revenue and expenditure sides. In Volkov, "Problemy," 1975, p. 76, we are told that the income part of the budget does not reflect the balance of foreign trade operations and that just this—reflecting the balance—would be more "expedient." And there are other citations.

23. This idea was suggested to me by J. Gillula.

24. In Feonova, et al., *Organizatsiya*, 1974, p. 61, we read: "Buyers pay suppliers for goods delivered for export at wholesale prices excluding turnover tax (except goods supplied by cooperative organizations) with allowance for price markups and discounts approved in accordance with standard practice." On page 78 of this book it is asserted that turnover tax is not directly collected on imported goods, i.e., it is collected not from organizations of MFT but from those organizations that process and/or resell these goods.

In A. Birman, *Ocherki*, 1972, p. 58, it is rightly said that if turnover tax is collected on exports it means that "the state budget pays turnover tax to itself."

25. In Vakhrin, *Formirovaniye*, 1974, p. 14, it is said that there were 200,000 persons working in foreign trade in 1970. Taking expenditures on wages as 50 percent of the total amount of expenditures and wages as 2,000 rubles per year, we get 800 million rubles. I think that even for 1970 this represents a minimum.

26. As I have already pointed out, expenditures for foreign trade are jumping around. At least partially, this should be explained by changes in retail prices. Besides, in transactions of foreign trade organizations with purchasers of foreign equipment, special coefficients, implemented beginning July 1, 1967, are used (Shelikov, *Spravochnik*, 1970, p. 154).

27. Kostinsky, *Foreign*, 1976, p. 7 and personal communication.

28. Garbuzov, "Finansovya," 1977, p. 10. Alec Nove pointed this statement out to me (in Europe they receive Soviet literature faster than we).

This statement, indirectly but all the same quite definitely, is supported by another statement: "In the financial resources of the Soviet state during the past decade, receipts from foreign trade increased significantly, which was a result of the expansion of the foreign economic relations of the Soviet Union" (Garbuzov, et al., *Problemy*, 1977, p. 13).

29. This must be connected with changes in the structure of foreign trade and especially with price changes.

30. Garbuzov, "Uspeshno," 1962, p. 11.

31. Ladygin and Zotova, *Sotsialisticheskaya*, 1977, p. 310.

32. Only the relatively small sales of gold for industrial uses are included in foreign trade amounts.

33. Because of the recent jump in world market gold prices the USSR has excellent possibilities to increase its earnings of hard currency.

34. In particular the actual amount of payments may differ substantially from the actual amount of imports and exports—a large part is paid for with credits, there are inventories of goods in warehouses, etc.

35. Ivanitskiy, *Ekonomika*, 1977, p. 29.

36. When I first began to work as a planner in 1950, we had such an assignment.

37. Garbuzov, "Byudzhet," 1966, p. 16.

38. In Garbuzov, "Byudzhet," 1971, p. 15, it is asserted that in 1970 these amounts should enter the budget "at the level of the plan."

In Dementsev, "Finansovyye," 1975, p. 9, it is stated that in four years of the five-year plan 3.7 billion rubles entered the budget from the reduction of expenditures on management. This is equal to the plan amounts for 1971–74 (table IV-5).

39. In examining column 1 of table IV-5 a natural question arises—why did the amounts of the economy increase rapidly until 1970, and then begin to fall rapidly? There are two answers. In Garbuzov, "Byudzhet," 1973, p. 15, it is stated that "in the past two years" many administrative links were reduced, which led to a reduction of the expenditures on management. Hence, of course, the possibilities for giving the assignments for further cuts in these expenditures were eliminated. The second factor is that those enterprises converted to the new planning system pay this economy to section 17 of the classification of revenues (Millionshchikov, *Nenalogovyye*, 1967, pp. 32–33). But I cannot explain why the amounts jumped again in 1976.

40. Millionshchikov, *Nenalogovyye*, 1967, p. 31.

41. Shekhovtsev, *Svodnoye*, 1976, p. 95. The same value is also cited in Bobrovnikov, *O gosudarstvennom*, 1974, p. 20.

42. *Byudzhet 76*, pp. 7, 75, 105. In the republic budgets these amounts should be included in "other revenues."

43. According to table I-1 (appendix I) the share of the union budget in the USSR State budget in 1965 was 43 percent, while in 1970 and 1975 it was somewhat more than half.

44. This correlation (that I did not choose by accident) is confirmed by data on the planned amounts of receipts from reducing administrative and managerial expenses in the budget of the RSFSR reported by Fadeyev, *O gosudarstvennom*, 1970, p. 20: Fadeyev, *O gosudarstvennom*, 1973, p. 19; etc.

45. In particular, when determining the income and expenditure of the population (see chapter VI and appendix B) I had to resort to estimates.

46. For example, "since the total revenues of Gosstrakh are greater than its expenses the remainder is placed at the disposal of the state budget. It is used as a general budget resource" (A. Birman, *Ocherki*, 1968, p. 68).

"The profit received by the state insurance system is transferred directly to the revenues of the state budget and is used for financing the building of socialism. A considerable portion of the temporarily surplus funds, which form in the accounts of state insurance organs as a result of the lag of the receipt of premiums and reimbursement for losses, is allocated for increasing the credit resources of Gosbank"—Tsapkin, *Finansy*, 1972, p. 141.

47. Aleksandrov, *Gosudarstvennyy*, 1965, pp. 30–31.

48. Khodorovich, "Dokhody," 1975, p. 62. A list of types of insurance, for which deductions are made, is also found in Motylev, *Gosudarstvennoye*, 1975, p. 148 while on p. 150 of the same book it is stated that these funds "are included in the revenue of the budget of union republics." According to Galimon, *Finansy*, 1976, p. 203, 4 percent of the amounts of insurance of kolkhozes go for preventive measures. It is interesting to note that according to the same source only 2 percent of the amounts of insurance for kolkhozes go for the expenses of the organs of Gosstrakh.

49. Motylev, *Gosudarstvennoye*, 1975, p. 18.

50. Ibid., pp. 310–11.

51. Volkov, *Perspektivnoye*, 1976, p. 53. In Voluyskiy, *Svodnyy*, 1970, pp. 78–79, it is proposed to introduce in the financial plan the article "Payments of Indemnification on Property and Personal Insurance and Other Expenses of Gosstrakh" and to show the results of the operations for Gosstrakh in detail. From this it unquestionably follows that now these results are shown as a balance. I do not see why the budget should be arranged differently here than the consolidated financial plan.

52. In speaking about the insurance payments of kolkhozes, Semenov writes in *Rol'*, 1973, pp. 182–83: "Insurance payments were reimbursed during 1959–1967 only in the amount of 63.2 percent, which created a rather large revenue from insurance even with the exclusion of the 15 percent deductions for preventive measures and the maintenance of state insurance organs. The unutilized deductions from insurance payments for preventive measures at the end of the year were closed and transferred to the revenue of the budget." This unquestionably contradicts some of the above-cited quotations, but it is easy to see that the corresponding amounts (if Semenov is at all correct here) went to the republic budgets.

In chapter II it was noted that according to Kurchenko, *Balansovyye*, 1973, pp. 108–109, there is a separate section of the classification of budget revenues "Deductions from Insurance Payments, which are Converted to Cover Expenses." First, nowhere is the existence of this section mentioned again. Secondly, even if such a section did exist, judging from the exact meaning of the name it should be a question of those amounts about which we have already spoken above, that is, the deductions for the local budgets.

53. A. Birman, *Finansy*, 1975, p. 325. These payments are clearly mentioned also in Reynin, *Spravochnik*, 1974, p. 89.

54. Shekhovtsev, *Svodnoye*, 1976, p. 95.

55. I hope to complete a long manuscript on Soviet capital construction statistics within one or two years.

56. The simplest way to calculate them is to subtract the indicators of column 1 in the table in *Narkhoz 75*, p. 505, from the indicators of column 2 in the table on p. 502. As a result we obtain the noncentralized capital investments in "comparable prices." They are equal during the Seventh, Eighth and Ninth Five-Year Plan periods respectively to 25.8, 58.5 and 88.3 billion rubles (excluding kolkhozes).

57. Garbuzov, "Byudzhet," 1978, p. 15.

58. According to Daynauskas, "Tseny," 1978, p. 38, the actual savings from the reduction of equipment prices "does not reach 30 percent of the amount taken into account in the plans for financing capital investment."

59. Garbuzov, "Byudzhet," 1976, p. 13; and *Garbuzov*, "Byudzhet," 1978, p. 15.

60. Galimon, *Finansy*, 1976, pp. 205–206.

61. *Narkhoz 58*, p. 899.

62. In A. Birman, *Ocherki*, 1972, p. 57, the "upward price adjustment" is spoken about, not as a budget revenue, but rather as an element of "other monetary revenues"—see appendix J.

63. Kurchenko, *Balansovyye*, 1973, p. 109.

64. Tkachevskiy, *Sovetskoye*, 1971, p. 34.

65. Azarkh, *Spravochnik*, 1972, p. 161.

66. Maslennikov, "Vypolneniye," 1976, p. 14.

67. Yevdokimov, *Kontrol'*, 1974.

Chapter V

Balances of Budget Funds: Budget "Profits"

Already in chapter I it was noted that the constant excess of revenues over expenditures in the budget, the existence of a constant, so to speak, "budget profit" is a puzzle and evokes distrust. Nearly all the Western specialists with whom I spoke about the deficit nature of the Soviet budget immediately cited as a counterargument precisely this fact. It is impossible not to agree with them—indeed, the simultaneous existence of both a budget deficit and an excess of revenues over expenditures is very strange.

The easiest thing is to assume that there are no budget profits, that the Soviets are simply fooling us (as well as the Soviet readers) and concealing thereby the deficit nature of the budget. This is not so—indeed, in spite of the deficit nature of the budget, each year amounts which constitute its profits are actually formed. In order to explain what is going on, we can take an example from . . . American practice. The U.S. federal budget has been constantly in deficit for a long time, but there are instances when the planned expenditures (that is, those permitted by Congress) are not fully made, and in principle it would be quite possible to declare that such an underexpenditure—the excess of the funds earmarked for spending over those actually spent—is the "budget profit." With this example I have, in fact, stated the main point of this chapter and the remainder of it is devoted to some explanations, illustrations and calculations.

I have already indicated that we have the least data of all for the union budget, as well as, correspondingly, for the USSR State budget.[1] This also pertains to the problem in question. According to the data on the USSR State budget we know only the amounts of its profit, as presented in table I-5. Fortunately, there is considerably more information for republic and local budgets, and we will deal first with them.

A careful examination of the data on these budgets, which are regularly published in the *Byudzhet* handbooks, reveals a large number of indicators on the surpluses of budget funds at the beginning and end of each fiscal year, on the part of these funds that is converted to cover expenditures, and on the profits of these budgets. All these data are interconnected.

How do surpluses of funds in the budgets arise? In exactly the same way as in the American budget, for in itself the allocation of budget funds according to the plan certainly does not mean that all the money will actually be issued and spent.[2] It is possible to name at least five instances of this.

First of all, organizations often do not fulfill various aspects of their plans. This pertains in particular to construction, for which, as is known, not once has the plan been fulfilled. The budget funds for capital investments are issued mostly in conformity with the actual amount of work performed.[3] Similarly, "underexpenditures" can result, for example, due to underfulfillment of the plan "for the expansion of the network and personnel of budget-carried institutions."[4]

Secondly, usually the actual receipt of budget funds is based on allocations by article of expenditure, and it is impossible to transfer money from one article to another. Furthermore, the receipt of budget funds may involve some additional conditions. Thus, if some position at a budget-carried institution is vacant, forced savings result because it is impossible to hire a worker for another position on this account or to spend this money for other needs. The payment of bonuses is also typical of this. The amounts of bonuses are stipulated in the planning budget and, if not all the conditions for receiving the bonuses are met, this money cannot be spent.

Thirdly, in many instances the organizations cannot obtain the materials or equipment they need, and the funds allocated for this are not spent.

Fourthly, the plan, according to the well-known expression, is not a dogma, but a guide to action. In the process of fulfilling it some unforeseen circumstances always arise. As a rule, they cause additional expenditures, but there are instances when such circumstances lead instead to savings. I have already written above, in chapter III, about how in 1972 previously earmarked allocations were taken away from all ministries in order to channel them into agriculture. Overall, this should have led to an increase in expenditures, but for some types of outlays the expenditures actually decreased.

Finally, fifthly, the reserve funds of the Councils of Ministers of the USSR and the republics are formed according to the planning budget. It is quite probable that these reserves are not always entirely exhausted.[5]

Therefore, it is quite understandable how large surpluses of unspent funds, which reach billions of rubles, can be formed annually. Having clarified why the surpluses are formed, we now have to discuss a number of other questions:

(a) The examination of the data on the planned and actual budget expenditures during 1965–76[6] would seem to contradict what I said above—it turns out that in all years both the total expenditures for the budget (excluding only 1972) and its individual components (there are somewhat more exceptions here) exceeded the plan indicators. However, there is no real contradiction here. Above I have already noted that during the fulfillment of the budget it is revised, and some allocations are reduced, while others are increased.[7] At the same time we should not confuse two very different things—the expenditures for some budget article as a whole and the expenditures of individual organizations. For example, in 1966 the total budget expenditures for both health and physical culture were 140 million rubles more than stipulated in the plan.[8] However, it is possible to assert with confidence that the funds allocated according to the plan to many health and sports organizations were not entirely spent. It is clear that a portion of the funds allocated to these organizations was, in the course of events, taken away and used for other purposes, but it is also clear that the assets were not taken away in time from some organizations, and surpluses were formed.[9] Furthermore, the redistribution of funds is usually so drawn out that it is not possible to spend all the additional funds obtained.[10] As soon as the fiscal year has ended, all the budget allocations are immediately terminated;[11]
(b) Thus, the actual expenditures for the budget as a whole are always more than according to the plan, but, on the other hand, the actual revenues for the budget as a whole are also always greater than according to the plan.[12] Moreover, since the excess of the actual revenues[13] over planned revenues is always greater than the actual expenditures over planned expenditures, the actual budget profit is practically always greater than according to the plan (see table V-5). This also explains why large surpluses of budget funds are always formed.

It is quite appropriate to be interested in why the actual budget revenues are greater than the planned revenues. How does this occur? A number of different factors are in effect here, and they are not always clearly distinguishable at first glance.

One of them is connected with a phenomenon which has already been noted above—the prohibitions of every possible kind against the shifting of funds from one section (article) to another. The second factor is the formulation of the plan at all levels with certain "concealed" reserves so that it is nearly always possible to overfulfill it.[14]

In this regard, it is interesting to examine the data on the elements of the budget[15] to see precisely for which elements the plan on revenues is overfulfilled. Not all the planning data on budget revenues are regularly published, and, as a result, it is difficult, in particular, to determine the amount of the "overfulfillment of the plan" of the gap in the income part of the budget being studied in this book. However, by using some summary data (as was done in the cited work of the CIA), it is possible to say with confidence that in fact, so to speak, the plan for the gap itself is regularly and considerably overfulfilled. From all this it is possible to draw the following conclusion.

As the budget is implemented, not only additional expenditures but also additional revenues appear. In particular, during some years the budget in fact receives more turnover tax and/or payments from profits than anticipated in the plan. Although we do not have any data on this, it is quite possible to assume that at times (and perhaps often) the actual revenues from foreign trade also are more than the planned revenues. At the same time it is possible to assert with complete certainty that the constant excess of the actual amounts of the gap over the planned amounts shows best of all that the shortfall in real revenues is covered precisely by this excess. As will be shown in chapter X, the amount of bank credits to the budget needed in order to cover the planned budget deficit are anticipated already as the plan is being formulated. If the actual deficit is greater, once again this source of escape is resorted to, and the budget actually receives more of these credits than was planned;

(c) The reasons for the great fluctuations in the amounts of budget profits from year to year—see table V-2—are, unfortunately, not very clear to me. The profits are increasing practically constantly for local budgets, and the fluctuations occur basically in the profits of the union budget, which once more speaks in favor of the assertion made just above.

It seems that there is no single reason that can explain these fluctuations; apparently a set of causes is in effect. Among them are the "lean years," when it is necessary to "tighten the belt" at once (for example, this evidently can explain the sharp increase of budget profits in 1973 right after the serious crop failure of 1972); changes in the regulations for dispersing funds (it is possible that precisely for this reason a sharp decrease took place in 1965); and so on. It is also possible that this is in some way connected with changes in revenues during these years—in particular, from foreign trade;

(d) A fundamentally important question for us is: to what extent does

this process of the formation of surpluses of unutilized budget funds pertain to the union budget? Having no data on the union budget, it is possible only to guess at this. More precisely, there is no doubt that in the accounts of the union budget the surpluses are formed in exactly the same way as in the accounts of other budgets, but it is not entirely clear how great they are and how they are used. We will soon return to this question.

Thus, we know that surpluses are formed in the accounts of the budgets, we know their amount for republic and local budgets, and now is the very time to discuss the question of their use. As can be judged from data in the *Byudzhet* handbooks, the situation is as follows.

Above all there are the so-called carry-overs of budget funds. Their amounts for the republic and local budgets are regularly published. These amounts are gradually spent during the year, and then at the end of the year are restored by the new surpluses that have accumulated. These carry-overs do not remain constant from year to year—they are always changing and according to the general trend are increasing in conformity with the increase in the size of the budgets.

Of the total amount of surpluses accumulated by the end of the year, a portion is allocated for the increase of these carry-overs (very rarely, for local budgets, expenditures are greater than revenues; then the amounts of the carry-overs decrease). Another portion of the accumulated surpluses is allocated for the partial coverage of expenditures of the next year and is included in the revenue of the corresponding budget. The remainder is taken as the excess of the revenues of the corresponding budget over its expenditures (its "profit").

Why does everything happen precisely in this way; what is the sense of such a division of the surpluses? In particular, why are the carry-overs necessary? Financing should be carried out continuously, but the planning of the dispersal of funds takes place discretely and is always late. The USSR Supreme Soviet approves the budget only in December. After this the sessions of the Supreme Soviets of the republics and the local soviets must take place, and the long and complicated process of coordinating the plans in all respects with all the numerous organizations must be completed. Therefore,

> In the budgets of the union republics and the corresponding local budgets a current cash balance is formed from the surpluses of funds at the beginning of the year being planned, the amount of which is determined when approving the budget. These funds are used during the year to cover temporary cash gaps, which might appear during the fulfillment of the budget (these funds should be restored during the same year to the approved amounts).[16]

This quotation is important not only because it confirms my interpretation of the meaning of the carry-overs. It is very significant that it speaks about the carry-overs only for the republic and local budgets. This means they do not exist in the union budget.[17] It is clear why, as I have already noted above, the USSR State Budget, and hence the union budget, are approved in December and the bureaucratic apparatus manages to withdraw funding of the union budget immediately, on 1 January.

It would be incorrect to think that surpluses are not formed at all in accounts of the union budget. They of course exist[18] and it is they that form the profits of the union budget. But it is not very clear whether these surpluses are used to cover expenditures of the next year; and if so, how? Since this entire arrangement is not described in the literature and I had to guess at many things, it is not surprising that I cannot answer the following questions of evident interest:

—it is not clear why the amounts of the excess of revenues over expenditures are shown in the statistical handbooks for only the USSR State budget and the state budgets of the union republics, but not for local budgets. These amounts are calculated below, but it is not completely certain whether this is entirely valid;
—as mentioned above, it is not known whether all the surpluses of the union budget are included in its profits. This certainly seems to be the case, but it cannot be proven;
—the proposed arrangement more or less explains by what means the amounts of the carry-overs can increase. However, it is also necessary to explain where the funds, which are formed when the amounts of the carry-overs decrease, actually go. The explanation suggests itself that these amounts increase the total amount of the surpluses and can go to cover expenditures, that is, they enter the revenue of the budget of the following year and/or go for the formation of the budget profit. But according to data in the *Byudzhet* handbooks this is not so;
—the question of the use of the profits of republic and local budgets requires clarification. In one textbook it is asserted:

> The amounts of the excess of revenues over expenditures for republic and local budgets, which are formed as a result of the overfulfillment of the plans on revenues or economizing on expenditures (with the exception of the funds allocated to ministries for capital investments) remain at the disposal of the executive organs and are spent at their discretion.[19]

From this follows a very important conclusion for us—the profits of the republic and local budgets do not enter the union budget.

But the question remains, where, nevertheless, are these profits put, how do the republic and local budgets use them?[20]

Let us turn now to the examination of the specific data. Table V-1 presents the data on the surpluses of budget funds (less those used to cover expenditures) for the state budgets of the union republics and for local budgets. As their difference (column 3) I calculated the surpluses of funds for the republic budgets themselves. In the first of the handbooks used here (*Byudzhet 57*), the carry-overs are shown only in the table on the revenues of the state budgets of the union republics. However, beginning with the next handbook (*Byudzhet 62*) the amounts of the surpluses are also shown in the tables of expenditures. Here the surpluses as of the beginning of the year are given in the tables on revenues, while in the tables on expenditures they are cited as of the end of the year.

I have found no explanation for the following curious fact. In *Byudzhet 62* the amounts of the surpluses at the beginning and end of 1950 and 1955 according to the tables on revenues and expenditures are different, which is quite natural. But, beginning with the indicators for 1960, and in all subsequent handbooks, the values of the surpluses at the beginning and end of each individual year are reported as the same.[21]

As is evident from table V-1, each year the amounts of the surpluses change and we are left to assume that the change takes place at some elusive moment of time precisely on New Year's eve. And this is not the only point. I am not able in any way to understand what sort of funds are transferred in connection with the change of the surpluses. It would seem that the increase of the carry-overs should constitute an expenditure and, correspondingly, their reduction—a revenue of the budget.

Nothing of the sort is evident in the *Byudzhet* handbooks. True, in *Byudzhet 57*, p. 15, "funds stipulated according to the budgets of the union republics for the increase of carry-overs at the beginning of the year" are shown for 1954, but even here I was not able to balance this amount with the other indicators.

This is shown differently in the handbooks with respect to the local budgets. The "excesses of revenues over expenditures" are not singled out here (as in the tables on expenditures for the state budgets of the union republics). Also, the surpluses at the end of the year, which are shown here, are substantially greater than the surpluses at the beginning of the year in the tables of revenues.

It might seem that the surpluses of budget funds at the end of the year for local budgets are substantially greater than the surpluses at the beginning of the year due to the fact that the former include the

Table V-1. Surpluses of Budget Funds for Republic and Local Budgets, at the Beginning of the Corresponding Year
(in millions of rubles)

Year	State budgets of union republics	Local budgets	Difference—republic budgets themselves
	1	2	3
1940	100	na	na
1950	287	177	110
1951	293	na	na
1952	296	na	na
1953	300	na	na
1954	327	na	na
1955	376	260	116
1956	386	288	98
1957	458	312	146
1958	761	440	321
1959	663	391	272
1960	847	469	378
1961	1,099	494	605
1962	1,033	560	473
1963	1,037	652	385
1964	1,248	628	620
1965	1,347	668	679
1966	1,272	700	572
1967	1,231	759	472
1968	1,573	883	690
1969	1,730	993	737
1970	1,683	1,012	671
1971	1,777	1,089	688
1972	1,860	1,095	765
1973	1,957	1,179	778
1974	2,219	1,275	944
1975	2,479	1,408	1,071

Sources: Column 1:
1970–75—*Byudzhet 76*, p. 77
1965–69—*Byudzhet 72*, p. 78
1950, 1955, 1960–64—*Byudzhet 66*, p. 72
1956–59—*Byudzhet 62*, p. 70
1940, 1951–54—*Byudzhet 57*, p. 15
Column 2:
1970–75—*Byudzhet 76*, p. 99
1965–69—*Byudzhet 72*, p. 102
1950, 1955, 1960–64—*Byudzhet 66*, p. 95
1956–59—*Byudzhet 62*, p. 93
Column 3: column 1 less column 2.

surpluses which are transferred to cover expenditures, but an elementary check shows that this is not so. For example, for 1970:[22]

surplus at the beginning of the year	1,011.5 million rubles
surplus used to cover expenditures	1,076.9 million rubles
surplus at the end of the year	2,000.6 million rubles
difference of surpluses	989.1 million rubles

Thus, the difference of the surpluses is almost 100 million rubles less than the amounts used to cover expenditures.

It might seem that the difference of the two surpluses being examined here is the sum of the excess of revenues over expenditures for local budgets. However, as is evident from table V-2, if on the whole this assumption appears plausible, for 1961 the calculated amount of the profits of local budgets (442.3 million rubles) is more than the entire amount of the profits for the same year for the state budgets of the union republics (312.2 million rubles), which, of course, should not be.

Hence the amounts of the carry-overs for local budgets are not only the excess of revenues over expenditures. To all appearances, the surpluses formed are partly taken as budget profits and are partly used for the change of the very amounts of the carry-overs.[23] For this reason the values in column 3 of table V-2 should be overstated and, correspondingly, the values in column 5 should be understated. Nevertheless, both of these columns on the whole show the trends of changes in the given amounts.

We will analyze the indicators in table V-2 somewhat later, but now let us return to the question of the surpluses of the budget funds. The main question which interests us here is: what can the surpluses of funds in the accounts of the union budget be? The data in table V-1 will help us a little in this respect. If we compare the values of the surpluses presented here with the total amounts of the revenues for the corresponding budgets—table V-3—we find that the surpluses for the local budgets constitute a slightly greater percentage of the total amount of expenditures for these budgets. The explanation is obvious—a significantly greater number of organizations, although they are smaller, are financed from local budgets, and they have, so to speak, more opportunities not to spend the allocations earmarked for them. But from this it can be concluded that there should be a similar relation between the union and the republic budgets, that is, the percentage of the surpluses for the union budget should be smaller than for the republic budgets.

But let us even assume that this is not quite so. Let the ratio of the

Table V-2. Profits for Different Budgets (in millions of rubles)

Year	USSR state budget	State budgets of union republics	Local budgets[1]	Union budget	Republic budgets[1]
	1	2	3	4	5
1940	589.1	171.7	—[2]	417.4	—
1950	953.1	203.7	177.1	749.4	26.6
1951	2,730.0	279.4	na	2,450.6	—
1952	3,750.0	147.3	na	3,602.7	—
1953	2,510.0	69.3	na	2,440.7	—
1954	470.0	123.4	na	346.6	—
1955	2,480.7	112.9	75.1	2,367.8	37.8
1956	2,244.4	105.7	47.2	2,138.7	58.5
1957	1,959.9	458.9	205.8	1,501.0	253.1
1958	2,960.5	221.7	136.1	2,738.8	85.6
1959	3,615.4	572.5	252.1	3,042.9	320.4
1960	3,952.2	617.4	208.9	3,348.8	408.5
1961	1,744.4	312.3	442.3	1,432.1	−130.0
1962	2,152.0	541.9	541.8	1,610.1	0.1
1963	2,539.1	1,046.7	429.3	1,492.4	617.4
1964	2,176.9	1,000.2	571.1	1,176.7	429.1
1965	703.3	508.9	452.3	194.4	56.6
1966	720.2	550.1	536.4	170.1	13.7
1967	1,918.6	1,510.0	828.5	408.6	681.5
1968	2,277.4	1,893.2	886.7	384.2	1,006.5
1969	1,502.3	1,208.0	783.1	294.3	424.9
1970	2,102.8	1,720.5	989.1	382.3	731.4
1971	1,804.6	1,421.6	740.8	383.0	680.8
1972	1,897.6	1,536.8	892.4	360.8	644.4
1973	3,795.8	2,511.6	1,082.0	1,284.2	1,429.6
1974	3,943.3	2,566.3	1,240.2	1,377.0	1,326.1
1975	4,248.2	2,738.3	1,482.3	1,509.9	1,256.0
1976	5,500.0				
1977	5,000.0				
1978	5,600.0				

Sources: Column 1:
1976–78—*Narkhoz 78*, p. 533;
1970–75—***Byudzhet 76***, p. 7;
1965–69—***Byudzhet 72***, p. 10;
1950, 1955, 1960–64—***Byudzhet 66***, p. 8;
1940, 1956–59—***Byudzhet 62***, p. 5;
1951–54—***Byudzhet 57***, pp. 5, 7.
Column 2:
1970–75—***Byudzhet 76***, p. 77;
1965–69—***Byudzhet 72***, p. 80;
1950–55, 1960–64—***Byudzhet 66***, p. 74;
1940, 1956–59—***Byudzhet 62***, p. 72;
1951–54—***Byudzhet 57***, p. 17.

Column 3: (Difference between the surpluses of budget assets at the beginnin[g] and end of the year in the tables of expenditures and revenues for loca[l] budgets)

1970–75—*Byudzhet* 76, pp. 99–100;
1965–69—*Byudzhet* 72, pp. 102–103;
1950, 1955, 1960–64—*Byudzhet* 66, pp. 95–96;
1951–54—*Byudzhet* 62, pp. 93–94.

Column 4: column 1 less column 2
Column 5: column 2 less column 3.

[1]See the full explanations in the text.
[2]In *Byudzhet* 62, p. 93, no entry is given for "surpluses at the beginning of the year." See the explanation in *Byudzhet* 57, p. 13.

surpluses to the total amount of the expenditures for the union budget be the same as for the republic budgets or even higher—equal to that for the local budgets. We obtain the amounts shown in table V-4.

A quite strange picture results. No correlation is found between the amounts of the surpluses that we calculated and the profits of the union budget—for two years the profits are greater than the surpluses, for the other four years it is just the opposite. How can this be explained? Of these two series we can be certain only of the values of the profits; we calculated the surpluses quite arbitrarily.[24] It is possible that the actual surpluses of funds in the accounts of the union budget are substantially less, but for two years—1955 and 1960—the profits are greater than the surpluses, and it is not clear where they came from.

Table V-3. Ratio of Surpluses of Funds to the Total Amount of Expenditures for Republic and Local Budgets (in billions of rubles)

	1950	1955	1960	1965	1970	1975
Republic budgets						
Amount of expenditures	3.0	6.3	28.6	37.3	45.2	66.4
Surpluses	0.1	0.1	0.4	0.7	0.7	1.1
Percent	3	2	1	2	2	2
Local budgets						
Amount of expenditures	6.6	7.8	14.4	21.1	28.8	38.4
Surpluses	0.2	0.3	0.5	0.7	1.0	1.4
Percent	3	4	3	3	3	4

Sources: Amounts of expenditures: Appendix I
Surpluses: table V-1.

The explanation can be only the following. To all appearances we are greatly overstating the amounts of the surpluses for the union budget in table V-4. Besides, apparently the profits of the union budget themselves are only in part made up of the surpluses of funds in the accounts of this budget.

Table V-4. Estimated Surpluses for the Union Budget (in billions of rubles)

	1950	1955	1960	1965	1970	1975
1. Expenditures of the union budget	31.7	39.9	30.1	43.2	80.6	109.7
2. Percent of surpluses for local budgets	3	4	3	3	3	4
3. Estimated surpluses for the union budget	1.0	1.6	0.9	1.3	2.4	4.4
4. Profits of the union budget (for comparison)	0.8	2.4	3.3	0.2	0.4	1.5

Sources: Line 1: Appendix I
Line 2: table V-3
Line 3: calculated from lines 1 and 2
Line 4: table V-2.

Let us now return to table V-2. In it, by using the fact that the data on the total amount of the profits of both the USSR State budget and the state republic budgets are regularly published, I calculated the values of the profits for the union budget, which can be accepted with confidence. As I have already noted above, we apparently are overstating the profits of the local budgets somewhat and, consequently, are understating somewhat the profits of the republic budgets. But all in all this is not extremely important for the main goals of our study. The main thing is that this table shows the dynamics of the profits of the union budget and the state budgets of the union republics.

One is struck by the sharp decrease of both in 1961[25] and a second sharp decrease in 1965. It is also interesting that since 1965, when the profits of the union budget decreased to one-sixth of their amount in the previous year (!?),[26] the profits of the state budgets of the union republics begin, quite substantially, to exceed the profits of the union budget.

We took as self-explanatory the fact that the budget profits are the surpluses of the allocations not used at the end of the year less those that are included in the budget revenue. However, this explanation is apparently insufficient to explain the constant and very sharp jumps in the amounts of the profits—for example, the sharp rise from 1950 through 1952, and then a no less sharp decline, or the sharp crash in 1965–66. It is significant here that the amounts of the profits do not increase as the sizes of the budgets increase; compare, for example, the amounts of the profits in 1952, 1960, and 1973. This suggests that the profits, particularly for the union budget, are formed (or are regulated) in some artificial way.

In recent years, only about a third of the profit has formed in the union budget. Nearly all the surpluses of funds and, consequently, the entire profit of the state budgets of the union republics remain at the disposal of the republics.[27] However, it is not at all clear here just what the republics do with this profit, and further study of this question would be of considerable interest. At the same time, precisely because the profits of the republic and local budgets are not centralized, in the calculations of the resources of credit extension in chapter IX only the data on the profits of the union budget are used.

Although in nearly all the sources it is stated that the budget profits (this must be interpreted as the profits of the *union* budget) are used as a credit resource, in some sources it is also asserted that these amounts are also used for other purposes. Thus, in one source it is asserted that "the reductions of retail prices were carried out" using these profits.[28]

The last thing that is worth noting here is that the total amount of the profits of the budget is always several times greater than stipulated by the plan, as shown in table V-5. This coincides completely with our notion of the budget profits as the consequence of the fact that a part of the funds appropriated is actually not used. But, at the same time, the following natural question arises—why is such a reserve nevertheless placed in the plan (the planning budget)? After all, since the funds are not used annually, it is clear beforehand that precisely this will happen—why earmark more allocations? Let us note that the amount of the planned profit remains essentially unchanged.

One explanation is quite obvious. In a bureaucratic system no one will agree beforehand to be given less money only because in the past he did not use all the money.

Another explanation is that if allocations are cut back beforehand so that large surpluses are not formed, in some years surpluses would not be formed at all—we have already seen how the amounts of surpluses jump. But the Soviets do not want this at all—propagandistically it is very advantageous for them to end up the budget with an excess of revenues over expenditures annually. This demonstrates both the strength of the financial system and the fact that the budget is not running a deficit; (both of these are incorrect).

Table V-5. Planned and Actual Profits of the Budget (in billions of rubles)

Year	Budget profit: According to the plan	Budget profit: According to the report	Year, No. and page in the journal *Finansy SSSR* where the plan data (column 1) are indicated
	1	2	3
1965	0.165	0.7	1965, no. 1, p. 4
1966	0.141	0.7	1966, no. 1, p. 5
1967	0.235	2.0	1967, no. 1, p. 4
1968	0.308	2.2	1967, no. 12, p. 5
1969	0.2	1.5	1969, no. 1, p. 4
1970	0.3	2.1	1970, no. 1, p. 4
1971	0.2	1.8	1971, no. 1, p. 4
1972	0.2	1.9	1972, no. 1, pp. 5, 6
1973	0.232	3.8	1973, no. 1, p. 5
1974	0.2	3.9	
1975	0.2	4.2	
1976	0.2	5.5	1976, no. 1, p. 4
1977	0.2	5.0	1976, no. 12, p. 5
1978	0.231	5.6	1978, no. 1, p. 5

Source: Column 2: table I-5.

At the same time, on the basis of this circumstance in particular, I would like to note the following: all of the points we have raised during the discussion in this chapter together lead us to the conclusion that our explanation of the budget profits only by the surpluses of unspent funds is obviously inadequate. I have the feeling that this explanation is quite correct with respect to the republic and, apparently, the local budgets, but with respect to the union budget it should be supplemented. Namely, it is impossible to rule out the possibility that the profits of the union budget are partially formed by increasing the revenues of the union budget by the necessary amount. In other words, somewhere at the end of the year it is reckoned precisely what profits of the union budget there should be, and the amount that is injected into the budget revenues in excess of its actual revenues is correspondingly adjusted. Such is my hypothesis, but the word "hypothesis" means that there is no proof.

Let us summarize. We were not able to answer all the questions, and apparently the further study of this entire question would be useful. At the same time it is possible to draw the following conclusions: (1) The budget profits are nothing other than the surpluses of unspent budget funds, which are formed at the end of each fiscal

Table V-6. Second Adjustment of the Gap in the Budget Revenues (in billions of rubles)

Year	Amount of gap after first adjustment	Revenues from foreign trade	Economy from reduction of expenditures on management	0.5 percent of total amount of budget revenues	Remaining gap: Total	Remaining gap: Percent of total revenues
	1	2	3	4	5	6
1940	1.2	0.3	0	0.1	0.8	4
1950	3.7	1.9	0	0.2	1.6	4
1951	4.7	2.6	0	0.2	1.9	4
1952	5.2	3.3	0	0.2	1.7	3
1953	9.8	3.6	0	0.3	5.9	11
1954	12.4	4.1	0	0.3	8.0	14
1955	7.2	4.0	0	0.3	2.9	5
1956	5.8	4.7	0	0.3	0.8	1
1957	6.8	5.0	0	0.3	1.5	2
1958	8.2	5.6	0	0.3	2.3	3
1959	9.9	6.6	0	0.4	2.9	4
1960	10.3	7.1	0	0.4	2.8	4
1961	10.6	7.0	0	0.4	3.2	4
1962	10.7	7.7	0	0.4	2.6	3
1963	10.7	8.2	0	0.4	2.1	3
1964	10.9	8.7	0	0.5	1.7	2
1965	12.7	8.8	0	0.5	3.4	3
1966	11.7	8.4	0.3	0.5	2.5	2
1967	14.0	9.4	0.4	0.6	3.6	3
1968	18.3	10.7	0.7	0.7	6.2	5
1969	21.1	12.1	0.7	0.7	7.6	5
1970	24.4	14.2	0.9	0.8	8.5	5
1971	25.5	15.5	0.8	0.8	8.4	5
1972	28.3	18.9	0.4	0.9	8.1	5
1973	33.1	19.0	0.3	0.9	12.9	7
1974	33.9	18.8	0.4	1.0	13.6	7
1975	40.6	21.5	0.4	1.1	17.6	8
1976	46.4	24.0	0.7	1.2	20.5	9
1977	48.2	25.3	0.4	1.2	21.3	9
1978	54.0	29.1	0.5	1.3	23.1	9

Sources: Column 1: table III-3
Column 2: table IV-3
Column 3: table IV-5
Column 4: 0.5 percent of column 1 in table I-5
Column 5: Column 1 less sum of columns 2–4
Column 6: Column 5 as a percentage of column 1 of table I-5.

year. The existence of such profits in no way contradicts the fact that the budget itself can simultaneously run a deficit;

(2) At the same time there are some grounds to believe that at least in part these profits are formed artificially for the union budget—the amount of the budget revenues is inflated so that in some years these profits would be a little larger;

(3) Not all the profits of all the budgets, but only the profits of the union budget are used for state-wide purposes, in particular, for the consolidation of the credit resources of the banks;

(4) To all appearances, the unspent surpluses of the union budget are not included in its revenues. Therefore, in table V-6 we do not take these amounts directly into account, although we take them into consideration in the "0.5-percent addition."

* * *

Thus, we have completed the examination of all the imaginable budget revenues and can now make the next adjustment of the gap in the revenues (table V-6). In this and the preceding chapter we established that in addition to the amounts calculated in table III-3 it is also necessary to take into account the revenues from foreign trade, as well as those from economizing on expenditures on management. I repeat that we almost certainly are overstating the budget revenues from foreign trade, and considerably so. However, to be absolutely sure of our results, let us take above all this another 0.5 percent of the total amounts of the budget revenues for each corresponding year. This 0.5 percent (and, as is evident from column 4 in table V-6, it is also not at all a trifle) should cover what we did not take into account—for example, the revenues from the labor of prisoners and/or the use of the surpluses of the union budget as its revenues.

It turns out that even with these, I repeat, maximum assumptions, there remain very considerable amounts of budget revenues—column 5. These amounts are present every year without any exceptions and their size fluctuates from 1 (only once) to 9 percent of the total amount of the budget revenues for each corresponding year.[29] Beginning 1966 it has had definite upward trend, and the growth is especially fast for the last few years.

I would like once again to repeat that our detailed analysis did not reveal any other possibilities of real budget revenues, while the remaining inexplicable amounts are almost certainly understated.

Notes

1. More accurately speaking, we have practically no data on the union budget (only the total amounts of revenues and expenditures of the union budget are published), although in some cases we can obtain them by subtracting from the amounts for the USSR State budget the corresponding data on the state budgets of the union republics.

2. Precisely because the budget in fact deviates significantly from the previously approved amounts, for sake of legality the Supreme and local soviets approve at their sessions not only the budget for the next year, but also the report on the fulfillment of the budget for the past year.

3. "For a long time the monetary assets for the financing of capital investments were issued on the basis of the annual plan of capital investments and in the event of its nonfulfillment were withdrawn to the budget"—Senchagov, "Finansovyye," 1975, p. 82.

4. Lavrov and Plotnikov, *Gosudarstvennyy*, 1975, p. 359.

5. There are, of course, other instances. For example a portion of the receipts for section 60 of the classification of budget revenues is not planned—Shirkevich, "Voprosy," 1975, p. 37.

6. The data are collected in: CIA, *The Soviet*, 1977, pp. 26–27.

7. See the description in Lavrov and Plotnikov, *Gosudarstvennyy*, 1975, Chapter XXVII, §2.

8. CIA, *The Soviet*, 1977, p. 26.

9. Anyone acquainted with large bureaucratic structures (not necessarily Soviet) will agree that in searching for additional funds it is far from always possible to reduce allocations for those types of expenditures that will not be made, even when it is clear that the funds will not be spent.

10. Such an instance also occurred in my own practical work when I was working as the chief of the planning division of a plant. We were allocated insufficient capital investments, and we complained for a long time. At the very end of the year the additional funds were finally given, but we were no longer able to use them.

11. "The funds from budget accounts are issued during the current year through 31 December inclusively, while the amounts not utilized this year are turned over by all institutions to the bank. The credits not used by the end of the year are withdrawn, while the funds remaining in the current accounts are included in the account of financing during the new year" (Lavrov and Plotnikov, *Gosudarstvennyy*, 1975, p. 362).

12. CIA, *The Soviet*, 1977, p. 24.

13. Here, perhaps, it is more correct to speak not about the "actual," but the "reported" revenues.

14. This question is too complicated to discuss here in detail. Briefly, I am referring here only to plans for value indicators; as is known, the plans in physical terms are generally not fulfilled. It is also significant that budget planning is carried out year by year and not by five-year periods.

15. CIA, *The Soviet*, 1977, pp. 34–35.

16. Zlobin, *Finansy*, 1967, p. 335.

17. The so-called reserve funds of the USSR Council of Ministers (just as the reserve funds of the councils of ministers of the republics) have a completely different purpose.

18. The existence of such surpluses in the accounts of the union budget is clearly mentioned in Massarygin, *Kreditnaya*, 1974, p. 92. See also Goloshchapov, et al., *Byudzhetnyy*, 1963, p. 103.

19. Zlobin, *Finansy*, 1967, pp. 335–36.

20. The question of interactions of the union budget, the republic and local budgets is quite complicated and confuses the problem being examined even more.

It is my pleasant duty to note that J. Gillula turned my attention to this question, and while discussing with him the interactions of different budgets I arrived at the idea of writing this chapter.

21. Possibly this is connected with the fact that at the end of the year, as was already noted above, the amounts of the carry-overs should be restored, but then it is unclear why this was not done earlier, before 1960.

22. *Byudzhet 76*, pp. 99–100.

23. It is possible that this procedure was not used earlier. Thus, according to *Byudzhet 57*, p. 17, in 1951 and 1955 funds were spent on increasing the carry-overs for the state budgets of the union republics at the expense of the article of expenditures "Other Measures." In the tables on revenues these funds are shown after the final balancing entries (Ibid., p. 15).

24. If we use the percentage for the republic, and not the local budgets the picture will be very similar.

25. This possibly is a false correlation, but nevertheless let us take into account the monetary reform that took place precisely on 1 January 1961.

26. It is quite possible that this is somehow connected with the elimination of the *sovnarkhozy*, which was carried out at that time, and with the transfer of the financing of most of industry back to the union budget.

27. In Rusin and Eydinova, *Gosudarstvennyy*, 1975, p. 18, it is stated that the bulk of the budget surpluses for republic budgets cannot be withdrawn to the revenue of the union budget, with an exception of the unused surplus of funds for capital investments. This is also attested to by the fact that in the *Byudzhet* handbooks the profit for the state budgets of the union republics is shown below the total of the expenditures, among which is included the transfer of funds to the union budget.

28. Batyrev, *Denezhnoye*, 1959, p. 145.

29. The "jump" of the amounts of the gap in 1953–54 draws attention. It is difficult to say so with certainty, but it is quite possible that the "heirs of Stalin" loosened the belt slightly.

Chapter VI

Emission of Cash

At the end of the preceding chapter the preliminary results of the examination of the budget revenues were tallied, but nothing was said about one additional source—the emission of cash into circulation. As far as I know, in Western literature emission has not been examined precisely as a source of revenues of the Soviet budget. It seems to me that this may be due to the complexity of the question, to the peculiarity of the Soviet financial system as compared to the Western systems, and primarily to the fact that this problem, like the entire problem of Soviet finances in general, has been studied less than it deserves.

The question is important for us methodologically as well. While not having much of the necessary data, I make a number of rough estimates below and according to them the amounts of emissions cannot entirely explain the remaining gap in budget revenue. But the examination of the question of the emission of cash brings us directly to the idea that the emission, so to speak, of noncash money, which apparently is formed by loans to the budget from the bank, can also be a budget revenue. We will deal with the question specially in chapter X.[1]

Simplifying to a certain extent, it is possible to say that three different types of money are used in the USSR:

(1) Cash (*nalichnyye den'gi*) serves commodity-money relations of the state with the population, as well as transactions within the population itself;
(2) Noncash (*beznalichnyye sredstva*) serves the transactions between state (cooperative) organizations as well as between them and the state;
(3) Currency (*valyuta)* serves for internaltional payments.[2]

We will not touch in the book upon the question of currency for foreign trade. In this chapter, as well as in the next one, we will examine the circulation of cash, while later we will have to deal in detail with the noncash turnover.

Although cash and noncash transactions have a number of common features, they differ in important ways, and their separation for purposes of analysis follows their separation in real economic practice.[3] Thus, about cash.

In principle, for any state the emission of money (additional to that which is intended for the replacement of worn-out bills and coins) is a revenue of the state treasury. In all of world history the instances when some state would withdraw money from circulation, thereby bearing additional expenditures, are very rare.[4] It is also clear that the economic basis of sound emission is the overall growth of the economy and, consequently, the increase in the volumes of commodity and money transactions. Inflation (more accurately, increase of prices) demands more money in circulation as well.

In Western economies the additional emission of money creates only indirect financial obligations of the treasury; in itself this emission does not produce a corresponding state debt. In the USSR, where the main commodity and money transactions occur between the population and the state, the emission of money not only, so to speak, supplies these transactions (money turnover) with bills and coins; on one hand, the state, exactly as any other state, uses the emission to cover expenditures; on the other hand, in specific Soviet conditions, the state, in issuing this money, is obliged to offer the equivalent amount of goods and services.[5] By emitting an additional sum of money (additional to what is normally required for circulation), the state can consider it (and does!) a budget revenue, but only a temporary revenue, for the state debt increases at the same time and in the same amount (on the premise of the invariability of prices). It seems that it is quite legitimate to liken Soviet cash to Western non-interest-bearing state "bonds."

A significant subtlety is that in both Western and Soviet economies, if emission takes place within the limits of the needs of money circulation itself, it is, so to speak, a net revenue of the budget (treasury).[6] If, however, more money is emitted than is necessary, in both instances this has a negative influence on the market and causes inflation. And, understandably, just such an emission of money that is greater than necessary, under Soviet conditions directly creates an additional state debt. Therefore, strictly speaking, only money which is in excess of the amount needed for "normal" circulation can be likened to Western non-interest-bearing state "bonds."

In the Soviet literature it is fully recognized both that from time to time emission occurs and that emission is a budget revenue. This is stated most clearly in respect to war times—many works directly indicate that those special conditions made it necessary to cover part of state expenditures by emission, and that emission is a budget revenue.[7] In some instances it is stated that the emission was "too excessive," i.e., if it were done to some normal extent, everything would be fine.

As is known, soon after the end of the war (at the end of 1947) an exchange of money took place. The population was allowed to exchange old money for new money at a ratio of 10:1 and thereby practically all the monetary savings of the population were withdrawn.[8] By this simple means the state wiped out its domestic debt, which had arisen primarily precisely due to emission. The exchange of money—the monetary reform of 1947—was accepted quite calmly at the time by the population. The moral justification of the exchange was the fact that only dishonest people (speculators) could have accumulated considerable monetary savings by the end of the war. The majority of the population was so impoverished during the war that there was no question of savings.[9] The state declared that this was another and the last sacrifice that it was asking of the population, and that this was the consequence of the most difficult war in the entire history of the country, which was quite true. Moreover, at the same time prices were revised and the ration system was abolished, "old" money had been devalued up to this time and was treated accordingly. Thus, there was no serious dissatisfaction in the country, although at the time one of the cruelest regimes in the history of mankind reigned; the population, if it had wanted to, could not have expressed such dissatisfaction.

In order not to return again to past monetary reforms, let us add a few words about the exchange of money of 1 January 1961. Officially money was exchanged so that the population did not lose anything. In fact, the entire scale of monetary calculations—prices, wage rates and so forth—was changed identically, and it was said that this had been done in order to simplify all transactions and to create conditions for the introduction of vending machines. However, in reality the population also suffered with this reform. First, for those who had accumulated very substantial monetary savings illegally, it was difficult to exchange them. Second, and considerably more significant, this exchange psychologically prepared the population for the superficially not very appreciable, but quite substantial increase of prices in state and cooperative trade. Making calculations in ten-kopeck pieces instead of rubles helped greatly in this respect. This was manifested most graphically on the kolkhoz markets, where soon after the exchange prices increased very substantially.[10]

But let us return to the question of emission. I have already stated that direct indications of emission as a source of budget revenue exist only in respect to war times. However, there are indirect statements in the literature which quite definitely say that emission was also used as budget revenue after the war. Among them is, in particular, a statement of the former Minister of Finance.[11] "We must not permit economically unjustified emission in the plan . . . unfounded, economically unjustified emission has an adverse effect on the economy of the country." In other words, "substantiated," "economically justified" emission is quite permissible; it "will not have an adverse effect." In this indirect manner the Minister of Finance is saying that "economically justified" emission, at least at that time, was taking place. We will discuss further what kind of emission can be considered justified, but now another, comparatively recent and even more definite piece of testimony:

> . . . along with the increase in the amount of marketed goods and paid services as well as the wages being paid to the population and other payments, the amount of money necessary for circulation is increasing . . . in recent years the amount of credit formation by Gosbank has increased at an exceptionally fast rate, and, as is known, among the resources for extending credit, the emission of money is in far from last place.[12]

A well-known Soviet financial expert states in a very tactful form, yet quite definitely:[13] ". . . it would be unscientific to overlook this possibility during the theoretical analysis of the problem."

And here is another bit of evidence:

> In connection with the increase of the monetary income and expenditure of the population, the retail trade turnover, and the overall economic turnover, as a rule, the amount of money in circulation also increases annually. Its growth is used to increase the credit resources of Gosbank. According to established practice, currency emission is not taken into account in the plan estimates, but is reserved for possible deviations from the plan drafts and the implementation of measures not stipulated by the plan. The increase of money in circulation is shown only in the reported balances.[14]

You could not say it more directly. Here the systematic ("as a rule, annual") emission of money is definitely stated.

Two things are also interesting in the quotation. Firstly, as we see, it is asserted here that the increase of money in circulation is shown in the "reported balances." The balance is not the budget, but it is likely that in fact emission is not planned; it is resorted to only when it is ascertained that it would be impossible to cover expenditures by other measures.[15] This is consistent with the well-known fact that the five-year programs for increasing the standard of living have not ever been fulfilled and that the plans for the development of agriculture are also regularly not fulfilled.

Secondly, it is stated here that the growth of money in circulation is used to increase credit resources, and we will return to this question nearer the end of the chapter.

At the same time it is worth citing a long quotation from a quite old book, in which the negative consequences of emission are on the whole explained correctly:

> Of the greatest importance for ensuring the stability of the monetary system is the strict and consistent application in practice of the principle of the *deficitlessness of the budget,* that is, the prohibition of resorting directly or indirectly to the use of an emission resource to cover any expenditures of the state budget (including expenditures on financing the national economy).
>
> This prohibition is connected with the fact that when using emission to cover expenditures of the state budget that are not balanced by revenues, the increase in the amount of money in circulation can exceed the actual requirements of trade turnover for means of circulation. In turn this will violate the economic law of money circulation, will overfill the channels of circulation with currency notes, and, as a result, will have an adverse effect on the stability of money. In order not to permit a decrease in the purchasing power of money, it will be necessary to withdraw from circulation the excess currency notes, to implement a number of measures for mobilizing monetary assets by some financial methods, or to cut back some expenditures of the state budget.[16]

It is impossible not to agree with the author—the consequences of emission to cover the budget deficit are adverse, as we will see in chapters VII and X. However, the author had to mention that some "normal" emission is quite permissible to the extent that commodity and money turnover grows, and here I agree. Still the latter quotation is, so to speak, theoretical; in practice emission took place both at that time, before 1957, and afterwards.

In the literature we find not only theoretical discussions of emission, but even some figures. From 1950 through 1956 "the issuances of cash from Gosbank increased by 37 percent," while "the aggregate money turnover through Gosbank in 1956 increased in comparison with 1948 by 73 percent."[17] In 1958–1965 the cash turnover through Gosbank increased by another 56 percent.[18] It is clear that "the aggregate money turnover"[19] depends not only on the amount of money in circulation, but also on the rate of turnover (see below). But such a large increase could not be only a consequence of the increase in the volume of transactions; there was also direct emission.

Thus, we do not need any special evidence of the fact that emission takes place. It is clear that it happens at least to the extent of the increase in cash circulation (see below). But it would be desirable to have figures in order to estimate the extent of the phenomenon. For such, if only rough, estimates, we need above all to estimate the monetary income and expenditures of the population. Since this question is quite complicated and does not in itself have a direct relationship to our main theme, I have analyzed it in appendix B, and here, in table VI-1, I cite only the final results of these calculations.

Table VI-1. Balance of Monetary Income and Expenditures of the Population (in billions of rubles)

	Income			Income less expenditures	
Year	according to our estimate	according to official data	Expenditures	using our income estimate	using official income data
	1	2	3	4	5
1960	82.7	87.4	90.4	−7.7	−3.0
1961	90.4	95.5	93.4	−3.0	2.1
1962	97.1	102.6	100.8	−3.7	1.8
1963	102.7	108.5	106.5	−3.8	2.0
1964	110.4	116.7	111.9	−1.5	4.8
1965	122.7	129.7	123.4	−0.7	6.3
1966	133.6	140.3	134.5	−0.9	5.8
1967	144.5	151.8	146.5	−2.0	5.3
1968	159.7	167.8	161.0	−1.3	6.8
1969	170.2	178.8	174.2	−4.0	4.6
1970	183.0	192.3	189.3	−6.3	3.0
1971	195.0	206.6	200.4	−5.4	6.2
1972	207.1	219.4	214.5	−7.4	4.9
1973	220.7	233.8	227.4	−6.7	6.4
1974	237.2	251.3	243.9	−6.7	7.4
1975	252.0	266.9	262.9	−10.9	4.0
1976	265.7	281.5	275.9	−10.2	5.6
1977	277.7	294.2	291.2	−13.5	3.0
1978	291.0	307.8	306.4	−15.8	1.4

Sources: Columns 1 and 2:
Appendix B, table B-3, columns 3 and 4
Column 3:
Appendix B, table B-4, column 12
Column 4:
column 1 less column 3
Column 5:
column 2 less column 3

A very curious picture emerges. In the calculations in appendix B, I took into consideration all official data on money incomes and expenditures of the population and whenever necessary I made some estimates. When the resulting figures on money incomes of the population (column 1) are compared with the expenditures (column 3), it turns out that the population systematically year by year spends substantially much more than it receives (column 4). Of course, it is impossible to believe this; it just cannot be. I should say that similar calculations have been done previously by other Western scholars and they obtained practically the same results.[20] However, indicators of the aggregate money income of the population for three five-year periods have been published only once (in *Narkhoz 75*). These figures are substantially bigger than the ones I calculated, and they are shown in column 2. Using them, it turns out that the money income of the population is systematically larger than its money expenditures (column 5). True, for one year—1960—even income according to official data is less than expenditure but we should bear in mind (see appendix B) that I calculated income for this year by interpolation, which means that the real numbers can be somewhat different.

In order not to return again to my estimates of the income of the population, let us direct our attention to the figures in column 4. Although there are some fluctuations, these figures as a whole increase quite stably. Hence, I think it is possible to conclude that in our calculations we have not simply made some mistake, but we have regularly not taken into sufficient account some type of income (quite possibly a few such types), and this leads to the systematic understatement of the monetary income of the population.

When comparing the expenditures of the population (including the increase of deposits in savings banks) with the official data on its income,[21] a completely different picture results, and we will analyze it. However, we must note that having obtained understated estimates of the income of the population, we cannot fully rely on our estimates of the expenditures. We have to take into account the following circumstances:

Firstly, it is by no means ruled out that I made some mistakes in estimates of the expenditures (appendix B). My estimates of the volumes of trade on commission are quite rough; there is a possibility that the values of insurance payments should be adjusted upward; and there is no concrete certainty of the values of paid services. Nevertheless, we could not have overlooked major types of expenditures,[22] and the adjustments should be of a comparatively partial nature.

Secondly, the substantial excess of the monetary income of the population over its monetary expenditures[23] completely conforms to a widely-known fact: the population has enormous monetary savings not only in savings banks, but also on hand, directly in money form. We will analyze this in detail in chapter VII.

Thirdly, if we accept the values obtained in column 5 in table VI-1, it turns out that during 1960–78 the population received 79.4 billion rubles more than it spent. In addition, already by 1961 the population had some monetary savings. In other words if we simply accept these figures, it means that the savings of the population in cash now (1979) constitute something more than 80 billion rubles.

More on intuition than on precise knowledge, I believe that this is too high an estimate. I will therefore proceed quite arbitrarily as follows—for all our further calculations, I will reduce the values in column 5 of table VI-1 by one-third. In other words, I take the following as the amounts of the excess of monetary income over expenditures:

1961–65	—	11 billion rubles
1966–70	—	17 billion rubles
1971–75	—	19 billion rubles
1976–78	—	7 billion rubles
Total	—	54 billion rubles

The occupation of economist has accustomed me to calculation, to basing my conclusions on figures, not on feelings. However, the same occupation has also accustomed me to the fact that often intuition is by no means useless; as the well-known expression goes, "information is the mother of intuition." It is difficult for me to explain exactly why 54 billion rubles in this case is better than 45 (or, say, 60) billion rubles, but I should note that the *qualitative* conclusions of this research are practically identical in both cases.

I understand that all this sounds not very convincing, but I can invite critics not only to indicate my errors, but also to make their own calculations. I sincerely hope that other researchers will be able to refine these figures. However, it seems to me that the figures correctly reflect the general trends and state of affairs in the Soviet economy, and I will use them below for further analysis without significant reservations.

Thus, we see that during all of the last three five-year periods the monetary income of the population has very substantially exceeded its expenditures, but these amounts are significant only absolutely. If we compare the adjusted values of the excesses of monetary income over expenditures to the official data on income, these excesses are 2.0 percent in 1961–65, 2 percent in 1966–70 and 1.6 percent in 1971–75 and 0.8 in 1976–78. Perhaps precisely the fact that this was such a relatively small, and decreasing, percentage to a certain extent reassured the Soviet financial managers and rulers. However, the absolute amount of these values and the very substantial abundance of money in the hands of the population has led to such serious consequences as the increase in the shortage of consumer goods, the decline of interest in wages and so forth. This also corresponds to a number of statements in the literature where the consequences of the rapid increase of monetary savings are quite distinctly, though not directly, discussed.

> The existing system of the organization, planning and regulation of money circulation was formed under the conditions of the insufficiently complete balancing of the monetary income and expenditures of the population for some consumer goods [said very delicately, but quite clearly]. Such a lack of balance in recent years has been expressed, even at the stage of the drafting of national economic plans, in the establishment of additional targets for retail trade turnover, which attested to the insufficient volume and inferior structure of the planned supply of goods and services for covering the planned amount of monetary income of the population . . . the time has come when drafting national economic plans to unconditionally exclude nonconformity between the physical-material and value structures of the fund of consumption of material goods and to exclude the incomplete balancing of the monetary income and expenditures of the population . . . .[24]

Another author expresses himself no less tactfully and no less clearly:

> "As is known, the state of the money circulation of the country reflects the general state of the process of socialist reproduction, its positive and negative aspects, and is to a certain extent an indicator of the extensiveness and intensiveness of economic development, attests to the existence of disproportions [how true—why do Sovietologists study this most interesting phenomenon so little?] . . . . One of these negative indicators, which attests to the fact that an unfavorable correlation is forming between the consumer demand of the population and its satisfaction, is the gap, which has been increasing in the past 3–4 years, between the price index for consumer goods in state and cooperative trade and the price index on the kolkhoz market . . . the dynamics of prices on the kolkhoz market continue to be an indicator of the existence of specific phenomena in the socialist economy under current conditions.[25]

The author accompanies this very accurate discussion with a large number of reservations, but the "unfavorable correlation" itself is quite clearly named and demonstrated by reference to a widely-known fact.[26]

Both of these quotations speak about the connection between the question of the income and expenditures of the population and the question of money circulation. We will now deal precisely with this.

What should the volume of money circulation and the amount of circulating currency notes be? The corresponding formula is elementary—the total amount of cash payments during the year must be divided by the number of times money turns over, that is, by the indicator that characterizes the number of repeated returns of money to the bank during the year.[27]

The majority of wages are paid twice a month, that is, 24 times a year. Since paydays are not the same at different organizations and institutions, if at the end of each pay period all the money were spent by the population without any left over, the rate of turnover would be on the average 7.5 days (half of a half-month period); that is, the number of turnovers a year should be approximately 50. However, there are a number of factors which substantially slow down the turnover of money. Three of these are:

(*a*) Pensions, stipends, grants and wages of servicemen are paid only once a month. According to tables B-1 and B-3 (see appendix B) we see that these payments constitute, roughly speaking, 20 percent of all the monetary income of the population. So, as is easy to calculate, the number of turnovers should be 45 a year;
(*b*) The population spends money not only on everyday purchases of foodstuffs,[28] but also on the payment once a month for housing and municipal services, on the purchase of relatively expensive things, as well as on vacations. Let us assume that the people deposit the money for vacations in a savings bank and this, consequently, does not influence our calculations (see chapter VII). As to the payment for housing and municipal services, this constitutes, roughly speaking, 2–3 percent of the total monetary expenditures of the population (tables G–1 and B–4). A complicated thing is the purchase of nonfood consumer items. Their share in the total trade turnover from 1960 through 1978 changed negligibly and was in the range of 45–48 percent.[29] Among the nonfood consumer items are those which are purchased daily—soap, tobacco, haberdashery items and so on. It is clear that the purchases of expensive durable goods—televisions, radios, watches, clothing, furniture, and so forth[30]—should directly and immediately slow down the turnover of money. However, first, the proportion of the corresponding purchases is increasing very slowly (in 1978 the expenditures on furniture, carpets and beds, radios, bicycles and motorcycles, watches, jewelry, sewing machines, all footwear, all clothing, linen, hats and furs were only 21 percent of the total commodity turnover against 19 percent in 1960);[31] secondly, a substantial portion of these purchases are made with savings in savings banks, and, thirdly, the population purchases a portion of these goods on credit (see below). For all these reasons it would be rash to believe that the growth of the amounts being spent by the population for these goods changes the turnover rate of cash substantially. Let us assume more or less arbitrarily that these factors decrease the number of turnovers to 40 a year;
(*c*) The participation of the rural population also has a very substantial influence on the turnover rate. The following points are important here.

Firstly, as is asserted in a quite thorough source, in the sphere of kolkhoz trade ". . . money circulates considerably more slowly . . . the relatively large amount of money hoarded by the rural population in the form of cash plays a decisive role in slowing down the money turnover."[32] Unfortunately, our calculations in appendix B single out the monetary income only of kolkhoz farmers, not of the entire rural population, and the share of the money wages of kolkhoz farmers in the total monetary income of the entire population from 1960 through 1978 increased only from 5.5 percent to 6.2 percent (tables B–2 and B–3). This result greatly surprises me. According to my many personal observations, according to the assertions of my former friends and colleagues, and even according to the literature,[33] the income and standard of living increased considerably more rapidly for the rural than for the urban population.[34] As is evident from tables B–2 and B–3, the income of the rural population from the sale of produce to the state is also increasing more slowly than total income of the whole population.

Sales on the kolkhoz markets, by means of which money is transferred from the urban to the rural population, are also not increasing very fast. From 1960 through 1978 they increased by only 67 percent,[35] while the total amount of all money income of the population during the same period increased more than three-fold (table B–3).

For all that, secondly, the money turnover and its rate should be influenced not so much by the indicators of the share of the rural population in the total money income of the entire population as by the absolute amounts themselves of the monetary income of the rural population, which have indeed increased very substantially. According to the sources just indicated[36] in 1960 the total amount of the income of kolkhoz farmers from the kolkhozes and the income of the entire agricultural population from the sale of produce to the state and at kolkhoz markets was 8.3 billion rubles, while in 1978 the amount was already 24.2 billion rubles. However, in order to obtain the total amount of income of the rural population it is also necessary to add to this the wages of the workers of sovkhozes and others.

Thirdly, as is correctly noted in one already quite old book:

> . . . The way in which workers and employees spend their income is a factor which influences the rate of circulation of money. If purchases are made in state and cooperative trade, the money quickly proceeds from stores to Gosbank. When money is spent by the population at the kolkhoz market, the money proceeds first to the kolkhoz peasantry and then through the channels of circulation to the bank.[37]

All this (see also note 49) pertains not only to trade at kolkhoz markets, but also to other types of payments of the population to the population—services, commission trade in nonfood consumer items and so on.

Thus, let us assume more or less arbitrarily that due to the cumulative effect of various circumstances connected both with the participation of the rural population in the money turnover and with the payments of the population to the population, the turnover of money should be still slower, say, something like 30 turnovers a year.

Before proceeding one more point should be made. In discussing the influence of the income of the rural population on our calculations, I made remarks which call its very amount into question. From this the reader might conclude that we are underestimating the income of the rural population and, consequently, of the population as a whole. I cannot completely deny this possibility, but, it seems to me, the explanation lies in the fact that there is a significant *redistribution* of money income between urban and rural population. True, according to the official data this is not entirely so—in 1965, 1970 and 1978 the sales volume on the so-called kolkhoz markets was respectively 3.6, 4.2 and 6.2 billion rubles.[38] But just these data arouse serious suspicion; they seem improbably low.[39] Therefore we are by no means exaggerating the income of the Soviet population, but we are almost certainly understating it. Nevertheless, it is necessary to look for some sort of additional income and not only in the countryside (see appendix B).

I indicated above the factors which are slowing down the turnover of money in comparison with some theoretical level, but there are also contrarily influencing factors. Among them are noncash payments and deferred payments (which are becoming more and more widespread), the fantastically rapid increase of deposits in savings banks, the interregional movement of money[40] and so on.[41]

Now about some published indicators: In 1936 the number of turnovers of cash was 10.4, and this indicator had doubled in comparison with 1930.[42] (In 1931 the amount of money in circulation was 0.4 billion rubles, while in 1933 it was 0.8 billion rubles).[43] In 1939 the number of turnovers of cash was 8.39.[44]

I was not able to find any data on money turnovers or the amount of money in circulation for the postwar period (and, it should be assumed, this is not accidental) except one reference by a well-known specialist who, I hope, was relying not on speculative reasoning, as I have to do, but on experience. This specialist accepted in one example 20 turnovers a year.[45]

Thus, my preliminary estimates of the number of turnovers are substantially overstated (although, as we see, the general trend is toward an increase in the number of turnovers). The whole point is that the surpluses of money in the cashiers' offices of enterprises, organizations and Gosbank itself,[46] as well as in the hands of the population, also influence the indicator of the rate of turnover of money. For this reason, for the practical calculation of the turnover of money in the national economy "the entire amount of money received by Gosbank during the year is divided by the average annual amount of money in circulation."[47]

The indicator of the number of circulations that I obtained on the basis of estimates is more than four times greater than the published indicators for the prewar period and two times greater than the approximate indicator for the end of the 1950s. In my opinion, this must be due precisely to the fact that my estimates did not take into account the large amounts of money in the hands of the population (the monetary assets in the cashiers' offices of enterprises, organizations and Gosbank should be comparatively small). Since these amounts increased very substantially after the end of the 1950s (see below), I would not be surprised if the actual rate of turnover of money now is less than 10 turnovers a year.

The more turnovers an amount of money makes, the less of it that is needed for circulation. Let us try to make some estimates. We will assume first that money makes 20 turnovers a year,[48] and, secondly, that the amount of a turnover is equal to the total monetary expenditures of the population (column 12 of table B-4). Here, we are overstating the amount of money actually necessary since taxes are included in these values, but, on the other hand, we are not taking into account the turnovers of money within the population itself. On the whole, these values seem to be somewhat overstated, which makes the calculations based on them minimum estimates.[49]

Thus with 20 turnovers a year[50] the needs for money circulation are:

1960	90 : 20 =	4.5 billion rubles
1965	123 : 20 =	6.2 billion rubles
1970	189 : 20 =	9.5 billion rubles
1975	263 : 20 =	13.2 billion rubles
1978	306 : 20 =	15.3 billion rubles

What follows from this calculation?

Above we assumed that in 1961–78 the population was paid 54 billion rubles more than it spent. This unquestionably means that emission was made in just this amount and in our further calculations in table X-1 we will take precisely this amount as the budget revenues from emission.

As is evident from our calculation, for the normal maintenance of money circulation it would be quite sufficient to increase the amount of money in circulation during 1961–78 by 15.3–4.5 = 10.8 billion rubles. Consequently, the emission of 54.0–10.8 = 43.2 billion rubles was economically unjustified and was *excess emission.*

This value—54 billion rubles—also has additional significance. In chapter VII we will turn to the monetary savings of the population and their importance for the overall economic situation in the country. The importance of knowing the amount of savings in cash for the analysis of this question is clear. There are no data on the accumulation of cash savings up to 1960, so we will reason as follows. The unspent money held by the population during 1960–78 (54 billion rubles) was 5 times greater than the increase in the money supply needed to maintain commodity and money circulation. Let us assume arbitrarily that at the beginning of 1948, after the monetary reform, the population did not have any monetary savings left at all. During 1948–59 the money income of the population increased more slowly than during 1960–78, and the very amounts of this income were substantially less. Therefore, it is unlikely that we would be greatly mistaken if we assume that the population had a total of 10 billion rubles by 1960, of which, as was already noted, 4.5 billion rubles served normal commodity and money circulation, while 5.5 billion rubles, consequently, were savings in cash.

From this we can conclude that at the beginning of 1979 the population had 60 billion rubles in cash savings, and distributing this amount in accordance with the indicators of emission and the amount of money necessary for normal money circulation, we obtain the figures in table VI-2.

In spite of the gross assumptions that have been resorted to here, the possible errors cannot be very significant.[51] Taking into account such factors as the movement of money between different groups of the population, seasonal fluctuations, the migration of money, and noncash transactions with the population cannot, in my opinion, substantially change our results. The critical question here is our estimate of the monetary income-expenditures of the population.

The amounts of credits to the population have a very direct relationship to the question of the monetary savings of the population and emission. However, these amounts are very small, and they do not have a substantial influence on money circulation. There are two types of credits to the population—commercial and long-term.

The former are given to consumers when purchasing goods which otherwise sell poorly. Their amounts are relatively small and are increasing very slowly; data on them are given in chapter VII.

Table VI-2. Calculation of the Monetary Savings of the Population (in billions of rubles)

	1947–60	1961–65	1966–70	1971–75	1976–78
Emission of money	10.0	11.0	17.0	19.0	7.0
Amount of money normally necessary for circulation by the end of the period	4.5	6.2	9.5	13.2	15.3
Increase of this amount during the period	4.5	1.7	3.3	3.7	2.2
Savings by the population of cash at the end of the period	5.5	16.5	33.5	52.5	59.5
Increase of savings	5.5	11.0	17.0	19.0	7.0

Source: see text

Long-term credits to the population are of even less importance. They are given primarily for the construction of houses in rural areas. In 1960 the total amount of these credits was slightly more than 1 billion rubles. They have decreased gradually and in 1978 were equal to only 0.6 billion rubles.[52]

With respect to credits to the so-called housing-construction cooperatives, we have data only on their balances at the end of the year. Initially, after cooperative construction was permitted, the amounts of these credits grew quite rapidly. But, subsequently, in the 1970s, this growth was significantly curtailed, which may be at least in part explained by repayments of amounts issued earlier.

The year-end balances of these credits for cooperative housing construction for a series of years, 1965–1978, were as follows:[53]

1965	627 million rubles
1970	2,069 million rubles
1975	3,104 million rubles
1976	3,178 million rubles
1977	3,255 million rubles
1978	3,318 million rubles

Since, to repeat, there are not other data and, in particular, we cannot calculate data on the increment of these credits, it is difficult for us to deal with them.

As a whole, the credits to the population are not great, and their amounts change slowly. Therefore, I ignored them in the calculations of the income and expenditures of the population (appendix B), and they will not be taken into account here.

Thus, during the foregoing analysis we saw that considerable emission is taking place in the country, and we estimated its amounts. However, all this was done primarily for only one purpose—to estimate the amount of the corresponding budget revenues.

The question of precisely why it is possible to consider emission a budget revenue was already examined above. By printing (coining) money and putting it into circulation, the state receives and uses additional financial resources to meet its financial obligations to the population. Two things are significant here. Firstly, there is no reason to believe that emission covers some particular financial obligations of the state. This money is, so to speak, depersonalized; any payments can be and are made by using it. Secondly, it would be incorrect to divide emission here into "normal" and "unfounded" emission. True, I indicated above that the emission of money in excess of the normal requirements for money circulation is in reality an increase of the domestic state debt. This money can ultimately be presented for payment, and normally it would be necessary to pay off this debt (see chapter VII). But at the moment of issuance it is unquestionably a budget revenue and, actually, it is issued precisely for this. This point must be especially stressed. The negative consequences of the excessive emission of money are quite well known to Soviet specialists, which is seen from the literature. The need to balance the money income and expenditures of the population is persistently stressed in many books and articles. This is discussed, for example, in the above-cited quotation from the book by the former Minister of Finance, and many more similar quotations could be cited here. But this is reflected not only in the literature. The planning and financial organs compile a special planning balance of the money income and expenditures of the population,[54] the aim of which is to reveal inconsistencies between the amount of the income of the population and their opportunities to spend this income. However, in spite of all the good intentions (it is known, the road to hell is paved with them) it is not possible to do this, and therefore "unfounded" excessive emission must be regularly accepted. We will examine the consequences of this in chapter VII.

It would seem that everything is clear, but this is not quite so. In the Soviet literature it is persistently emphasized that the emission of money is not a budget revenue, but . . . one of the types of credit resources of Gosbank. This question is of fundamental importance for us and it must be examined in more detail on the basis of a number of quotations. Here, for example, is what is said in a book written by the chief of the Economic Planning Administration of the Board of Gosbank, that is, by an author who should know precisely what he is talking about:

> Since currency emission in the USSR is of a credit nature, the money which is in circulation is one of the resources of short-term credit operations. It is used for the extension of credit in strict conformity with the demands of the turnover of cash, which are regulated in a planned manner by the compiling of annual balances of the income and expenditures of the population and quarterly cash plans of the Gosbank, which are approved by the government. The credit plan takes into account the entire amount of money which is in circulation during the given planning period and also the emission of money or its withdrawal from circulation in the amounts stipulated by the cash plans of Gosbank.[55]

This should not be taken as some new procedure. Practically the same thing is said in a book published over 15 years ago that was written under the editorship of a very well-known financial specialist:

> When an increase in the amount of money in circulation is stipulated in the cash plan as an increase in the emission resource for the extension of credit to the national economy, the amount of the excess of issuances over receipts according to the cash plan coincides exactly with the amount of the increase of the emission resource for the extension of credit to the economy.[56]

Another quotation, also from a quite reliable source:

> In the socialist countries the state budget comes out with an excess of revenues over expenditures. In connection with this the need to use currency emission to cover the budget deficit does not arise. The assets formed as a result of currency emission are a credit resource of Gosbank and are used by it for credit formation in the national economy.[57]

This quotation is interesting in many respects. Firstly, the fact of currency emission is actually recognized here. Further, which merits particular attention, not only the USSR but also the "socialist countries" are spoken about here; that is, we have every reason to believe that a similar mechanism is used there as well.[58] Let us ignore for the time being the formally correct but essentially wrong assertion of the "profitability" of the budgets: we will discuss this question in chapter X. The important thing here is that once again the same thing is asserted—"the assets formed as a result of the emission of money" are a credit resource of Gosbank, but do not directly enter the budget.

Thus, it would seem obvious that emission is only one of the sources for increasing the credit resources of the bank, but in reality this very "only" does not follow from the two cited quotations and, in fact, is incorrect. But, before explaining and demonstrating this, here is one interesting item. The author of the book just quoted is attempting to convince the reader (we will see why in chapter X) that emission is not a budget revenue. In particular, he says:

> In the Soviet Union the need does not arise to use emission as a financial resource for the needs of accumulation, for defense or other resources of the state (this

can be required only under such special conditions as were created, for example, during the first years of the Great Patriotic War), since they are completely provided for by the growth of the national income.[59]

Although it is not stated directly here that emission is not used (that would be a blatant lie) it is said that it can be used only when the need arises under some "special" conditions. However, realizing that this is, to put it mildly, not very convincing, the author states in another passage[60] that "additional currency emission is carried out ... in conformity with the plan," i.e., he acknowledges the fact of the existence of emission. But in another passage he embarks on the following machinations:

> If the population, after receiving a certain amount of money income from the socialized sector, does not use it completely for the purchase of goods and other payments to enterprises and organizations, the amount of money in the hands of the population will increase. This, at the same time, causes the payments of enterprises and organizations to the population to exceed their monetary receipts from it—currency emission will take place. Consequently, enterprises and organizations and the socialized economy as a whole will require additional means of payment. Gosbank supplies them by issuing loans (entries on accounts) in amounts which exceed the inflow of its resources by the amount of the additional money put into circulation, that is, by means of emission.
>
> In this case the amount of the social product that is allocated for personal consumption will be less than the amount which the population will receive in the form of monetary income. A portion of the material funds may also be switched over for the purposes of accumulation or for increasing the public consumption funds, and the physical form of this portion of the social product should change correspondingly. As a result an additional revenue from currency emission will appear in the consolidated financial balance sheet.[61]

What is actually said here? It is directly stated that emission will lead to the formation of additional revenue in the "consolidated financial balance sheet," (that is, in the budget) and this revenue is formed not directly, but as a result of some production processes. This is a very clear discussion of whether emission is legitimate and to what economic results it can lead. The author is attempting to find a means to convince the reader that emission is in principle fruitful. Having declared, incidentally, that emission can be used as a credit resource, he cites an argument in favor of emission[62] and states that in the end emission will lead to the additional production of goods. Such a discussion in the literature of the legitimacy and positive consequences of emission is quite rare.

Thus, the very fact that emission takes place and the amount of emission is taken as a credit resource can be considered proved, but here it is appropriate to raise the quite natural question—why are these amounts used precisely as a credit resource and not as a direct revenue of the budget? It turns out that the one does not contradict the other, that emission *simultaneously* is taken as a credit resource and a budget revenue. The following quotations speaks more or less specifically about this:

> ... the credit form of emission can be accompanied by the use of emission not only for the extension of credit for current production and circulation, but also for the needs of the state budget. In other words, being bank-oriented in form, emission can be of a budget nature and by its economic nature come close to the emission of paper currency.... In the USSR during the first years of the Great Patriotic War currency emission, which stemmed from the disproportions in the economy that were caused by the burdens of war, was carried out in part in the form of the payment of the bills of the state budget from its account at Gosbank. Formally it was carried out by means of credit, although in essense it was of a budget nature.[63]

Before analyzing this quotation, it should be noted that some Soviet economists, including our author, differentiate the notes of a bank, which they assume are properly backed, and paper money, which in their opinion is issued without the proper backing and thus gives rise to inflation.[64] But to continue, this quotation clearly asserts that the credit form of emission (i.e., the emission of notes) "can be accompanied" by the extension of credit to the state budget and not only used as a source of credit resources for current production and circulation. The example cited by the author completely confirms this—during the first war years emission was carried out in part "in the form of the payment of the bills of the state budget from its account at Gosbank." And when the author says that this operation "formally was carried out by means of credit, although in essence it was of a budget nature," this means the same thing—the bank paid the bills of the budget and covered these expenditures by emission, and by emission in excess of the needs of the economic turnover itself. We may say that the bank extended credit for the expenditures of the budget: *it issued credit to the budget in the amount of the emission.*

Let us not forget that the author speaks only about the "partial use of this mechanism, so other forms are possible. However, the very existence in principle and the use of this means—*currency emission giving rise to a budget revenue through bank credit*—is quite obvious.

That this statement is not accidental is evident from the following quotation from a comparatively recent book:

> ... during the first war years Gosbank advanced monetary assets to the economic turnover in excess of the requirements stemming from the volumes of the production and turnover of the national product, in connection with the strain on the economy of the country and the short-term deficit of the state budget. This led to a worsening of the structure of the means of payment in the aggregate money turnover (an increase in the share of the emission of cash) and the resources of the bank.[65]

This quotation states that Gosbank issued more money than conformed to "the volumes of the production and sale of the gross national product," and that this increased the share of the emission of cash in the aggregate money turnover and led to inflation. Another interesting thing in this quotation is the reference to how such things occur—it turns out that Gosbank "advanced" the money to the economic turnover. But "to advance money to the turnover," to issue more assets than should be, means under Soviet conditions to extend credit to the budget. Indeed, by issuing money to enterprises and organizations, Gosbank is performing "the cash functions of the budget" in addition to "the cash service" of enterprises and organizations. In principle Gosbank can issue just as much money as is stipulated by the budget, for, once again, in principle the budget is needed for the balancing of revenues and expenditures. By issuing more money Gosbank has, if not in essence then in form, extended credit to the budget.

If this is not enough, the following example shows how the same mechanism operates in a slightly different case. In a book published under the editorship of the chief of the Main Administration of Savings Banks, it is stated:

> ... on 1 January 1963 the system of savings banks with all assets and liabilities was transferred from the jurisdiction of the USSR Ministery of Finance to the jurisdiction of USSR Gosbank ... starting in 1963 the funds attracted by savings banks as deposits were used by USSR Gosbank for extending credit to the national economy ....
>
> In practice the deposits in savings banks also served earlier as one of the sources of the credit resources of Gosbank. Thus, assets in the amount of not less than 3 percent of the total balance of deposits, which represented the cash reserve of savings banks necessary for supporting the operations they perform, were deposited in current accounts in Gosbank and were directly a part of its credit resources for the extension of short-term credit. The remaining amount of deposits received was transferred to the state budget in the form of the acquisitions of loans of savings banks and, thus, increased the revenues of the budget, which exceeded its expenditures. In turn the corresponding amounts from these funds were planned as continuing liabilities according to the credit plan of Gosbank, that is, were earmarked for the formation of the loan fund.[66]

Let us think over carefully what this means. According to the quotation the deposits in savings banks, both earlier and now, served as one of the sources of the credit resources of Gosbank. Practically no changes have occurred here. Indeed (this is worth repeating) "Not less than 3 percent of the total surplus of deposits ... were directly a part of ... credit resources," but the remaining amount," that is, the other 97 percent, which "was transferred to the state budget" and "increased the revenues of the budget," also "was earmarked for the formation of the loan fund."

We are going to discuss credit resources in chapter IX, and we will return to this question again there. Here I will only say once more that from this point of view nothing has changed: both before and after 1963 the amounts of deposits formed the loan fund either directly or as continuing liabilities (*ustoychivyye passivy*). True, the text speaks about "the corresponding amounts from these funds," but, as far as I remember Russian bureaucratese, in this case "the corresponding amounts" simply means nothing since the entire amount of the deposits can be fully attributed to the continuing liabilities.

Hence, this transformation could not have been of any significant importance for the loan fund. Then why was all this done; why was the budget deprived of one of the sources of revenue—especially under conditions when there were not enough budget revenues? The only answer which can explain all this is that the budget in fact was not deprived of this revenue, that only the form, but not the essence, changed. Alas, I do not have direct proof or even indirect literary evidence, but from all the circumstances it indisputably follows that whereas earlier this money entered the budget as special loans of savings banks, starting in 1963 the budget received the same assets in the form of Gosbank loans.

One more point. In one of the Soviet textbooks on finance it is stated that:

> ... certificate and noncertificate (*obligatsionnyye* and *bezobligatsionnyye*) loans were issued .... The noncertificate loans were intended as a way to invest the reserve funds of Gosstrakh and the stable balances of deposits of savings banks. The assets deposited by these organizations in the loans issued were not formalized by the purchase of bonds, but were taken directly into account by the Main Administration of Savings Banks ...
>
> In connection with the fact that the assets of the population and juridical entities (Gosstrakh and savings banks) were invested in loans, along with the issuing of term loans, termless loans were also issued. The reserve fund of Gosstrakh and the stable balances of the deposits of savings banks were invested in the latter.[67]

A number of things in this quotation are interesting. Above all, perhaps only here is it stated that the reserve funds of Gosstrakh were (and certainly are now) a source of budget revenues. We have already dealt with this question in chapter IV. We are told here how all this technically occurred—the budget utilized the relatively small amounts of the reserve funds of Gosstrakh and the much larger amounts of the balances of the population's deposits in savings banks as its own revenues in the form of "nonfunded loans." And the budget, of course, did not pay the savings banks and Gosstrakh any interest for them. It is interesting that these loans were "termless," i.e. from the very start no term at all was set for their repayment. And right here it is appropriate to raise a direct question. We are told that since 1963 the deposits of the population have no longer been used to form budget revenues. Let us assume all this is true. On 1 January 1963 the balance of deposits of the population in savings banks (excluding deposits in Gosbank) was 12.7 billion rubles (table VII-1), and as we just saw, the amount of "noncertificate loans" to the budget was practically the same. One would like to know, did the budget return this money, if not to the savings banks themselves at least to their new boss—Gosbank? This elementary wording of the question—of course the money was not returned, there is no place in the budget expenditures for this return—shows the complete formality of this entire operation of transferring savings banks to the jurisdiction of Gosbank and, in connection with this, eliminating the practice of "noncertificate" and "termless" loans. So, it looks like in this case only the form changed in some way, but by no means the essence; the budget as before receives and enters in its revenues both the money from the increment of the deposits of the population in savings banks and the money from increases in the reserve funds of Gosstrakh. But if the deposits of the population in savings banks are used both as a credit resource and at the same time as a budget revenue, in principle it is also quite legitimate to treat the cash savings in the hands of the population the same way. Indeed, the fact that the total amount of savings is divided into two parts—the deposits in savings banks (as well as the assets in 3 percent loan bonds) and the amounts on hand, the cash—is a strictly formal distinction since a deposit can be withdrawn at any time from the savings (and vice versa). It can even be said that it is more profitable for the state when the money is in the hands of the population—then it is not necessary to pay interest on it.

It would seem that the persistent efforts to attract deposits in savings banks, including the payment of interest, contradict this, but this is not quite so. The payment of interest creates a certain (not too great) stimulus among the population to defer the spending of money, to spend tomorrow, or even the day after, what can be spent today. But, I repeat, there is no difference here in the meaning of the use of this money as a credit resource and at the same time as a budget revenue.

Let us try to summarize the lengthy discussion in this chapter. Above all we were able to estimate, if only approximately, the amounts of emission and to break this down into "normal" emission and emission which created enormous savings of the population in cash.

Furthermore, we discussed in detail the question of how precisely emission is taken as a budget revenue. It turns out that this is done through the mechanism of credits which are granted by the bank to the budget. Actually, just this conclusion is methodologically the most important for us—it clarifies the question of how the entire budget deficit is covered using bank credits. We will address this question in chapter X, but for the time being let us examine some other issues.

Notes

1. When I told Dr. Rush Greenslade about budget revenues from emission, he immediately connected this with the possibility of "noncash emission." I mention this both to give him his due and to demonstrate the obvious unity of these seemingly different phenomena.

2. It is possible to subdivide currency further. Foreign trade with Western countries takes place in hard currency, while that with the majority of "socialist countries" is in so-called *invalyutnyy* (foreign currency) rubles. Furthermore, within the country the sale of some consumer goods to certain groups of the population takes place in so-called "currency checks," though these amounts are very small.

3. This question has been described in detail in the literature, and there are differing points of view on its many aspects. See, for example, Rybin and Shrayber, "Nekotoryye," 1977.

4. The withdrawal of money from circulation takes place when there is an exchange of currency—the most typical example is the exchange of money in Germany in the 1920s. However, here it is quite significant that, under such circumstances, while withdrawing the "old" money, the state at the same time emits "new" money, and it is not at all necessary that on the whole it loses in this; everything depends on how the old money will be exchanged for the new money.

Another example—rather recently the United States bought up quite a large number of dollars on the world currency markets in order to support the declining dollar. Such an action is more or less typical, but in any similar case it is necessary to compare the sums of emittings and withdrawings. I repeat, on the whole the main trend in all countries and at all times is emission.

5. The money emitted by a Western state is to serve transactions mainly between private individuals and organizations. The Soviet state is the main supplier of the population with goods and services.

6. This additional money settles in the channels of money circulation.

7. In Z. Atlas, *Denezhnoye*, 1957, p. 122, where the causes of the shortage of funds during the first years of the war are described, we read: "The deficit of the state budget was covered by the emission of currency notes, and also by the material reserves and stocks of past years."

The words about reserves and stocks here hardly mean anything; it is well known that there were few stocks and they were located mainly in the western regions of the country, i.e., areas quickly occupied by the Nazis.

Furthermore, this source states that in four years "the total amount of payments of the population reached 27 billion rubles or more than 26.4 percent of all state revenues and nearly half of all the direct military expenditures."

In M. Atlas, *Razvitiye*, 1958, p. 222, we read: "During the first three years of the war the amount of money in circulation increased as compared with prewar times 2.4-fold."

8. There were special conditions of exchange on deposits in savings banks, but their amount was relatively small. At the same time state bonds were also exchanged at a ratio better than 10:1.

See the description of the exchange in M. Atlas, *Razvitiye*, 1958, chapter VII. §4; Z. Atlas, *Denezhnoye*, 1957, chapter V, §4; as well as Gusakov and Dymshits, *Denezhnoye*, 1951, p. 167ff.

9. Although I cannot, unfortunately, document this, it was undoubtedly primarily the rural population that suffered from the reform. On the one hand, peasants accumulated more funds from the sale of agricultural products, and on the other they were reluctant to use savings banks. Public opinion was against the peasants, and the rulers were worried least about their mood. However, certainly very far from all peasants in all regions succeeded in accumulating savings.

10. A Soviet author in a work on the monetary savings of the population, in characterizing his calculations, writes: "The indicators for savings for 1960, 1961 and 1962 have been excluded. This is connected with the fact that the conditions of the implementation of the 1961 monetary reform had a substantial influence on their amount" (Ivensen, "Voprosy," 1973 p. 58).

11. Zverev, *Natsional'nyy*, 1970, p. 148.

12. Gusakov, *Planirovaniye*, 1974, pp. 208–209, 233–34.

13. A. Birman, *Ocherki*, 1968, p. 119.

14. Voluyskiy, *Svodnyy*, 1970, p. 52.

15. A curious result follows from this. As will be shown below, the ever growing gap in budget revenues may be, in fact must be, explained by emission and by loans to the budget by Gosbank. The corresponding calculations according to the reported budget results are presented in chapter X. I do not compare the planned and reported budgets in this work (the relevant data are shown in CIA, *The Soviet*, 1977), but the differences between them are not too great. If the emission of money is not in fact included in the planned budget, then the planned budget must include a correspondingly larger amount of revenue from Gosbank loans. Possibly such calculations can be made.

16. Z. Atlas, *Denezhnoye*, 1957, pp. 168–69.

17. Yampol'skiy, *Resursy*, 1974, p. 126.

18. Ibid., p. 12.

19. As I understand it, "the aggregate money turnover" characterizes both the receipt of money by the cashier's offices of Gosbank and its issuance.

20. For example, Schroeder and Severin, "Soviet," 1976.

21. In *Narkhoz 75*, p. 55, all that is said about these amounts is that they are "money incomes of the population." It is quite probable that these values include not only direct payments from the state but also changes in the balance of the amounts of fund transfers (usually by telegram) and something like Western travelers' checks. In Gosplan, *Metodicheskiye*, 1974, p. 454, it is stated that the balance of money income and expenditures of the population includes "money received through fund transfers and travelers' checks (less the transferred or deposited amounts)." It should be clear that the corresponding values for the country as a whole should be relatively small. It is also probable (though somewhat less certain) that this amount includes income of the population from various transactions, for example, income from the sale of agricultural products to the population. If this is the case, the amounts of savings of the population calculated later are correspondingly overstated, but as also indicated later I reduce the resulting amount by one-third "just in case," which should more than compensate for any possible mistake here.

22. Among the relatively small expenditures which we did not take into account

are, for example, the expenditures on lotteries, the payment of interest for the use of commercial credit and so forth.

23. According to the data for the first part of the period in question in Poskonov, *Kreditno*, 1967, p. 156, all the issuances of cash from Gosbank in 1959–66 increased more rapidly than the overall turnover of money. The latter consists of issuances and receipts. Hence, the issuance of money was increasing faster than the receipts.

24. Kashin, "Nekotoryye," 1973, p. 30. The author should know well what he is talking about; his post is deputy chief of the Monetary Circulation Administration of Gosbank (the title is indicated in the journal *Den'gi i kredit*, No. 2, 1974, p. 30).

25. Gusakov, *Planirovaniye*, 1974, pp. 221–22.

26. I do not have the corresponding statistics, but can confirm, on the basis of personal experience, that during all of the 1960s and the beginning of the 1970s the prices on kolkhoz markets increased very appreciably, even in Moscow, where the supply of produce through the network of state stores is incomparably better than in other regions.

27. Of course the number of times money turns over depends on the rate of turnover, and, certainly, a lot depends on the differing velocities of turnover during different time periods. For the sake of simplicity I ignore these factors here. The slowing down of the turnover rate resulting from the accumulation of cash by the population will be examined below.

28. In the USSR people walk to food stores every day, instead of driving there once a week, as in America.

29. *Narkhoz 70*, pp. 582–83, *Narkhoz 78*, pp. 438–39. This fact is in itself curious and deserves special attention. Apparently a big factor here is the very fast increase of consumption of alcohol.

30. This book is intended for Sovietologists, and they, of course, understand that such things as watches, clothing and shoes are indeed expensive in the USSR.

31. *Narkhoz 78*, pp. 438–39. *Narkhoz 72*, pp. 584–85.

32. Gusakov, *Planirovaniye*, 1974, p. 182.

33. See, for example, Mayer, "Aktual'nyye," 1977, p. 49.

34. It is noted that there are data other than those I used on the share of the money wages of kolkhoz farmers, and if we use these data, the income of kolkhoz farmers comes out to be slightly more, but far from enough to explain the strange result we obtained. At the same time we should take into account the possible explanation that the growth of the expenditures of money significantly lagged behind wages in the countryside.

35. *Narkhoz 70*, p. 573; *Narkhoz 78*, p. 429.

36. Appendix B, table B-2; *Narkhoz 70*, p. 573; *Narkhoz 78*, p. 429.

37. Gusakov and Dymshits, *Denezhnoye*, 1951, p. 190.

38. *Narkhoz 78*, p. 429.

39. Gur Ofer (Israel) is of the same opinion. He came to this conclusion when studying, together with Aron Vinokur, the results of a survey of the family budget of the Jewish population of the USSR. As he presumes, the sales on the kolkhoz markets should be at least 10 billion rubles a year.

40. In the Soviet literature much attention is devoted to the migration of money, but it seems to me that the actual influence of this factor on the rate of circulation is not very great.

41. Among these other factors particular mention should be made of the seasonal fluctuations in the payments of money to kolkhoz members and in the payment for procurements of produce. It would seem that these fluctuations should be of substantial importance. However, as is evident from the data in Shvarts, *Beznalichnyy*,

1963, p. 103, even in 1961, that is, when in practice there still was no monthly wage of kolkhoz farmers, this was not so—the seasonal fluctuations of the issuing of cash were only 2–4 points.

42. Gusakov, *Planirovaniye*, 1974, p. 177. However, according to M. Atlas, *Razvitiye*, 1958, p. 173, in 1936 there were only 8.25 turnovers.

43. M. Atlas, *Razvitiye*, 1958, p. 130.

44. Ibid, p. 201. It is also curious that in 1940 the total amount of receipts of Gosbank was 18.1 billion rubles, including trade receipts of 14.8 billion rubles. At the same time just that part of the income of the population that can be directly estimated was 14.5 billion rubles at that time (table B-1), while the retail trade turnover of state and cooperative trade during that year was 18 billion rubles (*Narkhoz* 76, p. 531).

45. Batyrev, *Denezhnoye*, 1959, p. 312.

46. Here, of course, I am referring only to the so-called till cash of Gosbank, and not to the total amounts.

47. Z. Atlas, *Denezhnoye*, 1957, p. 178. E. Domar pointed out to me that "this is not a Western concept of velocity of circulation." This is not quite so, but let me emphasize that here, as in other cases concerning the Soviet economy and the Soviet statistics, we should use Soviet definitions.

48. In the opinion of V. Shlapentokh the so-called second economy decreases the velocity of money turnover. Indeed, the value of transactions in the second economy is big and constantly increasing, which demands correspondingly larger sums of money.

In regard to the second economy the following phenomenon is interesting as well. As is known, a significant part of the second economy is stealing from enterprises and kolkhozes. In principle such cases increase incomes of the population in kind and even its total sum of monetary incomes. For example, comrade A steals something from his (her) enterprise and sells it to comrade B. In this case the monetary income of comrade B is not changed, but the monetary income of comrade A is bigger. Hence the combined monetary income of this comradeship increased.

Thus, in principle, the sums of monetary incomes of the population in this chapter and in appendix B should be higher than according to my calculations. I have not adjusted them for two reasons. Firstly, one cannot say how to do it—we have no data. Secondly, and even more important, in our calculations we need to know the balance of the monetary incomes and expenditures of the population and not their absolute sizes. This balance is not affected by stealing (except stealing of money from the state). Indeed, in our example the total monetary income of comrades A and B increased, but their total monetary expenditure increased by exactly the same sum. Hence the balance did not change. See my estimates of the size of the second economy in "Second and First Economics and Economic Reforms" (in Russian), Occasional Paper of the Kennan Institute for Advanced Russian Studies, Washington D.C., 1980.

49. In particular, it would be possible to take into account the increasing receipt of wages by the population directly through savings banks. These amounts were 6.5 billion rubles in 1973, 8.5 billion rubles in 1974, and 10 billion rubles in 1975 (Zakharov, "Rabota," 1976, p. 23).

50. Certainly, the same number of turnovers for 1960–75 is an additional simplification.

51. In two recent sources some data on the increase of the cash turnover were published without any references (Pchelin, *Gosudarstvennyy*, 1976, p. 5, and Barkovskiy, "Problemy," 1977, p. 54). In appendix B an attempt is made, without particular success, to use these data for checking the calculations on the income and expenditure of the population. My attempts just to apply these data in some way to the analysis of money

circulation were also unsuccessful. In particular, according to these data in each of the years for which figures are given (1970–75), the increases of "the turnover of cash through the cashier's offices of Gosbank (according to receipts and expenditures)" are less than the increases of "the receipts of cash at Gosbank." Hence, seems, it should follow that the "expenditure," i.e., the issuing of money to the population, was decreasing. It is hard to believe this, although perhaps a sharp increase in the noncash issuances to the population is showing up here (see note 49).

52. *Narkhoz 70,* p. 735; *Narkhoz 78,* p. 538.

53. *Narkhoz 78,* p. 538.

54. See, for example, Gosplan, *Metodicheskiye,* 1974, p. 453.

55. Barkovskiy, *Organizatsiya,* 1973, p. 57.

56. Ikonnikov, *Denezhnoye,* 1962, p. 41.

57. Kosyachenko, *50 let,* 1967, p. 159.

58. From this it follows that it is worth studying the question of budget revenues in the other "socialist" countries—this is the idea of M. Feshbach. It is possible that there are more direct descriptions of the mechanism itself in the literature of these countries.

59. Ikonnikov, *Denezhenoye,* 1962, p. 219.

60. Ibid, pp. 223–24.

61. Ibid., p. 218.

62. Of course, it is possible to regard this quotation also as substantiation of the fruitfulness of the "deferred demand" of the population, but one does not contradict the other. On deferred demand, see chapter VII.

63. Batyrev, *Denezhnoye,* 1959, p. 209.

64. Indeed, as we will see in chapter VII, Soviet money is backed neither by gold nor by the corresponding commodity resources. And this very distinction of the notes of the bank and paper money, was of importance only in the 1920s and now makes no real sense.

65. Melkov, *Kreditnyye,* 1969, p. 101.

66. Chetverikov, *Sberegatel'nyye,* 1972, pp. 24–25.

67. Zlobin, *Finansy,* 1967, p. 251.

Chapter VII

Savings of the Population. Inflation in Cash Circulation

The monetary savings of the population and inflation have, strictly speaking, only an indirect relation to our basic theme, the budget deficit. Nevertheless I am devoting a separate chapter to it both because of the exceptional importance of this particular question and because some of the estimates made in the course of this study lead to a number of conclusions.[1]

In chapter VI we determined the amount of "excess" cash received by the population and thus made an estimate of the savings of the population in cash form. In addition the population has monetary savings, first, in savings banks and secondly, in bonds. Let us first consider the savings in savings banks.

The appropriate data are given in table VII-1.[2] The most striking thing about these data is the extremely rapid increase of savings in savings banks and, correspondingly, their fantastically large amount.

As for the increase itself, in my opinion a careful study of these data with the use of some additional material will yield much food for thought and, perhaps, some conclusions. It must be kept in mind, of course, that the growth of savings is the result of not one but a whole complex of complicated factors. For example, if the sharp jump in the growth of savings in 1953 can apparently be explained by the regular (and last!) mass reduction of prices, which was implemented at the beginning of that year, there is no obvious explanation for the slower growth of savings in the following year, 1954. The very sharp drop in the growth of savings in 1958 is also not very understandable, although perhaps this was connected with the reduction of the size of the army at that time (having been demobilized, the officers could withdraw their savings from their savings accounts). A detailed analysis, I repeat, promises to be very interesting,[3] but here let us talk about what pertains directly to our theme.[4]

In 1960 and 1971 two appreciable declines in the growth of deposits took place. In the first instance this was undoubtedly connected with the exchange of money declared at that time on 1 January 1961. Many looked upon this with bewilderment and preferred at any rate to keep

Table VII-1. Deposits of the Population at Savings Banks and Gosbank (in millions of rubles)

Year	Amount of deposits at end of corresponding year			Increase of deposits during the year
	Savings banks	Gosbank	Total	
	1	2	3	4
1940	725	—	725	—
1948	1,288	223	1,511	—
1950	1,853	181	2,034	—
1951	2,192	140	2,332	298
1952	2,664	101	2,745	413
1953	3,865	103	3,968	1,223
1954	4,835	107	4,942	974
1955	5,366	111	5,477	535
1956	6,375	114	6,489	1,012
1957	8,058	117	8,175	1,686
1958	8,719	120	8,839	664
1959	10,056	124	10,180	1,341
1960	10,909	127	11,036	856
1961	11,671	147	11,818	782
1962	12,745	135	12,880	1,062
1963	13,992	133	14,125	1,245
1964	15,707	128	15,835	1,710
1965	18,727	129	18,856	3,021
1966	22,915	131	23,046	4,190
1967	26,869	128	26,997	3,951
1968	32,360	140	32,500	5,503
1969	38,397	140	38,537	6,037
1970	46,600	143	46,743	8,206
1971	53,215	154	53,369	6,626
1972	60,732	157	60,889	7,520
1973	68,660	156	68,816	7,927
1974	78,905	169	79,074	10,258
1975	90,985	169	91,154	12,080
1976	103,000	174	103,174	12,020
1977	116,700	179	116,879	13,705
1978	131,100	167	131,267	14,388

Sources: Columns 1 and 2:

1977–78—*Narkhoz 78,* p. 415
1940, 1965, 1970, 1975–76—*Narkhoz 76,* p. 515
1971–74—*Narkhoz 75,* p. 597
1950, 1960, 1969—*Narkhoz 70,* p. 562
1968—*Narkhoz 69,* p. 585
1966–67—*Narkhoz 68,* p. 597
1958, 1964—*Narkhoz 65,* p. 600
1963—*Narkhoz 64,* p. 595
1952, 1959, 1961–62—*Narkhoz 62,* p. 492
1948—*Narkhoz 61,* p. 607

Column 1:

1956–57—*Narkhoz 59,* p. 810
1955—*Narkhoz 60,* p. 854
1951, 1953–54—*Narkhoz 56,* p.282

Column 2:

1951, 1953–57—estimated according to the trend

Column 3:

sum of columns 1 and 2

Column 4:

calculated from column 3

their money closer at hand.[5] Something similar also occurred in 1971. Precisely at that time, as I well remember, rumors of monetary reform were widespread (we will soon see that this was not without reason) and people were once again less willing than before and afterwards to carry their money to savings banks.

The level that the total amount of savings reached[6] merits the closest attention, for it characterizes the state of affairs in the Soviet economy as, if we are not afraid of precise words, catastrophic. But before examining this question in the greatest possible detail, let us talk about the savings of the population in bonds.

Firstly, the 3-percent loan: here we encounter our next riddle. The data on the balances of assets of the population in these loans are not published and, it would seem, they can be calculated according to the data published in *Narkhoz* yearbooks on the receipts of funds from these loans by the budget and on the payments and expenditures on these loans, although beginning with *Narkhoz 72* the publication of the latter data was for unknown reasons stopped.[7] The data on the receipt of funds by the budget are published separately for the 3-percent loan, but the data on the expenditures and payments are given as a whole for all types of loans (although this is not specified). Beginning in 1958 the obligatory loans were halted; therefore, the data on the expenditures of the budget on loans should pertain only to the 3-percent loan. On the other hand, the costs of making the loans[8] and the winnings are included in the amounts of the expenditures, but the former cannot be very significant, and I assume that all the expenditures are payments to the population.[9]

Data on the budget receipts and the expenditures for the 3-percent loan are given in table VII-2. Since expenditures on old loans were made until 1959 and they were not reported separately, we have data on expenditures on the 3-percent loan only beginning in 1959. The population accumulated quite a few of these bonds by 1959. Nevertheless, the fragmentary data for the preceding years show that their purchases were quite modest,[10] while the very large expenditures during 1959–62 show that the savings which existed up to that time had been nearly wiped out. As a result of all these calculations we find that during 1959–78 the population accumulated 1.3 billion rubles in these bonds, and it is not clear what the result was for the preceding years; our data are insufficient for this. This result surprises me; according to my personal impressions this figure should be much greater. And indeed in a recent article by the chief of the Main Administration of the Savings Banks we read:[11] "In 1976 . . . 580 million rubles were received from the 3-percent bonds which are 13.2 percent of the amount of the bonds in the hands of the population."

Table VII-2. The 3-Percent Loan (in billions of rubles)

Year	Budget revenues	Budget expenditures	Difference
	1	2	3
1940	0.02		
1950	0.1		
1953	0.1		
1955	0.1		
1956	0.1		
1957	0.1		
1958	0.1		
1959	0.2	0.7	−0.5
1960	0.1	0.7	−0.6
1961	0.04	0.8	−0.8
1962	0.1	0.8	−0.7
1963	0.1	0.1	0
1964	0.1	0.1	0
1965	0.2	0.1	0.1
1966	0.2	0.1	0.1
1967	0.1	0.2	−0.1
1968	0.3	0.2	0.2
1969	0.4	0.2	0.2
1970	0.5	0.1	0.4
1971	0.3	0.1	0.2
1972	0.3	0.1	0.2
1973	0.4	0.1	0.3
1974	0.4	0.1	0.3
1975	0.6	0.1	0.5
1976	0.6	0.1	0.5
1977	0.6	0.1	0.5
1978	0.6	0.1	0.5
Total for 1959–78	6.1	4.8	1.3
Total for 1963–78	5.7	1.8	3.9

Sources: Column 1:
1976–78—*Narkhoz 78*, p. 533
1970-75—*Byudzhet 76*, p. 9
1965–69—*Byudzhet 72*, p. 12
1950, 1955, 1960–64—*Byudzhet 66*, p. 11
1940, 1956–59—*Byudzhet 62*, p. 9
1953—*Narkhoz 59*, p. 800

Column 2:
1972–78—estimate
1965, 1970, 1971—*Narkhoz 22–72*, p. 481
1969—*Narkhoz 70*, p. 730
1968—*Narkhoz 69*, p. 769
1966–67—*Narkhoz 68*, p. 774
1964—*Narkhoz 65*, p. 781
1963—*Narkhoz 64*, p. 770
1962—*Narkhoz 63*, p. 654
1959–61—*Narkhoz 62*, p. 635.

This means that at the beginning of 1976 4.4 billion rubles of these bonds should have been in the hands of the population, and in addition 0.5 billion rubles more was received in 1976 excluding expenses, while according to our calculations (table VII-2) this sum should be only 0.3 billion rubles in 1976.

Apparently, the relatively large amounts of expenditures on bonds in 1959–62 are connected with the payments on old bonds; at any rate we have no grounds not to trust the information cited in the last quotation. Therefore, let us assume that in 1978 the population had about 6 billion rubles in these bonds.

The second type of loans are those which were issued through 1957 by subscription, that is, were practically obligatory. On 1 April 1958 "the state debt" on them was "in round figures 26 billion rubles."[12] At the 24th CPSU Congress it was declared that by 1990 this old debt would be completely paid off (of course, without interest), and since 1974 the paying off of this debt has been taking place.[13] At present the population has about 20 billion rubles in these bonds, which represents the amount of the state debt.

Before proceeding to the analysis of the influence of these savings on the economic situation in the country, a few words on the presentation of this question in Soviet literature are in order.

It is understandable that the enormous increase of the savings of the population in general and in savings banks in particular ("in particular" because only these data are published) could not but be reflected in the literature. However, in speaking of this, Soviet authors for the most part stress the positive aspects of the increase in savings which, in their opinion, above all characterizes the increase of the standard of living of the population. Generally speaking, to a certain extent this is indeed so; poor people do not save, this is the privilege of the rich.[14] Saying the same thing in different words, savings arise (under normal conditions) only when primary needs are met. At the same time, as I will try to show below, this enormous increase of savings attests not so much to the increase of the standard of living of the population as to the enormous difficulties of the Soviet economy.

In the Soviet literature a number of causes of the rapid increase of savings are usually listed. Let us examine them:

(a) Most often it is stated that the commodity structure of consumption is changing. The proportion of expensive goods is increasing, and purchasing them requires preliminary savings. This is not entirely so. First, as a Soviet author correctly indicates:

> ... this factor can have only a short-term influence on the formation of the monetary savings of the population. The accumulation of durable goods is conducive to an increase in annual savings only during the period of the formation of the market for these goods. As the consumer demand for this type of goods is satiated, the influence of this factor on the level of savings weakens and becomes little felt.[15]

Secondly, as the data on the commodity credit to the population show[16]—table VII-3—only a small portion of the population needs this credit, since its amounts are comparatively small and are increas-

Table VII-3. Sale of Goods to the Population on Credit (in millions of rubles)

Year	Sales volume during year	Increase (decrease) during year
	1	2
1960	633.0	
1961	1,110.0	477.0
1962	1,583.2	473.2
1963	2,132.7	549.5
1964	2,752.5	619.8
1965	3,371.7	619.2
1966	3,314.8	−56.9
1967	3,049.0	−265.8
1968	3,342.5	293.5
1969	3,307.1	−35.4
1970	3,122.1	−185.0
1971	3,766.1	644.0
1972	4,265.7	499.6
1973	4,463.9	198.2
1974	4,601.8	137.9
1975	4,696.0	94.2
1976	4,907.3	211.3
1977	5,039.1	131.8
1978	4,994.3	−44.8

Sources: Column 1:
1960, 1965, 1970, 1975–78—*Narkhoz 78,* p. 437
1971–74—*Narkhoz 76,* p. 541.
1961–64, 1966–69—*Narkhoz 70,* p. 581

Column 2:
Calculated from column 1.

ing very slowly.[17] Indeed, since the interest on deposits in savings banks is small and the interest for the use of credit is also comparatively small, people would use credit far more if they did not have money in savings.[18] It is also not unimportant that credit is extended only on goods that do not sell well.[19] Thirdly, a more specific examination of the question would show that all the annual expenditures of the population on the purchase of expensive goods—refrigerators, televisions, cooperative apartments, cars and so on—are many times less than the existing amounts of savings;

(*b*) Of approximately the same nature is the reasoning that people save money for trips to resorts.

In response to this, we must note that those who go to resorts in most cases do this each year, and their corresponding savings, therefore, can be only of a seasonal nature. In most cases a trip to a resort (to a vacation home, or on a tourist trip) is not a very expensive matter, and special long-term savings are not needed for this. Trips to resorts themselves pertain only to a relatively small portion of the population. In connection with this, let us turn our attention to the data on payments for services in appendix G, table G-1. In 1975 the population spent 9.2 billion rubles on payments for all types of transportation. But intra-urban and suburban transportation, the fare for business trips and personal trips (not to resorts) also belong here. In other words, the population spends annually on trips to resorts hardly more than 2 billion rubles, and, I think, only somewhat more on vacations.[20] I do not study the movement of money from some groups of the population to others in this work and I do not have data on payments for dachas or payments to private individuals for housing in resort areas. But even with the boldest of assumptions the corresponding amounts cannot be more than a billion rubles a year.

Consequently, this argument—that people putting away money for vacations leads to a very fast growth of savings—does not hold;

(*c*) The line of reasoning about savings for retirement is considerably more serious, and no doubt a significant part of all savings are for this purpose.

At the same time it should be borne in mind that pensions are (relative to the existing standard of living) quite good. In principle people save for retirement not because they have to, but because they have an opportunity to do this.

It is extremely difficult to estimate even approximately just when amounts of savings are connected with this phenomenon. Let us turn our attention to the total number of deposits—more than 127 million at the end of 1978.[21] This means that one inhabitant in two has a deposit; hence, far from only future retirees have money in accounts at savings banks;[22]

(d) Little is said in the Soviet literature about this line of reasoning, but in principle the change in the age composition of the population has a great influence on the amount of savings. On the whole the Soviet population is "aging" appreciably,[23] and not only is the proportion of retirement age increasing, but the proportion of children is decreasing. Of substantial importance in connection with the former point is the fact that the proportion of the age cohorts that are approaching retirement age (particularly in the 40–49 age group) is increasing. The decrease in the proportion of children is also of particular importance.[24]

However, it must be borne in mind that there are other factors here as well. The very ageing of the population and the change of the numbers in different age groups are not occurring very rapidly, and more precisely, the demographic changes themselves are very significant, but they are not excessively great relative to the enormous growth of savings. It is also significant that as people retire those who saved earlier should begin to spend these savings;

(e) The gradual reduction of the proportion of the population with a very low income and the increase of the proportion with a relatively high income should be of great importance. I do not have the corresponding data, but the overall trend here is quite clear. In particular, the number of people holding academic degrees is increasing rapidly; there are quite a large number of well-paid workers and kolkhoz farmers (on the rural population, see below). The increase in the number of deposits attests indirectly to this. I already noted that the number of deposits now exceeds 127 million, and since 1965 it has more than doubled. This unquestionably means that representatives of practically all the groups of population now have deposits.[25]

At the same time it would be very rash to think that at some time in the recent past there was such a change in the standard of living of large groups of the population that their needs were met to the extent that they switched to planned regular savings. We will discuss this question specifically below, but right here I will note that the main reason for savings is the impossibility of spending the money. The increase in the standard of living of the population is of relatively secondary importance here.[26]

Before turning to the next item in the list of reasons for saving, I will cite a recent article, in which the arguments examined above are discussed:

> There are various opinions on the nature of the increase of savings. Often it is explained by unmet demand, that is, by the lack of the goods needed by the

> population in the trade system. However, it does not seem entirely correct to us to consider unmet demand as the sole or even the main reason for the increase of savings. First, money is being saved for major purchases and for enrollment in housing construction cooperatives. This supposition is all the more probable as the sale of goods to the population on credit during 1966–75 increased by only 38 percent, while the sale of all nonfood consumer goods increased by 2.3-fold. The purchase by the population of goods, which require large monetary expenditures that as a rule are impossible without preliminary saving, increased significantly. Thus, the sale of passenger cars to the population from 1965 through 1975 increased 15-fold (in comparable prices), jewelry—7-fold, furniture—2.1-fold, refrigerators—3.3-fold, and so on. The capital investments of the population in the construction of their own homes and apartments in 1975 alone were 1,821 million rubles. The increase of savings is also connected with the desire of workers to ensure a specific standard of living after retirement and so forth.[27]

This quotation is interesting in several respects. Firstly, it is quite clearly stated here that "often" the increase of savings is explained precisely "by the lack of the goods needed by the population in the trade system." Hence I am far from the only one of this opinion. Secondly, our author himself says that this point of view is "not entirely correct," but not "entirely incorrect," that is, in his opinion there are specific reasons for this point of view. Thirdly, his arguments against this point of view, if we examine them more closely with the figures available, are very unconvincing. We have already spoken in part about this above, but the question is too important to worry about being repetitive. Indeed, I have already indicated above that the total amount of expenditures of the population on the purchase of expensive goods is small in comparison with the amount of savings. Not at all by chance does our author cite the relative rather than the absolute figures. Suffice it to say that the total sales of fur goods, furniture and jewelry in 1975 was 6.6 billion rubles,[28] while the sale of refrigerators and passenger cars was not more than 7 billion rubles.[29] Even if we assume that all these goods were purchased by means of preliminary savings, the corresponding amount is only less than 15 percent of all the savings at savings banks in 1975, and it is no less important that far from all these goods were purchased by means of preliminary savings, especially by savings at savings banks. It is obvious that the savings of the population for the construction of their own homes and apartments are even less significant, for according to the figures of the author it is clear that these amounts are practically negligible in comparison with the amounts of savings. Finally, fourthly, this quotation is noteworthy for the fact that it once again shows how important the question is from the Soviet point of view, and this is far from the only case of the discussion of the question in the Soviet press;[30]

(*f*) The question of the dependence of savings on the sizes of the shares of the population living in the city and in the countryside is very interesting. In principle it is clear that the urban population is considerably more inclined to use savings banks; therefore, in itself the process of the rapid increase of the urban population and the gradual decrease of the rural population (these data are given in table VII-5) should lead and is leading to an increase of deposits. At the same time the slow turnover of money and the appearance thus (given, of course, an increase of monetary income) of the possibility for savings conform considerably more to the conditions of rural life.

Under Soviet conditions, where 44 percent of money wages are spent on food,[31] and where private plots supply a very large portion of the food ration of the rural population, the pattern of expenditures of the rural population is very different from that of the urban population,[32] and the problem of how to spend money arises to a considerably greater extent there than in the city. This question is quite complicated and many-sided and we will soon return to it. But one point can be made here—the rural population is inclined to keep its accumulation in cash and not in savings banks.

Thus, the different factors we have examined, which influence the monetary savings of the population, are very conflicting. Here it is necessary to stress one very important thing. Even those factors which are conducive to an increase in savings do not act in such a way that they should lead to the very sharp increase in deposits observed; their effect could have had and, in fact, did have only a relatively modest influence. At any rate all these factors cannot explain how in the past 18 years—from 1960 through 1978—the total amount of deposits increased more than 12-fold![33]

Let us now turn to the analysis of the monetary savings of the population as a whole and include other forms of savings in our examination.

It might be thought that the astronomical rate of increase of the amounts of deposits at savings banks contradicts my estimates of the rapid increase of savings in cash. It seems to me that the situation is just the opposite. And it is not only that the rapid increase of deposits demonstrates that the population has a large amount of money and, consequently, all types of savings should increase.

We have, in particular, the following testimony:

> As the analysis of the balances of the monetary income and expenditures of the population and the cash plans of Gosbank shows, the possibilities of attracting assets for deposits in savings banks are still very great. Taking into account that most of the increase in the amount of deposits comes from new depositors, and

the coverage of the population by savings banks in a number of republics, krays, oblasts, cities and rayons is still far from great, savings banks have extensive prospects.[34]

What is more, an analysis of the deposits at savings banks leads us to interesting results. Table VII-4 gives the data on the amount of deposits and the size of the population by republics and the average deposit per inhabitant by republic.[35] The most interesting thing for us is the fact that in the Central Asian republics and Azerbaydzhan the average deposit is much smaller. Why? On one hand, according to some calculations based on Soviet statistics, both average wages and, particularly, monetary income per capita in these republics, are lower than in other republics.[36] But on the other hand these indicators

Table VII-4. Deposits at Savings Banks by Republics at the End of 1978

	Amounts of deposits (billions of rubles)	Size of population (millions)	Average size of deposit per person (rubles)
	1	2	3
Total for USSR including:	131.1	262.4	500
RSFSR	76.1	137.5	553
Ukraine	27.7	49.8	556
Belorussia	5.2	9.6	542
Georgia	2.8	5.0	580
Lithuania	2.8	3.4	824
Moldavia	1.2	3.9	308
Latvia	1.5	2.5	600
Armenia	1.7	3.0	567
Estonia	1.0	1.5	667
Total for these nine republics	120.0	216.2	555
Uzbekistan	2.8	15.4	182
Kazakhstan	5.0	14.7	340
Azerbaydzhan	1.3	6.0	217
Kirgizia	0.8	3.5	229
Tadzhikistan	0.6	3.8	158
Turkmenia	0.6	2.8	214
Total for these six republics	11.1	46.2	240

Sources: Column 1: *Narkhoz 78*, p. 415.
Column 2: *Narkhoz 78*, p. 10.
Column 3: column 1 divided by column 2.

contradict a mutual opinion in the USSR (such are my own impressions as well) that the real standard of living in these republics is not worse than elsewhere in the country. The explanation is three-fold. First, all calculations on the basis of official data underestimate the real amount of production on private plots, which is a very important source of incomes in these republics. Secondly, the calculations cannot take into account the redistribution of monetary incomes among various groups of the population. But it is very well known that kolkhozniks of these republics sell a lot of agricultural products outside these areas. And, thirdly, muslims do not consume alcohol, which dramatically changes the entire picture. Because of the first two reasons we can safely conclude that in spite of the statistics, real income in these republics per capita should be roughly equal to average income in the country as a whole. So if we assume that for these six republics the average size of the deposit were equal to the average deposit for the RSFSR (553 rubles), it turns out that the total amount of the deposits here should be $46.2 \times 533 = 25.6$ billion rubles, which is almost 15 billion rubles more than the actual number. It seems to me that this attests to the fact that the *minimum* amount of monetary savings in these republics (in reality it should be much more, particularly because of the third reason) is not less than 15 billion rubles.

We turn now to table VII-5. It is also interesting in many respects. Note that the average amount of a deposit in the countryside (line 5) has surpassed the average size of a deposit in the city beginning in 1970. This means that if in the countryside money is now being deposited in savings banks, it is in earnest. But the number of deposits in the countryside is much smaller (in 1978, with an adjustment for the size of the population—nearly one-half as many) in spite of the fact that there are many more savings banks in the countryside. Let us also take into account that there are considerably fewer deposits per rural inhabitant than per urban resident (line 3), although this difference decreased sharply during the period in question.

It seems that these data attest not to the fact that in the countryside there is little money (where, then, would such a large average size of deposit come from?), but to the fact that rural inhabitants deposit far from all their cash in savings banks.

I will specifically state that I do not at all think that the monetary income of the rural population is now much greater than that of the urban population. At the same time the monetary expenditures of the rural population are substantially less. As a result, and this is far from my opinion alone, there are now large amounts of cash in the countryside.[37]

In addition to the arguments cited above here is another point.

Table VII-5. Deposits of the Urban and Rural Population in Savings Banks

	1940	1950	1960	1965	1970	1975	1978
1. Population (millions)							
urban	63.1	73.0	107.9	123.7	138.8	155.1	160.6
rural	131.0	108.6	108.4	108.5	105.1	100.5	99.5
2. Amount of deposits in savings banks (millions of rubles)							
in cities	576	1,647	8,728	14,028	34,053	66,077	96,000
in the countryside	149	206	2,181	4,699	12,547	24,908	35,100
3. Deposits per capita (rubles)							
in cities	9	22	81	113	245	426	598
in the countryside	1	2	20	43	119	248	352
4. Number of deposits (millions)							
in cities	11.6	10.4	38.3	42.2	58.9	78.9	95.1
in the countryside	5.7	3.9	13.9	15.2	21.2	27.7	32.3
5. Average deposit (rubles)							
in cities	50	151	228	332	578	837	1,009
in the countryside	26	52	157	309	591	900	1,087
6. Number of savings banks (thousands)							
in cities	10.3	11.2	19.5	22.3	23.5	24.1	24.9
in the countryside	31.3	29.1	47.0	51.3	54.8	55.8	55.7

Sources: Line 1 (all data are for the end of the corresponding year, excluding 1940 —the beginning—and 1978—on July 1): *Narkhoz 78*, p. 7
Line 2, 4, 5, 6
1978—*Narkhoz 78*, p. 415
1940, 1965, 1970, 1975—*Narkhoz 76*, p. 515
1950, 1960—*Narkhoz 70*, p. 562
Line 3
line 2 divided by line 1.

Specialists know that the data regularly published in the *Narkhoz* yearbooks on the patterns of the expenditures of the family of an industrial worker and the family of a kolkhoz farmer arouse serious suspicions—at the very least because much is unclear about the compilation of these tables, and it is difficult to use them confidently. Nevertheless, these tables assert that "savings (the increase of cash, deposits at savings banks and others)" constitute a considerably greater proportion in the aggregate income of the family of a kolkhoz farmer than in the aggregate income of the family of a worker. The corresponding data are as follows:[38]

	1965	1970	1975	1978
Proportion of savings in aggregate income:				
family of an industrial worker	3.4	4.6	6.8	7.2
family of a kolkhoz worker	12.1	10.6	10.1	13.1

These data, if we examine them jointly with the previously cited data showing that the per capita deposit in the countryside is substantially less than in the city (table VII-5) decisively confirm that there is an especially large amount of savings in cash precisely in the countryside. True, one might disagree with me, pointing out that an important link in this reasoning has been omitted—the relative levels of per capita income in the city and in the countryside. Unfortunately, I do not have such data, but from many indications and personal impressions I conclude that the gap which existed at one time between the income of the worker and the kolkhoz farmer has slowly been closing since about the second half of the 1960s when a guaranteed monetary income of kolkhoz farmers was introduced. The fact that the families of kolkhoz farmers are larger, that is, the income is distributed among a larger number of members of the family, should also be of substantial importance. In spite of all this, the differences in the proportion of savings in aggregate income are so substantial that it is possible to assert that a considerable portion of the savings in the country occurs in the form of cash held by the population.

Unfortunately, our calculations in appendix B do not demonstrate this. For example, in 1978 the monetary income of kolkhoz farmers from kolkhozes as well as from payments for procurements of produce was only 23.9 billion rubles (table B-2), that is, only 8 percent of the total amount of monetary income of the population according to our estimate (table B-3). The following considerations are important in discussing this.

Firstly, the possibility cannot be ruled out that our disagreements with the official data on the total monetary income of the population (see chapter VI) at least in part are explained precisely by the fact that we have in some way not taken into sufficient account the income of the rural population.

Secondly, the income of the workers of *sovkhozes* and other state agricultural organizations and enterprises are not taken into account in these calculations. In 1978 the payments of wages to the workers of state agricultural organizations and enterprises were 19 billion rubles.[39] Not included in this amount are the payments to workers and employees of various organizations and enterprises of a nonagricultural nature that are located in the countryside.

Thirdly, our calculations of the income and expenditures include only the settlements of the population with the state. Precisely the rural population receives by way of redistribution large amounts from the urban population for the sale of produce, and, as I have already noted above in chapter VI, these amounts apparently now constitute something on the order of 10 billion rubles, that is, about two times more than according to the official statistics on the sales volumes at *kolkhoz* markets.

Fourthly, let us take into account the fundamentally different pattern of expenditures of the rural population, which spends considerably less of its money income on food than the urban population (although the share of *total* income, as I said in note 32, is higher).

For all these reasons I believe that several billion rubles are annually accumulated in savings precisely in the countryside.

Thus, the data on savings at savings banks do not contradict our estimate of the very large monetary savings of the population in cash. It is quite possible for us to believe that the population has these amounts (shown in table VI-2) in addition to the amounts of deposits in savings banks and the amounts in bonds, as well as the amounts of short-term commodity credit and long-term credits,[40] and in addition to insurance amounts. In order to simplify our calculations, I will not take into account all these latter amounts (all the more as I do not know the insurance amounts), and this slightly offsets our possible error in the estimate of savings in cash (in reality I believe that we are *understating* it).

What is the significance of these savings? First of all it is necessary to point out one thing that is of decisive importance for the proper understanding of the entire problem—the Soviet population does not have opportunities for investment; money is not saved (and not invested) in order to earn new money using it. The interest paid by savings banks is too low to serve as a real stimulus, and the fact that only 30 percent of all savings are in term accounts clearly shows that money is not deposited in a savings bank in order to obtain the interest. In point of fact the only purpose of savings is their subsequent spending on consumer goods, that is, so to speak, deferred demand.[41]

Another important factor is that in the USSR saving for unforeseen circumstances—possible unemployment, illness, the education of children and so on—is not widespread. I did indeed say above that the savings for retirement age are of substantial importance, but I pointed out there that they should not be overestimated.[42]

As I understand it, the main reason for the fantastically rapid growth of savings is the sharp and increasing imbalance between the monetary income of the population and its possibilities for spending this money. Simply speaking, the monetary savings of the population in all forms are increasing due to the fact that there are not enough goods and services; a goods famine exists in the country.[43] Therefore, in order to correctly evaluate the importance of savings it is necessary first of all to compare the savings with their backing by goods. Precisely this has been done in table VII-6 (for the sake of simplicity I don't take into account here state bonds). Here, I use the amounts of monetary expenditures, and not the income, of the population because the former are more reliable, and for simplicity I do not reduce this amount either by taxes or by deposits in savings banks.

The results obtained are startling to me. Indeed, the Soviet population can now go for seven months without working;[44] they will have enough savings for all expenditures. For all the unreality of this assumption it nevertheless very clearly characterizes the state of affairs.

Further it turns out that the savings of the population would be enough for nearly 83 percent of the total amount of their annual purchases in state and cooperative trade. Finally, the savings now are 3 times greater than all the commodity stocks both in retail and wholesale trade and in industry.[45]

Table VII-6. Comparison of the Monetary Savings of the Population With Other Indicators (in billions of rubles)

	1960	1965	1970	1975	1978
1. Total amount of monetary expenditures of the population	90.4	123.4	189.3	262.9	306.4
2. Expenditures of the population on purchases in state and cooperative trade	72.9	98.2	146.8	200.4	230.0
3. Commodity stocks in retail and wholesale trade and in industry	24.5	35.7	45.7	58.1	60.3
4. Savings of the population, total	16.5	35.4	80.2	143.7	190.8
a) at savings banks and Gosbank	11.0	18.9	46.7	91.2	131.3
b) in cash form	5.5	16.5	33.5	52.5	59.5
5. Savings as a percentage of:					
a) total amount of expenditures	18	29	42	55	62
b) expenditures on purchases	23	36	55	72	83
c) commodity stocks	67	99	175	247	316

Sources: Line 1: column 12 of table B-4
Line 2: column 5 of table B-4
Line 3: *Narkhoz 78*, p. 442
Line 4: total of lines 4a and 4b
Line 4a: column 3 of table VII-1
Line 4b: table VI-2.

The relation of savings to the indicators in question has increased by a factor of three to five in 15 years—a change that follows directly from the rapid increase of savings.

The consequences are obvious. Firstly, in spite of the obvious increase in the production of consumer goods, in spite of the rapid development of the service sphere, the goods famine in the country is intensifying; the lines are getting longer. Of course, this causes great dissatisfaction among the population, although the possibilities for openly displaying these attitudes are minimal.[46]

Secondly, and no less important, the interest in wages is gradually decreasing, especially if it is necessary to work more (harder) in order to receive a larger wage. Whereas earlier the authorities solved problems by creating material stimuli and attracting people to especially important sectors or regions by large wages,[47] now the decline of interest in larger wages is becoming more and more noticeable. In particular:

—the number of those moving to Siberia and the Far East has for a long time been less than the number of those moving away. Meanwhile, the rapid development of Siberia is now one of the most important economic and strategic problems;
—in the rich agricultural regions—the Kuban', the Southern Ukraine, the Central Asia and so on—the kolkhoz farmers do not want to work more, even if they are paid substantially more for the additional work;[48]
—in all the sociological studies among workers, it turned out that wages are not first on the list of what determines the place of work. We should not overestimate the significance of these studies,[49] but all the same it is clear that one of the reasons for the declining growth of labor productivity is, once again, the qualitatively different attitude toward high wages.

Thirdly, money circulation itself is in a state of disorder. In order to evaluate this properly, suffice it to make the following comparison. As is asserted in a reliable source:[50] "The amount of money in circulation increased four-fold during the entire period of the war," and this lead to the necessity of carrying out a radical monetary reform soon after the end of the war. Meanwhile, as our estimates show, in 19 years (1960–78) the savings of the population in cash form alone increased 9-fold (table VI-2) and the deposits of the population in savings banks increased even more. True, 19 years are not 4 years and during the latter period the amount of goods increased substantially, but the amount of money which the population has all the same cannot in any way be regarded as normal.[51]

What are the possible alternatives for the Soviet rulers? The first is to do nothing, to continue the same policy. It is very likely that today's leadership—"the Brezhnev team"—will not undertake anything. The consequences are obvious—the situation will deteriorate, money will further depreciate, the lines at stores will grow, the population will be more and more dissatisfied. It is significant here that those strata and groups of the population which have a relatively low monetary income and, among them, millions of teachers, physicians, rank and file engineers, secretaries, laboratory workers and so on, will especially suffer from the continuation of this policy. Since the depreciation of money leads to the direct reduction of income, the authorities will practically be forced to continue and even extend the practice of "fattening" those who are at the highest and intermediate levels of the leadership by granting them various privileges, which will increase the irritation of the population.

In spite of all this, it is unlikely that any sharp outbreak of dissatisfaction can occur in the near future; the Soviet regime is in quite firm control of the political situation in the country.

The situation for the "heirs of Brezhnev" will be considerably more difficult. Indeed, they will be faced with the following choice. The continuation of today's policy threatens to completely destroy the economy. The continuing depreciation of money and the decline of interest in wages will be considerably more serious factors underlying falling rates of growth than the shortage of oil or even labor resources. The situation could be radically altered by a sharp increase of labor productivity, but this cannot be counted on in the Soviet economic system.

The further increase of prices for consumer goods is an absolutely necessary alternative.[52] In principle this path has already been followed for quite a long time; only recently the prices for vodka,[53] gold, fur, coffee and transportation were increased; inexpensive goods are disappearing from the market. However, such a measure would be extremely unpopular. An outburst of dissatisfaction would be inevitable, and it is extremely doubtful that it would be possible to maintain political control under these conditions. For the present the authorities have not decided on this.[54]

However, even a relatively sharp increase of prices in itself is inadequate. It is necessary in some way to eliminate or at least freeze the savings of the population. It seems to me that among specialists there is a certain misunderstanding of the importance of these savings, a misunderstanding based on Western experience. Thus, in one discussion I was told that the situation with savings could become a crisis only if the population en masse were to rush to withdraw money from the bank, just as Americans rushed to the banks in 1929. It is not that this is untrue; indeed, if the population were to rush to the savings banks, this would not be good, but this obviously underestimates the fact that the gigantic savings *already* have an extremely negative influence on the economic situation, since these savings for the most part are *forced.*

In order to demonstate this, let us make a simple assumption. Assume that the authorities were able to equalize the balance of monetary income and expenditures of the population—that the increase of savings was halted. Would the lines at stores in this case shorten? If so, not by much, for the purchasing power of the population now is determined not only by current income, but also by savings. Psychologically it is quite understandable why many in the West do not understand this quite clearly—it is necessary to become divorced from the usual idea in the West that it is necessary only to have money in order to buy everything needed. In the USSR money is a necessary condition, but not a sufficient one. It can be stated with certainty that the authorities will absolutely be forced in some form or another to take away the savings of the population, and this cannot but have serious political consequences.

This chapter's title speaks not only about savings of the population, but about "inflation in cash circulation." What does this mean?

In the following chapters we will discuss the differences between the cash and noncash spheres of circulation in the Soviet economy in detail, but here I would like to say that inflation in each of these spheres has a very different nature and should be considered separately. Furthermore, if inflation in the circulation of cash is a fact of Soviet life, there can be some doubts (though I don't have any—see chapter 10) about inflation in noncash circulation.

Official Soviet data do not show growth in either wholesale prices in industry[55] or in retail prices—the index of the latter has been 1.0 for more than two decades.[56] This entire book is based on Soviet statistics, and it is my deep conviction that generally speaking these statistics are rather reliable. But we may by no means trust these price statistics; they are a shameless lie. For me—a former Soviet economist and (perhaps even more important) a former Soviet citizen—it is absolutely evident. Nevertheless for my Western readers I shall say that during the last 25 years prices of many important consumer goods (alcohol, meat and meat products, furniture, cars, books, furs, gold, air fares, etc.) were raised many times and very substantially. The prices of some goods were reduced, but not so substantially. It may seem that in constructing a price index Soviet statisticians use as an excuse the fact that the quality of such goods as radio and TV sets, watches, clothing, shoes, refrigerators, washing machines and the like is increasing faster than their prices. The question was never discussed in the USSR openly, so we apparently should think that just this line of reasoning serves to justify their tricks with price indexes; no other explanation seems feasible. But this explanation cannot be taken seriously either. Having bought many such goods, I could never agree that, say, a radio set for 150 rubles was twice as good as a radio set which I had bought 10 or 15 years earlier for 75 rubles. What I am saying is that the prices of these goods were clearly growing faster than their quality.

Having no direct true statistical information about inflation, let us nevertheless consider some indirect evidence. According to official data on "the growth of real incomes of the population" per capita incomes in 1978 were 221 percent greater than in 1960.[57] Quite a remarkable achievement especially if we forget that this growth took place from an extremely low level and that even now, after this achievement, the standard of living of the Soviet people is scandalously low for such a superpower.[58] And it is especially remarkable if we trust these data. Personally, I have no doubts that the standard of living in 1978 was higher than in 1960, and I have no doubts that the growth was not so fast. But this doesn't matter here. My point is that in 1978 all monetary expenditures of the population were 343 percent greater than in 1960 (see column 12 of table B-4). The population growth was 120 percent,[59] so monetary expenditures (including the increment of savings in savings banks) per capita grew by 343 : 120 = 286, which is substantially higher than the official growth of the standard of living.

Of course, the Soviets include in their calculations of "growth of real incomes of the population" so-called free services[60] provided by the state. The growth of these services from 1960 to 1978 was 314 percent, which is very close to the growth of monetary expenditures of the population.

In other words, even if we trust Soviet official calculations of the standard of living—221 percent—it is much lower than growth of monetary expenditures per capita and growth of free services. This can be explained only by the fact that Soviet statisticians take into account rather substantial increases in prices for consumer goods.[61]

I cannot even roughly estimate the rate of inflation, but some comments are in order.

The main thing is that Soviet inflation is of the repressed type. It follows from all our discussion in this chapter that if there were a free market in the USSR prices would immediately jump up and, consequently, savings of the population in all forms would be much less.

The state completely controls the economy, including prices and wages. In attempting to solve some social problems for political reasons and in trying to stimulate higher labor productivity, the state systematically raises wages (as we see in table B-1, the average monthly wage in 1978 was 159.9 rubles as compared with 64.2 rubles in 1950 and 80.6 in 1960). But the state cannot provide the appropriate amounts of goods and services, so it is practically forced to raise prices. On the other hand, a too rapid growth of prices, especially for goods of primary necessity, is politically dangerous[62] and the Soviet rulers are maneuvering by raising the prices of luxuries (such as cars, furs, gold, caviar, carpets, etc.) and of alcohol, by stopping the production of many cheap goods, and by raising the prices of many goods at a faster rate than their quality is improving.

Actually all this is a little aside from my main theme, so I will limit myself to the following. There is inflation in the USSR and the growth of the savings of the population demonstrates it. The basic reason for inflation is low productivity in the Soviet economy; it cannot provide enough goods and services. At the same time inflation is of the repressed type, and just because of this there is too much cash in circulation with all the consequences of this.

As I already said above, the state will continue to raise prices, inflation will be worse, and where this leads we will see in a few years.

To sum up it must be said that the entire situation with cash circulation in the country is of an extremely critical nature, which affects the very foundations of the regime, and there are no easy ways to overcome this crisis.

Quite unexpectedly for me, precisely this point was probably the most debatable in this entire study. G. Schroeder expressed some doubts concerning this, and the participants in a seminar of the Russian Center of Harvard University cited very serious doubts (if not objections).

A quite reasonable question that arises here (M. Goldman formulated it), is: if money is indeed becoming cheaper, why do the Soviet people work at all and, in particular, why is a so-called second economy developing? A. Bergson stated this question in a more theoretical form—if this is indeed so, the marginal value of labor should tend to zero.

I repeat, these questions are reasonable, but in our analysis it is necessary to take into account at least the following:

(a) The existence of enormous amounts of money in the hands of the population as a whole does not at all mean that everyone has money. Soviet society has by no means achieved the socialist ideals of material

equality—the inequality of incomes is extremely substantial, and there are enormous strata of the population for which wages are meager; for them the marginal valuation of labor is quite positive;
(b) It is possible that the following example goes to extremes, but nevertheless I will allow myself to ask: what is the marginal valuation of money for American billionaires? The existence of even enormous wealth by no means subverts the attempt to increase this wealth;
(c) I spoke above about the difficulties of making purchases in the USSR, about the goods famine, but this should not be understood too broadly. The majority of everything that the population buys is purchased in state and cooperative trade, and money for this, i.e., wages, are needed. I do not at all wish to understate the importance of the fact that the population as a whole has in savings about 70 percent of its annual income (wages), but at the same time let us take into account that the very *increase* of savings in a year is less than 10 percent of the wages;
(d) It would be untrue to say that people do not want to work for wages at all. In fact the formula is as follows: people do not want to work harder, more, or longer for more wages.[63] There are many contradictory examples, but the overall trend is just this. Recall that I spoke above about the sharp decline of the stimulus provided by good wages for increasing labor productivity; this is exactly what we are talking about here.

It is possible to point out some additional things, but, limiting myself to these, I will allow myself to draw the following conclusion. It would be incorrect to say that cash circulation in the country has been completely upset, that money has lost all value, that people are ceasing in general to work since they do not need additional wages, and I am not asserting this. I am only saying that the country is moving rapidly in this direction, that the process has become threatening and that no easy ways of resolving the crisis are evident.

Why do most American sovietologists disagree with me on the issue? Because they unreservedly believe in modern Western economic theories which, they think, are universal. Not true, since their premises are not universal, since the subject—a Western economy and/or an economy of the Third World—are very different from a Soviet-type economy. That is why scholars who follow the theory make mistakes in judgements on financial matters, standard of living, GNP accounts, etc. That is why a special theory of the Soviet-type economy is badly needed.

Notes

1. Due to the lack of some data and time, my analysis is far from exhaustive. The problem is so important for the understanding of various economic and political processes in the USSR that it would be very important to study it further. Some aspects of the problem are analyzed in my articles "Dokatilis'," *Novoye Russkoye Slovo*, New York, 6 and 7 December 1979 and "Ugroza", Vremya i my, No. 53, 1980.

2. The values given here include not only the deposits of the population in savings banks, but also the comparatively small amounts in the accounts of the population in Gosbank. What are these Gosbank deposits? In Plotnikov, *Byudzhet*, 1948, pp. 259–296, we read that in 1941 winners of the Stalin prize, artists and composers, were permitted to transfer their savings from savings banks to Gosbank, where they could use them with fewer restrictions than were then in force at savings banks. On page 297 of the same book we read: "In addition to savings banks, there were so-called field offices of Gosbank which accepted deposits from servicemen."

In Gusakov and Dymshits, *Denezhnoye*, 1951, p. 161, we read: "In order to attract the free assets of the population (primarily rural) at the end of 1942 institutions of Gosbank began to accept the deposits of private individuals in the amount of 300 rubles or more."

In Pchelin, *Gosudarstvennyy*, 1976, p. 32, we read that in 1970 there were 51,900 "accounts for deposits of citizens" in Gosbank, while in 1975 there were only 38,500 of them. It is easy to calculate that in 1975 the average amount per deposit at Gosbank was 4,400 as against 954 rubles in savings banks (see the latter in *Narkhoz 76*, p. 515). Overall, it seems that these deposits in Gosbank are the monetary assets of some exceptionally well-off (by Soviet standards) individuals—famous writers, artists, stars, composers, arms designers. It is also possible that part of these assets belong to those working abroad—diplomats, generals and officers of occupation forces.

3. According to V. Treml, the drop in the amounts by which savings increased in 1954–55 was a result of the reduction of the rate of interest paid on deposits at that time (prior to 1954, 3 percent was paid on ordinary deposits and 5 percent on term deposits). He is also of the opinion that the reduced growth of deposits in 1958 was due to a sharp increase in the construction of housing in rural areas (it nearly doubled in comparison with 1957).

4. According to the data in M. Atlas, *Natsional'nyy*, 1977, p. 324, an enormous increase in the amounts of deposits in savings banks is typical for all the CEMA countries in 1960–75.

5. I have discussed this question with V. Treml, and he believes that people must have remembered that it was precisely those who did not keep their money in savings banks who were "burned" in the exchange of money in 1947. He also points out that the drop in the growth of savings occurred primarily in the deposits of the rural population (see *Narkhoz 62*, p. 492) and that there was a sharp jump in the volume of trade turnover in 1960, i.e., people tried to spend more money (*Narkhoz 62*, p. 511). His arguments are quite reasonable, but, as I noted above, in this as in other similar cases such phenomena are explained by a complex of different reasons. In other words, in addition to the factors Treml rightly mentions, there was a purely psychological factor at work—in uncertain circumstances many people (but far from all) prefer to have the possibility of maneuvering quickly. As is evident from table VII-2, the same factors also influenced the operations with the 3-percent loan.

6. The published data on the total amounts of deposits in my opinion also include the deposits of party and some other organizations which, strictly speaking, are not savings of the population. But the corresponding amounts are small. On the contrary, the deposits of mutual assistance funds at savings banks (their amounts are also small) are one of the forms of monetary savings of the population.

7. Perhaps this was in some way connected with the paying off of the state debt on old loans, which was announced in March 1971 (by the 24th CPSU Congress) and begun at the end of 1974—see below.

8. The expenditures include primarily (in addition to the winnings, which should be 3 percent in all) the costs of buying and selling of bonds. Since the prices for the bonds are slightly different at their purchase and sale, the bulk of these expenditures should be covered by this difference in prices.

9. It is completely incomprehensible why the data on the revenues from loans with a breakdown by their types are regularly published in the *Byudzhet* handbooks, while the data on the expenditures on them are not published.

10. Quite large amounts in these bonds could have been accumulated during the war, but with the monetary reform of 1947 their exchange was carried out at a ratio of 5:1 (Z. Atlas, *Denezhnoye*, 1957, p. 126).

11. Ryndin, "Bol'shiye," 1977, p. 21.

12. Zlobin, *Finansy*, 1967, p. 252.

13. In 1974–75, 1 billion rubles each year; in 1976–80, 1.2 billion rubles each year; in 1981–85, 1.5 billion rubles each year; in 1986–89, 2 billion rubles each year; in 1990, 2.3 billion rubles (CIA, *The Soviet*, 1977, p. 18).

14. At the same time this is true, so to speak, only according to the trend, and there are at least some contradictory factors. I may cite my own experience. In the USSR small loans to each other "before payday" are very widespread. During the last 12 years before emigrating I worked as a division chief in research institutes and my income was exceptionally high in comparison with the income of the rank and file staff members of the institutes. Quite often I borrowed some small amount from my friends before payday, and it was practically always easy to borrow from those who received considerably less. Why? There are several reasons here and all of them are significant for our theme. Above all I will note the very fact that with my own high income I borrowed. The explanation is that in having a high income and being certain that I would receive such an income in the future, I was quite free with my money and was not afraid to spend a lot. I did not consider it obligatory to have savings and I often had "unplanned expenses." I cannot say that *everyone* receiving a high income acts precisely this way, but this was not an exception. On the other hand, at times it was difficult to borrow from those who also had a high income, because, first, many of them lived the same way I did, that is, they had no savings, and secondly, those with a high income, who regularly saved and lived economically, were not always inclined to lend money. Finally, it is important that many (of course, not all) people with a low income acted in just the opposite manner; precisely the low level of their income forced them not to spend everything down to the last kopeck; they had spare money.

These circumstances to a considerable extent explain the fact that there are 127 million deposits in savings banks and the fact that very significant amounts in cash savings are distributed among a large portion of the population.

15. Ivensen, "Voprosy," 1973, p. 56.

16. It is worth noting that trade organizations are granted credit in these amounts by Gosbank (Poskonov, *Kreditno*, 1967, pp. 84 and 134). In other words, a corresponding adjustment should be made in the published indicators of the breakdown of credits into credit to enterprises and organizations and credit to the population (for example, *Narkhoz 76*, pp. 656–57).

17. The series presented in table VII-3 is quite interesting in itself. In particular, an explanation is needed for why the total amount of credit remained stable during 1965 to 1971.

18. Credit replaces the cash in circulation and, thus, increases inflation even more.

For simplicity henceforth I do not take the amounts of credit into account, since they are small in comparison with trade turnover and money circulation.

19. Soviet consumers see many slow-selling goods, and they get the impression that there are actually very many goods that simply cannot be sold. But in fact this is not so. True, the amount of goods that the population does not want to buy because of low quality or our-of-date fashion is increasing but while total retail trade turnover grew by 228 percent during 1965–78, inventories grew by only 167 percent (*Narkhoz 78*, pp. 429, 442). Note also that price reductions for such goods are relatively rare and in relatively small amounts.

20. In 1978, 59 million people vacationed at vacation homes and sanatoriums (without dispensaries). Of the 19 million people who visited tourist centers (all figures are from *Narkhoz 78*, p. 423) only a small portion can be assigned to this category. Vacations, particularly to vacation homes and on tourist trips, are relatively inexpensive; a big part is paid for by trade unions and at the expense of the funds of enterprises.

21. *Narkhoz 78*, p. 415.

22. See also note 25 below.

23. *Narkhoz 74*, p. 33.

24. The previously cited article by Ivensen, "Voprosy," 1973, is devoted precisely to this question.

25. Here it must be kept in mind that in the case of so-called term savings accounts, a separate account is opened for each individually deposited amount. Therefore, the real number of depositors should be less than the number of deposits. "For every 1,000 inhabitants receiving an income there are 612 deposit accounts" (Gnutov, "Sberkassa," 1974, p. 20): deposits, not depositors.

26. Of course, this is true only in a statistical sense; there are many individual contradictory examples. I will again refer to my personal experience. My wife and I had a very high (for the USSR) level of income, more than 900 rubles a month. We had a very good apartment by Soviet standards, a car and so on. However, I repeat, this high level of income was sufficient only for everyday needs; by the time of our emigration we had practically no savings. In other words, the increase in the level of monetary income in itself, while in principle creating the possibility of savings, is by no means necessarily in all cases realized in monetary savings. For many in the USSR (I do not believe that we were an exception in this respect) an increase in income leads to an increase in expenditures, and not to savings. It is usually a question of the possibilities of spending the money and the relative priorities of different groups of the population.

27. Belyavskiy, "Sotsial'no," 1978, p. 64.

28. *Narkhoz 76*, pp. 543–44.

29. This is an estimate based on data from *Narkhoz 76*, p. 510.

30. ". . . in recent years the growth of monetary income has not been accompanied by an improvement of the conditions for utilizing it, since the effective demand of the population has not been fully met. Therefore, today life makes it necessary to advance the task of gradually meeting the effective demand of the population to the foreground . . . ." (Mayer, "Aktual'nyye," 1977, pp. 54–55.)

31. This follows from an elementary calculation. In 1978, 125.9 billion rubles were spent for foodstuffs in state and cooperative trade (*Narkhoz 78*, p. 438), 5.9 were sales on kolkhoz markets (table B-2) and 2.2 at the intravillage (*vnutriderevenskyy*) market, while the total amount of expenditures of the population was 306.4 billion rubles (table B-4). Of course, this involves some approximations (a portion of the purchases in state and cooperative trade is not made by the population; it is necessary to take into account the expenditures of the population at kolkhoz markets and so on), but on the whole a true picture is obtained.

32. According to obviously unreliable data on the budgets of the families of workers and kolkhoz farmers (for example, *Narkhoz 78,* pp. 391–92) it turns out that kolkhoz farmers spend somewhat more on food as a percentage of their income.

33. Taking into account population growth, savings increased 10 times. However, the calculation of total deposits in per capita terms must include the caveat that changes in the age structure of the population should also be considered.

34. Gnutov, "Sberkassa," 1974, p. 19. Let us also note here that this statement is based on the analysis of precise, though unknown to us, data—the balance of the monetary income and expenditures of the population and the case plan of Gosplan—and the fact that it is stated here that "the possibilities . . . are *very great*".

35. A number of things are mysterious here, among them—why is the average size of the deposit rather low in Georgia hardly higher than in Armenia. On the other hand, the highest deposit per capita within the second group—in Kazakhstan—corresponds with the fact that the share of the nonmuslim population is also the highest in this Central Asia republic.

I would also like to note, using this example, that considerably more attention should be given to studies by republics—they are important not only in themselves, but also can substantially help to understand many things pertaining to the country as a whole.

36. Schrouder, "Regional," 1973, pp. 174, 188.

37. Such was the opinion of many with whom we discussed this question in Moscow six years ago; such an opinion is, in fact, widespread. In 1973 my friend, a correspondent of *Izvestiya,* told me about the following case. Shortly before this he was told at the Volga Motor Vehicle Plant that for some time they (with special permission) had sold *Zhigulis* to the inhabitants of the rural regions of Saratov Oblast. The buyers paid 5,500 rubles for the cars mainly in one-, three- and five-ruble notes. It is understandable that they could only have saved such denominations, "under mattrasses", and did not receive them in such amounts at a savings bank.

And there is also some more recent evidence. An article by Tarasevich and Leshkevich, "Gde," 1978, recounts the results of a survey conducted "in seven Belorussian villages" among kolkhoz members in several oblasts. It turned out that "One half of the peasants included in the survey had personal savings that were entirely sufficient for constructing a first-class individual house. More than 20 percent of those questioned stated that they could construct a house with the help of their relatives. And only one-fourth of the villagers intended to get credit from the state."

I would not begin to underestimate this evidence. In fact a "first-class individual house" should now cost something like ten thousand rubles, and half (!) of those questioned said that they had this kind of money while almost another fourth knew that they could get the money from relatives. And the other 20 percent who "intended to get credit from the state" very likely considered their money income sufficient to later repay this credit. There is money in the countryside.

38. *Narkhoz 78,* pp. 391–92. The data on the period before 1965 and those for 1966–69 are not published in the yearbooks (with the exception of 1940).

39. Calculated according to *Narkhoz 78,* pp. 366, 372.

40. We did not examine above the amounts of long-term credit to the population since they are relatively small and, incidentally, are decreasing, which once again attests to the abundance of money in the hands of the population.

41. "The savings of workers in both cash and noncash forms (in savings banks) are caused to a considerable extent by the lack of goods of the appropriate quality and variety or are the funds saved for the purchase of durable goods in a period to come" (Belkin and Ivanter, "Finansovyye," 1977, p. 63).

Here also is the following rather long citation (without the footnotes in it) from a relatively recent article in a very respected journal. The citation is internally inconsistent, but the basic sense of it is obvious without my commentary:

> In recent years the question of the economic nature of the organized money savings of the population and the reasons for their being so highly dynamic have been discussed in the economic literature. Two extreme points of view exist: part of the economists consider the unsatisfied demand for basic consumer goods as the reason for savings, and other say the increase in the people's well-being is the basic reason for savings. In our opinion, the growth of monetary savings is a natural process—a result of the increase in the people's well-being—but, without a doubt, a part of savings is engendered by a lack of the necessary material goods at any given moment. Some economists reject the influence of unsatisfied demand on monetary savings. According to calculations of other economists, the unsatisfied demand accumulated in the monetary savings of the population amounts to about 75 percent of the savings. Such an estimate seems substantially overstated to us.
>
> According to our approximate calculations, the amount of deposits of the population in savings banks—the equivalent of the unsatisfied effective demand—currently amounts to a quite weighty sum and has increased by almost 30 percentage points in comparison with the same figure in 1968 (Aleksandrova and Fedorovskaya, "Rost," 1978, p. 75).

42. It is necessary, in particular, to take into account the fact that only those who earn a lot and who, consequently, count on receiving the maximum pension, have, so to speak, excess money to put away for retirement.

43. The authors quoted above referred to a significant point in this respect: "The coincidence of the total amounts of income and trade turnover still does not guarantee the complete satisfaction of the effective demand, since the unmet demand for some groups of goods cannot be offset to a significant extent by the supply of goods of other groups" (Belkin and Ivanter, "Finansovyye," 1977, p. 62).

44. In fact longer, since we took taxes and deposits in savings banks into account in the expenditures of the population. Moreover, the length of this period continues to grow.

45. This, incidentally, characterizes very vividly the well-known official thesis that Soviet money is backed "by all the property of the USSR," including primarily commodity stocks.

46. This is not directly connected with our theme, but nevertheless it is appropriate to say that the majority of the Soviet population do not worry much about civil rights and political freedoms. But everything that concerns the standard of living is a most serious thing in the relations of the population to the regime.

47. It is worth mentioning that immediately after the United States exploded the first atomic bomb, a commission chaired by Molotov was formed to prepare proposals on increasing the salaries of scientists. It is well known that Stalin at the time personally ordered the wages of scientists to be increased by several (!) times. In a short time the Soviet atomic, and then hydrogen bombs were exploded, and finally sputnik was launched.

48. It is well known that since 1965 a policy of monetary pay for kolkhoz farmers has been pursued, and in many cases their pay is of a regular nature and does not depend on the overall results of the work of the kolkhoz. One of the consequences of this was . . . the reduction of the production of meat and dairy products on private plots. Having obtained a guaranteed monetary wage, kolkhoz farmers began to work less hard on their own plots. It is important here that the prices for meat and dairy products on kolkhoz markets increased, but kolkhoz farmers already have money and do not want to work more in order to earn even more.

49. As affirmed in a recent article—Kapelyush, "Tipichen," 1978—a recent questionnaire in two Voronezh villages found that a very significant part of those asked would have preferred to have more interesting, even if lower paying, work. This sort of preference is even more widespread among those who have a secondary or higher education.

50. Poskonov, *Kreditno*, 1967, p. 57. This does not contradict the quotation cited at the beginning of the chapter that during the first three years of the war the amount of money increased 2.4-fold—inflation also continued at the end of the war.

51. In some recent Western works, the so-called marginal propensity to save of the Soviet population was compared with corresponding figures for Western countries, and on this basis it was concluded that savings in the USSR are "normal." One of the readers of this manuscript (a very famous economist) suggested that I carry out such a comparison for the savings of the population in the USA and other countries. It is hardly necessary to prove here that all this is absolutely untrue. It is sufficient to point out the simple fact that savings as investment in Western countries is totally absent in the USSR, saying nothing about the fundamental fact that in the Western economies supply is always bigger than demand and the Soviet economy is an economy of shortages.

52. It is necessary to increase prices not only in order to bring the monetary income and expenditures of the population into greater conformity. There are many absurd correlations in the prices for different goods that need to be rectified.

53. The sale of alcoholic beverages in 1978 was 161 percent of that in 1970. (*Narkhoz 78*, p. 410) Although it is indicated here that the table was compiled in "comparable prices," it is difficult to believe that this is really so.

54. On the front page of *Izvestiya*, No. 18829 of 23 March 1978, a quite unprecedented statement was published (I do not recall anything like this in all my not so short life). Here it was officially made clear that "an increase of retail prices for food products is not being proposed." Obviously the rumors had become very widespread.

55. *Narkhoz 78*, pp. 138–39.

56. During the last war retail prices increased very substantially, and during 1947–53 they fell. However, by 1955 retail prices were much higher than in 1940. According to official data the index of prices of all consumer goods is the same now as in 1955 (see *Narkhoz 60*, p. 717; *Narkhoz 67*, p. 740; and *Narkhoz 78*, p. 447).

57. See *Narkhoz 65*, p. 593 and *Narkhoz 78*, p. 387.

58. Surprisingly there are very few convincing comparative calculations of the standard of living in the USSR and elsewhere. My very rough estimate is that a Soviet citizen lives 4 times worse than his/her counterpart in the other superpower.

59. *Narkhoz 78*, p. 7.

60. In 1978 the population received free benefits "from all sources" (excluding stipends, pensions and the like which I included in monetary incomes) of 64 billion rubles (*Narkhoz 78*, p. 390) and in 1960, 17 billion rubles (*Narkhoz 70*, p. 537). The growth of population—120 percent (see above). So the growth of these incomes was $64:17:120 \times 100 = 314$ percent.

61. Certainly it would be better to include in our calculations consumption in kind, but on the one hand the data are lacking and, on the other, it will not change our conclusion.

62. Maybe some of my readers don't remember this, but Soviet rulers remember very well what happened in Poland in December of 1970, when prices of meat were raised.

63. This point was brought to my attention by an old friend and recent emigré, L. Aliyevskaya.

Chapter VIII

Noncash Circulation and Bank Credit

Noncash transactions in the USSR are quite similar to those in the West, with two peculiarities.

The first is that practically all transactions of the state with enterprises, institutions and organizations, and of these with each other, are made in noncash form, primarily through Gosbank.[1] In the West any payments can in principle be made in cash as a matter of convenience, but in the USSR this is regulated by law.[2]

The second—all organizations have diverse financial ties not only with each other and with banks, but also with the state. On the one hand, enterprises, as we saw in chapter III, pay to the state the turnover tax, and make various deductions from profits. Budget-financed organizations, as we also saw in chapter III, turn over all their revenues to the state. On the other hand, enterprises receive state funds for construction, and sometimes for capital repair, for the replenishment of working capital, and for covering losses. Budget-financed organizations receive from the state all the funds for their operation. All these settlements with the state are carried out only by means of noncash transactions.

Noncash transactions occupy the main position in the total volume of money payments. In 1966 the share of the noncash transactions in this total was 90 percent as against 83 percent in 1940.[3]

All noncash transactions pass through the banks; there are no direct settlements between enterprises (for example, using bills of exchange) or, all the more, between enterprises and the state. The banks not only technically carry out the transfer of funds, but also have quite serious functions of control, as well as regulation.

There are three main banks: the USSR State[4] Bank *(Gosbank)*, the All-Union Bank for Financing Capital Investments *(Stroybank)* and the USSR Foreign Trade Bank *(Vneshtorgbank)*.[5]

The first one handles all settlements except those for construction (although it does finance construction at kolkhozes) and foreign trade. It is the only emission center of the country. This bank alone carries out operations with cash.

Stroybank carries out the financing and extension of credit to construction, except to kolkhozes, while Vneshtorgbank deals exclusively with foreign trade. It makes settlements on imports and exports with foreign organizations in convertible currency,[6] and, in addition, makes settlements with Soviet organizations in "normal" Soviet money and issues credits to them. Because of the growth of foreign trade the volume of settlements of Vneshtorgbank is becoming more and more significant.

Thus, enormous flows of funds pass not only between enterprises and organizations, but also between them and the state by means of noncash transactions through the banks, and, as we saw, flows involving the state are in many respects counterflows. We will not discuss here the expediency of these counterflows; they have their own logic, although it may be disputed. Regardless of our opinion on this, the situation is in principle as follows. Every enterprise (except budget-financed) must in general cover its own expenses with its own revenues and turn over a portion of its profits for expenditure on state-wide needs. Using these profits the state not only pays for such needs as defense, education, health care, the state apparatus and so forth, but also financing the expansion of production, although in recent years the financing of the expansion of enterprises using their own assets has assumed a larger role.

These functions—the redistribution of funds—are also performed by the budget. It accumulates funds, and primarily just the funds of state enterprises, and not of the population,[7] and channels them into the necessary (considered necessary) directions. Financing from the budget is considered a free grant, but this is not entirely so. There is of course a fee for capital that is paid to the budget.[8] Of even more substantial and fundamental importance, however, is the obligatory payment to the budget of the so-called free remainder of profits.[9] It is possible in principle to say that the withdrawal of the latter is the return of previously-assigned budget allocations. Nevertheless, financing from the budget is considered formally an outright grant, and in addition, repayable financing in its direct form—through bank credits—is being used more and more extensively. We will now examine the question of credits together with the question of noncash money transactions for several reasons.

Firstly, credits are given (issued and repaid, when they are repaid) in noncash form (although often credit is given for payment, for example, of wages, in cash form).

Secondly, the extension of credit is not only connected with the circulation of money;[10] but in the opinion of some Soviet authors it also serves to replace cash (currency notes),[11] which is quite true.

Thirdly, as is actually already clear from the foregoing, credit is closely connected with budget financing; in a number of cases one replaces the other.[12]

I stress the fact that in practice bank credit and budget financing are complementary, and, it seems to me, the difference between them is often only of a formal nature. Here, for example, is what one book says:

> The draft of the consolidated credit plan of Gosbank is brought into line with the planning for the state budget. This includes determining the possibilities of using budget funds for the extension of credit and the amounts of the allocations from the budget for the repayment of credits with temporarily replaced budget assets.[13]

Thus, in principle it is incorrect to study budget allocations without examining credits at the same time. This is true because the budget covers its own deficit with credits, while credits are backed in part by budget allocations and also because the Soviet state is able to maneuver, utilizing both credits and budget allocations simultaneously for different purposes. It should especially be emphasized that, when studying the sources for covering expenditures for military purposes, on no account should the analysis be limited by the obviously narrow framework of the potentials of the budget itself.

We have already spoken about the extension of credit to the population in chapter VI and have seen how modest its amounts are. The extension of credit to enterprises and organizations, however, has assumed an enormous scale.

There are short-term and long-term credits. Some authors also distinguish intermediate-term credits. Without describing credits in detail—all this is in the literature[14]—let us note only that credits are very diverse and are issued for quite different needs.[15]

It is very difficult to draw a distinct line between financing and the extension of credit. The practical difference, however, is also not extremely significant; it consists merely in the fact that interest is collected on credit. However, the amount of interest is not very great,[16] while withdrawing the free remainder of profits makes this even less significant.

To a certain extent the development of credit forms is based on an illusion of the possibility of organizing truly cost account (*khozraschetnyye*) relations in the Soviet economic system. It is not by chance that credit began to increase rapidly after the so-called economic reform of 1965 (there are also other reasons). To answer the natural question—why are different bank methods, including credit, used at all in the Soviet system?—is possible only on the basis of a detailed analysis of the entire Soviet economic system and the theoretical notions of Soviet economists, and this is not part of my task here.[17]

It is practically identical under Soviet conditions whether the state gives money to enterprises by way of direct financing (including permission to use "internal" assets) or by way of bank credit, since this is money from one and the same source, from the same "state pocket."

In the next chapter we will especially examine the question of the resources for the extension of credit, but right here I will note that the availability of credit resources in itself creates the potential possibility for their use, and in this case supply gives rise to demand. It is no less important that the availability and use of the credit mechanism itself suggest the quite natural (although by no means necessarily correct) idea of using this mechanism in cases of the especially acute need for money even beyond the limits of the real (or considered real) credit resources.

Changes in the total amounts of credits to enterprises and organizations are shown in table VIII-1. Both their rapid growth and the existing volumes are impressive.[18] In table VIII-2 the growth of credits is compared with data on the growth of the budget. The amount of credits is increasing much more rapidly, and the overall balance of credits now slightly exceeds the amount of the budget. Among the budget expenditures the share of the expenditures on the national economy is increasing slightly,[19] but the growth of the amount of credit is so precipitous that credits are increasingly supplanting the direct budget financing of the national economy, although the absolute amounts of the latter are themselves also increasing very rapidly.[20]

The total amount of short-term credits at the end of 1978 was 54 percent of the value of all working capital in the economy.[21] Taking into account also the other sources of working capital—credits received (*kreditory*), continuing liabilities (*ustoichivyye passivy*)—we find that internal assets and other equivalent assets (*priravnennye k nim sredstva*) account for only 25 percent of all working capital.[22]

The data presented give a static picture of short-term credits. Since by their very definition they are allocated for a short term, the total amount of credits issued for a year is an astronomical amount. As far back as 1971 the amount of credits issued during the year was 934 billion rubles,[23] while in 1976 the amount issued was 1.334 trillion rubles.[24] Note also that in 1971 the volume of noncash money transactions through Gosbank alone was 1.48 trillion rubles,[25] while in 1976 this volume was to have been 2.13 trillion rubles.[26] It is clear that by volume of transactions Gosbank is the largest bank in the world.[27]

Table VIII-1. Balances of Bank Loans to State Enterprises and Organizations, Cooperatives and Kolkhozes (in billions of rubles)

Year	Short-term credits: at the end of the year	Short-term credits: increase during the year	Long-term credits: at the end of the year	Long-term credits: increase during the year
	1	2	3	4
1940	5.6	—	0.7	—
1950	17.3	—	1.4	—
1952	21.4	—	1.6	—
1955	21.1	—	2.6	—
1958	33.2	—	3.9	—
1959	39.5	6.3	4.0	0.1
1960	42.7	3.2	3.6	−0.4
1961	47.4	4.7	4.0	0.4
1962	50.8	3.4	4.5	0.5
1963	56.0	5.2	5.1	0.6
1964	63.2	7.2	6.5	1.4
1965	66.7	3.5	6.5	0
1966	77.3	10.6	9.5	3.0
1967	87.8	10.5	12.5	3.0
1968	96.8	9.0	15.6	3.1
1969	101.0	4.2	18.6	3.0
1970	104.7	3.7	20.8	2.2
1971	111.6	6.9	24.8	4.0
1972	120.9	9.3	29.1	4.3
1973	134.7	13.8	33.6	4.5
1974	149.3	14.6	38.9	5.3
1975	160.7	11.4	42.8	3.9
1976	177.9	17.2	49.5	6.7
1977	194.2	16.3	59.3	9.8
1978	206.6	12.4	67.8	8.5

Sources: Columns 1 and 3:
1940, 1965, 1970, 1975–78—*Narkhoz 78*, p. 538*
1971–74—*Narkhoz 75*, pp. 746–747
1950, 1960, 1969—*Narkhoz 70*, pp. 735–36**
1967–68—*Narkhoz 68*, p. 779–80**
1958, 1963, 1964—*Narkhoz 64*, pp. 774–75**
1952, 1959, 1961–62—*Narkhoz 62*, pp. 639–40
1955—*Narkhoz 60*, p. 849,** *Narkhoz 61*, p. 766

**Narkhoz 74*, p. 760 gives slightly different indicators for 1965 and 1970.

**When using these handbooks the amounts of credits for new equipment, for production of consumer goods and for other measures are added to the amounts of the long-term credits.

Table VIII-2. Comparison of the Growth of Credits and the Budget

Year	Amount of short- and long-term credits			Budget expenditures		
	Total, billions of rubles	as a percent of		Total, billions of rubles	as a percent of	
		1950	1960		1950	1960
	1	2	3	4	5	6
1950	18.7			41.3		
1960	46.3	248		73.1	177	
1965	73.2	391	158	101.6	246	139
1970	125.5	671	271	154.6	374	211
1975	203.5	1,088	440	214.5	519	293
1978	274.4	1,323	593	260.2	630	356

Sources: Column 1:
the total of columns 1 and 3 of table VIII-1
Column 4:
table I-5, column 2.

The question of the connection of the cash and noncash spheres of circulation in the USSR is of fundamentally great importance. In the West these spheres are closely connected and it is not always possible to draw a clear line between them. The situation is entirely different in the USSR. In the literature there are various opinions on this, which in itself attests that this is not a very simple matter. Here, we will discuss only what directly pertains to our theme.

I have already noted that these two spheres of circulation differ sharply, and most attention is devoted to cash circulation. Thus, the emission of cash is under especially strict control—currency emission is carried out according to a plan specially approved by the government; emission in excess of that officially permitted is considered a criminal offense. The receipt of cash at the bank by enterprises and organizations and the immediate turning over of cash received from the population are especially and very strictly controlled. A persistent effort is made to accelerate the turnover of cash and to replace a part of it by noncash transactions. Nothing similar is observed with respect to the noncash sphere, and the very attempt to replace a part of the cash turnover by noncash transactions clearly attests to a different attitude toward them.

Why? It is believed that the population's demand[28] for goods and services arises precisely through the cash turnover, and this demand is "unplanned"—it is not regulated—while the needs of state organizations and enterprises for the goods and services of other state enterprises and organizations yield to easy regulation and even control under the conditions of a planned economy. A simple example to illustrate. If someone has a specific amount of cash, in principle nothing will prevent him from trying to buy a commodity or service for this amount.[29] (As I have already stated above, and this is worth repeating again, the very availability of cash in the hands of the population is a state debt.) However, when an enterprise or organization has some amount of money, this money is only an entry at the bank, and the practical significance of this is radically different—in order to spend this money the enterprise must have the appropriate allocations, limits and so forth. (It is important that if, as we saw in chapter VII, cash exerts pressure on the market, the noncash assets of enterprises, even if there is too much of them, do not create particular problems; they are withdrawn by the state.)

The following consideration is also significant in this connection. Money in noncash form, using Soviet politicoeconomic language, does not change owners.[30] The movement of money from one enterprise to another or even the settlements between enterprises and the budget are settlements within the large "USSR and Company." It is quite possible, for example, to liken these transactions to the settlements of one division of General Motors with another. But in a cash transaction, money changes owners; this is like settlements of General Motors and General Electric.

I began this description with the phrase "it is believed," and not by chance. The point is that this description, which reflects a very widespread point of view, is true only in part. More correctly, in reality cash and noncash transactions differ sharply; it is true that in moving from one enterprise to another the money remains "state" money, but it would be incorrect to reduce the significance of money settlements between enterprises only to some formal entries and not to see behind them the real commodity-money relations (but many Soviet economists do not see this).

Precisely this attitude toward noncash transactions "helped" to a considerable extent to create enormous inflation in the noncash sphere and to create a very serious financial crisis here as well. What is important here?

Until some moment when the entire management of the economy was clearly centralized, when there could be no question of any economic independence of enterprises, when enterprises did not strive to obtain a profit, the attitude described above toward money and commodity-money relations was fairly well founded. However, gradually, as the economy grew and its management became more complicated, as the difficulties of solving everything only in Moscow increased, as the interest of enterprises in obtaining profits was enhanced and so on, money settlements have gradually become more and more important, and the previous attitude toward them has become incorrect. Certainly, much that was said above about the fact that an enterprise cannot without any restrictions spend money, that it needs allocations and limits, that the withdrawal of the free remainder of the profits radically undermines the interest of enterprises in having a larger profit, remains true today. However, everything has at the same time become more complicated and in many respects the consequences of inflation in the noncash sphere are similar to those of inflation in the cash sphere.

We will examine the inflation in the noncash sphere and its results specifically in chapter X, but for the time being I will note that Soviet authors (at any rate, some of them) are beginning to understand that the previous separation and even the opposition of the cash and noncash spheres are fraught with very serious consequences.

Thus, in the journal of Gosbank there has been sharp criticism of the opinion that the noncash sphere differs fundamentally from the cash sphere, that a noncash transaction is only the right to demand money and not its real movement.[31] The same author writes in another article:

> It seems that emission should be understood to mean the additional placement into circulation of means of purchase and payment, which are necessary for the realization of newly produced goods and services, and this refers to both the cash and noncash money turnover.[32]

Let us note that precisely the volume of noncash transactions is increasing especially rapidly. Thus, in comparing the data on the noncash transactions for 1940, 1950–65, one author indicates that[33] "during this period the noncash turnover increased more than 10-fold, while the entire cash turnover through the cashier's offices of the bank increased only 6-fold." The same author writes that "for a socialist economy the more rapid growth of the noncash sphere as compared with the sphere of cash payments is a typical feature," although he stipulates that: "This situation may be of importance only when planning for the distant future" (since) "first of all it is necessary to take into account the increase and reduction of the prices for the goods being sold in the retail trade network."[34]

In other words, this author in 1974 predicts in the near future an increase of the prices for "goods being sold in the retail trade network," and here I completely agree with him. But in respect to the idea that a more rapid increase of the volume of noncash transactions is typical for the "socialist economy," this in principle contradicts the idea of the unity of the cash and noncash spheres; it is in essence a relapse to the notion of settlements between enterprises being purely technical operations that do not have a real economic content.

Why am I saying this here? Because, without such notions, without such "theoretical grounds" the Soviet authorities would not go so far both in maintaining a constant excess of budget expenditures over budget revenues and in furiously increasing credits.

I will note in conclusion that this rapid increase of the volume of noncash transactions, formally speaking, has created additional sources for expanding the extension of credit (including the extension of credit to the budget). The following connection has been formed (and is forming)—the more credit is given, and the more money the budget gives, the more the volume of money circulation (primarily in the noncash sphere) grows, and the more sources for the extension of credit there are as a result. Following this superficially correct (but in essence, extremely faulty) logic, the country has arrived at a far-reaching crisis of the entire financial system.

Notes

1. An exception, but one that is strictly limited, is some purchases in the retail network—a part of the so-called small-scale wholesale trade (*melko-optovaya torgovlya*)—see appendix B. This also includes payments for transportation expenses for business trips.

2. The former chairman of the Gosbank board once wrote: "There is no economic difference between the money which is in circulation in the form of currency notes and the money which is in the accounts of enterprises and organizations at Gosbank and other Soviet credit institutions" (Sveshnikov, "Denezhnyy," 1974, p. 49). As we see, this is not entirely so.

3. Konnik, *Zakonomernosti*, 1968, p. 17. It is possible that these data are somewhat imprecise—see Shvarts, *Beznalichnyy*, 1963, p. 105. Shvarts gives data on the noncash turnover only for Gosbank and it seems to me that during 1960–66 the share of the noncash turnover should have increased.

4. As in many other titles of Soviet organizations and institutions, the word "state" here is nothing more than an anachronism.

5. Earlier there were other banks—among them were *Sel'khozbank* (Agriculture Bank), *Tsekombank* (Central Municipal Bank), *Torgbank* (Trade Bank). There are Soviet banks abroad. There is also a special CEMA bank in Moscow.

6. With the "socialist" countries (though not with all), settlements are usually made in nonconvertible currencies including rubles.

7. Even if we add the turnover tax (which is, for the most part, an indirect tax) to the receipts from the population in 1978, almost 60 percent still remains for all other receipts—see *Narkhoz 78*, p. 534. However, considering the fact that the budget deficit is included in this amount, perhaps it is worth refining this point of view somewhat.

8. In 1978 the fee for capital reached 29.6 billion rubles—almost 10 percent of all budget revenues (*Narkhoz* 78, pp. 533–34).

9. This is rather far from our theme, but a brief explanation is necessary. After all the reforms, enterprises can actually use only a portion of profits, and this portion is strictly limited. What is left is called the "free remainder" and is fully withdrawn—in part by superior organizations, but primarily for the budget. Under these conditions it is all the same to enterprises whether they will have a profit higher than a certain level. And even more than that, due to planning from the achieved level, enterprises avoid having too large a profit.

10. "The money turnover is directly connected with the credit turnover. In issuing credit, the bank is giving enterprises monetary assets, which influences the amount of the noncash and cash turnover. Consequently, bank credit acts as an economic tool for regulating the money turnover, the satiation of the economy with monetary assets and the channels of circulation with cash" (Rybin and Shrayber, "Nekotoryye," 1977, pp. 62–63).

11. See, for example, Shenger, *Ocherki*, 1961, p. 59. Here the points of view of other authors are set forth, but on p. 60 the author declares that he does not agree with them and with remarkable logic says: "The fact that as a result of the development of credit an enormous saving of real money takes place is unquestionable .... In the socialist economic system of the USSR, owing to its advantages, this saving is achieved to an even greater, to the highest degree."

12. Credit replaces direct budget financing, but on the other hand the budget grants funds for increasing credit resources. Here is another example. In Z. Atlas, *Denezhnoye*, 1957, p. 201, it is stated about the 1941–45 war period: "The repayment of prewar credits by enterprises, which had suffered from the effects of the war, was deferred. These credits to a considerable extent were repaid after the war using assets of the state budget."

13. Voluyskiy, *Svodnyy*, 1970, p. 131.

14. See, for example, Massarygin, *Kreditnaya*, 1974,

15. In Russian (as in English) the word "credit," and especially the term "extension of credit" can be understood in two ways depending on the context. Basically credit (the extension of credit) is the loaning of money, that is, with its subsequent return. But in some expressions this can mean simply the allocation of funds, and it is not implied that this money will be returned. In this entire work I use these terms only in their first sense.

16. See the interest rates for credit, which were in effect in 1955, in Z. Atlas, *Denezhnoye*, 1957, p. 242, and those now in effect in Lavrushin, *Ekonomicheskaya*, 1977, p. 64.

Note that banks do not pay interest on the funds of enterprises and organizations in their accounts. The only exception is the funds of savings banks.

17. In the opinion of many economists and financial experts the extension of credit instead of outright grant financing conforms more to the principles of cost accounting and has a great stimulating role. In itself this is not incorrect. However, in order for this to be truly so, a number of serious changes in the economic system itself are necessary. Of most significance is that the replacement of direct financing by the extension of credit for this purpose should not increase the total amount (volume) of financing and the extension of credit. Meanwhile, these total amounts have increased greatly, and precisely this was the main role of the expansion of credits.

It is also difficult to agree with the opinion of many Soviet economists that the extension of credit instead of financing enhances the economic independence of enterprises. In particular it must not be forgotten that the bank uses credit "in order to achieve specific goals which stem from the requirements of the economic policy of the state" (Shvarts, "O roli," 1973, p. 23).

18. The amounts of the credits of both Gosbank and Stroybank (as well as, it seems to me, the credits of Vneshtorgbank to Soviet organizations) are shown here. The data on the credit formation of Gosbank alone are in Levchuk, *Ssudnyy*, 1971, p. 97, as well as in Pchelin, *Gosudarstvennyy*, 1976.

19. See for example, *Narkhoz* 78, p. 534.

20. However, as follows from my research on budget expenditures, an ever-increasing portion of the budget expenditures on the national economy in reality is allocated for the financing of military expenditures.

21. Calculated according to *Narkhoz* 78, pp. 538 and 521. In *Narkhoz* 78, p. 522, a slightly different indicator is cited because kolkhozes are not accounted.

22. *Narkhoz* 78, p. 522.

23. Barkovskiy, *Organizatsiya*, 1973, p. 5.

24. Chernov, "Kadry," 1977, p. 7.

25. Barkovskiy, *Organizatsiya*, 1973, p. 6.

26. Chernov, "Kadry," 1977, p. 7.

27. In 1975, 180,900 people worked at Gosbank, excluding cost accounting organizations, tekhnikums, savings banks and Vneshtorgbank, which are subordinated to it (Pchelin, *Gosudarstvennyy*, 1976, p. 29). I do not believe that there is even one other bank in the world with a staff of this size.

28. In the Soviet literature, that which the people would like to have, which they need (or it seems to them that they need it) is usually called "requirements" (*potrebnosti*), while that which they could really pay for is called "demand" (*spros*). This is seen best of all from the term "effective demand" (*platezhesposobnyy spros*).

29. However, it is of little avail—the necessary goods must also be in the store, and this does not always happen.

30. For simplicity, I am ignoring here the noncash transactions with kolkhozes and cooperatives. However, as is known, both kolkhozes and cooperatives are only formally not state organizations.

31. Mochalov, "O masse," 1973.

32. Mochalov, "O priroste," 1974, p. 33.

33. Gusakov, *Planirovaniye*, 1974, p. 151.

34. Ibid., p. 161.

Chapter IX

Sources of Credits

As we saw in tables VIII-1 and 2, the extension of long-term and, especially, short-term credit is of a truly extensive scale. The natural question arises: what are the sources of these credits? In the literature the following types of credit resources are listed:[1]

—the funds of banks;
—the assets of the state budget;
—the assets in the current and other accounts of enterprises and organizations;
—the assets of credit institutions (Stroybank and Vneshtorgbank);
—deposits of the population;
—money emitted;
—the profit of Gosbank;
—other resources.

We will now examine all these types of resources in as much detail as possible and attempt to make quantitative estimates of them. In principle this classification is quite complete. Practically all authors either simply repeat it or say in essence the same thing, although frequently in a different order. One definition must be noted:

> The main sources of the state loan fund are [a little above the author explains that the loan fund is the state-wide fund for the extension of credit to the national economy]:
>
> 1) the temporarily idle monetary reserves of socialist enterprises, which arise in the process of the circulation and turnover of productive capital and are collected in bank accounts. As a result of the fact that the rate of the circulation and turnover of capital in various enterprises and sectors of the national economy differs sharply depending on the duration of the production period, the formation of temporarily idle monetary assets on the scale of all social reproduction is of a continuous nature;
>
> 2) the assets of the state budget in the form of state monetary reserves, which have been accumulated as a result of revenues exceeding expenditures, and current budget resources, which are formed in the process of the implementation of the budget by institutions of Gosbank, since the payment of funds to the budget and their expenditures do not coincide in time;

3) the current, temporarily idle, monetary reserves and the monetary savings of the population, which are accumulated primarily through the network of savings banks.[2]

This lengthy quotation is very interesting. The learned author of this article did not even consider it necessary to mention the authorized (*ustavnyy*) and reserve capital of the banks. Indeed, as we will see, this own capital of the banks is now something of the order of 1.5–2 percent of the total amount of credits issued.

She also says nothing about how the maximum amount of credits is determined. In point of fact, as follows from this quotation, there is no real backing of credits at all, since the credits are themselves backed by credits. The author indicates as the first in order of importance source of credits the accumulation of the temporarily idle monetary assets of enterprises in bank accounts. But I have already noted in chapter VIII that only less than 30 percent of these assets are the enterprises' own assets and those equated with them, while more than 70 percent are borrowed assets that have been obtained primarily from the bank through credits.[3]

I wish least of all here to criticize this system. In Western economies borrowed assets are also quite considerable; no production begins without bank credit. However, an obvious fact—no natural limit to credit resources is evident—is extremely important, and in fact, this chapter is devoted primarily to just this question.

Also interesting in this quotation is the definition of the excess of the revenues of the budget over its expenditures as "state monetary reserves,"[4] and the fact that the assets of the population are accumulated as a credit resource through deposits at savings banks only "primarily," that is, there are other forms of use of these assets. Thus, what was said in chapter VII about the use of the monetary savings in the hands of the population as a credit resource is indirectly confirmed here.[5]

I was not able to find precise indications of the differences in the sources for the extension of short-, intermediate- and long-term credit. In one book[6] it is stated that the Stroybank fund for the extension of long-term credit "is formed primarily at the expense of state-wide resources," while the fund for the extension of short-term credit is formed by Stroybank "at the expense of its own assets, the temporarily idle assets of its clientele, and budget allocations."

In other words, this asserts that budget allocations (from the context the reference must be to the surpluses of the budget) are channelled into the formation of the sources of not only long-term, but also short-term credits. There are similar assertions in other works.[7]

Let us now examine the credit resources by type and attempt to estimate their amount by the end of 1975.

Bank Funds

They consist of the authorized and reserve capital. The amount of the authorized capital of Gosbank is 1.5 billion rubles.[8] The reserve fund cannot exceed the authorized capital;[9] thus, together they should amount to 3 billion rubles. The authorized capital of Stroybank is 250 million rubles, while the reserve fund also cannot exceed the authorized capital.[10] Consequently, the total amount of internal capital of both banks is 3.5 billion rubles.

The assets of Vneshtorgbank are also not very great—all of its joint stock puts only 300 million rubles at its disposal.[11] Henceforth for simplicity we will not take it into account.

Two additional comments. Firstly, the reserve fund is apparently not always precisely equal to the limit; in particular, at the beginning of 1967 the reserve fund of Stroybank was 58 million rubles below the limit.[12] Secondly, there is also the so-called "fund for the extension of long-term credit" of Stroybank, and at the beginning of 1967 it was 1.502 billion rubles.[13] Since it must be assumed that this fund is formed from budget profits, we will take it into account later when examining profits as a source of credit resources.

Profits of Gosbank

We will examine this source of credit resources "out of order" because the profits of Gosbank are closely connected with its assets; namely:

> . . . 50 percent of the profit of the bank is allocated for the replenishment of the reserve fund, while the remainder is transferred to the budget. Since the profit remains on the balance sheet of the bank until it is allocated and until the completion of the redistribution carried out after the approval of the annual report, it serves as a resource for the extension of credit.[14]

Until recently the profits of Gosbank were small because bank interest rates were so low, and even now they are not very significant. When examining this question in chapter III, we did not come to a specific conclusion; but here it is possible to assume that these profits in recent years have been on the order of 1 billion rubles. As follows from the quotation just cited, the profit of Gosbank serves as a credit resource only temporarily.

Approximately the same procedure of using profits exists at

Stroybank, and given the considerably smaller volume of operations, the profit there should be substantially less.

We can assume without the risk of great error that on the average the credit resources from the profits of Gosbank and Stroybank are 0.5 billion rubles.

Thus, the internal assets and retained profits of the banks are truly a negligible amount in comparison with the amounts of credits issued. Any capitalist bank would be green with envy.

Assets of the State Budget

In speaking about the resources for the extension of credit, one specialist writes:

> The assets of the state budget are in the form of long-term and current reserves. Among the long-term reserves are the amounts formed as a result of the excess of budget revenues over expenditures during all preceding years, while among the current reserves are the temporary, carry-over balances of assets in the accounts of the union budget, the republic and local budgets.[15]

It seems that this definition is not entirely accurate. It is not only that the author does not separate the profits of the union and the other budgets, although they are used in quite different ways. It is also that, as we saw in chapter V, only a portion of the budget profit can be attributed to "long-term reserves"; it is also used for other needs.[16]

In table IX-1 the balances of the long-term credits are compared with the amounts of the budget profits (both the USSR State budget and the union budget separately). The balances of the long-term credits are always less than the cumulative total of the profits of the USSR state budget (remember that we calculated this total beginning only with 1950) and even less than the total profits for the union budget. But in 1975 the balances of credits exceeded the total profits of the union budget. In other words, it would be an oversimplification to believe that the resources for long-term credits are approximately equal to the accumulated amount of budget profits—this is a much more complicated situation.

The special discussions of the author of a book on the resources for short-term credit add little clarity to this matter. He distinguished "assets which are created as a result of the excess of revenues over expenditures for the budget during the current period" and demonstrates that their purpose is the extension of short-term credit to enterprises for working capital.[17] Further, he states that:

> In practice this occurs not in the form of allocations from the budget for

increasing the authorized capital of Gosbank, but by the transfer of amounts formed from the excess of budget revenues over expenditures to the bank for the replenishment of the resources for the extension of short-term credit.[18]

A little below we read:

The assets of the budget from the excess of revenues over expenditures during past years are a stable amount which is constantly in the bank and is used for the extension of credit (including long-term) to the national economy.[19]

In another book it is explained that:

In addition to the use of enterprise profits, almost all the needs of operating enterprises for an increase of working capital and capital investments, and in part for those expenditures on new construction that are rapidly recovered, are met by means of credit. Budget financing is concentrated primarily in investments in new construction with longer payback periods and in the nonproductive sphere.

In conformity with this, credit resources are partially replenished from budget assets—the reserves of the budget, which are formed as a result of the excess of its revenues over expenditures and are transferred to the banks in the form of special allocations for the extension of long-term credit to industrial construction and agriculture.[20]

All this seems quite logical, but only seems so. At least the following

Table IX-1. Comparison of Budget Profits with the Amounts of Long-Term Credits (in billions of rubles)

Year	Balance of amounts of long-term credits at end of year	Amount of budget profits by cumulative total since 1950	
		USSR State budget	Union budget
	1	2	3
1950	1.4	1.0	0.7
1955	2.6	12.9	12.0
1960	3.6	27.6	24.7
1965	6.5	36.9	30.6
1970	20.8	45.5	32.3
1975	42.8	61.1	37.2
1978	67.8	77.1	n.a.

Sources: Column 1:
column 3 of table VIII-1
Columns 2 and 3:
calculated from columns 1 and 4 of table V-2 (column 2, 1978—table I-5).

questions are not very clear. Firstly, it is asserted here that there are some "special allocations" for the extension of long-term credit. Perhaps this is so, but I would like to know how all this is done. Secondly, the fact that for quite a long time there were relatively few long-term credits is a little perplexing. The sharp increase in long-term credits (table VIII-1) beginning at about the time that the book in question was published—in 1967—was not accompanied by any abrupt change of the amounts of the budget profits. Thus, only a part, and at that a small part, of the budget profits was used up to that time for the creaion of resources for long-term credit.

Another thing. Up to some point in time, the budget profit to all appearances was not considered a credit resource. At any rate, in two relatively old books devoted specifically to credit, this source is not even mentioned in characterizing credit resources.[21] The impression is formed that the budget profit began to be considered a credit resource somewhere around 1960. In this connection it is also worth noting that at the end of 1960, of the total balance of long-term credits of 3.794 billion rubles (this amount in itself is not very large), only 389 million rubles were given to "state and cooperative enterprises and organizations."[22] Therefore, it is quite possible that the budget profits began to be considered a source of credit resources at approximately the time that the practice of granting long-term credits (instead of direct budget financing) to state enterprises began to be sharply increased. But, to repeat, this is no more than an impression.

What can be inferred from all this? The attempt to single out the resources for the extension of long-term credit is clearly not successful.[23] As to the total amounts of the excess of the revenues of the budget over its expenditures—the budget profits—it is quite clear that they are used as a source of credit resources (although perhaps only beginning in approximately 1960), but it is not entirely clear what portion of them.

The author of one textbook, when characterizing the credit resources, writes:

> The assets of the state budget include: the amounts of the excess of the revenues of the union budget over its expenditures during past years and the budget assets which are in accounts at Gosbank owing to the existence of a gap in time between the receipt of the revenues and the making of expenditures. The assets of the republic and local budgets are taken into account in accordance with this article.[24]

These two phrases are not an example of clear writing, but nevertheless the impression is created that the profit of only the union budget is used as a credit resource. Since, I repeat, this does not follow unquestionably from the quotation itself, I will add that it is not clear to me how (by means of what technical operations) the profits of the republic and local budgets are withdrawn and allocated to Gosbank.[25]

Therefore, in my calculations of credit resources below, I take only the accumulated profit of the union budget (as it is shown in table V-2), and I use this entire amount, i.e., incuding all profits accumulated since 1950. Of course, this cannot be precise, but I do not see a better method. Let us add to these amounts the carry-overs of assets in the accounts of the republic and local budgets—table V-1.

For verification let us use the assertion repeated in several sources[26] that the balances of assets in the accounts of the state budget at the end of the 1950s were about 40 percent of the total amount of the credits resources of Gosbank. According to table V-1, in 1959 (at the end of the 1950s) 0.7 billion rubles were in the accounts of the republic and local budgets. I have no data on the amounts of the balances of credits of Gosbank itself at this time. However, by using the data on the balances of the credits of Gosbank on 1 January 1961 and taking their share in the total amount of credits (94.8 percent)[27] as the same in 1959. we find that the total amount of the balances of credits of Gosbank at the beginning of 1959 was[28]

$$37.2 \times 0.948 = 35.2 \text{ billion rubles.}$$

If we now assume that the credits issued were equal to the amount of the credit resources, it turns out that the amount of credit resources which remains for the budget profit is:

$$(35.2 \times 0.4) - 0.7 = 13.6 \text{ billion rubles.}$$

Meanwhile, according to table V-2, during the period 1950–58 alone the profits of the union budget were over 18 billion rubles.

This calculation confirms that a considerable portion of the profits of the union budget were allocated for purposes other than the creation of credit resources.

Since all the references we have found to the effect that the budget profits were used for other purposes pertain to the 1950s, we will proceed as follows. Let us assume that up to 1959 precisely 13.6 billion rubles went for the creation of credit resources from the profits of the union budget, but beginning in 1959 the entire profit of the union budget was used only for the creation of credit resources. We then obtain (see table V-2) 32.4 billion rubles (remember we are calculating credit sources by the end of 1975).

As to the balances in the accounts of the budget, in 1975 they were 2.5 billion rubles for the republic budgets (table V-1). It is possible to add to them the balances in the accounts of the union budget (that are used until the moment at the end of the year when they are taken as budget profits), which we arbitrarily estimate at 1 billion rubles. The total is 3.5 billion rubles.

In an already familiar textbook we read: "The assets of enterprises, economic organizations, institutions, credit institutions, and the assets of citizens in the form of deposits in their accounts at the bank and at savings banks are customarily called attracted resources."[29] From this it follows that not only the funds of the bank and the assets of the state budget but also the money put into circulation are considered the bank's own credit resources.

Above, in chapter VI, a long quotation was cited, in which, in particular, it is asserted: "The entire amount of money in circulation during the given planning period is taken into account in the credit plan."[30]

Formally everything here is in order. Indeed, the money in circulation, that is, money temporarily not used for payment, is the "deferred demand"; the state (bank) has in fact been given in this amount. But, as I have already noted in chapter VII, this is all a matter of proportions, of the amount of this very "deferred demand." The whole trick is that if we ignore the problem of the volume of money in circulation, the simplest means of increasing credit resources would be to increase emission as much as possible.[31] In chapter VII it was shown that the limit of the reasonable, normal amount of money in circulation was already surpassed long ago, that the corresponding credit resources are only formally backed by money in circulation.

According to the estimate in table VI-2, at the end of 1975 13.2 billion rubles served the needs of circulation, and the population had in addition as savings in cash another 52.5 billion rubles.

One stipulation is important here. Our conclusion on the use of the entire amount of money in circulation as a credit resource is based only on indirect evidence. In the two quotations cited above, there is no direct assertion of this, and in the second quotation it is merely stated that the money emitted "is taken into account" in the credit plan. And, of course, we are forced to use rough estimates of money in circulation and "under mattresses."

Having now finished up with the bank's own assets, let us turn to borrowed assets as a source of credit resources.

Assets in the Current and Other Accounts of Enterprises and Organizations

These assets constitute a very appreciable amount and correspondingly play an important role. However, the published indicators of these balances, though believable in themselves, lead to strange results in comparison with other data.

In one official publication it is stated that the monetary assets of enterprises, organizations and kolkhozes in all their accounts at Gosbank were 11 billion rubles in 1966 and 16.1 billion rubles in 1971.[32] In an article published a year later in the same journal, there are data on the monetary assets in the current accounts of industrial enterprises, which coincide with the data just cited, followed by the statement: "whereas at the beginning of 1966 Gosbank could meet 56 percent of the economy's need for credits from assets of the economy and the deposits of the population, at the beginning of 1971 it could meet 78 percent of the need."[33]

In table IX-2, I compare values of credit resources calculated accordingly with the amounts of credits actually issued in 1966 and 1971. During both of the years in question Gosbank issued substantially more credits than it had assets for. Since this result on the one

Table IX-2. Comparison of Credit Resources with the Short-Term Credits Actually Issued by Gosbank (in billions of rubles)

	Assets in accounts at bank	Balance of deposits of population	Total	Percent of all resources	Amount of credit resources	Credits actually issued	Difference
	1	2	3	4	5	6	7
Beginning of 1966	11.0	18.9	29.9	56	53.4	64.7	−11.3
Beginning of 1971	16.1	46.7	62.8	78	80.5	100.0	−19.6

Sources: Column 1
"Dannyye," 1971, p. 49
Column 2
table VII-1, column 3
Column 3
column 1 plus column 2
Column 4
Andreyev and Svirodova, "Nekotoryye," 1972, p. 62
Column 5
column 3: column 4 × 100
Column 6
"Dannyye," 1971, p. 46
Column 7
column 5 less column 6

hand seems strange and, on the other, is in itself of great importance, it is worth stipulating that:

firstly, I have used data on credits issued not from a random publication, but from the official organ of Gosbank, and if we do not trust these data, it is not clear what in general can be trusted;

secondly, in principle all other data used in this calculation in themselves seem quite reliable;

thirdly, column 6 of table IX-2 shows data not on all credits, but on the credits issued by Gosbank, as it should be. (The total amount of short-term credits issued during these years by Gosbank and Stroybank, as is evident from table VIII-1, is substantially greater and, incidentally, it would be interesting to know where Stroybank got the additional credit resources.);

fourthly, if we examine carefully the differences between the total amount of the resources (column 5) and that portion of them backed by the assets in the accounts of enterprises and organizations at the bank and deposits of the population (column 3), they turn out to be too small (especially for 1971) to include all the remaining types of credit resources—the assets of the state budget, the assets of credit institutions, the profit of Gosbank, other resources, and, of most importance, the money put into circulation;

it might be thought that the strange result we obtained is explained by both the fluctuations during the year of the credit resources themselves and of their use. Indeed, the amounts of the resources issued fluctuate quite greatly during the year,[34] but we, fifthly, are using data for the end of the year.

Thus, although it is difficult as I humbly hope, to find a big mistake in our estimates and reasoning, there is an obvious disparity between the amount of credits actually issued and the credit resources. That this disparity is no accident, namely, that there is no real correspondence between the amount of credits issued and the amount of credit resources, we will see at the end of the chapter.

For the present let us proceed as follows. We have only the data on the balances of the assets of enterprises and organizations in 1971 and only those at Gosbank—16.1 billion rubles. By comparing them with the data for 1966—11 billion rubles—we see that they increased by 1 billion rubles a year. Assuming some acceleration, it is reasonable to conclude that in 1975 these balances were 21 billion rubles. Let us assume that 10 percent of these amounts were in Stroybank. The total is 23 billion rubles.[35]

Assets of Credit Institutions—Stroybank and Vneshtorgbank

In our discussion we are following the list of credit resources of Gosbank; consequently, that is why we should take into account the assets of Stroybank and Vneshtorgbank that are in their accounts at Gosbank. These assets cannot be very considerable, but in passing I will note that there must be rather significant amounts at these banks themselves in their own accounts. True, with available sources it is difficult to determine their amount very precisely,[36] but there is no doubt that on the whole the assets of Stroybank and Vneshtorgbank yield several billion rubles of credit resources.

We will take these sums into account below.

Deposits of the Population

Considering everything it turns out that this money is the most significant source of credit resources. Thus, in a recent book on credit resources, we read: "The amount of the deposits is continuing to increase rapidly; this resource is equal to approximately 50 percent of the total amount of the assets used by Gosbank for the extension of credit to the economy."[37]

The balances of deposits at the beginning of 1974 were 68.8 billion rubles (table VII-1), while at the same time the balance of the short-term credits issued (including Stroybank and Vneshtorgbank) was 134.7 billion rubles (table VIII-1). By comparing the data on the credits of Gosbank in 1966 and 1971[38] with the total amount of credits during the same years (table VIII-1), we find that the credits of Gosbank were correspondingly 95 and 92.5 percent of the total amount of short-term credits for the national economy. With allowance for this adjustment it turns out that the deposits of the population indeed were "approximately 50 percent of the total amount of assets used by Gosbank for the extension of credit."

At the same time let us note that this quotation speaks not about credit resources, but about "the total amount of assets for the extension of credit."

We will take the amount of deposits of the population by the end of 1975 according to table VII-1, as 91.2 billion rubles.

Other Resources

It is difficult to say what this is. Maybe this is the depreciation charges that are accumulated by enterprises and some organizations, but, on the other hand, these amounts quite possibly are included in the "balance of assets in the accounts of enterprises and organizations at banks." It seems that this item is primarily insurance payments. The fact that insurance funds are used as credit resources is asserted, for example, in one of the textbooks:

> The purpose of personal and property insurance in the USSR is to render material assistance to citizens in the case of natural disasters and accidents. But since the funds being accumulated are not immediately paid out as indemnification and insurance benefits, the state in the public interest temporarily uses them for the financing of the national economy and the consolidation of the credit resources of the country.[39]

What might the magnitude of these amounts be? Apparently we can assume that all the insurance funds being accumulated are credit resources. In one book it is written:

> An important role of life insurance for the national economy, as is known, is the fact that by providing it a large reserve fund is accumulated in a special account. During the entire history of life insurance in the USSR, this fund has remained inviolable and is used in the national economy along with the balance of deposits in savings banks.[40]

This source indicates that the amount of the reserve of deposits for life insurance was 132 million rubles in 1957 and 1.124 billion rubles in 1967. Since that time, all types of insurance have increased several fold.[41] It can be roughly assumed that by 1975 the total amount of the "other" credit resources was not less than 10 billion rubles. This value takes into account both the fact that the amounts of insurance funds are increasing rapidly and the very real possibility that we are omitting some other types of credit resources.

In particular, the amounts of state loans to the population are taken into account in the direct revenues of the budget. However, it is quite likely that these amounts are also taken as backing for credits issued.

We are also including in this 10 billion rubles the assets of Stroybank and Vneshtorgbank, which are in Gosbank.

Let us now summarize. In table IX-3 I have brought together all our estimates of the credit resources to compare them with the amounts of long-term and short-term credits actually issued by the end of 1975. Our estimates above were in a number of cases quite rough, and we cannot be entirely certain of our judgments about some things. For example, although it is well known that money in circulation is taken as a source of credits, it is not completely clear whether the total amount of money in circulation is taken as such (moreover, our estimate of the amount of money in the hands of the population may be subject to doubt). Also, in no way can we be entirely certain that only the profits of the union budget are credit resources.

Table IX-3. Credits Resources at the End of 1975
(in billions of rubles)

1. Bank funds	3.5
2. Profits of banks	0.5
3. Assets in accounts of the budget	3.5
4. Accumulated budget profits	32.4
5. Assets in money circulation	
a) everyday turnover	13.2
b) savings of the population	52.5
6. Assets in the accounts of enterprises and organizations at banks	23.0
7. Deposits at savings banks and Gosbank	91.2
8. Insurance amounts and others	10.0
Total	229.8

Source: text of chapter IX.

Nevertheless, it seems to me that the result obtained deserves careful attention. And this result is very curious: the amount of credit resources we obtained—229.8 billion rubles—is considerably more than the total amount of the balances of short-term and long-term loans at the end of 1975—203.5 billion rubles (table VIII-1).

In table IX-2 we obtained just the opposite result; there the amount of credits issued was substantially more than the amount of resources. Given all the inevitable assumptions and approximations we have made, I am more inclined to trust the latter result—if we put aside the trivialities and reason on a broad scale; *if*, moreover, *we accept the Soviet concept of what precisely can be credit resources, then on the whole there are more credit resources than there are balances of long-term and short-term credits.*[42] At the same time there are at least the four following "buts."

"But" Number One

All this is true on the assumption of the productivity, so to speak, of the credits being used, i.e., that the money issued on credit is used in such a way that it yields an additional revenue as compared with the case in which the corresponding credit resources remain unutilized and are wasted. In particular this pertains to the use of the money in the accounts of enterprises, the budget profits and so forth, as credit resources. This question is too broad and complicated to discuss here and I will only note that the continuing decline in efficiency in the Soviet economy (there is extensive literature concerning this) will call into question the expanding use of credits. Or, in other words, it leads to more and more inflation (see chapter X).

"But" Number Two

As we have already seen, more than half of the credit resources are the assets of the population itself: deposits at savings banks and money put into circulation; and the largest part is savings in cash. We saw in chapter VII that a significant portion of these savings are of a forced, artificial nature, which raises the serious question of the reliability of the backing of such credits. As was also noted in chapter VII, it is quite likely that with the forthcoming change of leadership the new rulers will in some way reduce the amount of savings of the population (for example, by an exchange of money). Then the credit resources would correspondingly decrease sharply, and more than half of the actually issued credits will turn out to be backed by nothing at all.

"But" Number Three

As is plainly seen from the literature, there is no agreement among Soviet authors on the real limits of credit resources. The literature speaks in detail about what can be considered credit resources (can form the loan fund); it is repeated importunately that the planning of credit is achieved by the balancing of credit resources with the credits;[43] but nowhere is a single word said about what to do when imbalances arise, i.e., if the demand for credits is greater than the resources, or vice versa.

But this is not even the most interesting thing. For all the statements about the need to balance the credits with the resources—and such balances are indeed compiled[44]—there is still a lengthy discussion in the literature on what in general can be considered credit resources. Here, for example, is what is said in a work already cited above:

> ...in Soviet economic literature there are two concepts of the nature and essence of credit under socialism... According to the first concept bank resources are formed mainly at the expense of deposits (i.e., the monetary resources of the population, the economy and the budget) and emission. Moreover, of course, the amount of credit formation of the bank is always governed by the size of its loan fund (including the magnitude of currency emission). According to the second concept credit resources arise as a result of the bank continuously advancing more and more new assets into the economic turnover of the country, into the social product. In this case the deposits, or the so-called attracted assets, do not constitute either the physical or the economic basis of the increase of the bank's credit resources... The credit formation of the bank is determined here not by the amounts of its resources, but by the volume of the gross social product.[45]

It seems to me that the "second concept" is in principle quite logical. With the normal management of the economy, if the new credit is used productively and leads to an increase of the social product and the national income, issuing it is entirely founded, even if in this case certain limits of backing are violated. But, in the end, it is not a matter here of my understanding but of the fact that in the literature this question is discussed from various points of view, and the authors are far from unanimous.

The authors of two articles in the official organ of Gosbank, the journal *Den 'gi i kredit*,[46] argue actively with each other about this. The editor-in-chief of this journal, in a long review of a book already mentioned above, primarily demonstrates the contradictions of various statements of the author of the book on this issue, but carefully avoids stating his position which, it must be said, is unusual for Soviet reviews.[47]

The following statement of the chief of the Credit and Monetary Circulation Department of the USSR Ministry of Finance is very typical.

> It seems to us that the resources for the extension of credit exist objectively and can be calculated on the basis of the plan of national economic development and the state budget for the corresponding period. The amount of the resources is the constraint on the amount of credits which can be issued.[48]

Thus, the authors adhere to the view of credits that no more of them should be issued than there are resources.

In a book published 15 years ago there is a discussion of the following theme—is the granting of credit the use of temporarily idle assets or does credit itself arise from the need to support the seasonal fluctuations of the demand for assets?[49] Of course, credit resources should not arise at all in the second question.

Hence, it seems that we can say with confidence that in spite of the formal compilation of balances, in principle there are no strict rules which actually could precisely regulate the amount of credits being issued by any natural, objective limits. Therefore, the result we obtained, that the amount of credits issued was less than the available resources, in general does not prove anything; quite possible it is just the opposite—that is, more credits can quite possibly be issued than there are resources for them. This is exactly the point of:

"But" Number Four

In the next chapter we will finally examine a phenomenon which has already been mentioned—the regular deficit nature of the budget, which is covered by bank credits. These credits are substantial enough to permit the assertion that there are no untapped credit resources left.

What follows from all this, what can be said in concluding the chapter? It seems quite unquestionable that as the national economy develops, as the savings of the population in various forms increases, the credit resources of the Soviet financial system are increasing sharply. In spite of the fact that we have not been able to get precise figures, it is nevertheless possible to assume that, on the whole, so to speak, the normal credits—long-term and short-term—are at any rate more or less formally backed. However, a substantial excess of credit resources over this normal use is not found, and therefore the credits issued to the budget, about which we will speak in the next chapter, are not backed.[50]

Notes

1. See, for example, Solovov (he is a deputy chief of the Economic Planning Administration of the Gosbank Board) "Organizatsiya," 1975, p. 24, and Barkovskiy, *Organizatsiya*, 1973, chapter III.

2. M. Atlas, "Kredit," 1974, p. 60.

3. According to *Narkhoz 78*, p. 522, at the end of 1978 only 25 percent of working capital was "own and equivalent assets." Bank credits accounted for 46 percent, accounts payable (i.e., loans from other enterprises, which very likely ultimately means bank assets) accounted for 22 percent.

4. It seems that this definition is suitable only for the profits of the union budget—see chapter V.

5. It is possible, however, that our author was not thinking about this here but had in mind only the loans and assets of Gosstrakh.

6. Massarygin, *Kreditnaya*, 1974, p. 85. In the textbook by Barkovskiy, *Organizatsiya*, 1973, the special section (no. 5) of chapter XVII on the Gosbank plan for the extension of long-term credit gives rise to more questions than it answers.

7. See, in particular, the quotation from Yampol'skiy, *Resursy*, 1974, p. 71, a little below.

8. Poskonov, *Kreditno*, 1967, p. 95. Until 1960 the authorized capital of Gosbank was 400 million rubles (M. Atlas, *Razvitiye*, 1958, p. 344).

9. "The reserve fund is formed from deductions from the bank's profit; it is intended for covering losses which can appear in the operations of the bank after the approval of the annual plan. The deductions for the reserve fund are made until they reach an amount equal to the authorized capital. After the approval of the annual report, 50 percent of the profit of the bank is transferred to the union budget, while the remainder is entered in the reserve fund" (Ikonnikov, *Denezhnoye*, 1962, p. 83). See also Barkovskiy, *Organizatsiya*, 1973, p. 50.

10. Poskonov, *Kreditno*, 1967, p. 251; also, see below.

11. "Ustav," 1963, p. 91. It is unclear to me in precisely what money this amount is expressed, but it is quite possible that it is in "normal" rubles.

I will note in passing that it is very unclear how much credit Vneshtorgbank gives to Soviet organizations, in particular to foreign trade associations, to pay for exports. The amount of credits to "other sectors" (*Narkhoz 78*, p. 538) is too little for us to think that Vneshtorgbank credits are shown here. Apparently they are included in the total amount of credits to trade.

12. Poskonov, *Kreditno*, 1967, p. 251.

13. Ibid.

14. Barkovskiy, *Organizatsiya*, 1973, p. 50.

15. Massarygin, *Kreditnaya*, 1974, pp. 91–92.

16. It has already been noted in chapter V that according to Batyrev, *Denzhnoye*, 1959, p. 145, the reduction of retail prices was carried out at the expense of budget profits. It is also stated there that "the needs of Gosbank for resources for the extension of short-term credit are met" with budget profits.

In one, quite old book (Kisman and Slavnyy, *Sovetskiye*, 1958, p. 33) it is stated: "... a portion of these assets was used to offset the devaluation of commodity stocks as a result of the reduction of wholesale prices and to make up the shortage of internal working capital of enterprises and economic organizations. The remainder serves as a resource for the expansion of credit investments in the national economy."

In Melkov, *Kreditnyye*, 1969, p. 106, we read: "As is known [to whom?], at times a portion of the amount of the excess of budget revenues was used for implementing various measures, including for reducing prices, but nevertheless a considerable portion of this amount could [a very mysterious word, the author just said that all this is "known"] remain in the accounts at the bank."

17. Yampol'skiy, *Resursy*, 1974, p. 69.

18. Ibid., p. 70.

19. Ibid., p. 71.

20. Kosyachenko, *50 let*, 1967, p. 158.

21. Gusakov and Dymshits, *Denezhnoye*, 1951, p. 276ff; Z. Atlas, *Denezhnoye*, 1957, p. 352. Incidentally, in this book on p. 351 in the list of resources of Gosbank there is mention of "the assets of the union budget from its implementation during past years." Note the word "union."

22. *Narkhoz 64*, p. 774.

23. Quite typical is the statement in Gerashchenko, *Denezhnoye*, 1970, p. 336: "The assets of the state budget that are allocated for the extension of long-term credit" are sources of the assets of Stroybank for the extension of long-term credit. This statement can be understood as you like.

24. Ibid., p. 332.

25. The fact that the profits of only the union budget are used as a credit resource also follows from the following quotation: "Only that part of credit formation that is carried out with budget assets allocated for the consolidation of the credit resources of banks is currently reflected in the balance of financial resources of the state. This includes both the assets allocated from the budget for the extension of long-term credit and the free budget assets in the form of the excess of revenues over expenditures for the union budget, which are used by Gosbank mainly for the extension of short-term credit" (Voluyskiy, *Svodnyy*, 1970, p. 53).

Further on it is stated here that "the increase in credit formation by banks using the temporarily idle assets of enterprises and economic organizations... are not now reflected in the planning balances of financial resources. This procedure is motivated by the desire to avoid duplication, bearing in mind that the temporarily idle assets of the economy are formed mainly from the profits, amortization deductions and other resources of economic organs that are taken into account in the main articles of the balance." It is difficult not to agree with the wisdom of the statement about "duplication," but according to all other sources in fact the assets of enterprises and organizations are nevertheless taken into account as a credit resource.

26. For example, Melkov, *Kreditnyye*, 1969, p. 106.

27. Calculated according to Poskonov, *Kreditno*, 1967, p. 304.

28. *Narkhoz 64*, p. 774.

29. Barkovskiy, *Organizatsiya*, 1973, p. 50.

30. Ibid., p. 57.

31. More strictly speaking, the credit role of currency emission should also conform to the main purpose for issuing money. Excessive currency emission leads to its depreciation; the real credit role of a given nominal amount of money is then correspondingly decreased.

32. *Dannyye*, 1971, p. 49. Need I say that in the breakdown of these data by sectors (industry, agriculture, procurements, transportation and communications, trade) there is a gap—2.77 billion rubles for 1971. It is difficult to say what this is. For the current accounts of Gosstrakh this is very little and, incidentally, it is not clear where the assets in its current accounts are reflected. Perhaps this is the amount of the balances of the assets of organizations of the so-called nonproductive sphere.

In M. Atlas, *Razvitiye*, 1958, p. 280, there are data on the balances of assets in the current accounts at Gosbank in 1951–56. In 1956 these balances were 3 billion rubles (judging from this table, incidentally, the gap just noted is partially explained by the existence of assets in the special accounts for capital repair).

There are data on the balances of assets in accounts at Gosbank for 1961 and 1966 in Poskonov, *Kreditno*, 1967, p. 150. According to these data it might be thought that the gap noted above is explained by the rather large assets of "trade union, public and other [?] organizations."

33. Andreyev and Sviridova, "Nekotoryye," 1972, p. 62.

34. See San'kov and Ol'khova, *Kredit*, 1975.

35. In M. Atlas, *Natsional'nyy*, 1977, p. 322, we read: "... in the USSR during the period from 1961 through 1975 the assets of state enterprises and economic organizations in accounts at Gosbank increased from 9.2 billion rubles to 39.8 billion rubles, or 4.3-fold, while the assets of cooperative enterprises and organizations increased from 1 billion rubles to 6.7 billion rubles, or 6.7-fold." If we believe this, and not the official indicators, a substantially different picture is obtained.

36. In particular, in Pchelin, *Gosudarstvennyy*, 1976, p. 58, some data on Vneshtorgbank for 1971–75 are cited, but it is not very clear in what currency these indicators are given.

37. Yampol'skiy, *Resursy*, 1974, p. 30.

38. "Dannyye," 1971, p. 46.

39. Motylev, *Gosudarstvennoye*, 1975, p. 11.

40. Reytman, *Lichnoye*, 1969, p. 60.

41. Many data on this are given in Kulikov, "Zadachi," 1973, as well as in "Gosudarstvennoye," 1975. According to the latter sources in 1974 the payments for accident insurance alone were 3.5 billion rubles (p. 59), while all types of insurance payments in 1974 amounted to 6 billion rubles (p. 61).

42. Apart from the estimate in table IX-2, there is another piece of evidence in favor of the fact that perhaps I am incorrect, to conclude, that the amount of credits being issued is less than the resources of the loan fund. As is asserted in Massarygin, *Kreditnaya*, 1974, p. 37, "the total amount of the credit fund at present is approximately one-third of the annual national income of the country." The produced national income in 1974 was 354 billion rubles (*Narkhoz 75*, p. 563). One-third of this amount is 118 billion rubles, which more or less agrees with the data in table IX-2.

In another passage in the same book (p. 91) it is stated: "The bank's own assets take up a comparatively small proportion in the total amount of its credit resources (approximately 5–7 percent)." It is explained here that the bank's own assets are its authorized and reserve capital and the redistributed profit. The authorized and reserve capital, as we saw above, is 3.5 billion rubles and in no way more. Hence, the undistributed profit is 2.4–4.8 billion rubles. This is too much! Therefore doubts quite naturally arise as to whether it is possible at all to believe the author in his calculations.

43. See, for example, Barkovskiy, *Organizatsiya*, 1973, chapter XVII.

44. The balance is compiled by the Ministry of Finance and Gosbank, but to all appearances Gosplan does not participate in this. At any rate in Gosplan, *Metodicheskiye*, 1974, not a word is said about this. In recent years the literature has spoken more and more about the compilation of a consolidated financial plan, which should include the plan of the utilization of credit resources as one component.

45. Massarygin, *Kreditnaya*, 1974, pp. 11–12.

46. Yampol'skiy, "Resursy," 1975; Zaydenvarg, "Kreditnyy," 1975.

47. See the review, Titarev, "Resursy," 1975, of the book by Yampol'skiy, *Resursy*, 1974.

48. Zakharov, "Voprosy," 1976, p. 48. The title of the author is indicated in the journal *Finansy SSSR*, No. 4, 1976, p. 17.

49. Shvarts, *Beznalichnyy*, 1963, p. 179ff.

50. It would seem that if Soviet financial experts do not have objective limits of credit resources and can issue as much of them as they like, then why does the literature again and again speak about the need for the economy and mobilization of every kind of resource, including credit resources? Not only is all this spoken about, but persistent efforts are being made to attract deposits in savings banks and so forth. The explanation is elementary. The overutilization, so to speak, of credit resources, like a number of similar things, has led to a very difficult financial and economic situation of the country. More credits are being issued than necessary and the budget deficit is being maintained not because of the good life, but out of grim necessity generated by the faulty system of management of the economy.

Chapter X

Bank Loans to the Budget. Inflation in the Noncash Sphere

I already mentioned that the budget receives loans (outright credits) from Gosbank and uses them to cover its deficit. In this chapter we are to make the final calculations, to substantiate this conclusion, and to explain its importance. But before this let us review some results of the entire foregoing discussion.

The initial mystery was that on the revenue side of the budget there are considerable amounts of revenues about which nothing is known. A very detailed examination of all the known (as well as some assumed) revenues of the budget in chapters III and IV helped us to narrow the initial gap considerably (primarily because of the revenues from republic budgets and from foreign trade) as well as to set aside some possible explanations as incorrect. Nevertheless, in spite of a number of risky maximum assumptions when estimating some revenues, it was not possible to explain the gap entirely; a few billion ruble annual excess of the total amount of the revenues of the budget over the amount of its individual components remains.

In chapter V we examined the question of the so-called amounts of the excess of the revenues of the budget over the expenditures. It was ascertained that there is nothing mysterious behind them—the corresponding amounts are the balances of the budget appropriations not spent at the end of the year—and it was also shown that the existence of these balances, which is explained by purely technical causes, in no way contradicts the possibility that the budget at the same time runs a deficit.

Further in chapter VI it was shown that the emission of cash should be a source of budget revenues among others, but these amounts (see below) also cannot explain the entire gap at least for the last few years. A very interesting thing ascertained there is that the corresponding amounts are transferred to the budget revenues not directly, but through the use of the mechanism of credits of the bank to the budget; simply speaking, the bank extends to the budget credit for this amount.

Finally, in chapter VIII we saw that credits (short-term and long-term) are a source of enormous and ever increasing in importance financial resources. Our attempt in chapter IX to determine some objective limit of the credit resources ended in failure; we obtained rather conflicting indicators. At the same time, as I tried to show, Soviet specialists do not have a unanimous opinion on the question of the very existence of such a limit. Many assume that the amounts of credits are determined only by the demands for them, and there are simply no limits of their issuance.

Before proceeding, let us return for another but now the last time to the cardinal question—are there any other sources of budget revenues which we have not examined? A recent work already cited above gives a summary of the existing ideas on this account. Here three things are indicated.[1]

First, the suggestion is made that the budget receives revenues from the repayment of the amounts of aid to other countries. In itself this possibility exists, but I do not believe that it is realized; and if nevertheless this is so, the corresponding amounts should be very small.

It is not only that both the "aid" and the repayment should take place either in foreign currency or in "transferable rubles" (it is extremely doubtful that the corresponding settlements would be made in "domestic" rubles). We must take into account here that the foreign debt of the USSR in hard currency is increasing and has reached levels that are threatening for the lenders. Therefore, even if (when) repayment of aid takes place, it should go to cover the foreign debt and not to the budget. It is also difficult to name countries that would in reality be in a position to repay aid received earlier—Cuba,[2] Vietnam and Egypt are not suited for this. Finally, the total amounts of assistance, as far as we can know this, are small.[3]

Secondly, it is stated in this report that the budget earns on emission.

Thirdly, it is asserted that the budget even since 1963 has regarded the savings of the population at savings banks as a budget revenue, and the suggestion is made that this can be done in the form of bank loans to the budget.

If the first assumption, as we saw, does not seem plausible, the second is completely true, while the third is likely, which is not surprising since the author of the report cited (Sheldon T. Rabin) learned all this from me.

Thus, there are no other possibilities except those examined in the preceding chapters of explaining the remaining gap between the total amount of the revenues and the part accounted for, and it remains for us to conclude that there simply are no such revenues; the Soviet budget is therefore a deficit budget. Precisely this fact is the basic one; how this deficit is ultimately formalized is a secondary, technical matter. From a large number of indications there is a high degree of probability that the deficit is covered by the bank granting (it is practically certain that all this is formalized through Gosbank) something like loans to the budget.

I cannot stake my life on the fact that the corresponding amounts are indeed called loans or credits. However, the phenomenon itself is unquestionable and, without fear of repeating myself, I summarize the arguments proving this below. But first let us make the final calculations in table X-1. The starting point is the last gap determined in table V-6. From this we subtract emission in cash circulation (column 2). The amounts for 1961–75 were calculated in chapter VI. With respect to 1950–60, recall that, in table VI-2, I assumed that in 1960 4.5 billion rubles were needed to maintain "normal" money circulation, that the total amount of cash was 10 billion rubles, and that 5.5 billion rubles were held as cash savings of the population. Let us assume that by 1950 40 percent of this amount, i.e., 4 billion rubles, circulated, which means that emission in 1950–60 was 6 billion rubles. Having no basis on which to break down this amount by years I do it arbitrarily in proportion to the gap. In other words, 6 billion rubles are 19 percent of the total budget gap for 1950–60, which is 32.5 billion rubles, and I use this percentage to calculate the values in column 3 for these years.

In order not to return any more to my calculations of cash emission, let me once more repeat that my estimations in chapter VI cannot be precise; in particular I could be in error for individual years. At the same time it is not highly likely that I substantially underestimated savings of the population "in stockings" and amounts in normal circulation. Thus, I could not have overestimated the total amount of the emission for all years in consideration.

So, the amount of emission which we subtract from the gap in the budget revenues is a maximum, and the remaining gap cannot be explained in any other way than as a deficit of the budget, which can be covered only by loans from Gosbank.

True, one may say that the remaining deficit is covered by some amounts that are more or less equivalent to the increase of the deposits of the population at savings banks. In chapter VI, I noted that this practice existed until 1963, and these amounts were included in the revenues from the population and that then a termination of this practice was announced. Generally speaking, the total amount of

Table X-1. Last Refinement of the Amounts of the Gap in the Budget Revenues (in billions of rubles)

Year	Previous Remaining Amount of Gap	Emission	Difference—budget deficit	Increase of deposits in savings banks (for comparison)
	1	2	3	4
1940	0.8	?	?	
1950	1.6		1.3	
1951	1.9		1.5	
1952	1.7		1.4	
1953	5.9		4.8	
1954	8.2		6.7	
1955	2.9	6.0	2.4	
1956	0.8		0.6	
1957	1.5		1.2	
1958	2.3		1.9	
1959	2.9		2.4	
1960	2.8		2.3	
1961	3.2	1.4	1.8	
1962	2.6	1.2	1.4	
1963	2.1	1.4	0.7	1.2
1964	1.7	3.6	−1.9	1.7
1965	3.4	4.1	−0.7	3.0
1966	2.5	3.9	−1.4	4.2
1967	3.6	3.5	0.1	4.0
1968	6.2	4.5	1.7	5.5
1969	7.6	3.1	4.5	6.0
1970	8.5	2.0	6.5	8.2
1971	8.4	4.1	4.3	6.6
1972	8.1	3.3	4.8	7.5
1973	12.9	4.3	8.6	7.9
1974	13.6	5.0	8.6	10.3
1975	17.6	2.7	14.9	12.1
1976	20.5	3.7	16.8	12.0
1977	21.3	2.0	19.3	13.7
1978	23.1	1.0	22.1	14.4

Sources: Column 1:
table V-6, column 5
Column 2:
1961–75, two-thirds of column 5 of table VI-1; 1950–60, see text
Column 3:
column 1 less column 2, except 1950–60—81 percent of column 1
Column 4:
table VII-1, column 4

the differences according to column 3 for 1963–78 (108.9 billion rubles) is less than the increase of the deposits in savings banks during this period (118.3 billion rubles), and this assumption does not seem unlikely. However, in order to be logical, it is then necessary to explain the difference during the years preceding 1963, when the increase of the deposits *was included* in the budget revenues.[4]

The point here is not only that the assumption about covering the budget deficit with deposits of the population in savings banks was officially abolished in 1963, but also that since then the deposits have been used as a basic source of credits (chapter IX). I cannot understand how the same amount of money can be used at the same time for both purposes. The only explanation can be that the deposits are used as a credit source and the deficit is covered by bank credits. At least formally it looks more or less logical.

Considering column 3 of table X-1 we see that for several years the amount of the deficit is very small, and for three years we even obtained a "negative deficit," i.e., in fact, a surplus of revenues over expenditures. However, since in estimating the values of revenues for which we do not have direct information I consistently took the highest possible estimate, these "negative deficits" may not in fact be true budget surpluses.

Under Soviet conditions the budget deficit has practically almost the same significance as the issuing of credits. We have already seen in chapter VIII the amounts that these credits have reached, and later in this chapter we will examine the budget deficit and the credits together.

Let me also specify that to simplify matters, I was purposely a little inaccurate in terminology, but now is high time for correction. Indeed, in determining the size of the budget deficit I take incomes from emission as something natural and normal. Indeed, if the emission is not excessive, i.e., if it supplies the economy with money only for circulation, then it is a quite normal source of covering the budget expenditures. But when too much cash is poured into the economy, which, as we saw in chapters VI and VII, is precisely the case, then we have every right to say that such an emission is covering the budget deficit. So, without a doubt, the real size of the budget deficit is much bigger than shown in column 3 of table X-1. Nevertheless let us now consider a part of the deficit which is not covered by the emission of cash.

In discussions I have had, a few doubts and objections were voiced, and it would not hurt to list my arguments now.

The main one is that this is the only feasible explanation of the remaining gap in the budget revenues. Having studied in detail all the possible and probable budget revenues, having overstated at least part of them and having taken into account the revenues from emission, we nevertheless obtained quite substantial gaps and I do not see any other ways of explaining them.

True, the amounts of the deficit determined for 1950–1968 are rather modest and they could be the result of some errors in calculations.[5] But the amounts of the deficit for 1969–78 are so large that they should not be explained as my mistakes and misjudgments (we will soon return to the question).

My next argument is that looking attentively at how the Soviet economy works we see a lot of various facts which in their totality draw a very definite picture—there is too much money in the economy. We discussed these facts in regard to cash circulation in chapter VI. We will discuss them in regard to noncash circulation below, in this chapter. In this connection I should also say that, knowing all the difficulties of the Soviet economy, its failures and shortcomings, it would be very unlikely that the Soviet rulers actually managed to maintain a balance of revenues and expenditures in the state budget that is, to avoid budget deficits.

It is significant that we have in point of fact an analog of this mechanism—the transfer of the revenues from emission to the budget not directly, but through bank credit to the budget. The mechanism of the use of the amounts of the increase of the balances at savings banks as budget revenues was of the same nature until 1963.

It is of significance also that all this pertains only to the union budget. The revenues of the republic budgets are entirely broken down; all the gaps here are explicable. It is understandable why this is so. The use of the same mechanism in the republic budgets would reveal the carefully-kept secret of the deficit nature of the Soviet budget to a considerably larger number of people. Moreover, Gosbank is a very centralized organization; there are no separate Gosbanks of the union republics.[6] In principle it is not necessary to speak about the real separation of the union and the republic budgets; it is sufficient, in particular, to look at the volumes of the transactions between them.[7] Therefore it is quite likely that in some sense the republic budgets are financed precisely at the expense of the deficit, but in reality the deficit should relate only to the union budget.

Speaking of Gosbank, it should be stressed that it and only it implements the budget; all the budget operations are executed exclusively through Gosbank.[8] This is a quite technical point, but it unquestionably creates many conveniences for the realization of the indicated mechanism.

In what form can and should emission take place in the noncash turnover? As we saw in chapter VIII, this turnover takes place only by bookkeeping operations. Thus "the emission of bookkeeping operations" should take place, and this very expression seems rather funny, but only seems so; in essence it is absolutely correct. Two more things are to be noted in this connection.

Firstly, I have already noted in chapter VIII that necessary emission in the noncash turnover can to a considerable extent serve not only and not so much as a source of budget revenues but also as a source of credit resources. At the same time, by increasing the limits of the credit resources, this emission creates the principal possibility of expanding the credits to the budget.

Secondly, it must be said once again that, just as with the cash turnover, the emission of noncash money is normal only within certain limits, beyond which it will inevitably lead to inflation, and, as we will see a little below, it has.

M. Feshbach suggested that I look at how things happen in the other "socialist" countries. This is very reasonable advice, since these countries are utilizing Soviet experience extensively. In 1960–73 all the CEMA countries, even Poland, also had budget profits,[9] which should not be explained as anything other than tricks with financial statistics. Hungary alone has had (with the exception of 1970) a relatively small (about 1 percent) budget deficit, and, as is known, comparatively things there are not that bad. In my opinion, the case of Hungary completely proves my hypothesis. Indeed, the luxury of a small (!) deficit is quite permissible; this has not undermined the economy of the country under conditions of its growth.[10] But when growth is getting slower and the deficit bigger . . .

Finally, the last argument. A quite well-known author, the editor-in-chief of the journal *Finansy SSSR*, while participating in a discussion on improving the current classification of the revenues and expenditures of the budget, proposes:

> ". . . the set of budget revenues should be limited to four sections: Section I—Payments of State Enterprises and Organizations. Section II—Payments of State and Public Organizations. Section III—Payments of the Population. Section IV—State Credit."[11]

What does this mean? My first (and quite natural) reaction was that the author is directly and unequivocally confirming my conception. However, after reading the article more carefully again, I discovered in it that these sacred words about "state credit" can be understood as the amounts of loans issued by the state and this, then, means nothing peculiar. But, there is a considerably more interesting assertion here. As far as I know for the first time it is quite definitely stated in Soviet literature that there is a "rational idea" in the policy of "deficit financing, particularly when this pertains to the expenditures of the budget on capital construction."[12]

I would not say this if it were not for one strange circumstance. In the Soviet literature we do not find even a hint at the phenomenon in question, and it must be thought either that Soviet authors do not know what they are writing about or that they are all deliberately lying. On the whole I am inclined to believe that a narrow group of the highest officials of the Ministry of Finance have been let in on this secret, while the others simply do not know about all this.[13]

Let us now examine the objections which might be made to my assertion.

(*i*) The first objection was just examined. Indeed, I do not have references from the Soviet literature to even a theoretical discussion of such a possibility.

It would be more than naive to hope that something of the sort could slip through in the carefully censored Soviet literature. If this is so, then there inevitably arises the second objection—a question.[14]

(*ii*) Why is this so carefully hidden? I can only guess at this. To all appearances initially this mechanism was invented and began to be used as far back as the 1930s, when, in preparing for war and having suffered a number of very serious setbacks in agriculture and industry, the Soviet leadership had an acute need for money. Precisely because an additional need for money arose out of military needs, they kept the means of coverage secret. True, before the war much such information was published in the literature that later completely disappeared from all publications,[15] and, it seems to me, that was precisely the case. We will discuss this further below, but here I will indicate that in my opinion what we see in our calculations is only, as they say, the tip of the iceberg; it is possible to state with confidence that by means of the same mechanism considerable military expenditures are made *in excess of* the budget, which means that the actual deficit is even bigger.

The second reason could be that the use of this mechanism—the imbalance of the budget—sharply contradicts one of the pillars of the Soviet theory of the balanced development of the economy as well as many systematic propaganda statements that, say, only a capitalist economy is unbalanced and only there, in particular, can there be budget deficits.

(*iii*) If, as I just said, by means of loans to the budget they are hiding its imbalance, it would be possible to take a different route—to understate the real expenditures in the accounting publications.

As I have also just said, that is precisely what is being done: the total amount of the budget expenditures is obviously being understated at the expense of some portion of the military expenditures. Furthermore, the more intensive use of this means involves great difficulties. It is disadvantageous to reduce the published figures on the expenditures on sociocultural measures from a propaganda point of view, and it is complicated to achieve technically—for too many people are acquainted with the corresponding figures. It is also difficult to reduce the published expenditures on the economy, for this would lead to the distortion of a number of balance sheet ratios, which would immediately come out in the open.

(*iv*) The next objection—a question can be formulated as follows. As was shown in chapter VIII, various types of credit are developing rapidly in the USSR. Why not then, instead of issuing credits to the budget, reduce the budget allocations and correspondingly increase the issuing of direct credits for enterprises and organizations? Here the following points are significant.

On the one hand, additional difficulties would arise due to the substantial increase in recent years of the interest for the use of bank credit. A Soviet author indicates another thing:

> At present about half of the national income and the majority of net income are redistributed centrally through the channels of the state budget. Such enormous scales of budgetary redistribution do not conform, however, to the actual needs of the economy. A certain portion of the assets circulated through the budget (apparently, not more than 20 percent) do not undergo real redistribution, but only make idle turnovers: enterprises withhold for the budget specific amounts and receive them back by way of budget financing. This is explained only by the fact that the plans for the receipt of budget revenues are artificially overstated and are adjusted to a previously established percentage of growth, which creates the appearance of the 'constant' increase of the budget.[16]

Exactly: the Ministry of Finance, in conformity with the laws of the functioning of any bureaucratic system, is doing everything possible—and even the impossible—so that the USSR State budget would increase steadily and rapidly.

And one more thing. As I have already indicated, this phenomenon itself—the deficit nature of the budget and correspondingly the expenditures, so to speak, at the expense of the deficit—is closely connected with military expenditures. The formalization of these expenditures in the form of direct credits would seem strange and would not conform to the regular forms and methods of management. It is one thing that the budget, in receiving credits does not give them back; a completely different thing is the formalization of outright credits to the Ministry of Defense. How, in particular, would their repayment be formalized in this case?! If this is not done, even more people would be let in on the secret. Indeed, only a small number of bureaucrats in the USSR Ministry of Finance know this secret, and otherwise the financial staff of the Ministry of Defense would also be let in on it.

(*v*) I have already touched on the question of the size of the deficit, and, in fact, this is one of the most serious objections. In table X-2 the amounts of the deficit are again shown and compared with the totals of the budget revenues. We see that in addition to three years when the deficit was negative, for five other years the deficit was less than 2 percent of total budget revenues. Does it refute my conclusions? No.

First of all for 20 other years the deficit was greater than 2 percent, including 14 years when it was more than 3 percent and for a few years it was really very substantial.

Secondly, in spite of all the fluctuations, the deficit is a constant one, which shows (although it does not prove) that it is not an accidental mistake in our computations.

Thirdly, with all the fluctuations the rate of the deficit is more or less steady; it goes in step with the growth of the budget itself—one more reason to think that it is not a mistake.

Fourthly, the relatively small rate of the deficit for the most of the years supports (and does not contradict) its existence. Indeed, on the one hand, if the deficit were bigger the economy would have been in a very difficult situation long ago. On the other hand, the relatively small amounts of the deficit gradually convinced the Soviet rulers that this method of financing the economy could be used; they became bolder and in the extremely difficult economic circumstances of the last years permitted themselves to make the rate of the deficit much bigger.

Finally, let me once again say that if my hypothesis on the funding of military expenditures is right, the real size of the deficit is higher than is shown in tables X-1 and X-2.

In finishing with the question about the relative size of the deficit, I would like to mention that some additional analysis of the figures is needed. In particular, I am puzzled about the jump in the deficit in 1953–54 and the sharp decrease in 1963–67.[17] These figures should be analyzed together with figures on cash emission, the increment of bank credits, etc.

(*vi*) This last objection/question was posed by V. Shlapentokh—what is the cumulative effect of the budget deficit? We saw in chapter VII that cash emission led to enormous savings of the population. Continuing the same line of reasoning we may say that the budget deficit—noncash emission—led to "savings" of enterprises. Where is this money; where and how is it reflected?

Table X-2. Budget Deficit as a Percentage of the Total Revenues of the Budget (in billions of rubles)

Year	Budget Revenues, Total	Deficit Covered by Noncash Emission	Percent
	1	2	3
1950	42.3	1.3	3.1
1951	47.0	1.5	3.2
1952	49.8	1.4	2.8
1953	54.0	4.8	8.9
1954	55.9	6.7	12.0
1955	56.4	2.4	4.3
1956	58.6	0.6	1.0
1957	62.7	1.2	1.9
1958	67.2	1.9	2.8
1959	74.0	2.4	3.2
1960	77.1	2.3	3.0
1961	78.0	1.8	2.3
1962	84.3	1.4	1.7
1963	89.5	0.7	0.8
1964	94.4	−1.9	−2.0
1965	102.3	−0.7	−0.7
1966	106.3	−1.4	−1.3
1967	117.2	0.1	0.1
1968	130.8	1.7	1.4
1969	140.0	4.5	3.2
1970	156.7	6.5	4.1
1971	166.0	4.3	2.6
1972	175.1	4.8	2.7
1973	187.8	8.6	4.6
1974	201.3	8.6	4.3
1975	218.8	14.9	6.8
1976	232.2	16.8	7.2
1977	247.8	19.3	7.8
1978	265.8	22.1	8.3

Sources: Column 1:
table I-5
Column 2:
table X-1
Column 3:
column 2 as a percentage of column 1.

The obvious answer is that this money is in the working capital of enterprises (and organizations), as the following figures show[18]

	Working capital at the end of the year (billions of rubles)	
	Total	Stocks of goods and materials (excluding monetary working capital)
1950	42.2	29.3
1960	92.0	71.0
1970	211.8	163.4
1978	381.3	286.2

Certainly, a part of the growth of working capital is due to the increasing assets of enterprises themselves and, especially, to bank credits. But the budget deficit was an additional source of this rapid growth. So, the money, the accumulated budget deficit, is in the debts of enterprises to each other and to banks (see below).

It also seems to me that a big part of the budget deficit is in debts of kolkhozes to the state and, most likely, in debts of military to the state. We should also not forget in this connection the rapid growth of unfinished construction.[19]

Let us turn now to the significance of the deficit nature of the Soviet budget. In chapter VI we have already examined the question of the significance of inflation in the cash sphere. Since the deficit nature of the budget and its coverage by bank credits is also inflationary (in the noncash turnover), it is possible to speak of the overall inflation in the USSR,[20] and to a considerable extent to liken the consequences of the inflation of cash to the consequences of overall inflation.

I have already spoken above about the differentiation of the cash and noncash turnovers and, therefore, examined them separately. However these turnovers not only are closely interconnected but also have a number of common features. A well-known Soviet banking official is quite right when he writes that:

> ... the law of the amount of money in circulation is of universal importance. It is equally applicable both to the circulation of cash and to the noncash turnover, although there is a difference in the specific methods of calculating the amount of money in circulation in the individual parts of the unified money turnover.[21]

Above in this chapter I have already spoken about noncash emission and not at all by chance have just cited a Soviet author. Like him, I believe that an excess of money in the noncash turnover is in no way better than an excess of money in the cash turnover, and later I will attempt to demonstrate the negative consequences of noncash emission. Now, in order to clarify what we are talking about, let us examine a purely hypothetical situation.

Suppose there are no noncash transactions, and also no banks; it is impossible to write bills of exchange and other monetary documents. Then the entire money turnover by necessity will be carried out using cash—banknotes. How much of them will be needed? If we divorce ourselves from the fact that a noncash transaction is technically simpler and quicker (especially in transactions between different parts of the country), then approximately the same amount of cash will be needed as the amount of such means of payment as payment authorizations, checks, letters of credit, "limited checks", and so forth that are in operation in the country plus the volume of those monetary operations which are now carried out by simple bookkeeping operations. This is incontestable, but then it is no less incontestable that in the noncash turnover, as in the cash turnover, there should not be more money than is really necessary.

Two important conclusions follow from this. On the one hand, since the economy is growing, the normal volume, so to speak, of the monetary noncash means of payment is inevitably increasing. Therefore, strictly speaking, the increase of the amounts of these means cannot in itself be considered abnormal, and it also cannot be considered abnormal that the budget within some limits set by this *normal need* considers the increase of such means of payments in the noncash circulation as its revenue. At any rate this is by no means worse than considering as a budget revenue some limited increase of cash—a limited emission.

However, on the other hand, if these normal limits are exceeded, if more means of payment (even in the form of bookkeeping operations, although here it is not only a matter of the form) enter the noncash turnover than is really necessary, inflation in the noncash turnover occurs, and its consequences in many respects are identical to those which appear with inflation in the cash turnover.

What are the consequences? There are several. First of all, it is one of the reasons (not the only one) for the increase of wholesale prices in the USSR. Above, in chapter VII, I noted that the official indexes of Soviet retail prices are complete lies. There is no doubt that the indexes of wholesale prices are also false. The latter are published only for industrial goods and are practically the same since 1955,[22] which, of course, also does not correspond to the facts. This is not the place to discuss the question in detail, but let me assure the reader that the prices of industrial and agricultural goods as well as the prices of transportation are growing very substantially.

Secondly, inflation in the noncash turnover leads to a widely-known phenomenon—not only is the population not able to buy at stores what is needed, but enterprises experience constant difficulties with supply. In the literature the notable "*tolkachi*" and their romantic activity have been described many times, and it is correctly noted that such middle-man activity attests best of all to the imbalance of the Soviet planned economy. However, it seems to me that they fail to say that the activities of the *tolkachi* also attests to the disparity between financial and material resources, although this is sometimes spoken about in cautious terms even in Soviet literature:

> ... the problem of the material backing of the assets of enterprises and organizations is very acute. It is well known that the assets of the production development fund are far from completely backed by the corresponding material resources.[23]

Or, simply speaking, the enterprises and organizations have the money, but they cannot obtain for it "the corresponding materials resources." We can find such statements even in *Pravda*:

> It has been noted that the demand of associations and sectors for capital investments and working capital is constantly increasing and often exceeds all the possibilities of their efficient use. This is a direct consequence of the inadequate planned coordination of financial and material resources. As managers frequently say: 'If there were allocations of goods, the money would always be found ...'[24]

Thirdly, which is probably most important, inflation in the noncash turnover serves as very convincing evidence of the imbalances in the Soviet economy. Several things are significant here: the fact that the financial resources being allocated do not conform to the material and labor resources; the fact that under these conditions various monetary and financial indicators cannot serve as real measures of economic processes; and the fact that under these conditions various "stimulating mechanisms," which supplement the plan, do not work. The same article in *Pravda* speaks about all this:

> The 'excess' money in the economic circulation weakens the effectiveness of the plan assignments and cost accounting stimuli. If the physical indicators are coordinated and established for the five-year plan, the financial plans should also be unified, ... interconnected with them. Otherwise the lack of coordination of both will constantly prevent the increase of production efficiency.... As all the experience of the management of the socialist national economy convinces us, the balancing of the plans can be achieved only with the active utilization of a system of economic standards: payments to the budget, bank interest, prices and so forth.[25]

It is necessary to especially note, fourthly, another circumstance which is far from obvious. From the Soviet literature it is clear, and I have already pointed this out above, that continuing inflation is greatly worrying Soviet financial experts, who are seeking different ways to combat it. Since only inflation in the cash turnover is recognized, every possible effort is being made to decrease the cash turnover in favor of the noncash turnover—for example, they are introducing the transfer of wages to the accounts of workers and employees at savings banks instead of issuing them in cash. However, such a measure yields little. Moreover, as is correctly said in one of the theoretical works,[26] the development of the noncash turnover does not always promote the consolidation of the cash turnover. The point is that when some payments are transferred to the noncash turnover, although the need for cash for the maintenance of a portion of this turnover is thereby reduced, the balance of monetary income and expenditures of the population is not affected and no problem is solved.

Inflation in the noncash turnover automatically leads to an increase of wholesale prices (and, consequently, in the end, of retail prices) and no less automatically creates the potential (it is not always realized) for issuing more cash.

Thus, inflation in the noncash turnover also has a far-reaching influence on the state of the cash circulation.

In addition to all that has been said, I must note that the existence of inflation in the noncash sphere increases the amount of noncash means of payment needed and, thus, to some extent justifies a certain part of the budget deficit. Incidentally, this phenomenon explains in part just where the funds formed as a result of the budget deficit go—a question examined a little above.

Now, calculations. I already noted that the existence of a budget deficit is only a part of the problem; the rapid increase of the amounts of credits, the growth of expenditures from the profits of enterprises and so forth are of practically the same importance. First of all let us use the data published recently in one of the articles by Garbuzov on "the overall financial resources of the state."[27] From the context it is not obvious precisely what financial resources other than budget resources he is talking about, although it seems that it should be credits and the internal assets (working capital) of enterprises. In table X-3 I compare his data with total national income produced during the corresponding periods.

The results appear to be very important. They completely confirm the existence of inflation—financial resources are increasing considerably more rapidly than produced national income, and, let us take note, it is precisely the financial resources of the state other than budget resources that are increasing especially rapidly. In other words, the expenditures required per ruble of increase of national

Table X-3. Comparison of Financial Resources with the National Income (in billions of rubles)

	1961–65	1966–70	1971–75
1. Produced national income	861.1	1,228.8	1,673.7
2. Financial resources of the state,			
total	576.0	913.0	1,459.0
including			
budget	449.0	651.0	951.0
others	127.0	262.0	508.0
3. Financial resources as a percentage of national income			
total	67	74	87
budget	52	53	57
others	15	21	30

Sources: Line 1:
1966–70 and 1971–75, *Narkhoz 76*, p. 485; 1961–65, *Narkhoz 70*, p. 533
Line 2:
Garbuzov, "Resheniya," 1976, p. 6.

income are increasing more and more. The amounts of financial resources are growing more than proportionately, and just this is evidence of inflation.

Now a more detailed calculation. In table X-4 I try to calculate the total amount of financing of the national economy from different sources and to compare this amount with both the national income and the gross social product.

Let me first say that all these computations are rather provisional and may serve only as an illustration. I am trying here to determine what is spent on the economy in addition to what is included in basic production costs (*sebestoimost'*)—depreciation will be discussed below.

These expenditures include budget expenses for the funding of the national economy, i.e., investment and so-called operational expenses (for example—reclamation of land, geological prospecting, etc.). As specialists know there are also military-related expenses here, but the latter in my opinion are mainly investments in the development of production of military hardware and this contradicts nothing.[28]

A big and growing part of these expenditures is agricultural subsidies. If there were no such subsidies, then food prices would rise and many things in the economy would be different. However, such a hypothetical situation should be discounted; these subsidies are a reality and by taking them into consideration we are reflecting the real movement of money in the economy.

The next element is the increment of long-term and short-term

Table X-4. Trends in National Economic Indicators and Financial Resources (in billions of rubles)

	1950	1955	1960	1965	1970	1975	1978 amount	1978 as a percentage of 1950
1. Gross social product	117.4	196.8	304.0	420.2	643.5	862.6	992.1	845
2. Produced national income	54.7	93.7	145.0	193.5	289.9	363.3	422.5	772
3. Financing of national economy, total including:	18.1	29.6	47.6	66.8	118.9	176.2	229.4	1,267
a. Budget expenditures on the national economy	15.8	23.3	34.1	44.9	74.6	110.7	141.3	894
b. Increment of long-term credits	0	0.1	−0.9	−0.1	2.7	3.8	8.4	—
c. Increment of short-term credits	0	−0.1	3.2	4.8	7.2	11.4	20.9	—
d. Amortization (only for renovation)	0.7	2.3	3.7	9.2	14.4	28.9	37.1	5,285
e. Expenditures from profits	1.6	4.0	7.1	8.0	20.0	21.4	21.7	1,356
4. Financing of national economy in kopecks per ruble of gross social product	15.4	15.0	15.7	15.9	18.5	20.4	23.1	150
5. The same per ruble of produced national income	33.1	31.6	32.8	34.5	41.0	48.5	54.3	166

Table X-4 continued.

	1950	1955	1960	1965	1970	1975	1978	1978
For inquiries								
6. Balance of credits at the end of the year, total	18.7	23.5	45.5	72.6	123.5	200.4	271.1	1,450
including:								
a. long-term	1.4	2.4	2.8	5.9	18.8	39.7	64.5	4,607
b. short-term	17.3	21.1	42.7	66.7	104.7	160.7	206.6	1,194
7. Amount of working capital in the economy, end of year	42.2	62.0	91.7	137.2	211.8	314.0	381.3	904
including:								
a. in monetary assets	12.9	15.7	21.0	29.5	48.5	79.7	95.1	737
8. Profits of enterprises and organizations	5.2	12.6	25.2	37.0	87.0	104.5	114.3	2,198
8a. Percent of profits used for economic purposes	31.4	31.4	28.0	21.5	22.5	20.5	19.0	—

Sources: Line 1:
1965, 1970, 1975, 1978—*Narkhoz 78*, p. 41
1960—*Narkhoz 70*, p. 60
1955—calculated according to *Narkhoz 65*, p. 55 and *Narkhoz 70*, p. 60
1950—calculated according to *Narkhoz 70*, pp. 56 and 60

Line 2:
1965, 1970, 1975, 1978—*Narkhoz 78*, p. 385
1960—*Narkhoz 70*, p. 533
1950, 1955—calculated according to *Narkhoz 22–72*, p. 359

Line 3:
sum of the lines 3a, 3b, 3c, 3d and 3e

Line 3a:
1965, 1970, 1975, 1978—*Narkhoz 78*, p. 533
1950, 1955, 1960—*Byudzet 62*, p. 18

Line 3b:
calculated as the difference between the balances at the end of the given year and the

previous year. Credits to the population (including credits to housing for 1970, 1975, and 1978 cooperatives) are excluded.

1978—*Narkhoz 78*, p. 538
1975—*Narkhoz 75*, pp. 746–47
1970—*Narkhoz 70*, p. 735
1965—*Narkhoz 65*, p. 786
1960—*Narkhoz 60*, p. 849 and *Narkhoz 65*, p. 786
1955—(increment compared with 1953)—*Narkhoz 58*, p. 907
1950—no direct data; the increment was assumed to be very small

Line 3c:
(calculated as the difference between the balances at the end of the given year and the end of the previous year)
1978—*Narkhoz 78*, p. 538
1975—*Narkhoz 75*, p. 746
1970—*Narkhoz 70*, p. 735
1965—*Narkhoz 65*, p. 786
1960—*Narkhoz 65*, p. 786 and *Narkhoz 60*, p. 849
1955—(increment in comparison with the end of 1953)—*Narkhoz 58*, p. 907
1950—no data; the increment was assumed to be insignificant

Line 3d:
(there are no data on depreciation in kolkhozes)
1965, 1970, 1975, 1978—*Narkhoz 78*, p. 532
1960—*Narkhoz 70*, p. 729
1955—trend according to data in *Narkhoz 62*, p. 634
1950—*Narkhoz 64*, p. 769

Line 3e:
line 8 multiplied by line 8a divided by 100

Line 4:
line 3 divided by line 1.

Line 5:
line 3 divided by line 2.

Line 6:
sum of lines 6a and 6b.

Lines 6a and 6b:
(long-term credits to the population, including credits to housing cooperatives for 1970, 1975 and 1978, excluded. All data are for the end of the year.)
1965, 1970, 1975, 1978—*Narkhoz 78*, p. 538
1950, 1960—*Narkhoz 65*, p. 786
1955—*Narkhoz 58*, p. 907

Lines 7 and 7a:
(data on collective farms excluded; all data are for the end of the year)
1965, 1970, 1975, 1978 *Narkhoz 78*, p. 521
1950, 1960—*Narkhoz 65*, p. 761
1955—there are no data. Interpolation was made according to data for 1950 and 1958—*Narkhoz 62*, p. 640

Line 8:
(excluding profits of kolkhozes)
1965, 1970, 1975, 1978—*Narkhoz 78*, p. 515
1950, 1960—*Narkhoz 70*, p. 703
1955—*Narkhoz 60*, p. 843

Line 8a:
(only state enterprises and organizations; included are profits directed to capital investment, increment of working capital, funding planned loses of other enterprises, and half of what was directed to "other purposes")
1965, 1970, 1975, 1978—*Narkhoz 78*, p. 516
1960—*Narkhoz 70*, p. 704
1950, 1955—data of 1958 used—*Narkhoz 61*, p. 756.

credits. Since I am dealing here with financing of the economy, I do not consider credits to the population, including credits to housing cooperatives. The next element—depreciation—is a little more complex. In principle depreciation is a part of *sebestoimost'* and expenditures for it are reimbursed by the price of goods produced. Nevertheless, I included depreciation in our computations because the process of charging and using it is, once again, a real process of movement of money in the economy. And, of course, I include only a part of depreciation—the renovation part (excluding the part which is to cover capital repair expenditures)—and this part does not differ, economically speaking, from the corresponding budget expenditures or from long-term bank credits.

I understand that my position on this is not undisputable, so let us look at the following indicators (all data are from table X-4):

	1950	1955	1960	1965	1970	1975	1978
Financing of the national economy without depreciation (billions of rubles)	17.4	27.3	43.5	57.6	104.5	147.3	183.7
Per ruble of national income (kopecks)	31.8	29.1	30.0	29.8	36.0	40.5	43.5

As we see, in this case there are some fluctuations in 1955–65, but then the growth is constant and fast. In other words whether we take depreciation into account or not, the general tendency is very much the same.

Finally, about expenditures from profits: I take into account only the part of them that is spent on the economy, which means expenditures from these profits for investment and for the formation of livestock herds, as well as for the increase of working capital and covering the planned losses of other enterprises. In addition I take half of what is used for "other purposes."

Unfortunately, of necessity these computations involved a number of approximations and assumptions—some data do not include kolkhozes; in the calculations of profits (where, by the way, profits of kolkhozes are also not included) the percent of profit (line 8a in table X-4) pertains only to state enterprises and organizations and only to those which in fact received profits, etc.

Nevertheless, with all these reservations, it is my belief that the results of the computations—lines 5 and 6—are extremely significant and interesting.

Generally speaking, it is natural to interpret them as evidence of the diminishing efficiency of the Soviet economy. Indeed, for a long time (excluding 1955, about which, see below) constantly and noticeably more and more money has been needed to produce a ruble of gross social product and/or a ruble of national income.[29] The overall tendency is undisputable—the economy is getting, so to speak, more and more expensive. Continuation of this tendency will inevitably lead to stagnation; the country will not be able to increase production, to raise the standard of living (which is now disgracefully low) and will be forced to decrease its military expenditures. In spite of the importance of this problem, it does not pertain directly to my basic topic, so I will limit myself to these comments.

Considering the same figures from a narrower, purely financial point of view, we may say that simultaneously and to a great degree just because of the fact pointed out in the last paragraph, financial flows are growing faster than the volume of production. In other words, in order to achieve a certain result it is necessary to pump more and more money into the economy every year.

Thus, table X-4 demonstrates inflation and because we are talking here about production, it is inflation in noncash circulation. So, this table confirms the conclusion which we made in considering table X-3.

Some more comments about this table. All the figures are in current (not constant) prices. However, interestingly enough if the indicators of gross social product and national income here were in constant prices, the results of our computations would be very much the same.[30] So, we may conclude that the real level of production in 1978 was about 8 times higher than in 1950. I may witness, without any doubts, that this cannot be true—the growth of the economy was much slower. It is not only my personal opinion; many of my former colleagues were of the same conviction, but certainly could not say so in public. Many Western specialists have written about this. On these grounds we may say, first, that the price indexes are wrong, that prices were rising, which is one more bit of evidence of inflation. Secondly, the results of our computations—lines 4 and 5—must be even worse, which means that real financial flows per unit of *real* production have grown even more than shown in table X-4.

Next comment: line 6 explains why financing of the national economy from the budget is growing slower than from any other source. The budget financing is being replaced more and more with long-term bank credits, which are growing (lines 3b and 6a) very fast. Short-term credits are also growing very rapidly. Recall that in chapter IX we did not manage to find all sources of bank credits and concluded that they are not secured (in the Soviet concept of securing credits).

About working capital: I mentioned above that in my opinion money which is "produced" by virtue of the budget deficit goes at least partially into working capital. The data in table X-4 do not support this opinion: the total amount of working capital (line 7) is growing only a little faster than volumes of production, and the monetary part of working capital (line 7a) is growing even slower.[31] I cannot explain this.

One final comment about the table: it is very natural to ask why in 1955 we observe a downturn in our indicators, and why, as we saw above (if we do not take into account depreciation) another downturn occurred in 1965? I don't have a firm answer and may suggest only a hypothesis. It is likely that our figures for 1955 reflect the fact that by that time there was some reduction of military expenditures; in particular the number of servicemen was reduced and these people moved into the economy. Consequently in 1954–55 a rather sharp increase of production took place.[32] But it is much more difficult to explain what happened with 1965. According to the official data (lines 1 and 2, table X-4) the rate of growth in 1966–70 was even greater than in 1961–65. We may think that not only are these data overstated (which is beyond any doubt) but, in particular, the extent of this overstating was greater after 1965 than before this date.

Thus, in spite of the limitations of our calculations, a clearly traceable long-term trend of growth in the relative expenditure of financial resources is obvious, and it is no less obvious that the continuation of this trend will have the result that the growth of the Soviet economy will be more and more "expensive."

In table X-5 I make a similar comparison. Once again from these indicators we see that money turnover is increasing significantly more rapidly, which unquestionably attests to inflation, and very high inflation at that.[33] At the same time, these calculations should not be considered exact, since some figures here are in constant prices.

In 1969 a Soviet author, in citing data showing that noncash payments and credit formation during 1958–62 had increased substantially more rapidly than all the national economic indicators, wrote:

> Unquestionably it is impossible to assert that there should be some direct proportionality between the growth rates of the indicators of the development of the economy presented and credit formation. But at the same time the much more rapid growth rate of the payment turnover and credit formation, which is difficult to explain only by economic necessity, requires close attention. There

are grounds to assume that this increase at times is caused by inadequte attention to the noncash money turnover, by shortcomings in the planning and utilization of the credit resources of the bank.[34]

Translating these supercautious words into normal language, the payment turnover and credit formation are increasing significantly more rapidly than is required by "economic necessity," that is, their increase is economically unjustified.

Let us summarize. Above all it is necessary to consider as proven the deficit nature of the Soviet budget, and that the deficit is being covered both by the emission of cash and by loans to the budget from the bank.

Further, in its economic consequences the budget deficit is equivalent to other inflationary phenomena, primarily the insane increase in the amounts of credits issued.

The high inflation in the noncash turnover, which was generated as a result of all of this, is attaining threatening proportions—for the

Table X-5. Growth of Various Economic Indicators During 1940–78

	1978 as a percent of			
	1940	1960	197C	1975
	1	2	3	4
1. Gross social product	1,273	304	156	115
2. Produced national income	1,325	304	153	116
3. Total industrial production	1,986	377	166	116
4. Gross production of agriculture	258	166	117	114
5. Freight turnover of all types of transport	1,203	428	155	114
6. Capital investments	2,016	440	161	115
7. Retail trade turnover	370	414	154	114
8. Budget expenditures	1,495	356	168	121
9. Balances of loans for short-term and long-term credit at the end of the year	4,292	591	218	135

Sources: Column 1:
lines 1–7—*Narkhoz 78*, p. 33
line 8—*Narkhoz 78*, p. 533
line 9—*Narkhoz 78*, p. 538
Column 2:
line 1—*Narkhoz 75*, p. 49; *Narkhoz 78*, p. 34
lines 2–7—*Narkhoz 75*, pp. 49–50; *Narkhoz 78*, pp. 34–35
line 8—*Narkhoz 70*, p. 730; *Narkhoz 78*, p. 533
line 9—*Narkhoz 70*, p. 735; *Narkhoz 78*, p. 538
Column 3:
lines 1–7—*Narkhoz 78*, p. 34–35
line 8—*Narkhoz 78*, p. 533
line 9—*Narkhoz 78*, p. 538
Column 4:
line 1—*Narkhoz 78*, p. 34
lines 2–7—*Narkhoz 78*, pp. 36–37
line 8—*Narkhoz 78*, p. 533
line 9—*Narkhoz 78*, p. 538.

further development of the economy it is necessary to invest more and more assets, and more than are in fact available, which in turn increases the inflation.

One of the most important consequences of inflation is the fact that finances have ceased to be an effective instrument of the planned management of the economy. Indeed, it is impossible to plan and manage the economy with only physical indicators; various value indicators must be used. But under inflationary conditions, and especially when inflation is not recognized and all sorts of statistical tricks are used to conceal the real increase in prices and the budget deficit, value indicators become unreliable, and making judgements relying on them unavoidably leads to errors, miscalculations, and misjudgements.

I will not develop this theme here, but I will emphasize that it is precisely inflation and the corresponding distortion of all economic indicators that is one of the fundamental reasons for the failure of Soviet planning and the performance of the Soviet economy.

Notes

1. CIA, *The Soviet*, 1977, p. 23.

2. I already mentioned in chapter IV (note 6) that Cuba receives aid from the USSR to the amount of 6 million dollars daily—too much to return.

3. As already noted in chapter IV, according to M. Atlas, *Natsional'nyy*, 1977, p. 327, during the twenty years 1955–75 the USSR granted 15 billion rubles in credits to "the fraternal socialist countries."

4. As I have already noted in chapter IV, according to Zlobin, *Finansy*, 1967 p. 251, there was (and it is quite possible that there still is) a practice of using the reserve funds of Gosstrakh, and thus the increases of these funds are treated as budget revenues. Generally speaking, the operations of Gosstrakh are increasing very rapidly, but not so rapidly that they would explain the amounts of the deficit that we obtained in table X-1, especially for the last few years.

5. This point was made by A. Bergson. Methodologically he is absolutely right—when as the result of complicated economic calculations we obtain relatively small figures, a possibility of mistakes is the first thing to think about, but in fact the deficit does exist.

6. There are republic (as well as *oblast*) offices (*kontory*) of Gosbank.

7. For example, in 1975 305 million rubles were transferred from the union budget to the republic budgets. In addition 7.804 billion rubles were also received by republic budgets and 1.113 billion rubles were transferred to the union budget in counterflows. In 1970, all these amounts were even substantially greater (*Byudzhet 76*, pp. 75 and 77).

8. Stroybank and Vneshtorgbank perform their operations with the budget through their own accounts at Gosbank.

9. Sekretariat, *Statisticheskiy*, 1974, p. 60.

10. I met a Hungarian economist in Washington a few years ago, and he told me

that the budget borrows money from the bank. The fact that he told me this shows that this is done there openly.

11. Yevdokimov, "O klassifikatsii," 1976, p. 37.

12. Ibid., p. 33.

13. It is nevertheless worth noting that in Massarygin, *Finansovaya*, 1968, p. 25, the author reasons that the Soviet state "has the opportunity . . . using credit resources to increase the assets of the state budget." However, this can be understood in such a way that the author is speaking about loans from the population.

On the other hand, it is very easy to find examples in which Soviet authors write an obvious (perhaps nevertheless only for us) lie. ". . . the credit nature of Soviet money is determined by the fact that its emission (placement into circulation) is only of a credit, but by no means of a budget nature. This means that Soviet money is emitted for the advancement of the circulation of assets, and not for the implementation of budget expenditures, not for covering a budget deficit" (Levchuk, *Gosbank*, 1977, p. 35).

14. Dan Gallik asked me this quite natural question.

15. In particular, as M. Feshbach showed me, even data on the expenditures on the MVD were published.

16. Liberman, *Gosudarstvennyy*, 1970, pp. 269–70.

17. Possibly the post-Stalin team could "loosen the belt" a little, while the post-Khrushchev team, as far as we are aware, consolidated its position very slowly and prudently, but a budget deficit is not a very prudent measure. Interestingly enough, the sharp decrease of the deficit in the 1960s coincides with the abolishing of the use of deposits in savings banks as a budget revenue (see below).

18. *Narkhoz 65*, p. 761; *Narkhoz 78*, p. 521. These figures do not include the working capital of kolkhozes.

19. Usually both Soviet and Western literature take into account only unfinished construction itself—99 billion rubles by the end of 1978 (*Narkhoz 78*, p. 351; it does not include the unfinished construction of kolkhozes). But the so-called unfinished construction production (*nezavershennoye stroitel'noye pzoizvodstvo*) has the same economic meaning—by the end of 1978 it was 34.3 billion rubles (*Narkhoz 78*, pp. 521 and 527).

20. I will repeat that it is by no means of little importance in this connection that the USSR has a large foreign debt as well.

21. Barkovskiy, "Problemy," 1977, p. 50.

22. *Narkhoz 78*, pp. 138–39.

23. Belkin and Ivanter, "Finansovyye," 1977, p. 64.

24. Fedorenko, et al., "Parametry," 1978, p. 2.

25. Ibid.

26. Shvarts, *Beznalichnyy*, 1963, p. 29 ff.

27. Garbuzov, "Resheniya," 1976, p. 6.

28. Indeed, military hardware produced is included in the total amount of gross social product and national income.

29. I use just these indicators here and not Western calculations of Soviet GNP first because I use in this work only Soviet statistics and secondly because these Western calculations are not completely reliable (see "Conclusion").

30. Gross social product in current prices in 1978 was 845 percent of 1950, and national income was correspondingly 772 percent (table X-4). According to *Narkhoz 78*, p. 33, these figures (presumably in constant prices) are respectively 791 and 808. There is some puzzle here, but generally speaking it implies that for 1950–78 the overall price level did not change substantially.

31. Here only the growth of unfinished construction production, and not unfinished construction is taken into account.

32. *Narkhoz 55*, p. 29.

33. Note that the very rapid growth of capital investment is also greater than the growth of other indicators. Among other reasons, this shows that inflation in the area of capital investment was especially high.

34. Melkov, *Kreditnyye*, 1969, p. 118.

Conclusion

The main conclusions of this study were summarized in the preface and, now, it seems to me, it is appropriate to say a few words about their significance. It is clear that they are useful for our understanding of the operation of various Soviet financial mechanisms; the quantitative estimates made of a number of important phenomena should be also of interest. At the same time the main thing, in my opinion, is that the combination of circumstances examined in this work makes it possible to describe the entire financial situation in the country as extremely critical. Moreover, on the one hand, the financial crisis is an inevitable consequence of the overall economic crisis. On the other hand, the financial crisis complicates even more the overall economic situation and intensifies the economic crisis.[1]

The term "economic crisis," need I say this, means an acute disproportion between the supply of goods and the demand for them. But in our context its meaning is somewhat unusual. Indeed, in Western economies a crisis is the lack of money, less than full usage of productive capacities, and unemployment of the labor force. In the Soviet economy it is just the opposite: the economic crisis that I am talking about means too much money, the impossibility of expanding production because of a shortage of capacities, and of labor. To say the same thing with other words, the inadequate level of production is the main source of the overall crisis. It is inadequate not only in comparison with the incalculable natural wealth of the country and other unused possibilities, but also from the point of view of the increasing demands: the demands of the population, whose standard of living is disgracefully low for a modern superpower; the demands of the further development of production (in particular the conversion of agriculture to a modern technical basis), the development of transportation, the elimination of many imbalances, the necessary urgent, rapid development of the fuel and raw materials sectors; the demands (aspirations) of the rulers of the country, who are pursuing and wish to further pursue the policy of a global superpower.

Least of all would I want to be understood to be saying that one should anticipate a rapid collapse of the Soviet political system. It is well known that so far, due to a complicated set of different circumstances, by overcoming the most diverse difficulties the Soviet regime has by no means collapsed, and in some respects has shown impressive results. At the same time it is also well known that the difficulties of the regime are not diminishing, but increasing. I do not believe that a substantial transformation of the Soviet regime as such will take place as a result of the further increase of economic difficulties. However, it is quite possible that the USSR will be forced by the state of affairs in economic areas to turn above all to domestic problems and, consequently, to decrease its global pretensions. It is also practically inevitable that the USSR will be forced to continue to seek economic assistance in the West.

It is also appropriate to indicate here some questions which were not adequately studied in this work and require further efforts. I am not about to say by this that I have done everything else exhaustively and without any errors, but nevertheless it seems to me that precisely the following questions should become the main subject of further research and discussion. I hasten also to note that in the West there is literally not one specialist who would deal *constantly* with Soviet finances. There are a number of outstanding scholars who have turned to these problems from time to time and have reached very interesting results, but the urgent need for permanent attention to this theme is obvious. It should be stressed as well that this constant attention should not be limited only to the budget; in the end the budget is merely a part of the overall financial system.

It is expedient to divide the directions of further research into four such groups:

(1) *Major questions.* They, in my opinion, should be dealt with immediately and very seriously, for they are important both in themselves and for the problem examined in this book:

(a) the budget revenues from foreign trade. It is important not only to resolve ultimately just what is taken as budget revenues and how, and to correspondingly adjust my calculations. It is also very significant to determine precisely which goods are the most profitable for the USSR from this point of view. It would be useful to construct several hypotheses and to make the corresponding calculations;
(b) the amounts of emission. The most obvious way to adjust my estimates is to turn once again to the balance of the monetary income and expenditures of the population, particularly the estimates of the monetary income. At the same time the question of the cash turnover

should in general be dealt with in more detail, studying it from various angles;
(c) several times I mentioned in the text how the increase of prices influences processes to which the book is devoted. Unfortunately, we did not have more or less reliable data on the dynamics of wholesale and retail prices—official data are clearly wrong. It would be worthwhile to attempt to make some quantifications, even if hypothetical, and use them in analysis. The most important point here is to further study the question discussed in chapter X about the correlation between financial flows, the price level and volumes of production. Or, in other words, the flows of money (in both cash and noncash circulations) and goods and services should be studied together and with consideration of price changes.

I think that only in such an analysis will the question that I have not managed to answer—where does that part of the cumulative budget deficit, which is "covered" by "non-cash emission", and the accumulated amount of credits extended go?—be answered.

There are statements in the literature that the repayments are used as a source of subsequent credits; there are also statements that many credits to kolkhozes (and some credits to state enterprises, especially during the last war) were "forgiven." All these things should be considered together with the examination of credit resources;
(d) the study of the expenditures of the budget, it seems to me, would make it possible to determine more or less exactly, just how much the budget spends on defense. By knowing this, it would be possible to attempt to make at least a rough estimate of the expenditures for military purposes *in excess* of the budget and accordingly to estimate *the total amounts* of the budget deficit.

(2) *"Minor" questions.* I call them "minor," but their importance should not be underestimated: they are only relatively minor:

(a) an attempt should be made to improve my calculations of the amounts of the loan fund and its use for issuing short-term and long-term credit;
(b) a question that remains unclear is what happens with the amounts of the repaid long-term bank credits; also the very amounts of the repayments are very unclear;
(c) an attempt should be made to better understand the question of the so-called "other monetary revenues" (I examine this question in appendix J);
(d) it is necessary to clarify an entire group of questions on state (not social!) insurance. Apparently it is possible, in particular, to improve the estimates of the payments to the population (the indicators of the

payments to the population seem quite reliable). It is also necessary to attempt to determine the amounts of the insurance fund of Gosstrakh, and how it is used.

(3) *Theoretical questions.* I call the next two questions "theoretical," but they also have a quite practical importance:
(*a*) in some discussions of the preliminary results of this study, my formulation of the very serious consequences of inflation in cash circulation gave rise to serious objections. It seems to me that in part these objections were caused precisely by the incomplete theoretical elaboration of this problem. More accurately, theoretically this problem has been studied quite adequately in respect to Western economies, and it is necessary to attempt to connect the results of these studies with the peculiarities of the Soviet system.
(*b*) the same thing pertains to the question of inflation in the noncash circulation. Here there are considerably more peculiarities in the Soviet system, and it is necessary to attempt to understand how and to what degree inflation in the noncash circulation influences the economic life of the country.

(4) *Model of GNP.* Let us turn now to the very last question. This problem is extremely complex and by no means less important, and as the reader will soon see, it is directly connected with our theme. Unfortunately I can only demonstrate this connection, raise some questions, and pose in a few instances tentative suggestions. So, collective efforts are needed here and I hope that it is not out of place to finish the book with such a statement. But to the point.

First, a brief historical reference. As is very well known, the Soviet concept of gross social product and national income is quite different from the Western concept. This complicates the analysis of the Soviet economy and makes international comparisons next to impossible. About two decades ago A. Bergson worked out a special model of accounting for Soviet GNP (gross national product) on the basis of Western theory, made interesting calculations and published results of this work in a very well-known book.[2] After several years another book on the subject, by A. Becker, was published.[3] Here, the model was further developed; a lot of new statistical information was used, and calculations were made for years following those covered by Bergson's calculations. Then, as we may conclude from the literature, economists of the Office of Economic Research of the CIA made calculations for a later period, in particular for 1970.[4]

I must say that I have a very high opinion of the authors of all these works and of their results. Having lived in the West for a few years,

I have familiarized myself more or less with the works of Sovietologists on economics (of course, in the USSR this was impossible—all such literature is strictly forbidden) and should say that this model is one of the best accomplishments. But, nothing is perfect, and there is room for improvement of this model. What particularly do I have in mind?

I said already that the purpose of the model is to describe the Soviet economy on the basis of Western economic concepts. At the same time the model serves (should serve) as a tool to cope with Soviet statistics. Lacking a lot of data and knowing that at least some of the data are not reliable, those who created the model and used it hoped that in their calculations they would be able somehow to check and crosscheck the data. I think that this was a very reasonable approach, and if, as we will see below, it does not work completely this way, nobody can be blamed—the task is too difficult.

To make the next explanations understandable, I should remind the reader that the model divides the economy into two sectors—private and public.[5] An important requirement is that the incomes and outlays of each sector must be balanced. Certainly, this requirement is very evident and natural by itself, but one thing should be emphasized here. Because of difficulties with statistical information, the balancing serves the aim mentioned above—cross-checking of the information. In particular, if balances in both sectors are achieved, we may hope that the information used is accurate enough. Having this in mind let us observe the results of the last calculations by the CIA of GNP for 1970.

In the private sector incomes are less than outlays. This fact should not surprise the reader; in our calculations (chapter (V) we found similar results with the monetary incomes and expenditures of the population. True, in calculations of GNP both monetary and non-monetary (in kind) incomes and expenditures (outlays) are taken into account, but this does not make much difference. In my calculations I used data published recently on the total monetary incomes of the population, but the question is still open—we cannot explain satisfactorily, or even unsatisfactorily, what the difference between these total official numbers and our own calculations of monetary incomes is.

Economists of the CIA could not solve the problem either; they "simply" equated total incomes to total outlays and included in their breakdown of the incomes a special item "Unidentified money income and statistical discrepancy"—11,039 million rubles.[6] This is more than 5 percent of the total income of the population, but in addition nobody can guarantee that the total outlays of the population are not underestimated. If this is so, then automatically the "unidentified money income" is even greater than 11 billion rubles.

In this connection, two comments. Firstly, now it is rather fashionable to talk about the so-called "second Soviet economy." Theoretically speaking if we manage to estimate somehow its real magnitude it will lead to correcting many numbers in our calculations of the incomes and outlays of the population. At the same time, I think that the final results would not be changed dramatically. Indeed, a very big part of the second economy is *transactions* within the population; therefore these transactions will at the same time and at the same rate change both incomes and outlays. (See also note 48 in chapter VI.)

Secondly, it seems that the issue about the enormous savings of the population "in stockings" (chapter VII) must be somehow considered in this connection. It may be that my estimates of the amount of these savings are in error—I cannot insist on the numbers—but the savings are very very large; this is beyond reasonable doubt.

To conclude, the calculations for the private sector are far from perfect, and it is difficult to rely on them.

Now let us turn to an even more complicated question about the public sector. While in the private sector total outlays were used as a control total (because they happened to be higher than incomes), in the public sector it was done in just the opposite way. The reason is that the outlays of the public sector include military expenditures, which—we discussed this in chapter I—are underestimated in Soviet publications. There is a possibility that military expenditures are hidden in other items of outlays, and we will soon return to this point. Nevertheless economists of the CIA were actually forced to take as a control total incomes and not outlays. In doing so they, of course, ran into the basic riddle of this book (I mentioned this fact in the preface), but they could not decode it (and therefore I had something to do and wrote this book). So, in the article of incomes of the public sector titled "Taxes and other payments to the budget," they placed a special item "miscellaneous charges"—22,792 million rubles,[7] or 11 percent of the total income of the sector. Thus, the total amount of incomes was calculated; then the total amount of all known expenditures was subtracted, and the net result—21,038 million rubles—was proclaimed as "outlays n.e.c. (defense, net export, and unidentified outlays) and statistical discrepancy.

One may think that the situation with the public sector is the same as with the private sector—there is a shortage of revenues here and that is why the item "miscellaneous charges" appeared in the calculations. In the final analysis this is true, but only in the final analysis. The reader of this book already knows; "miscellaneous charges" are identified and quantified in this book, they are no longer "miscellaneous." It seems then that the incomes and outlays of the public sector are balanced, but there are two "buts."

The first is that the balance is reached with the deficit of the budget, which means that a part of incomes is not real income. So, at least theoretically the question—can real outlays be balanced with artificial incomes, and how?—must be considered.

The second "but" is no less significant. The balance is reached with the presumption that military expenditures (plus even some others) are 21 billion rubles, which fully coincided with previous estimates of the CIA. But these estimates were very much underestimated and the CIA soon admitted so publicly, stating that in fact military expenditures of the USSR were 40–45 billion rubles (I repeat, we are talking about 1970).[8] Naturally a new question sprang up—how to coordinate this new estimate with the results of GNP calculations?

The answer was given in a special publication of the CIA, where an attempt was made to show that the difference between the old and new estimates of military expenditures is hidden in some other articles of budget expenses—mostly in science (8 billion rubles) and investment (5 billion rubles). In addition, a part of the difference (6 billion rubles) is explained by revenues from foreign trade.[9]

I think that indeed the budget appropriations for science and investments, as well as some expenses of enterprises for science, partially are going directly or indirectly for the military build-up. But the point about foreign trade revenues here is a mistake. The reader knows that foreign trade revenues are a part of the gap in budget revenues, so they are included in the "miscellaneous charges" in the GNP model. And because of this fact the same money cannot simultaneously be used in the model as an additional source of military expenditures.

So, in the CIA explanations at least 6 billion rubles are not really explained. But even with these 6 billion rubles the total amount of military expenditures that they accounted for is only 40 billion rubles—the lowest level of the new range of these expenditures.

Why do I describe all this? Because, as I think, the riddle can be resolved at least partially on the basis of some of my conclusions.

I will repeat, but now for the last time, that in my opinion a part of military expenditures is funded at the expense of an even bigger budget deficit than was shown in chapter X. So, I suggest that this hypothesis be considered.

And the final suggestion: It seems to me that it would be useful to divide the public sector of the model into two parts. One—all enterprises and organizations—and another—the state (the Ministry of Finance and banks). It is not just a technical matter; if this is done the model will show interactions between the state and enterprises, in particular, bank credits. And when all these financial flows are shown, something, let us hope, will be much more clear.

On this optimistic note I conclude the book.

Notes

1. My manuscript was already finished when I reread a book by one of the best Soviet economists—I. S. Malyshev. The author was for many years the first deputy of a chief of the USSR Central Statistical Administration. Here is what he wrote more than 10 years ago:

> In the author's opinion, a disproportion, which has the most negative effect on the process of expanded reproduction in our national economy, is the excess of money in circulation (cash, and, equivalently, credit) compared with the total amount of material resources in the economy. This disproportion manifests itself most noticeably in the relation of monetary incomes of the population to the volumes of retail trade turnover of consumer goods . . . . a conciliatory attitude has also become widespread in the sphere of circulation of the means of production towards the disproportion between the amount of money and the amount of those material goods, the turnover of which is served by money. When plans are being worked out and in real practice, shortages of material products—even of such products as bricks, clay and sand—are always encountered. But shortages of money and financial resources are much more rare and not nearly as acute . . ..
>
> Thus, the country constantly experiences a 'goods famine' both for consumer goods and for the means of production . . . . The disproportion between money circulation and the turnover of material resources leads to various negative consequences. First of all, as a result of the shortage of material resources in comparison with monetary and financial resources, the improvement of the quality of goods produced is becoming an insoluble problem. The lack of goods to match the monetary income of the population weakens material incentives and, in addition to other negative consequences, leads to a decline in the rate of growth of labor productivity. The lack of goods to match the money appropriated for capital construction and for current production expenditures unavoidably disrupts the established plans and introduces elements of disorganization into the process of production. All of this restrains the growth of socialist production.

(Malyshev, *Vazhneyshiye,* 1968, pp. 20–21.)

2. A. Bergson, *The Real,* 1961.
3. A. Becker, *Soviet,* 1969.
4. CIA, *USSR,* 1975.
5. The latter includes state and collective farms, cooperatives, etc. It seems that dividing the public sector in two—state and all the rest—would improve the model. See also below.
6. CIA, *USSR,* 1975, p. 3.
7. Ibid., p. 5.
8. CIA, *Estimated,* 1976. I think (it is intuition, not knowledge) that these figures should be rather close to the truth.
9. CIA, *USSR,* 1978, pp. 12–13.

Appendix A

Profits of "Other" Sectors

As has been pointed out in chapter III, it is difficult to explain the gap in the amounts being received by the budget as payments from profits and the breakdown of these amounts by sectors in the *Byudzhet* handbooks.[1] A natural question is from where, from which sectors these additional profits come. The sectors industry and construction, agriculture, transportation, communication, housing and trade are already shown. In table A-1 this gap is compared with amounts of profits of "other sectors" in the *Narkhoz* yearbooks. The latter (with the exception of 1961) are always less in spite of the fact that only a part of the entire amount of the profits of the "other sectors" can be paid into the budget. In other words, profits of the "other sectors" in the *Narkhoz* yearbooks cannot explain the gap being considered.

We can only guess at the principle underlying the breakdown of sectors in the tables of the *Byudzhet* handbooks that show the distribution of payments to the budget from profits.[2] Therefore, for comparison in column 5 of table A-1 I cite the values of profit for supply and sales, since it is possible (although not very likely) that these amounts are included in the gap. It turns out that even if this is so, for many years the total amount of the profits for "other sectors" and for supply and sales is less than the gap in *Byudzhet* handbooks.

It is possible that profits in the *Narkhoz* handbooks are shown for "economic sectors," and not for sectors defined on an establishment basis, and this may explain the existence of the difference.

Notes

1. For example, *Byudzhet 76*, p. 8.

2. At the same time it is quite clear that there is no special reporting on this and the breakdown is made by workers of the Ministry of Finance. They almost certainly make this breakdown by ministries. It is possible that the payments of some enterprises and subsectors with a departmental affiliation that differs greatly from its real production purpose may be included in this gap.

Table A-1. Comparison of the Payments from Profits to the Budget and the Total Amount of the Profit of "Other Sectors" (in billions of rubles)

Year	Payments to the budget from profits: Total	Sum of sectoral values reported	Gap	Profit of "other" sectors	Profit of supply and trade sectors (for comparison)
	1	2	3	4	5
1960	18.6	16.9	1.7	1.6	0.8
1961	20.7	18.9	1.8	1.9	1.0
1962	23.9	21.7	2.2	1.9	1.2
1963	25.7	23.1	2.6	1.5	1.3
1964	28.7	25.3	3.4	1.9	1.3
1965	30.9	27.5	3.4	1.9	0.9
1966	35.7	30.9	4.8	2.1	1.7
1967	41.8	36.4	5.4	2.2	2.2
1968	48.0	44.3	3.7	1.9	2.9
1969	48.0	44.5	3.5	1.7	1.6
1970	54.2	50.3	3.9	1.8	1.7
1971	55.6	51.7	3.9	2.2	2.2
1972	60.0	55.8	4.2	2.3	2.5
1973	60.0	55.4	4.6	2.6	2.7
1974	64.4	59.2	5.2	3.0	2.7
1975	69.7	63.7	6.0	3.4	3.0

Sources: Columns 1 and 2:
1970–75—*Byudzhet 76,* p. 8
1965–69—*Byudzhet 72,* p. 11
1960–64—*Byudzhet 66,* p. 10
Column 3:
column 1 less column 2

Columns 4 and 5:
1965, 1970–75—*Narkhoz 75,* p. 725
1960, 1969—*Narkhoz 70,* p. 703
1966–68—*Narkhoz 68,* p. 743
1964—*Narkhoz 65,* p. 757
1963—*Narkhoz 64,* p. 747
1962—*Narkhoz 63,* p. 637
1961—*Narkhoz 62,* p. 627.

Appendix B

Monetary Income and Expenditures of the Population

This question has already been examined in detail in Western literature, particularly in a recently published work.[1] While rating this work very highly, I have nevertheless made my own calculations, which are presented below, for the following reasons.

First, the question is extremely important, but the results obtained by all of us in calculating the income of the population are unsatisfactory. As the reader will soon see, either we are all greatly mistaken about something or there are some deliberate distortions in the Soviet statistics. Additional efforts are needed to solve the riddle, and I have attempted (unfortunately, not very successfully) to exert these efforts. Secondly, in my calculations I have adjusted some estimates and used some new sources. Thirdly, I need these calculations for the analysis of problems both in the text of the appendix and in the text of the book itself.

Since we do not have much of the necessary data, I am forced in this appendix to make many of the calculations starting with 1960.

Let us begin with the *income*. It is appropriate to divide it into that part for which we have more or less reliable direct data (even if we do not have them for all years) and that part for which we have to resort to estimates. In table B-1, I have gathered data on the former.

The amounts paid to workers and employees (*rabochiye* and *sluzhashchiye)* as wages are of most importance here. It is very noteworthy that not once in any source have data been published on the total wage fund for all the workers and employees, although data on the wage fund for industry have been published.[2] Therefore it is necessary to calculate this fund as the product of the average annual number of workers and employees and their average monthly wage, which is done in table B-1.

Let us ask a simple and quite natural question—why is this so; why are data on the wage fund for the national economy never published? Perhaps the explanation is that the published indicators of the average wage include payments which have nothing to do with wages—see below.

Table B-1. Estimates of Monetary Incomes of the Population for Which there are Published Data (in billions of rubles)

Year	Number of workers and employees (millions)	Monthly wages (rubles)	Wage fund	Pensions	Grants	Stipends	Interest on deposits at savings banks	Old bonds	Total
	1	2	3	4	5	6	7	8	9
1940	33.9	33.1	13.5	0.3	0.5	0.2	0.03	—	14.5
1950	40.4	64.2	31.1	2.4	1.2	0.5	0.1	—	35.3
1955	50.3	71.8	43.3	4.0	1.9	0.5	0.2	—	49.9
1960	62.0	80.6	60.0	7.1	2.6	0.6	0.3	—	70.6
1961	65.9	83.9	66.3	7.7	2.7	0.6	0.3	—	77.6
1962	68.3	86.7	71.1	8.2	2.9	0.7	0.3	—	83.2
1963	70.5	88.2	74.6	8.9	3.1	0.7	0.3	—	87.6
1964	73.3	90.8	79.9	9.5	3.3	0.8	0.4	—	93.9
1965	76.9	96.5	89.1	10.6	3.5	0.9	0.4	—	104.5
1966	79.7	100.2	95.8	11.8	3.9	1.0	0.5	—	113.0
1967	82.3	104.7	103.4	12.6	4.3	1.1	0.6	—	122.0
1968	85.1	112.7	115.1	14.0	4.8	1.2	0.7	—	135.8
1969	87.9	116.9	123.3	15.0	5.3	1.3	0.9	—	145.8
1970	90.2	122.0	132.1	16.2	6.1	1.3	1.1	—	156.8
1971	92.8	125.9	140.2	18.0	6.3	1.4	1.2	—	167.1
1972	95.2	130.2	148.7	19.8	6.5	1.5	1.4	—	177.9
1973	97.5	134.9	157.8	20.8	7.0	1.9	1.6	—	189.1
1974	99.8	141.1	169.0	22.1	7.3	2.1	1.8	1.0	203.3
1975	102.2	145.8	178.8	24.4	9.2	2.2	2.1	1.2	217.9
1976	104.2	151.4	189.3	25.7	9.9	2.2	2.4	1.2	230.7
1977	106.4	155.2	198.2	27.1	10.0	2.3	2.7	1.2	241.5
1978	108.6	159.9	208.4	28.9	10.2	2.4	3.0	1.2	254.1

Table B-1 continued

Sources: Column 1:
1940, 1950, 1955, 1960, 1965, 1970, 1975–78—*Narkhoz 78*, p. 365
1971–74—*Narkhoz 76*, p. 461
1961–64, 1966–69—*Narkhoz 70*, p. 509

Column 2:
1940, 1950, 1955, 1960, 1965, 1970, 1975–78—*Narkhoz 78*, p. 372
1971–74—*Narkhoz 76*, p. 472
1961–64, 1966–69—*Narkhoz 70*, p. 519

Column 3:
column 1 multiplied by column 2 multiplied by 12 divided by 1,000

Column 4:
1940, 1965, 1970, 1975–78—*Narkhoz 78*, p. 390
1971–74—*Narkhoz 75*, p. 744
1950, 1960, 1969—*Narkhoz 70*, p. 537
1968—*Narkhoz 69*, p. 771
1966–67—*Narkhoz 68*, p. 776
1964—*Narkhoz 65*, p. 783
1963—*Narkhoz 64*, p. 772
1962—*Narkhoz 62*, p. 639
1961—*Narkhoz 61*, p. 765
1955—estimated taking into account two facts: pensions in 1958 were 6.4 billion rubles (*Narkhoz 65*, p. 783); the revision of pensions took place after 1955

Columns 5 and 6:
1940, 1965, 1970, 1975–78—*Narkhoz 78*, p. 390
1971–74—*Narkhoz 75*, p. 568
1950, 1960, 1969—*Narkhoz 70*, p. 537
1955, 1961–64, 1966–68—estimated by interpolation

Column 7:
1940, 1950, 1955—3.5 percent of column 3 table VII-1
all the rest—2.3 percent of column 3, table VII-1

Column 8:
1973–78—CIA, *The Soviet*, 1977, p. 18
1960–74—the population had negligible income from old bonds.
1940, 1950, 1955—I had no data and ignored these amounts.

Column 9:
sum of columns 3–8.

However, this explanation can serve as an official excuse but cannot be the real reason since the payments that have nothing to do with the wage fund could simply be shown separately. Taking into account that, as we will see below, we do not have "enough" income, I am inclined to the opinion that the real reason is that the published indicators of the number of workers and employees are understated.

A detailed examination of this question would take us far afield; therefore I will be very brief. First of all note that the standard indicators of the average registered number of workers and employees and the data on the number of workers and employees according to the 1970 census are clearly inconsistent with each other, and most of the disagreements are evident in the comparison not of the overall indicators, but of the subtotals. Further, as one might think, the average registered number of workers and employees does not include the prisoners working at camps (although this is disputable), as well as the personnel of the KGB and the MVD (I am almost certain of this). And the last point relevant here: A. Tretyakova has noted strange gaps in some totals for basic economic indicators such as the values of industrial output, amortization and so on. Her hypothesis, which merits testing, is that the figures for some defense sectors have been removed from all the published indicators, and it is quite possible that the corresponding figures are not included in any totals.[3] If this is indeed the case, the number of personnel in the corresponding sectors is also not included in the published data.

Later, in analyzing the results of our calculations, we will return again to this question; for the time being let us follow the published indicators on employment and the average wages. These data are not available for all years,[4] and some of the previously published data were subsequently adjusted.[5] I used the figures from the later publications.

As to pensions, I took the data on them from the tables in the *Narkhoz* yearbooks, which indicate the payment of pensions "from all sources" and not only the pensions paid from social insurance funds.[6] Up to a certain time the data on the payment of pensions "from all sources" were not published, but the notes to the table "Expenditures for the Budget of State Social Insurance" indicated the "total amount of expenditures on pensions from social insurance funds and the state budget."[7] In this phrase not one word is said about the pensions paid by kolkhozes. True, at the time kolkhoz pensions were quite small, but nevertheless a certain inaccuracy here is quite possible. Just as with the average wage there are some small inconsistencies in the data on pensions in the different yearbooks. For table B-1, I took the latest publications.

As to the indicators of grants and stipends, they have not been published for all the years of interest to us. Therefore, I had to interpolate the indicators for 1961–64 and 1966–69 according to the trend.

I used the data on grants (*posobiye*) "from all sources," and not only on those which are paid from social insurance funds.[8] There are data on the latter for all years, but they are substantially less than "all grants." In addition to grants from social insurance funds, probably also funeral subsidies and so-called material assistance should be included here. Moreover, the grants "from all sources" should include the amounts paid to kolkhoz farmers. Finally, I believe that the amounts of the so-called lump-sum assistance (*yedinovremennaya pomoshch'*), paid from the economic stimulation fund, is included precisely in the grants "from all sources"—see below.

I have not found other data on stipends except those cited in table B-1. It is not entirely clear which stipends are included here; in particular, are the stipends which are paid neither at higher educational institutions nor at tekhnikums included here? However, first, it is very likely that "all" stipends are shown, and secondly, even if this is not so, the corresponding amounts cannot be significant on the scale of our calculations.

The next type of income of the population, which is assuming increasing significance and which we can calculate quite accurately, is the interest on deposits at savings banks. The amounts of the deposits at savings banks (as well as at Gosbank) at the end of each corresponding year are cited in table VII-1. Savings banks pay 2 percent per annum on regular deposits and 3 percent on deposits held for a period of not less than 6 months, which is why they are called "time" deposits. Let us assume that on the average 2.3 percent is paid.[9] Since earlier the interest was higher (3 and 5 percent respectively) for 1940, 1950 and 1955 let us take this interest to be equal to 3.5 percent.

Finally, in column 8 we take into account the amounts of payments on "old" state loans; the loans were frozen at the end of the 1950s, but beginning in 1974 the state started to pay back its old debt.

Thus in column 9 of table B-1 we obtained the total of those monetary incomes of the population for which we can base our calculations mainly on data from the *Narkhoz* yearbooks and other official data. Let us now deal in table B-2 with the estimates of the income for which we do not have the corresponding data.

We will turn first to the monetary income of kolkhoz farmers. A portion of them—pensions, grants, interest on deposits at savings banks—has already been taken into account; we must only calculate their pay from the kolkhozes, as well as income from the sale of the

Table B-2. Estimate of Some Monetary Incomes of the Population (in billions of rubles)

Year	Payments to kolkhoz farmers								
	Total	Percent of monetary payments	Total monetary payments	Sale of produce	Traveling expenses	Personnel of MVD and KGB	Insurance amounts	Army	Total
	1	2	3	4	5	6	7	8	9
1960	7.4	62	4.6	1.9	1.2	0.9	0.1	3.4	12.1
1961	7.9	65	5.1	2.1	1.3	0.9	0.1	3.3	12.8
1962	8.5	68	5.8	2.3	1.4	0.9	0.2	3.3	13.9
1963	9.3	72	6.7	2.5	1.5	1.0	0.2	3.2	15.1
1964	10.2	76	7.8	2.7	1.6	1.0	0.2	3.2	16.5
1965	11.5	79.4	9.1	2.8	1.8	1.0	0.3	3.2	18.2
1966	12.8	85	10.9	3.2	1.9	1.0	0.4	3.2	20.6
1967	13.7	89	12.2	3.5	2.1	1.0	0.4	3.3	22.5
1968	14.3	90	12.9	3.8	2.3	1.1	0.5	3.3	23.9
1969	14.1	91	12.8	4.1	2.5	1.1	0.6	3.3	24.4
1970	15.0	93.6	14.0	4.4	2.6	1.1	0.8	3.3	26.2
1971	15.3	95	14.5	5.0	2.8	1.1	1.0	3.5	27.9
1972	15.6	98	15.3	5.0	3.0	1.1	1.3	3.5	29.2
1973	16.6	99	16.4	5.8	3.2	1.2	1.5	3.5	31.6
1974	17.1	99	16.9	6.6	3.4	1.2	2.2	3.6	33.9
1975	16.7	99	16.5	6.6	3.6	1.2	2.4	3.8	34.1
1976	17.5	99	17.3	6.3	3.8	1.2	2.6	3.8	35.0
1977	18.2	99	18.0	6.1	4.0	1.3	2.9	3.9	36.2
1978	18.6	99	18.4	5.9	4.2	1.3	3.2	3.9	36.9

Table B-2 continued

Sources: Column 1:

1965, 1970, 1975–78—*Narkhoz 78*, p. 261
1971–74—*Narkhoz 75*, p. 414
1960, 1969—*Narkhoz 70*, p. 383
1968—*Narkhoz 69*, p. 397
1966–67—*Narkhoz 68*, p. 423
1961–64, interpolation

Column 2:

1965, 1970—Zhurikov and Solomakhin, *Spravochnik*, 1973, p. 10; all the remaining years are by extrapolation or interpolation

Column 3:

column 1 multiplied by column 2 divided by 100

Column 4:

appendix C

Column 5:

2 percent of column 3 of table B-1

Column 6:

appendix E

Columns 7 and 8:

1960, 1965–75—Schroeder and Severin, "Soviet," 1976, p. 653
1961–64, 1976–78—by interpolation or extrapolation

Column 9:

sum of columns 3–8.

products of their private plots to the state and cooperatives. We do not need to take into account the monetary income of kolkhoz farmers and the rest of the rural population from the sale of produce to other groups of the population, since we will not further consider the corresponding monetary expenditures of these other groups of the population.

As to the income of kolkhoz farmers from kolkhozes, the yearbooks give summary data on payments both in money and in kind, but even these data are not available for 1961–64,[10] and I calculated them by interpolation. In one source[11] data are cited on share of the monetary payments for 1965 and 1970. Using these, I calculated the shares of monetary payments for 1966–69 (column 2 of table B-2) by interpolation, taking into account that in 1966–67 an abrupt increase in payments took place.[12] There was also an increasing trend for this share in 1960–64.[13] I also took the share of monetary income during 1971–78 arbitrarily according to the trend.[14] Some questions here remain unclear,[15] but on the whole, I believe, there should be no great errors.[16]

A very difficult question is the income of kolkhoz farmers as well as that of other rural inhabitants from the sale of produce to the state. There are no direct data on this in the literature, and this income must be calculated indirectly. This is done in appendix C; the end results of these calculations are cited in column 4 of table B-2.

Above in table B-1 we calculated the value of the wage fund of workers and employees, but this does not include all the compensation for their labor. According to the so-called "Methodological Explanations" in the yearbooks,[17] the indicators we calculated are not, strictly speaking, the indicators of the wage fund. On the one hand, the value of the average monthly wage that we used to calculate the wage fund includes "... the cost of free apartments, municipal services, products and items ... which are valued at state retail prices," as well as "amounts paid from the material incentive fund (except for lump-sum assistance), one-time and other bonuses which are not included in the wage fund." On the other hand, these indicators apparently do not include the payments to the so-called supernumerary staff (*nespisochnyy sostav*), or as they are still called, the "peopleless fund," or, for short, the *bezlyudka*. Let us try to work all this out.

As to the value of the payments in kind, I have not found any data for the appropriate calculation. We know that free apartments are given to the teachers of rural schools, but free state apartments and municipal services for other workers must be rather rare. It is also not very clear how to estimate the expenditures on special work clothing and "special food," although intuitively it seems to me that here are several hundred million rubles annually.

In the analysis of wages in an interesting and quite qualified work,[18] this is not mentioned at all, and I cannot understand this. At the same time, the author comes to the conclusion that in addition to the wage fund, which is calculated in the same way as we did this, in 1970 1.5 billion rubles were spent in industry alone. Unfortunately, his entire analysis is not very convincing, especially of the amount of the *bezlyudka,* since this figure for industry seems overstated to me.[19] More from helplessness than for any really good reasons, for our further calculations I take the amounts of the *bezlyudka* to be equal to the amounts of the payments in kind and therefore will not adjust the values of the wage of workers and employees that are calculated in table B-1.

As to the amounts paid from the economic stimulation funds, the above-cited passage from the "Methodological Explanations" states that only the amounts of "lump-sum assistance" are not included in the wage fund. I have already noted that the amounts of lump-sum assistance should be included in the amounts of the grants "from all sources"; therefore we should not take them into account separately. All the same, I estimate the approximate amounts of these grants in appendix D. The main purpose of this estimate is to demonstrate that even if I am mistaken, that is, if in fact the lump-sum assistance is not included in the amounts of grants "from all sources," the corresponding error cannot be very great. Therefore, incidentally, in these calculations I have tended to overstate the approximate indicators used.

The next type of monetary income of the population is travelling expenses and similar payments.[20] In the literature I found only one estimate of them, and then only for industry:[21] "the other monetary payments to workers and employees (such as travelling expenses, relocation allowances, and others) are estimated 'expertly' at 3 percent of wages." To verify this expert estimate,[22] let us make the following calculation. Assume that 5 million people[23] take business trips three times a year; each business trip lasts 10 days. Thus, their per diem expenses are (at 2.6 rubles a day) 390 million rubles, while their lodging expenses (at 1.6 rubles a day) are 240 million rubles. Let us assume further that the cost of transportation per trip in both directions is 50 rubles, i.e., another 750 million rubles. In all we obtain something on the order of 1.5 billion rubles a year. On the other hand, if we take the estimate of 3 percent of the wages for the entire economy, we obtain for 1965, 1970 and 1975 correspondingly 2.7, 4 and 5.4 billion rubles.

It is more or less clear that the relocation allowances, the field pay and other similar payments should total substantially less than the travelling expenses themselves. It is quite possible that in my calculation of the expenditures on business trips I underestimated the number of people taking business trips and perhaps their travelling expenses as well. Let us note in this connection that all expenditures on passenger transport in 1965, 1970 and 1975 were 4.9, 7.2 and 10.5 billion rubles.[24] According to estimates made at my request by A. Tretyakova,[25] it turns out that approximately half of these amounts are expenditures on rail and air transport. We can roughly assume that not less than half of these amounts represent payments of travelling expenses. This means that the transportation component of travelling expenses for the years in question should be approximately 1.2, 1.8 and 2.6 billion rubles.

It seems to me that everything is in order if we take into account that the expert estimate in question pertains to industry where there are considerably more business trips than in other sectors, especially agriculture, trade, and the sectors of the so-called nonmaterial production. On this basis I take the travelling expenses as 2 percent of the wage fund. I cannot in any way assert that this indicator is well-founded, but no better one is at hand.

Since this is a matter of quite large amounts, it is also appropriate to question whether the same percentage should be applied to the wage fund for all years. Against this is the fact that compaigns to reduce travelling expenses have been conducted constantly; the special limits on them have been reduced in every way. It is also quite important that all the rates of payments for business trips—per diems, lodging expenses, the payment for transportation—are in effect not dependent on the increase of wages. However, there are some contrary circumstances. Not only is the number of workers and employees and their wages increasing, which is directly reflected in the amounts of field, waterless, high mountain and relocation allowances, but the number of those categories of personnel that travel most extensively—scholars, authorities of all sorts, suppliers, workers of planning and installation organizations, geologists—is increasing, and quite intensively. Since 1960 the scope of the retraining of personnel has been increasing very rapidly, and hundreds of millions of rubles are being spent on their trips to the places of training. It is also significant that the proportion of trips by the most expensive type of transportation—by air—is steadily increasing.[26]

Therefore on the whole I think that it is possible without the risk of a very significant error to take an identical percentage for all years, and this was done in table B-2.

The question of the wages of prisoners is not very clear to me. Above I have already noted that, in my opinion, the number of working prisoners is not included in the published indicators of the average registered number of workers and employees. In chapter IV, I rejected the possibility that the revenues from the exploitation of the labor of prisoners are included in the budget revenues. As to the payments to prisoners for their labor, I believe that the corresponding amounts are included in the published indicators of the average wage. The reasons are as follows. In the Soviet system, all the payments to prisoners should certainly be controlled just as rigidly as any other payments of money to the population. The most widespread form of this control is the limiting of payments by means of specially approved plan indicators of the wage fund. Since the camps are run on a cost-accounting basis, there are no grounds to believe that any special forms of planning are applicable with respect to them—they are assigned a plan for the output of products and the appropriate wage fund should be given "for this plan." Actually we know this from the extensive literature (including Soviet) on the camps, in which it is stated that payments are made at the camps according to orders (*naryady*), that there are planners and so forth there.

Below we will examine the payments to the staff of the MVD and the KGB, and I believe that these payments are not included in the published indicators of the average wage. The point is that an examination of the breakdown of the average registered number of workers and employees, as well as the average wage, does not reveal a place for the personnel of the MVD and the KGB. But as to the prisoners the situation is much simpler—they can be shown in the sectors for which they actually work, primarily logging. It is natural to ask why I believe that the payments to prisoners are included in the calculation of the average wage, while their number is excluded from publications? The point is that the figures on wages are controlled very rigidly—in particular the bank will not issue money for wages without specifically formulated authorizations—while with respect to the number of workers there is no such rigid control. However, if I am mistaken in my assumptions, it is most likely with respect to the number, and not to the wages, and just the latter concern us here.

It is well known that prisoners are issued only a portion of their wage,[27] but the entire amount should pass through the wage fund if only for the technical but quite important reason that all of their wages should be subject to taxes.

For all these reasons, I assume that we should not take

the amounts of the wages of prisoners into account separately.[28]

I have already noted above that, in my opinion, the monetary income of the personnel of the KGB and the MVD is not taken into account in the published data. In appendix E, I make the corresponding estimate. It is based not on any even imprecise data, but simply on some ideas and approximate notions. Nevertheless I hope that there cannot be a great error here. Even if I am mistaken, that is, if the number of personnel of both these agencies is included in the published employment data, then as a result I am overstating the monetary income of the population, but in no way am I understating it. Meanwhile, as we will see, it is income that we "do not have enough" of, and not expenditures.

The next type of monetary income of the population is the monetary payments to servicemen. I could have made my own estimate, but I preferred to use an existing one.[29] Three things about this estimate bother me a little:

(*a*) it is not clear why there is a sharp drop in this estimate from 1955 to 1960. True, the size of the army at the time did actually decrease, but the reduction all the same seems too great;
(*b*) to all appearances the introduction of two new ranks (*praporshchik* and *michman*) are not reflected in this estimate;
(*c*) it is difficult to believe that during the 16 years from 1960 to 1975 the total amount of payments virtually did not change.

However, the pay of the army is quite low and a considerable increase of this estimate would require the assumption that the size of the Soviet army is very substantially larger.

Insurance of various types has a rapidly increasing role in the monetary income and expenditures of the population. There is extensive literature on this, and in principle it would be possible to study it in considerable detail, but this requires a substantial amount of time. Because I do not have it, I took the estimate of the expenditures of the population on the payment for various types of insurance from the work just cited.[30]

I do not examine and do not take into account here a number of other incomes, since they play a virtually negligible role. Among them are the profits distributed among the members of consumers cooperatives, lottery winnings[31] and so forth.

All the monetary income of the population, as it calculated, is summarized in table B-3 and the values obtained are compared with the only official publication of this indicator.[32]

The table clearly shows that the share of the incomes we estimated

Table B-3. Summary of the Monetary Income of the Population (in billions of rubles)

Year		"Exact" income	According to estimate	Total	According to the *Narkhoz* yearbook	Difference
		1	2	3	4	5
1960		70.6	12.1	82.7	87.4	4.7
1961		77.6	12.8	90.4	95.5	5.1
1962		83.2	13.9	97.1	102.6	5.5
1963		87.6	15.1	102.7	108.5	5.8
1964		93.9	16.5	110.4	116.7	6.3
1965		104.5	18.2	122.7	129.7	7.0
	Total of 1961–65			523.3	553.0	29.7
1966		113.0	20.6	133.6	140.3	6.7
1967		122.0	22.5	144.5	151.8	7.3
1968		135.8	23.9	159.7	167.8	8.1
1969		145.8	24.4	170.2	178.8	8.6
1970		156.8	26.2	183.0	192.3	9.3
	Total of 1966–70			791.0	831.0	40.0
1971		167.1	27.9	195.0	206.6	11.6
1972		177.9	29.2	207.1	219.4	12.3
1973		189.1	31.6	220.7	233.8	13.1
1974		203.3	33.9	237.2	251.3	14.1
1975		217.9	34.1	252.0	266.9	14.9
	Total of 1971–75			1,112.0	1,178.0	66.0
1976		230.7	35.0	265.7	281.5	15.8
1977		241.5	36.2	277.7	294.2	16.5
1978		254.1	36.9	291.0	307.8	16.8

Sources: Column 1: table B-1
Column 2: table B-2
Column 3: sum of columns 1 and 2
Column 4: totals for 1961–65, 1966–70 and 1971–75 *Narkhoz 75*, p. 55
All individual years are in proportion to the ratios of the totals for the five-year periods in columns 3 and 4. The 1961–65 ratio was used for 1960, and the 1971–75 ratio was used for 1976–78.
Column 5: column 4 less column 3.

(shown in table B-2) is relatively small. In other words, even if we were very substantially mistaken about some estimates here, this could not have radically influenced the overall results. Nevertheless the total indicators of the income of the population we obtained are substantially less than the official data. Hence we are making a definite mistake somewhere. Where?

It is significant that the gap between the official amounts of income and the amounts we calculated increases in absolute size but, roughly speaking, is approximately the same percentage; that is, our error to all appearances is of a regular nature.

In principle we should not entirely reject the possibility that precisely our indicators, and not the cited official data, are correct, but this is unlikely. In this case it would mean that the population regularly spends more than it receives (see below), and this contradicts all our notions of real Soviet life. Thus, it is necessary to find the error in our calculations.

The suggestion that Soviet publications understate the amounts of pensions and grants is improbable, and the suggestion that they understate the amounts of stipends is almost as improbable.

The population receives the most income in the form of wages. The indicator of the average wage has a serious propagandistic importance and it would sooner be more than less. But concerning the number of workers and employees, as I have already indicated above, there are very serious doubts. At the same time, the amounts of the gaps are so great that they can be explained (by accepting the official indicators of the average wage) only by assuming that the actual number of workers and employees was approximately 6 million greater in 1961–1970 and even 9 million greater in 1971–1975—too much.

On the whole it seems that the gaps obtained can be explained only by a set of different causes. It is necessary to look in the income of kolkhoz farmers,[33] perhaps in travelling expenses, and almost certainly in the pay of servicemen.

Let us turn now to the monetary *expenditures* of the population (table B-4). Here we are forced to make all types of estimates and to resort to indirect evidence.

The expenditures on the purchase of goods in the retail trade network—the indicators of the retail commodity turnover—constitute the bulk of the monetary expenditures of the population. The data on the commodity turnover in state and cooperative trade in current prices are published regularly. When using these indicators for calculation of the population expenditures the following things must be taken into account:

(*a*) these indicators encompass all the retail commodity turnover of state and cooperative trade, including public dining, as well as in part some types of services—see below. They do not take into account kolkhoz market sales, the volume of which is quite significant; for

example, in 1978 it reached 6.2 billion rubles.[34] However, these are basically sales of produce by the population itself to other groups of the population, and therefore the corresponding amounts should not interest us since we did not take them into account in the income of the population. The share of kolkhozes in kolkhoz market sales is negligible, constituting only 3 percent,[35] and therefore for simplicity we can ignore the corresponding amounts in our estimates;
(b) the retail commodity turnover includes so-called commission sales of various industrial (nonfood) goods. These sales once again involve the transfer of funds from some groups of the population to others and should be excluded from the commodity turnover (with the exception of the 7-percent commission fee levied on resale).

I have not found figures on the volumes of commission trade in the literature.[36] In a comparatively recent book an arbitrary example is cited,[37] in which commission trade—"the turnover on the sale of nonfood consumer goods, which are accepted on commission and are bought from the population"—is approximately 0.5 percent of the total commodity turnover. From personal impressions it seems to me that this is quite correct. Let us take into account that nonfood consumer items constitute approximately 44 percent of the total commodity turnover,[38] that commission trade encompasses only a part of the list of nonfood consumer items, that the network of commission stores is not very large, that the sale of items acquired through special buying centers at very low prices constitutes a rather significant portion of this turnover. Therefore I think that we will not be very mistaken by taking the amounts of commission trade as 0.5 percent of the total commodity turnover and by ignoring for simplicity the commission fee;[39]
(c) an important point is that the values of the retail commodity turnover include the sales to enterprises, kolkhozes and enterprises by so-called small-scale wholesale trade.

Judging from the results of a special study made in 1969, the small-scale wholesale trade constitutes only 5 percent of the total commodity turnover.[40] In another work this figure is analyzed and confirmed, and it is indicated that in 1960 this proportion was equal to 6.8 percent.[41] Finally, a third work[42] indicates that according to the data of the Trade Statistics Department of the Central Statistical Administration: "The sale of goods to organizations, institutions and enterprises increased from 2.8 billion rubles in 1950 to 8 billion rubles in 1972, although the proportion of this commodity turnover in the total commodity turnover decreased during the same period from 7.9 to 4.6 percent." On the basis of all this I calculated in table B-4 the trend

Table B-4. Estimates of the Monetary Expenditures of the Population (in billions of rubles)

Year	Total retail commodity turnover	Commission trade	Percent of small-scale wholesale trade	Commodity turnover without small-scale wholesale trade	Total expenditures on commodity turnover	Payments to the budget	Services for a fee	Membership dues	Intra-village market	Gosstrakh	Increase of deposits at savings banks	Total
	1	2	3	4	5	6	7	8	9	10	11	12
1960	78.6	0.4	6.8	73.3	72.9	6.9	8.6	0.9		0.2	0.9	90.4
1961	81.1	0.4	6.6	75.7	75.3	7.1	9.0	1.0		0.2	0.8	93.4
1962	87.3	0.4	6.4	81.7	81.3	7.6	9.6	1.0		0.2	1.1	100.8
1963	91.7	0.5	6.2	86.0	85.5	8.1	10.3	1.1		0.3	1.2	106.5
1964	96.4	0.5	6.0	90.6	90.1	7.4	11.2	1.2		0.3	1.7	111.9
1965	104.8	0.5	5.8	98.7	98.2	8.4	12.1	1.3		0.4	3.0	123.4
1966	113.0	0.6	5.6	106.7	106.1	9.3	13.0	1.4		0.5	4.2	134.5
1967	123.6	0.6	5.4	116.9	116.3	10.1	14.0	1.5		0.6	4.0	146.5
1968	134.2	0.7	5.2	127.2	126.5	11.4	15.1	1.7		0.8	5.5	161.0
1969	144.4	0.7	5.0	137.2	136.5	12.6	16.1	1.8		1.2	6.0	174.2
1970	155.2	0.8	4.9	147.6	146.8	13.8	17.1	2.0		1.4	8.2	189.3
1971	165.6	0.8	4.7	157.8	157.0	14.7	18.0	2.1	0.1	1.9	6.6	200.4
1972	176.4	0.9	4.6	168.3	167.4	15.8	18.7	2.3	0.5	2.3	7.5	214.5
1973	185.7	0.9	4.5	177.3	176.4	16.9	19.7	2.4	1.0	3.1	7.9	227.4
1974	196.6	1.0	4.4	187.9	186.9	18.3	20.7	2.6	1.4	3.7	10.3	243.9
1975	210.4	1.0	4.3	201.4	200.4	19.7	21.8	2.8	1.6	4.5	12.1	262.9
1976	220.1	1.1	4.2	210.9	209.8	20.9	22.9	3.0	1.8	5.5	12.0	275.9
1977	230.6	1.2	4.2	220.9	219.7	22.1	24.0	3.1	2.0	6.6	13.7	291.2
1978	241.3	1.2	4.2	231.2	230.0	23.5	25.2	3.3	2.2	7.8	14.4	306.4

Sources: Column 1:
1965, 1970, 1975–78—*Narkhoz 78*, p. 429
1960, 1971–74—*Narkhoz 76*, p. 536
1961–64, 1966–69—*Narkhoz 70*, p. 577

Column 2:
0.5 percent of column 1

Column 3:
1972—Cheremisov, *Resursy*, 1976, p. 47; 1969, Zaytseva and Moroz, "Izucheniye," 1971, p. 37
1960—Ryauzov and Titel'baum, *Statistika*, 1976, p. 80
All other years are extrapolated or interpolated

Column 4:
(column 1 × (100—column 3))/100

Column 5:
column 4 less column 2

Column 6:
table I-3, column 1

Column 7:
appendix G

Column 8:
appendix H

Column 9:
1960–69—ignored as negligible
1974—Fefilov, "Vnutrikolkhoznuyu," 1976, p. 16
1971—Abaturov, *Ekonomika*, 1975, p. 190; *Narkhoz 72*, p. 573
The remaining years are interpolated or extrapolated

Column 10:
1960, 1965–75—Schroeder and Severin, "Soviet," 1976, p. 658
1961–64, 1976, by interpolation and extrapolation

Column 11:
table VII-1, column 4

Column 12:
sum of columns 5–11.

of this indicator (column 3). Nevertheless very serious doubts remain about the correctness of this. The point is (I have already mentioned this above) that as a result of all our calculations we will obtain a more than strange conclusion—the monetary expenditures of the population are regularly greater than its income. Since this obviously cannot be, we have to find out where we might have made a mistake, and first of all it is necessary to take note precisely of the large amounts, such as the commodity turnover.

More specifically. On the one hand, certain doubts remain about whether the indicators of the small-scale wholesale trade include entirely the expenditures on the food and uniforms of the army and prisoners. It is also not entirely clear whether the expenditures on food at hospitals, pioneer camps and so on are completely taken into account in the indicators of the small-scale wholesale trade. On the other hand, we have a recent direct statement by an author who regularly writes about trade, and this statement should not be simply overlooked: "As is known, the sales volumes of the small-scale wholesale trade constitutes about one-tenth of the retail commodity turnover."[43] The words "as is known" are not very comprehensible—in the literature the 1969 study mentioned above is persistently cited—but it is very tempting to believe this particular author;

(d) the question of reusable glass containers merits a special study. As is shown in appendix F, it is a question of billions of rubles.

One textbook asserts:

> For the purpose of improving the receipt of empty glass containers from the population, in determining the total volume of the commodity turnover the amount of the forthcoming trade receipts is reduced by the value of the glass containers, i.e., net prices are used in the plan of the commodity turnover.
>
> At the same time in determining the wages of workers of trade enterprises, the actual volume of the retail commodity turnover is increased by the value of the glass containers received from the population and turned over to suppliers. The amount of the additional award for the fulfillment and overfulfillment of the plan of the commodity turnover is increased accordingly.[44]

From this it follows that glass containers are not at all taken into account in the volume of the commodity turnover, but this is not entirely accurate. In an official source it is stated:[45] ". . . the retail commodity turnover includes: . . . the value of the empty glass containers sold and *not* [my italics] returned by the population."

This is described in most detail and, apparently, correctly in another source,[46] and based on all this I do not include the value of reusable glass containers in my estimates. Nevertheless I do not wish in any way to completely put aside the possibility that statisticians, in wishing to inflate the figure on the commodity turnover, in fact include in it billions of rubles of the value of containers.

Let us turn now to the other monetary expenditures of the population in excess of its expenditures on the commodity turnover.

The situation is the simplest with various payments to the state—above all, taxes of various types, the purchase of bonds, and state revenues from lotteries. We have already calculated these in the main text of the work, in table I-3.

The next important type of expenditures of the population is the payments for various types of services: for housing and municipal services, transportation services, communications services, domestic and entertainment services and so on. The data on the expenditures on all these services are contained in two quite reliable works, but in order to use them in our estimates some recalculations are needed, and they are done in appendix G.

In appendix H an estimate of different types of membership dues—party, trade union and others—is made as well.

While examining the indicators of the commodity turnover above, we took into account only the population's purchase of various goods in the state and cooperative trade network. In addition to this the population purchases some product at the so-called intravillage *(vnutriderevenskyy)* market. It is[47] "the sale of produce to kolkhoz farmers and other groups of the rural population by kolkhozes." And: "The intravillage market underwent development with the conversion of kolkhozes to the money form of pay. Its proportion increased from 1.3 percent in 1960 to 2.4 percent in 1971."

Unfortunately, from this quotation and from the entire context it is quite difficult to understand what this is a percentage of, and it is possible only to guess that it is a percentage of the so-called kolkhoz trade. Then this means that the sales volumes of the intravillage market were 48 and 98 million rubles in 1960 and 1971 respectively.[48] During the three years from 1971 through 1974 this volume increased 14-fold.[49] Moreover, as is indicated in the same source, until 1970 "the development of intrakolkhoz trade was restrained" by the fact that these products were received from kolkhoz farmers at state retail, and not at domestic prices. However, two other circumstances, apparently, explain everything. First, precisely at this time the pay in kind at kolkhozes had practically been eliminated; thus kolkhoz farmers were forced to buy produce at the "intrakolkhoz market." And second, "intrasovkhoz" trade was permitted only recently.

In table B-4, I take into account the population's expenditures at the intrakolkhoz market beginning only in 1971 and assume that in 1975–76 its volumes should not have increased substantially.

In the monetary income of the population we took into account the payments of various insurance amounts; accordingly here in the expenditures it is also necessary to take into account the amounts of various insurance payments. I take the amounts indicated in an already cited work.[50]

The last element of the monetary expenditures of the population to be taken into account in our estimates is the increase of the deposits in savings banks—table VII-1.

What confidence can we have in the figures we have calculated in table B-4? We have already seen that the values we derived on the income of the population were substantially less than the official indicators; therefore it is quite possible that we have not taken something into sufficient account here as well.[51]

For verification let us compare our indicators of the monetary expenditures of the population with the indicators of the national income which is used for personal consumption. (These data used to be published regularly in the yearbooks, but starting with *Narkhoz 76* they were dropped.) This comparison yields rather strange results. According to the definition

> . . . the personal consumption of the population consists of the consumption of goods purchased in state and cooperative trade and at the kolkhoz market, the consumption of products received for work at kolkhozes, the consumption of products obtained from private subsidiary farming, and that part of the value of housing, which corresponds to the annual wear.[52]

Not everything is crystal clear in this definition, but we can nevertheless do something. It is easiest of all to determine the consumption of the population from "the products . . . received for work at kolkhozes." This is done in table B-5 using the data we have available. True, we do not have data on the consumption of products of private subsidiary farming or on the amount of the annual depreciation of housing, but let us try to do without these data, understanding that together this is many billions of rubles.

If we simply compare the sum of the pay in kind at kolkhozes and the monetary expenditures of the population (column 4) with the national income used for personal consumption (column 1), it turns out that the latter amounts are smaller beginning in 1965. It is possible that the amounts paid to the budget (primarily taxes)—column 5—should be subtracted from the amounts of the monetary expenditures of the population. Let us also try to subtract from the monetary expenditures of the population the increases of deposits at savings banks—column 6—although this is debatable. We see that even in this case the total amount of all the expenditures of the population in 1975, disregarding consumption of goods from private subsidiary farming and disregarding the depreciation of housing, is approxim-

Table B-5. Comparison of the Monetary Expenditures of the Population with the Part of the National Income used for Personal Consumption (in billions of rubles)

Year	National income used for personal consumption	Expenditures of the population: Pay in kind at kolkhozes	Amount of monetary expen-ditures	Total	Less taxes and other payments to the budget	Less taxes and increase of saving deposits
	1	2	3	4	5	6
1960	93.9	2.8	90.4	93.2	86.3	85.4
1961	96.7	2.8	93.4	96.2	89.1	88.3
1962	105.0	2.7	100.8	103.5	95.9	94.8
1963	110.3	2.6	106.5	109.1	101.0	99.8
1964	115.5	2.4	111.9	114.3	106.9	105.2
1965	124.9	2.4	123.4	125.8	117.4	114.4
1966	133.2	1.9	134.5	136.4	127.1	122.9
1967	144.0	1.5	146.5	148.0	137.9	133.9
1968	155.2	1.4	161.0	162.4	151.0	145.5
1969	166.1	1.3	174.2	175.5	162.9	156.9
1970	177.9	1.0	189.3	190.3	176.5	168.3
1971	187.8	0.8	200.4	201.2	186.5	179.9
1972	198.1	0.3	214.5	214.8	199.0	191.5
1973	207.1	0.2	227.4	227.6	210.7	202.8
1974	218.1	0.2	243.8	244.0	225.7	215.4
1975	231.8	0.2	262.9	263.1	243.4	231.3

Sources: Column 1:
1965, 1970–75—*Narkhoz 75*, p. 565
1960, 1966–69—*Narkhoz 70*, p. 535
1964—*Narkhoz 65*, p. 592
1961–63—*Narkhoz 64*, p. 578
Column 2:
difference between columns 1 and 3 in table B-2
Column 3:
table B-4
Column 4:
sum of columns 2 and 3
Column 5:
column 4 less table B-4, column 6
Column 6:
column 5 less table B-4, column 11.

ately equal to the amount of the national income used for personal consumption. This, of course, should not be.

There are two possibilities. Either the indicators of the national income have been calculated by some means incomprehensible to us, or in our estimates we overstated the monetary expenditures of the population. Some additional checks here seem necessary.

Here it is important that if we have indeed overstated the monetary expenditures, then the balances of the money not spent by the population, which are specified in chapters VI and VII, should be even greater.

I have also attempted for verification to compare our data with figures on the percentage increase of the money turnover through Gosbank during 1970–75.[53] These data, unfortunately, are incomparable with ours for a number of reasons, above all because only the outlays of cash are indicated there, i.e., the corresponding noncash payments and outlays (the transfer of money through savings banks,[54] the payment for credits for the purchase of goods by transfers from wages, and so on) are not taken into account. For all my efforts, in all cases I obtained different percentages from calculations than those given in this source. For example, according to our data (table B-1) the payment of pensions and grants in 1975 was 150.7 percent of 1970, while according to the source in question it was considerably more—158.5 percent. I do not know how to explain this.[55]

It is also worth noting that according to the same data the total turnover of cash through the cashier's offices of Gosbank increased by 31.9 percent between 1970 and 1975. According to my estimates the total amount of the monetary expenditures of the population during the same period increased by 38.9 percent (table B-4). This would seem to say that the monetary savings of the population in cash should have decreased, but such a conclusion contradicts all the other information we have.

It is quite possible that there is something here that we do not correctly (or not entirely correctly) understand. Thus, in a very reliable work we read:

> ...during 1948–58 the turnover of the cash functioning in the sphere of the monetary income and expenditures of the population increased approximately 1.9-fold, while the flows of money passing through the cashier's offices of Gosbank and directly planned by it have increased more than twofold.[56]

How this can be, i.e., how can the turnover of cash in this entire sphere increase more rapidly than the flow of money through the cashier's offices of Gosbank, which are the only center of this turnover? This is absolutely unclear to me.[57] And how, incidentally, was the actual turnover of money not through the cashier's offices of Gosbank taken into account? If we were able to answer this question, we would be able to understand better what was written above.

Notes

1. Schroeder and Severin, "Soviet," 1976.
2. For example, "Statisticheskiye," 1971, p. 87. Here the "wage fund of industrial

production personnel" is published for 1960–69, and the indicators of the fund are exactly equal to the product of average annual employment and the average wage.

3. It is possible that some sector (sectors) is completely excluded and/or that for some sectors only, say, 50 percent of all the real indicators is shown.

4. There are no data for 1941–49, 1951–54 and 1956–57.

5. Thus, in *Narkhoz 65,* p. 567, the data cited on the average wage for 1950, 1955, and 1960–64 are slightly different than the data in later yearbooks.

6. The pensions to kolkhoz farmers thus also belong here. As some of my estimates show, the pensions of a portion of former servicemen are paid from the budget appropriations on defense.

7. See, for example, *Narkhoz 61,* p. 765.

8. For example, in *Narkhoz 78* the former are on p. 535, while the latter are on p. 390.

9. "In the total balance of deposits approximately 70 percent are demand deposits and about 30 percent are time deposits" (Zakharov, "Rabota," 1976, p. 22). However, we are not very accurate here for two reasons. First, this ratio was not always precisely the same (Poskonov, *Kreditno,* 1967, p. 210). Secondly, we are taking not the average annual amount of deposits, but the end of the year balance. With respect to the lottery winnings, their amount is too small to play any significant role.

10. After this study was already completed, V. Treml pointed out to me that these data are reported in TsSU, *Sel'skoye,* 1971, p. 479. My interpolation turned out to give approximately the same figures, and there was no need to make the corresponding corrections.

11. Zhurikov and Solomakhin, *Spravochnik,* 1973, p. 10. This source was cited in the work CIA, *USSR,* 1975, p. 23. I mention this CIA study here not only because I found a reference to this source in it, but also because I drew from it a number of other useful data and ideas.

12. This corresponds to the fact that according to Kosyachenko, *50 Let,* 1967, p. 170, the monetary income of kolkhoz farmers from kolkhozes increased during these two years by nearly 20 percent.

13. The monetary income of kolkhoz farmers and the wage fund of the workers of sovkhozes increased during 1961–65 1.7-fold (ibid.). The wages of sovkhoz workers increased more slowly (see *Narkhoz 65,* p. 567, where the indicators of the wages for sovkhozes and subsidiary agricultural enterprises are given); hence the monetary income of kolkhoz farmers should have increased more rapidly. Still, the indicators I have used should be only approximately correct.

14. ". . . the majority of kolkhozes give preference to monetary payments and have rejected the distribution of income according to labor-days . . . . In 1972 only slightly more than 4 percent of the kolkhozes retained the distribution of income according to labor-days" (Gostrud, *Trud,* 1974, p. 436). In Fefilov, "Vnutrikolkhoznuyu," 1977, p. 16, the above-cited indicators of the share of monetary payments for 1965 and 1970 are confirmed, but then it is stated: "During the past five-year plan the share of the pay in kind of kolkhoz farmers was a few tenths of a percent."

15. There are, in particular, doubts as to whether in fact the pay at fishing kolkhozes belongs here.

16. In Semenov, *Rol',* 1973, p. 143, it is indicated that "in 1957 money payments were 56 percent of the pay of kolkhoz farmers, in 1964 it was 79 percent, in 1970 it was 98 percent."

It is difficult to say whom to believe here. I believed the work of Zhurikov and Solomakhin, since its data are confirmed by the work of Fefilov, cited above, which was published later. If Semenov is nevertheless correct, our error for 1964 is 0.3 billion rubles and for 1970 0.7 billion rubles.

17. For example, *Narkhoz 75,* p. 804. In *Narkhoz 76,* there are no methodological notes. These explanations were shortened in *Narkhoz 77,* p. 620, and shortened even more in *Narkhoz 78,* p. 596.

18. Sverdlik, "Mezhotraslevoy," 1976, p. 341.

19. It is extremely difficult to obtain funds for the *bezlyudka*—they are controlled very rigidly—and payments out of this fund are no less rigidly controlled.

Fees to writers, artists, performing artists for performances at concerts and so forth may also be included in the *bezlyudka.* Estimates show that on the scale of our calculations the corresponding amounts cannot be significant.

20. Among them are "field" payments, i.e., supplementary payments to workers under field conditions—geologists and construction workers; "waterless" and "high mountain" payments; "relocation" payments, i.e., the payment for moving to a new place of work; and the payment for official trips on intra-urban transport.

21. Sverdlik, "Mezhotraslevoy," 1976, p. 371.

22. As I understand it, in this context "expertly" means that the author does not know the precise figures and takes a very rough estimate based on intuition.

23. According to Kachalina, "Osnovnyye," 1976, p. 110, in 1977 there were 600,000 managers of organizations, institutions and industrial enterprises. Let us add to them two of their deputies, the chief accountants and directors of planning divisions. We obtain 3 million. Let us add half of the scientific workers—another 0.5 million. There remain 1.5 million for suppliers, (*tolkachies*), designers, installers and so on.

24. Komarov and Chernyavskiy, *Dokhody,* 1973, p. 209. See also table G-1.

25. I will note that her calculations do not exactly confirm the expenditures just cited on passenger transportation. Since these indicators are also of substantial importance for many of our other calculations, they should be studied further.

26. The rates for transportation were revised (upward!) in the spring of 1977.

27. In *Literaturnaya Gazeta* of 21 September 1977, p. 13, an article entitled "One Day with Justice Burger" tells about a visit of the Chief Justice of the United States to the USSR. It states that 70 percent of the wages of prisoners of colonies for juvenile delinquents are not issued to them and go to pay for their upkeep. It might be that in other camps, for adults, this percentage could be slightly less.

Only a very small portion of the amounts due to prisoners is issued to them; all the remainder is transferred to special accounts and is issued to them upon release from prison as a so-called release fund.

28. One problem is that if the wages of prisoners are indeed included in the wage fund calculated by us, then apparently only a third of the corresponding amounts are actually issued to them, while the remainder is withheld for the maintenance of the camps. Assuming that the number of prisoners is now in the order of 1 million and probably more than 80 percent of them work, and assuming their wage to be 50 percent of the average for the national economy, it turns out that the possible error for 1965, 1970 and 1975 will be 309, 385 and 466 million rubles respectively, i.e., not that much.

29. Schroeder and Severin, "Soviet," 1976, p. 653.

30. Ibid., p. 653. This is confirmed by the following statement: "The private and property insurance of the population has also been considerably developed. The payments of indemnity and insurance amounts in 1974 was 2 billion rubles or nearly 8 times more than in 1965" (Garbuzov, "30-letiye," 1975, p. 14). The indicators in the following statement practically coincide with the indicators cited in table B-2: "In 1971–75 the population was paid 8.2 billion rubles, which is 3.1 times more than during the Eighth Five-Year Plan" (Motylev, "Sovershenstvovat'," 1976, p. 17).

31. Moreover, on the whole, the population loses money on lotteries.

32. *Narkhoz 75,* p. 55. In Pchelin, *Gosudarstvennyy,* 1976, p. 4, it is indicated: "As against the Eighth Five-Year Plan the monetary income of the population increased [apparently in the Ninth Five-Year Plan] by 42 percent," which confirms this estimate.

33. At the same time it is worth noting that an indirect verification of the data on the income of kolkhoz farmers on the whole confirms our calculations. A well-known Soviet specialist on the income of the population (Mayer, "Aktual'nye," 1977, pp. 48–49) writes that "during the past two five-year plans" the income per kolkhoz farmer increased 1.7-fold, and he further indicates that the income of kolkhoz farmers from the public sector increased 3.2-fold during 1961-75. This agrees quite well with our calculations.

34. *Narkhoz 78,* p. 429.

35. Abaturov, *Ekonomika,* 1975, p. 190. Recall that in chapter VII this figure was questioned, but the volumes of kolkhoz trade are of importance only for the redistribution of monetary income between different groups of the population.

36. It is worth citing an example of how easy it is to come to wrong conclusions by using Soviet literature. In the book of a well-known and quite reliable author, Batyrev, *Denezhnoye,* 1959, p. 227, it is stated that the amount of the retail commodity turnover without commission trade in 1958 was 66.85 billion rubles, while according to *Narkhoz 62,* p. 515, the total amount of the retail commodity turnover during the same year was 67.72 billion rubles. It would seem that this is just what we need, but an elementary check shows that the difference of 0.87 billion rubles is "The turnover of consumer cooperatives on the sale of produce at prices established on the local markets"—*Narkhoz 62,* p. 511. In other words, Batyrev calls "commission" the commission trade by consumer cooperatives. In itself this is not incorrect; this term is used in the literature. But it usually stipulated precisely what commission trade is meant, and Batyrev does not make such a stipulation here.

37. Abaturov, *Ekonomika,* 1975, p. 138.

38. See note 31 in chapter VII.

39. It is nevertheless possible that I am underestimating the volumes of commission trade. On the one hand, the number of commission stores is rather significant—1,936 of the 93,500 state nonfood stores (*Narkhoz 78,* p. 453), and all these stores carry on a very brisk trade. On the other hand, the volume of commission trade in cars and books has been increasing sharply, especially in recent years.

40. Zaytseva and Moroz, "Izucheniye," 1971.

41. Ryauzov and Titel'baum, *Statistika,* 1976, pp. 78 and 80.

42. Cheremisov, *Resursy,* 1975, p. 47.

43. Orlov V. A., *Mezhotraslevyye,* 1975, p. 26.

44. A. Birman, *Finansy,* 1975, p. 66.

45. Gosplan, *Metodicheskiye,* 1974, p. 493.

46. Ryauzov and Titel'baum, *Statistika,* 1976, p. 59.

47. Abaturov, *Ekonomika,* 1975, p. 190.

48. The volume of kolkhoz trade during these years is calculated according to *Narkhoz 72,* p. 573.

49. Fefilov, "Vnutrikolkhoznuyu," 1977, p. 16.

50. These data basically conform to the indicators in Motylev, "Udarnym," 1975, p. 16. Moreover, these indicators are confirmed in "Plan," 1976, p. 48: "The total amount of [insurance] payments during the five-year plan was 26.4 billion rubles, including 15.4 billion rubles received from the population for voluntary types of insurance alone, or more than three times more than in the Eighth Five-Year Plan." However, in Motylev, *Razvitiye,* 1978, p. 41, these indicators are slightly higher.

51. In particular, we understate the expenditures of the population on lotteries. On

the average the population loses approximatley 50 percent of the total amount of the lotteries. The amounts of the lotteries during 1971–75 are cited in Zakharov, "Rabota," 1976, p. 24. During these years the population annually spent (on a net basis) 200–250 million rubles.

52. *Narkhoz 75,* p. 565.

53. Pchelin, *Gosudarstvennyy,* 1976, p. 5, as well as Barkovskiy, "Problemy," 1977, p. 54.

54. ". . . in three years of the Ninth Five-Year Plan (1971–73) 16.5 billion rubles entered the accounts of depositors at savings banks in noncash form as against 8.0 billion rubles during the first three years of the Eighth Five-Year Plan (1966–68)"—Sveshnikov, "Denezhnyy," 1974, p. 44. In 1976 savings banks received 11.7 billion rubles from the population in noncash forms, including 4.9 billion rubles of wages—Barkovskiy, "Problemy," 1977, p. 54.

55. Questions of this nature arise also with respect to similar data for 1956–60 in Poskonov, *Kreditno,* 1967, p. 85. In particular it is not clear here how the commodity turnover can increase more rapidly than the money turnover through the cashier's offices of Gosbank. However, perhaps this is explained by the fact that the payments of money from the bank have increased more rapidly than the receipt of money at the bank.

56. Poskonov, *Kreditno,* 1967, p. 83.

57. Considering the money turnover within the population itself (particularly for various services and illegal activities) should lead us to quite the opposite result.

Appendix C

Estimate of the Income of the Population from the Sale of Produce to the State

We will use the following data which are regularly published in the *Narkhoz* yearbooks:

(a) the shares of the purchases from kolkhozes, sovkhozes and other farms in the total purchases of the main agricultural products (e.g., *Narkhoz 78,* p. 203). It is clear that if, for example, all these farms supply 80 percent of the total amount of purchases, the remaining 20 percent are purchased from the population, which is what we need; *(b)* the total amounts of the payments to kolkhozes, sovkhozes and other state organizations and to the population for produce (e.g., *Narkhoz 78,* p. 204).

Applying the shares of the sales of the population to the total amounts of payments, we should obtain the amounts of the payments to the population. This is done in table C-1, but the calculations require some clarification.

First, there are some inconsistencies between the nomenclature of the tables with the shares and the tables with the amounts of payments: in particular there are no shares for fruits; the shares for potatoes and vegetables are given together, while the amounts are given separately. For fruits, I take into account that according to data in *Narkhoz 78,* p. 232, private subsidiary farming accounted for 44 percent of the gross harvest of fruits and berries (in tons) in 1978. However, the population consumes much of the fruit they produce and sells a lot of it at the kolkhoz markets. It seems to me that deliveries of fruits to the state from private plots are not widespread. If I have nevertheless made a mistake here, it is not serious—fruit is not the main element in the total amount. As to potatoes and vegetables, to my understanding, in the total amount of expenditures on potatoes and vegetables, potatoes should constitute the bulk—vegetables are sold in state and cooperative stores primarily for 2-3 months a year (except mainly for onions). Therefore, in determining the percentage of the purchases from the population, I took it to be closer to the indicators for potatoes than for vegetables. Once again,

Table C-1. Estimate of Payments to the Population for Deliveries of Produce (in millions of rubles)

	1960			1965			1970			1975			1978		
	All payments	Percent to the population	Total	All payments	Percent to the population	Total	All payments	Percent to the population	Total	All payments	Percent to the population	Total	All payments	Percent to the population	Total
	1	2	3	4	5	6	7	8	9	10	11	12	13	14	15
Potatoes and															
vegetables	519	28	145	1,638	20	328	2,487	12	298	3,780	12	454	4,785	19	909
Fruit	377	40	151	1,328	20	266	1,874	20	375	2,811	20	562	2,799	20	560
Livestock and															1,920
poultry	3,478	19	661	9,220	10	922	18,452	11	2,030	25,521	13	3,318	27,428	7	737
Milk	2,052	10	205	5,747	4	230	8,772	3	263	12,108	5	605	14,736	5	112
Eggs	286	52	149	826	26	215	1,634	11	180	2,950	6	177	3,740	3	387
Wool	778	20	156	1,209	14	169	1,967	14	275	2,375	16	380	2,419	16	313
Gap	1,081	20	216	1,288	20	258	1,547	20	309	2,034	20	407	1,664	20	985
Sales to trade	648	30	194	1,345	30	404	2,204	30	661	2,361	30	708	3,284	30	
Total			1,877			2,792			4,391			6,611			5,943

Sources:

Columns 1, 4, 7, 10, 13 (on gaps and sales to trade organizations, see text)

1965, 1970, 1975, 1978—*Narkhoz 78*, p. 204

1960—*Narkhoz 70*, p. 286

Columns 2, 5, 8, 11, 14

1965, 1970, 1975, 1978—calculated according to *Narkhoz 78*, p. 203 (explanations are in the text)

1960—table C-2

Columns 3, 6, 9, 12, 15—each of these columns is calculated as the product of entries in the two preceding columns.

Table C-2. Estimate of the Shares of the Sales of the Population in the Total Amount of Sales for 1960 (percent)

	Sales of kolkhozes and sovkhozes	Sales of the population	Sales of sovkhozes	Sales of kolkhozes and the population	Proportion of the population to kolkhozes and population
	1	2	3	4	5
Potatoes	76	24	25	75	32
Vegetables	93	7	47	53	13
Livestock and poultry	87	13	32	68	19
Milk	93	7	32	68	10
Eggs	63	37	29	71	52
Wool	86	14	30	70	20

Sources: Columns 1 and 3—
Narkhoz 70, p. 286
Column 2—
100 less column 1
Column 4—
100 less column 3
Column 5—
column 2 divided by column 4 and multiplied by 100.

if I am mistaken here, the effect of the error can hardly be very significant.

Secondly, there are gaps in the figures on the total amounts of payments (they are discovered in checking the totals separately for various crops and for individual products of animal husbandry) and it is not very clear what can be behind these gaps. Moreover, the amounts of the sales to cooperative and state trade organizations are not broken down by types of products. I took the amounts of both the gaps and the sales to trade organizations to pertain only to kolkhozes and the population (but not to sovkhozes) and arbitrarily assumed for all years that the population received 20 percent from the gaps and 30 percent from the sales to trade organizations.

Thirdly, for 1960 data are published on the amounts of payments not to all categories of farms, but only to kolkhozes and the population. Therefore for that year I had to make a special recalculation of the shares of the sales to the population—table C-2. I took the percentage of fruit for this year to be two times greater than for the remaining years, i.e., 40 percent.

It would also be possible to make similar calculations for the "intervening years," but I preferred to determine the indicators for them according to the trend. Here I assume that in 1972 and 1975 there was no increase of these amounts due to the crop failures. The decline in the total amount in 1978 relative to 1975, as shown in table C-1, was due to the sharp drop in the sale of livestock and poultry to the state.

In 1952 all organizations and the population were paid 3 billion rubles for deliveries of produce (*Narkhoz 58*, p. 367); it is very doubtful therefore that the population would have received in 1950 more than, say, 0.6 billion rubles. In 1955 all the payments were 6.4 billion rubles (ibid.); let us assume that the population received 20 percent of this amount, i.e., 1.3 billion rubles.

Thus we obtain (in billions of rubles):

1950 – 0.6	1965 – 2.8	1972 – 5.0
1955 – 1.3	1966 – 3.2	1973 – 5.8
1960 – 1.9	1967 – 3.5	1974 – 6.6
1961 – 2.1	1968 – 3.8	1975 – 6.6
1962 – 2.3	1969 – 4.1	1976 – 6.3
1963 – 2.5	1970 – 4.4	1977 – 6.1
1964 – 2.7	1971 – 5.0	1978 – 5.9

It seems to me that the order of magnitude of the figures we have derived is correct, and additional calculations would not improve them much. In speaking about the reliability of the figures obtained, it must be kept in mind that substantially more than half of the amounts that were calculated—livestock and poultry, milk, eggs, wool—are precise figures. In other words, the potential error cannot be very substantial.

One more thing in conclusion. In the *Narkhoz* yearbooks in the tables "Main indicators of the development of kolkhozes" data were previously published on "Receipts of kolkhozes (excluding fishing) from the sale of produce (monetary revenue in the prices of the corresponding years)." It would seem that it is simplest of all to subtract these figures from those that we already know, "Payments to kolkhozes, kolkhoz farmers, workers and employees for produce sold to the state, cooperative and state trade organizations," and we would obtain as the difference the monetary income of the population from the sale of produce. However, amazingly, this is not so. Here is what we obtain in this case (in billions of rubles):[1]

	1960	1965	1970
Payments for produce	14.1	21.5	33.0
Monetary revenues of kolkhozes	13.4	19.9	31.5
Difference	0.7	1.6	1.5

Let us now compare the differences obtained with the figures in table C-1. The differences are even less than those incomes of the population about which we are quite certain. In particular, the difference for 1970 is less than the income of the population only from the sale of livestock and poultry.[2] Therefore I believe that something (although I cannot say precisely what) is incorrect in the data on the monetary revenues of kolkhozes. However, perhaps all this is explained by the fact that until 1970 the purchase prices for the produce acquired from the population were substantially lower than for the produce of kolkhozes and sovkhozes, and after this the additional payment to kolkhozes and sovkhozes for above-plan production has had a significant influence.[3]

Notes

1. The data are from *Narkhoz 70,* pp. 286 and 382.
2. Moreover, some portion of the monetary revenues of kolkhozes is derived from the sale of produce on the kolkhoz markets directly to the population. This makes the indicators in question even stranger.
3. Shmelev, "Lichnoye," 1975, p. 86.

Appendix D

Estimate of Amounts of "Lump-Sum Assistance" from Economic Stimulation Funds

The amount of lump-sum assistance in industry is 6 percent of the economic incentive fund.[1] However, such assistance is given not only in industry, and it was given, although in very limited amounts, even before the implementation of the economic reform of 1965 and the formation of economic stimulation funds (there were some other funds before the reform).

The approximate estimate—see table D-1—is based on the following. Data on the amount of the economic incentive funds for industrial enterprises have been published for 1969–76. Industrial production personnel (*promyshlenno-proizvodstvennyy personal*), roughly speaking, constitute 30 percent of the number of all workers and employees in the national economy, but, at the same time, the possibilities for the payments of this assistance in industry are considerably better than in other sectors. The figures in column 3 were approximated on this basis, as well as on the basis of the fact that industrial enterprises have been converted to the new system of economic stimulation and, consequently, have formed the economic incentives funds not immediately, but gradually. For this and also in order to determine the indicators for column 5 for 1960–66, I made the quite natural assumption that the total amounts of the lump-sum assistance for the entire period in question should have increased.

Of course, the result calculated here cannot in any way be considered very accurate, but I do not see any other means and humbly hope that the possible error here will not be very great.

Notes

1. This indicator is cited in Sverdlik, "Mezhotraslevoy," 1976, p. 337, with a reference to another source.

Table D-1. Estimate of Amounts of Lump-Sum Assistance

Year	Economic incentive fund for industry (millions of rubles)	6 percent of column 1	All other sectors: relative to industry (percent)	All other sectors: (millions of rubles)	Amount of lump-sum assistance for national economy (billions of rubles)
	1	2	3	4	5
1960					0.1
1961					0.1
1962					0.1
1963					0.1
1964					0.2
1965					0.2
1966					0.2
1967	1,307	78	180	140	0.2
1968	1,773	106	150	159	0.3
1969	3,071	184	130	239	0.4
1970	3,739	224	120	269	0.5
1971	4,140	248	115	285	0.5
1972	4,399	264	110	290	0.6
1973	4,840	290	110	319	0.6
1974	5,247	315	100	315	0.6
1975	5,663	340	100	340	0.7
1976	5,892	354	100	354	0.7
1977	6,111	367	100	367	0.7
1978	6,166	370	100	370	0.7

Sources: Column 1:
1970, 1975–78—*Narkhoz 78*, p. 530
1971-74—*Narkhoz 75*, p. 739
1968–69—*Narkhoz 69*, p. 766
1967—*Narkhoz 67*, p. 885
Column 2:
6 percent of column 1
Column 3:
estimated, see text
Column 4;
column 2 multiplied by column 3 divided by 100
Column 5:
total of columns 2 and 4.

Appendix E

Estimate of the Expenditures on the Pay of the KGB and MVD

There is no need to explain that the estimate of the expenditures on the pay of the KGB and MVD, especially the KGB, involves great difficulties (and very much interest!). My attempt at this estimate is based on an elementary and simple idea—both the KGB and the MVD are organized, like the entire apparatus in the country, according to the territorial principle. Consequently, it is necessary to estimate how many people there should (can) be in each administrative unit. The wage of the employees of the KGB should be substantially higher than the average wage of workers and employees in the country, while that of the police (MVD) should apparently be only slightly higher than the average.

I have never had even indirect information about how much KGB employees are paid, but apparently they should be paid well. As to the police, the situation is as follows. First, in some cases I had occasion to know how much Moscow policemen are paid, and on the whole, I have gotten the impression that they are paid approximately the same as army officers, and this is slightly higher than the average wage of workers and employees. Secondly, let us take into account that whereas in Moscow practically all the policemen are officers, and a few of them are sergeants; in the provinces there are quite a few privates and sergeants. Thirdly, in some cases I had occasion to hear that the police have nearly feuded with the KGB, in particular, because they envy their privileged position and especially their wages.

It is also natural to assume that the average wage in the upper levels of the administrative hierarchy is substantially higher than in the lower levels.

As to the number, it seems to me that the civilians for both departments are included in the published indicators of the number of workers and employees, and my entire estimate—table E-1—pertains only to uniformed staff members of both departments.

I have no ideas about the "domestic force" (*vnutrennyye* or *konvoy-*

nyye voyska) of the MVD and the border guard of the KGB, although it nevertheless seems that the amounts of the payments to them cannot be very significant on the scale of our calculations. The point is that basically these units consist of privates.

Of course, I cannot know what in fact is the size of the central staffs of the KGB and MVD and it is just a guesstimate. It is quite clear that 30,000 people could not work at the building of the KGB at "Lubyanka" and several adjacent buildings, but I used this figure in my calculations—precisely in Moscow there is a very large number of various "staff members" ("sotrudniki"); also included here is the staff of various service organizations—the higher schools of the KGB and MVD, scientific research organizations, prisons and so on.

It also seems that if the central staff of the KGB should be larger than the central staff of the MVD, in the *oblasts* and *rayons* there should be the opposite correlation.

I will also stipulate that I am using average indicators. It is quite likely that in Kiev there are considerably more than 1,000 KGB staff members (the number which I took as an average for republics), while in Leningrad there are certainly more than 300 of them (not counting in both instances the *rayon* departments), but, for example, in Frunze and Tambov there should be considerably fewer.

The figures I obtained for the number on the whole seem reliable to me; but, of course, I cannot give any guarantees.

I have never heard (this does not mean that it is in fact not so) that the KGB pays informants; therefore the corresponding amounts are not in the estimate. I will also note that the numerous workers of the so-called first departments (*pervyy otdel*) of all enterprises and organizations, which are in fact subordinate to the KGB, receive wages at the expense of the funds of these organizations. Their wages are practically the same as those of the other workers of the same organizations and institutions. It might be thought that they receive some additional payment from the KGB, but the likelihood of this is doubtful. If, nevertheless, such an additional payment exists, it once again should not be significant on the scale of our calculations.

The estimate, which is based on all these premises, is presented in table E-1. The most difficult thing is to "attach" the indicators obtained to specific years. More from a feeling than from knowledge, I attributed the figures obtained to 1970. I can say nothing in respect to the KGB, but, as to the police, the feeling is that its size increased a little, especially in the post-Khrushchev era. Without particular proof let us assume that 1.1 billion rubles actually pertains to 1970, while the average annual increase of the amount for the KGB and

Table E-1. Estimate of Wages for the KGB and MVD

	KGB					MVD				
	Employment			Wage		Employment		Wage		
	Number of units	Per unit (people)	Total (thousands of people)	Average monthly (rubles)	Total for the year (millions of rubles)	Per unit (people)	Total (thousands of people)	Average monthly (rubles)	Total for the year (millions of rubles)	Total wages for the year (billions of rubles)
	1	2	3	4	5	6	7	8	9	10
Central staff	1		30.0	250	90.0		20.0	210	50.4	
Republic committees (ministries)	15	1,000	15.0	240	43.2	1,000	15.0	200	36.0	
Oblast (kray) departments and administrations of departments in cities having rayon divisions	264*	300	79.2	210	199.6	400	105.6	180	228.1	
Cities not having a rayon division and rayons	4,489**	25	112.2	170	228.8	35	157.1	140	263.9	
Total			236.4	198	561.6		297.7	162	578.4	1.1

Source: Column 1—*Narkhoz 75*, p. 44. All others are estimates—see text.

*It is arbitrarily assumed that 100 cities have a rayon division.

**There are 904 cities of republic and oblast subordination 3,118 rural rayons and 567 urban rayons.

MVD together is 2 percent. We obtain (in billions of rubles):

1960 – 0.9	1966 – 1.0	1972 – 1.1
1961 – 0.9	1967 – 1.0	1973 – 1.2
1962 – 0.9	1968 – 1.1	1974 – 1.2
1963 – 1.0	1969 – 1.1	1975 – 1.2
1964 – 1.0	1970 – 1.1	1976 – 1.2
1965 – 1.0	1971 – 1.1	1977 – 1.3
		1978 – 1.3

Two additional remarks. First, the estimate for the MVD does not include the expenditures on fire protection; it seems to me that firemen are included in the reported number of workers and employees. Secondly, I think that wages should constitute not less than 60 percent of the total amount of the expenditures on the pay of these organizations, and from this, one can get an impression of how much these two organizations cost the state—surprisingly, not so much (I have no idea what the KGB spends on foreign operations).

Appendix F

The Cost of Reusable Glass Containers

In the USSR bottles and glass jars (except for some imported ones) can be returned to the place of purchase or to special points, and their cost is entirely reimbursed. Accordingly, the price for glass containers is called the "deposit."

Our estimate is based primarily on the following quotation:

> Annually in state trade alone about 23 billion bottles and more than 2 billion glass jars are returned. The sale of food products in both these types of glass containers in 1975 as compared with 1970 will increase by 36 percent, reaching for food items alone 220 units (176 bottles and 44 containers) on the average per inhabitant.
>
> The return of glass food containers in 1972 was 82 percent, while in 1975 it is planned to increase it to 90 percent.[1]

The most widespread half-liter jar costs 5 kopecks, and the next most widespread liter jar costs 10 kopecks. Quite a few small jars costing 3 kopecks, as well as 3-liter jars costing 30 and 40 kopecks are also used. Let us assume that the average price per jar is 7 kopecks.

Among bottles, the half-liter bottle is also the most widespread, and a wine (vodka) bottle costs 12 kopecks, while a milk bottle costs 15 kopecks. There are also bottles for champagne, as well as other wine bottles holding 0.75 liters, which cost 17 kopecks each, and a comparatively small number of bottles holding 0.25 liters, which cost something (I do not remember exactly) on the order of 8 kopecks. On the whole more milk is sold than vodka, wine, beer and mineral waters, but the majority is sold "on tap" or in packages. Therefore, we may take 13 kopecks as the average price.

Then, for 1975 the estimate looks as follows (the article cited speaks about the *plan* data for 1975, but since the article was published at the end of 1975, we can regard these as the actual data).

In 1975 there were 254.3 million people in the country.[2] Hence the sale of food items (I am ignoring the sale of nonfood items in glass containers) in bottles was 44.8 billion units and in jars—11.2 billion units. The cost of glass containers was thus:

$$44.8 \times 13 + 11.2 \times 7 = 6.6 \text{ billion rubles.}$$

Taking into account that the return of glass containers was planned to be 90 percent, the total amount received in 1975 by the population for the return of glass containers was 5.9 billion rubles.

For 1970 it is necessary, first, to take into account that in 1975 the sale of products in glass containers increased by 36 percent and, secondly, that the return of glass containers should be on the order of 79 percent, taking the trend noted in the quotation of an increase of the percentage of returns from 1972 up to 1975. Thus we obtain:

$$(6.6/1.36) \times 0.79 = 3.8 \text{ billion rubles.}$$

Now it is necessary to formulate the series for the remaining years. If we simply extrapolate the indicators we just obtained for 1975 and 1970 to 1960, we will obtain a very small number. What is significant here?

Unfortunately, not only do we not have data on the glass containers themselves for the years in question, but it is also difficult to obtain data on the sale of the corresponding items. True, it is possible to ascertain that the rate of growth of the sale of milk and dairy products during 1970–75 was 25 percent, while during the preceding five years of 1965–70 it was more than two times more—59 percent, but there are no data for 1960–65 separately for milk and dairy products. The ratios are approximately the same for canned vegetables, fruits and berries,[3] which are sold mainly in glass jars.

At the same time, we do not know what part of the growth of the sale of milk and dairy products involves sales in small cities and in rural areas, where they are sold not in bottles but "on tap," or how much of them is sold in packages. As to canned vegetables, fruits and berries, very many of them are from East European countries in nonreturnable containers.

The situation is even worse with the data on the sale of vodka, wine, beer, and nonalcoholic beverages; we do not have here even indirect data.[4]

On the whole I have assumed that during 1960–70 the growth rate of these amounts were considerably lower than during 1970–78, although I do not have proof that this is actually correct. My estimates are (in billions of rubles):

1960 – 2.3	1966 – 3.0	1972 – 4.3
1961 – 2.4	1967 – 3.2	1973 – 4.7
1962 – 2.5	1968 – 3.4	1974 – 5.2
1963 – 2.6	1969 – 3.6	1975 – 5.9
1964 – 2.7	1970 – 3.8	1976 – 6.6
1965 – 2.8	1971 – 4.0	1977 – 7.3
		1978 – 8.0

Notes

1. Belobrov, "Sovershenstvovat" 1975, p. 23.

2. The adjusted average between the numbers on 1 January 1975 and 1 January 1976, *Narkhoz 76,* p. 7.

3. *Narkhoz 76,* p. 542

4. True, there are published data on the growth of the sales of alcoholic items, (e.g., *Narkhoz 76,* pp. 508–09), but it is difficult to use these data since prices have affected them.

Appendix G

Expenditures of the Population on Payments for Services

These expenditures are second in importance among the expenditures of the population,[1] but the data on them are not very reliable. In the literature there are two books in which the bulk of the data of interest to us is published.

In one[2] a rather detailed breakdown of these expenditures with data for 1965 and 1970 is given, and the plan data for 1975 are also cited. In the other[3] there are additional data for 1965 and 1972, but here a slightly different classification is used, and for some types the services for a fee are not singled out. The data on three types of expenditures of the population on services—passenger transportation, communications services and entertainment establishments—in both sources coincide, which is not surprising, since the authors of both books used the same third source.[4]

I have combined the data from both of these sources in table G-1 and rely mainly on the data of Komarov and Chernyavskiy, although I use some things from the book by Shneyderman, and for some indicators I had to use extrapolation.

The data of Komarov and Chernyavskiy on domestic services (*bytovyye uslugi*) include the so-called production services, which are included in the indicators of the retail trade turnover. Therefore, I used Shneyderman's data for the calculation of the totals. On the other hand, I could not use Shneyderman's data on housing and municipal services, since they include the subsidy for the maintenance of the housing stock, which, of course, is not attributable to the monetary income of the population.[5]

It is not entirely clear to me exactly what Komarov and Chernyavskiy included in "other services;" their amount is very large. It is possible that, in particular, payments for hotels and payments for some types of education and for paid clinics are included here.

It is also not clear to me whether the payment of parents for the care of children at kindergartens and nurseries is included in the amount of "others"; I believe that it is included, for otherwise it is

Table G-1. Services Paid for by the Population (in billions of rubles)

Types of services for a fee	1960	1965	1970	1972	1975 plan	1975 adjustment
Housing and municipal	2.2***	3.0*	4.6*	5.1***	6.6*	6.2***
Domestic		1.9*	4.0*		8.1*	6.6****
excluding nonproductive	0.3**	0.6**	0.9**	1.0**		1.3***
Entertainment	1.0**	1.2*	1.5*	1.5**	1.7*	1.6***
Transportation	3.3**	4.9*	7.2*	8.0**	10.5*	9.2***
Communications	0.5**	0.8*	1.2*	1.3**	1.9*	1.5***
Others	1.3***	1.6*	1.7*	1.8***	2.5*	2.0***
Total (excluding nonproductive)	8.6	12.1	17.1	18.7		21.8

Sources: *Komarov and Chernyavskiy, *Dokhody,* 1973, p. 209
**Shneyderman, *Statistika,* 1974, p. 62
***Estimate according to the trend
*****Narkhoz 76,* p. 567.

difficult to explain why the amounts of the "other services" are so great.

The extrapolation of the data on the total amount of the expenditures of the population on payments for services for all the years of interest to us is as follows (in billions of rubles):

1960 – 8.6	1966 – 13.0	1972 – 18.7
1961 – 9.0	1967 – 14.0	1973 – 19.7
1962 – 9.6	1968 – 15.1	1974 – 20.7
1963 – 10.3	1969 – 16.1	1975 – 21.8
1964 – 11.2	1970 – 17.1	1976 – 22.9
1965 – 12.1	1971 – 18.0	1977 – 24.0
		1978 – 25.2

Notes

1. In spite of the fact that following Soviet authors I call all these expenditures "expenditures of the population" for services, it should be kept in mind that this is not entirely so. The point is that also included here, in particular, are the expenditures for business trips which, of course, are not expenditures of the population in the precise sense of this word. Due to the difficulties of estimating them, these expenditures are not singled out, but this does not interfere with our estimates.

2. Komarov and Chernyavskiy, *Dokhody,* 1973, p. 209.

3. Shneyderman, *Statistika,* 1974, p. 62.

4. Buzlyakov, *Glavnaya,* 1971, p. 146. There are also rather interesting data in Azar and Pletnikova, "K voprosu," 1973.

5. For further study of the question, an attempt could be made to use some data from a quite recent work—Solov'yev and Shneyderman, "Metodologicheskiye," 1978.

Appendix H

Estimate of Membership Dues

Members and Candidates of the CPSU

Membership dues are paid from all wages in the amount of 1 to 3 percent; 3 percent is paid from wages of 200 rubles a month and more.

It is possible to roughly assume that the wages of communists on the average are 20 percent higher than the average wage for the country. The point is that practically all managers (*nachal'niki*) are party members; the communists among the workers and peasants also are usually paid better.

The corresponding calculation is presented in table H-1. In this table I arbitrarily took the increase of the average percentage of wages paid for membership dues to conform with the increase of the average wage. I ignored the entrance fees, which are paid both upon becoming a candidate and a member in the amount of 1 percent of the monthly money income.

Trade Union Dues

As far as I understand, practically all workers and employees are members of a trade union. However, in examining the official data it turns out that only approximately 95 percent of the published total number of workers and employees are members of a trade union.[1] Several million people working at kolkhozes (machine operators and specialists), as well as students of higher education institutions, *tekhnikums* and vocational and technical schools, are also members of trade unions. The membership dues of students are meager. The remainder pay 1 percent of the wage. On the whole it can be assumed that the total amount of the trade union dues (taking into account also the entrance fees) is 1 percent of the wage fund, as was done in table H-2.

I must note that there are difficulties even with this seemingly simple question. When the entire work was already completed, in one

Table H-1. Party Dues

Year	Number of communists (millions)	Average monthly wage per communist (rubles)	Percent of membership dues	Amount for the year (millions of rubles
	1	2	3	4
1960	8.7	96.7	1.5	151
1961	9.3	100.7	1.5	169
1962	9.9	104.0	1.6	198
1963	10.4	105.8	1.6	211
1964	11.0	109.0	1.6	230
1965	11.8	115.8	1.7	279
1966	12.4	120.2	1.7	304
1967	12.7	125.6	1.8	345
1968	13.2	135.2	1.9	407
1969	13.6	140.3	1.9	435
1970	14.0	146.4	2.0	492
1971	14.4	151.1	2.1	548
1972	14.6	156.2	2.2	602
1973	14.8	161.9	2.3	661
1974	15.0	169.3	2.4	731
1975	15.3	175.0	2.5	803
1976	15.6	181.7	2.5	850
1977	15.9	186.2	2.6	924
1978	16.2	191.9	2.6	970

Sources: Column 1:
(All data are at the beginning of the corresponding year)
1960–74—Shumakov and Zudin, *Knizhka, 1974*, p. 19
1975—interpolation
1976, Shumakov and Zudin, *Knizhka*, 1976, p. 20
1977–78—extrapolation

Column 2:
table B-1, column 2 × 1.2

Column 3:
estimate, based on the increase of the average wage

Column 4:
(column 1 × column 2 × 12 × column 3)/100.

source[2] I discovered plan figures for receipts of trade union dues for 1976—1,534 billion rubles, i.e., almost 16 percent less than my estimate. This is ultimately not very significant for our calculations in this work, and I did not attempt to re-do the calculations, all the more so since this is plan and not ex post data. Still. it seems to me that this question is worth some additional attention.

It may be that this apparent gap—i.e., the amount of trade union

Table H-2. Total Amount of All Membership Dues

Year	Party (millions of rubles)	Trade union (millions of rubles)	All others (millions of rubles)	Total (billions of rubles)
	1	2	3	4
1960	151	600	124	0.9
1961	169	663	132	1.0
1962	198	711	137	1.0
1963	211	746	141	1.1
1964	230	799	147	1.2
1965	279	891	154	1.3
1966	304	958	159	1.4
1967	345	1,034	165	1.5
1968	407	1,151	170	1.7
1969	435	1,233	176	1.8
1970	492	1,321	180	2.0
1971	548	1,402	186	2.1
1972	602	1,487	190	2.3
1973	661	1,578	195	2.4
1974	731	1,690	200	2.6
1975	803	1,788	204	2.8
1976	850	1,893	208	3.0
1977	924	1,982	213	3.1
1978	970	2,084	217	3.3

Sources: Column 1: table H-1, column 4
Column 2: 1 percent of column 3 of table B-1
Column 3: column 1 of table B-1 × 2 rubles
Column 4: total of columns 1, 2 and 3.

dues is so much lower than they seemed to be—can be explained by the fact that, as far as I know, people do not pay union dues from various types of additional earnings (the same would not apply to Party dues—things are much stricter there). This must also apparently be explained in part by the fact that total wage payments include payments to prisoners who, again, but in this case, because they do not belong to the unions, do not pay union dues. Still, the gap is so large (recall that entrance fees and dues of kolkhoz machine operators and specialists must also be taken into account) that a more careful examination of what this all means is in order.

Other Membership Dues

The other membership dues are for Komsomol, cooperatives, sports societies, the Red Cross and the Red Crescent, DOSAAF, and the society for the planting of trees and shrubs.

The membership dues in Komsomol are very small: with a wage of up to 50 rubles—10 kopecks a month, with a wage of up to 100 rubles—50 kopecks.[3] In Komsomol approximately 55 percent are workers and employees; moreover, there are students (primarily school pupils) and "others."[4]

A simple estimate shows that even with the enormous size of Komsomol of more than 30 million, the total amount of membership dues should be only several tens of millions of rubles.

For our purpose I arbitrarily assume that all the membership dues in question here, including the Komsomol membership dues, are on the average 2 rubles a year per worker (employee).

Notes

1. See the data on the number of members of trade unions in Bogolyubov, *Spravochnik,* 1977, p. 470.
2. Makarenko, *Sbornik,* 1976, p. 14.
3. Volchikhin, *Spravochnik,* 1975, p. 168.
4. Bogolyubov, *Spravochnik,* 1977, p. 472. "Others" here seems to mean servicemen, but the number is too small.

Appendix I

Share of the Expenditures of the Union, Republic and Local Budgets

	1950	1955	1960	1965	1970	1975
			In billions of rubles			
1. USSR State budget	41.3	54.0	73.1	101.6	154.6	214.5
2. Union budget	31.7	39.9	30.1	43.2	80.6	109.7
3. State budgets of union republics	9.6	14.1	43.0	58.4	74.0	104.8
4. Republic budgets	3.0	6.3	28.6	37.3	45.2	66.4
5. Local budgets	6.6	7.8	14.4	21.1	28.8	38.4
			In percent			
6. USSR State budget	100	100	100	100	100	100
7. Union budget	77	74	41	43	52	51
8. Republic budgets	7	12	39	37	29	31
9. Local budgets	16	14	20	21	19	18

Sources: Line 1
table I-5
Line 2
difference of lines 1 and 3
Line 3
1965, 1970, 1975—*Narkhoz 75*, p. 744
1950, 1955, 1960—*Byudzhet 66*, p. 74
Line 4
line 3 less line 5
Line 5
1970, 1975—*Byudzhet 76*, p. 100
1950, 1955, 1960, 1965—*Byudzhet 66*, p. 96.

Appendix J

"Other Monetary Accumulations"

The table "Monetary accumulations of the national economy (excluding kolkhozes)" has been published in the *Narkhoz* yearbooks since 1967.[1] The table gives the amount of all the accumulations and their breakdown into profit, turnover tax and "other accumulations." Data on other monetary accumulations are also contained in the *Byudzhet* handbooks beginning with the next to last edition.[2] In table J-1 I have written out all the data published in these sources. The following strange circumstances attract attention:

(*a*) the amount of the other accumulations "jumps" greatly from year to year;
(*b*) in two years—1950 and 1971—the amount is negative;
(*c*) the indicators for 1960, as well as those for 1965–69, are "rounded off," they are given (in the report!) to the nearest hundred million rubles.[3]

The explanations for all this in the literature are minimal. In the "Methodological explanations" to the *Narkhoz* yearbooks, it is stated that these are "a part of the net income of the national economy."[4] From the explanations the very first time they were published, it follows that these indicators pertain to "enterprises and organizations."[5] You would in no way say that these explanations actually explain anything.

The question of "other monetary accumulations" has only an indirect relationship to our main theme, but nevertheless I devote a special appendix to the question, since its clarification would help to better understand the overall picture of financial flows in the USSR and, as we will see, it is possible to obtain some estimate of the amount of the revenues from foreign trade.

The only source (which G. Schroeder pointed out to me) in which this question is discussed, is by a different Birman.[6] Here payments for social insurance are called a form of the "movement of the net income,"[7] and it is explained that deductions for social insurance must also be considered. According to the figures cited it can be

Table J-1. Amounts of Other Monetary Accumulations
(in millions of rubles)

1940	400	1970	3,303
1946	1,100	1971	−215
1950	−1,700	1972	1,111
1960	8,700	1973	1,821
1965	7,600	1974	2,625
1966	6,000	1975*	4,799
1967	8,900	1976	12,200
1968	4,500	1977	11,100
1969	4,500	1978	11,900

Sources: 1940, 1976–78—*Narkhoz 78,* p. 515
1946—TsSU, *Strana,* 1967, p. 39
1950—*Narkhoz 70,* p. 703
1960, 1965–69—*Byudzhet 72,* p. 15
1970–75—*Byudzhet 76,* p. 12

*According to *Narkhoz 78,* p. 515, 5.1 billion rubles. I take the latter number in table J-2.

understood that this means only the deductions of enterprises and organizations, which are published in the data on the revenues of the budget.[8]

Further on[9] it is correctly noted that the deductions of enterprises for trade unions should be attributed to the other monetary accumulations as well as a portion of the so-called other monetary expenditures (one of the items of the element-by-element classification of production cost is called this), and in particular the interest paid to the bank. According to the overall estimate of the book in question, in 1969 these latter amounts were 500 million rubles,[10] while the entire amount of the other monetary expenditures was about 9 billion rubles, but a considerable share of them is material expenditures, which have nothing to do with the matter at hand.

Finally[11] the question is examined more thoroughly and the following are listed by the author as being included in other monetary accumulations:

—wage deductions for social insurance benefits;
—customs revenues;
—payments to the budget (the algebraic sum) of the difference in prices for agricultural raw materials;
—various elements of the budget revenues;

—deductions for the construction of the warehouses of *Sel'khoztekhnika*[12] and roads;
—rental revenues of local soviets;
—accounts receivable and payable (*debitorskaya i kreditorstkaya zadolzhennost'*);
—the upward price adjustment of goods;
—various other receipts.

Let us examine all this in order. As to the customs revenues, A. Birman gives an explanation which fits what I described in chapter IV.

As to the differences in the prices for agricultural raw materials, as far as we know this is nothing more and nothing less than subsidies. True, A. Birman reasons that the difference for the budget can be both negative and positive, but this reasoning is only of theoretical importance. For further estimates I used recently published indicators of subsidies.

We know the rental revenues of the local budgets—table I-4.[13]

As to the accounts receivable and payable, as well as the revenues from the upward price adjustment of goods, we have no data to judge their amount. Nevertheless, it seems to me, the accumulations from the writing off of accounts receivable could not be substantial. In the USSR, where no bankruptcies of enterprises and organizations occur, such writings-off can be attributed only to some chance incidents. The revenues from the upward price adjustment of goods occur when a price increase takes place (one example of this was cited in chapter IV). Such revenues, as is evident from this example, may be substantial, but they are not of a regular nature. Therefore, I do not take either of these types of revenues into account in my further estimates of the other money accumulations.

Finally, as to the last type—"various other receipts"—in the opinion of A. Birman they are included in the other monetary accumulations improperly. The very fact that he expresses disagreement with existing practice attests that he knows this practice, that he is not speculating, but is discussing with a knowledge of affairs the real calculation of a real indicator. In general it should be taken into account that we are examining here the opinion of not only one of the major specialists, who unquestionably knows his business well, but also of a man very (by Soviet standards) independent in judgments. Therefore, there are no guarantees that his opinion fully coincides with the official point of view of those in the Ministry of Finance of the USSR who actually determine the published indicators. And so, this last group includes:

Table J-2. Estimates of Revenues from Foreign Trade Derived from Components of "Other Monetary Expenditures" (in billions of rubles)

Year	Total amount of other accumulations	Deductions for social insurance	Agricultural subsidies	Rent income	Other receipts	Customs Revenue (Income from foreign trade)
	1	2	3	4	5	6
1965	7.6	5.6	2.1	0.1	0.9	3.1
1966	6.0	6.1	3.6	0.1	0.9	2.5
1967	8.9	6.5	5.0	0.1	0.9	6.4
1968	4.5	7.2	7.6	0.1	0.9	3.9
1969	4.5	7.9	8.5	0.1	0.9	4.1
1970	3.3	8.3	14.8	0.1	1.0	8.7
1971	−0.2	8.8	16.2	0.1	1.0	6.1
1972	1.1	9.2	17.6	0.1	1.0	8.3
1973	1.8	9.9	16.7	0.1	1.0	7.5
1974	2.6	10.6	18.0	0.1	1.0	8.9
1975	5.1	11.3	20.1	0.1	1.0	12.8

Sources:
Column 1:
table J-1
Column 2:
1965, 1970–75—*Narkhoz 75*, p. 742
1969—*Narkhoz 70*, p. 730
1966–68—*Narkhoz 68*, p. 774
Column 3:
Treml, *Agricultural*, 1978, p. 8
Column 4:
table I-4
Column 5:
see text
Column 6:
columns 1 and 3 less columns 2, 4, and 5.

—the retail price markups for radios and televisions. They are 0.5–0.6 billion rubles a year;[14]
—the entertainment tax, which constitutes something on the order of 0.4 billion rubles a year—table III-2;
—the improperly utilized funds for the payment of bonuses for the introduction of new equipment, as well as the assets from the fund for the placement of new equipment into operation. From everything, it follows that these assets cannot be significant at all on our scale;
—deductions for geological prospecting, in instances when this money has not been spent. We saw in chapter III that these amounts probably cover the actual expenditures on geology.

On the whole I think that without risk of great error it is possible to take the total amount of the accumulations for this group to be 1 billion rubles.

In table J-2 I attempt on the basis of the data examined to make some estimates. As a result of these estimates it is possible to approximate the amount of revenues from foreign trade. Unfortunately, I have data on a major element of my calculations—subsidies to agriculture—only for 1965–75, so table J-2 is only about this period. Let us compare the figures obtained here with those which were obtained in table IV-3.

It should be especially stressed that since the amounts of the revenues from foreign trade obtained in this estimate, are *less* than we used in our basic estimate (table IV-1), this in no way contradicts the main conclusion of this book about the budget deficit.

At the same time I should note that a very strange case remains unexplained—the fact that the reported indicators of the other monetary accumulations for a number of years are rounded. This suggests the idea that this indicator is calculated artificially (at any rate for these years).

And the last thing. A. Birman speaks in the above-cited list about the algebraic difference of the prices for agricultural raw materials. It is obvious that it would be more precise to speak about the total amount of the subsidies to agriculture, i.e., including the subsidies for fertilizers and agricultural equipment, and that is what I did in my calculations. However, another question remains open. As we know, there are state subsidies to unprofitable industrial enterprises, and it is not clear to me whether the amounts of the profit are correspondingly reduced in the tables "Monetary accumulations of the national economy." If not, our estimates should be correspondingly adjusted, that is, roughly speaking, the amounts of the revenues from foreign trade, which we obtained in table J-2, will be a few billion rubles more. Unfortunately, we do not know the amounts of the subsidies to unprofitable enterprises.[15]

Notes

1. This table opens the "Finances and Credit" section of the yearbooks. For example, *Narkhoz 67,* p. 857; *Narkhoz 68,* p. 743 and so on. Previously (see for example, *Narkhoz 65,* p. 757) instead of this table there was a table with data on profits and turnover tax. The data on "other monetary accumulations" were published for the first time in TsSU, *Strana,* 1967, p. 39.
2. *Byudzhet 72,* p. 15 and *Byudzhet 76,* p. 12.
3. The indicator for 1970 was also initially "rounded off" (*Byudzhet 72,* p. 15).
4. For example, *Narkhoz 75,* p. 809.
5. TsSU, *Strana,* 1967, p. 39.
6. A. Birman, *Ocherki,* 1972.
7. Here A. Birman cites Batyrev, *Tovarno,* 1970, p. 113.
8. A. Birman, op. cit., p. 46.
9. Ibid., pp. 46–47.
10. Ibid., p. 47. This estimate is interesting in connection with our discussion of the possible amount of the profit of banks—chapter III and IX. From the context it turns out that the profits of banks "should" be attributed to the other monetary accumulations and that in fact they are not included in these amounts. If I have nevertheless taken them into account, the amounts of the revenues from foreign trade in calculations in this appendix would be even less (see below).
11. A. Birman, op. cit., pp. 57–60.
12. This is the only reference I know of about this type of budget revenues. I did not examine these revenues in the main text of this book, but they certainly should be included in the revenues of the local budgets and cannot be significant.
13. I would not be surprised if the forestry revenue and the revenue from entertainment were also included here.
14. CIA, *The Soviet,* 1977, p. 22.
15. The only hint of this is in Yevdokimov, *Kontrol',* 1974, p. 141.

Appendix K

Hidden Budget Revenues in 1944–45

Because of the lack of more or less systematic data for years prior to 1950, I am concerned little with this period in this book. However, we can make some use of the quite detailed data for 1944–45 given in the book by Plotnikov, *Byudzhet*, 1948. I am doing this separately, I repeat, because of the lack of data series. It is also significant that there practically could not be revenue from foreign trade in these years.

On page 259 of the book, a table is given which shows the basic budget revenues for these years, and on page 268 we read:

> In addition to the decisive revenues, which in the budgets of the war years were turnover tax and deductions from profits, there were also small revenues from socialist enterprises and organizations: income tax collected from cooperative organizations, the tax on noncommodity operations, the entertainments tax, forestry revenue, revenue from machine-tractor stations, collections of traffic violations, revenues from the sale of unregistered evacuated freight, etc. The budget revenues from these payments comprised relatively small amounts.

Some figures on these additional revenues follow in the corresponding calculations presented in table K-1.

For both of these years one-fourth of all revenues cannot be explained, and we can quite confidently conclude that approximately these amounts—i.e., 6.6 billion rubles in 1944 and 7.8 billion rubles in 1945—were emission of cash and also, partially, bank loans to the budget.

More precisely, the emission of cash during these years could not have been more than these amounts, and it is possible that emission was less by the amount of bank loans to the budget.

Table K-1. Data on Budget Revenues for 1944–45 (in millions of rubles)

	1944	1945
Total budget revenue	26.87	30.20
of which:		
1. turnover tax	9.49	12.31
2. deductions from profits	2.14	1.69
3. taxes and duties from the population	3.70	3.98
4. state loans	3.26	2.90
5. "defense and Red Army funds"	0.33	0.05
6. state insurance funds	0.90	1.04
7. income tax from cooperative organizations	0.15	0.13
8. tax on noncommodity operations	0.05	0.05
9. entertainments tax	0.11	0.15
10. forestry revenue	0.05	0.06
11. revenues from machine-tractor stations	0.05	0.07
Sum of components	20.23	24.43
Gap, absolute	6.64	7.77
as a percentage of total revenue	24.7	25.7

Sources: Lines 1–6: Plotnikov, *Byudzhet*, 1978, p. 259
Lines 7–8: Ibid., p. 268
Lines 9 and 11: 1944—extrapolation; 1945—Ibid., p. 269
Line 10: Ibid., p. 269.

Appendix L

The Puzzle with Social Insurance Funds

As noted in chapter III, there is a very strange inconsistency between the figures for social insurance funds for the state budget of the USSR and the sum of the state budgets of union republics. I have gathered the corresponding data in table L-1, and they show that beginning in 1958, with the exception of only two years, the latter are greater than the former.

V. Treml pointed this out to me, and then I discussed it with G. Schroeder. She also noticed that for two years in the budgets of the Ukrainian SSR and the Latvian SSR, social insurance funds were not shown at all, while data were given for three other years.[1] In another handbook, there is not even a line for social insurance funds in the table on revenues of the budget for Latvia.[2]

This is even more than strange. One possibility, that republic budgets have some sort of revenues which are not included in the total amount of revenues of the state budget of the USSR, completely contradicts everything that we know, and we must discard it immediately. Another possibility is that in fact different things are being called by a common name in different budgets. Indeed, as one textbook states:

> State social insurance funds, except for the amounts of payments of pensions transferred to the republic budgets of union republics, are included in the union budget.[3]

We find a little more definitive statement in the text of the law "On the budget rights of the USSR and union republics." The revenues that enter the state budgets of union republics are listed here, and then it is stated that "above" these revenues, the "state social insurance funds for payment of pensions" are transferred to these budgets.[4]

It seems to me that the conclusion that follows from this is that while the line "state social insurance funds" in tables on the state budget of the USSR represents the amount of funds entering that budget from the corresponding deductions of enterprises and organizations, in republic budgets the line of the same name characterizes the funds received by those budgets from the union budget. Since we know that the budget always spends on social insurance (and also on social security from state social insurance funds) about twice as much as it receives in revenues, everything would seem to be explained.

However, in fact another question quickly arises here, for which I do not see a clear answer. The point is that in the tables on republic budgets all transactions with the union budget are shown separately, and the impression is formed that allocations to republic budgets for

Table L-1. Budget Receipts of the Amounts of Deductions for Social Insurance (in millions of rubles)

Year	USSR State budget	Republic budgets	Difference
	1	2	3
1940	845	199	646
1950	1,932	520	1,412
1955	2,613	871	1,742
1956	2,795	1,256	1,539
1957	3,286	2,733	553
1958	3,264	3,269	−5
1959	3,583	3,740	−157
1960	3,739	4,222	−483
1961	4,153	4,767	−614
1962	4,414	5,223	−809
1963	4,631	5,697	−1,066
1964	4,949	6,105	−1,156
1965	5,562	6,513	−951
1966	6,003	7,142	−1,139
1967	6,394	7,756	−1,362
1968	7,123	8,393	−1,270
1969	7,778	7,430	−348
1970	8,203	7,968	−235
1971	8,708	8,618	−90
1972	9,143	9,255	−112
1973	9,747	9,716	31
1974	10,407	10,309	98
1975	11,064	11,630	−566

Sources: Columns 1 and 2:
1970–75—*Byudzhet 76,* pp. 9, 75
1965–69—*Byudzhet 72,* pp. 112, 78
1950, 1955, 1960–64—*Byudzhet 66,* pp. 11, 71
1940, 1956–69—*Byudzhet 62,* pp. 9, 60
Column 3:
Column 1 less column 2.

social insurance are not included in these amounts. It seems to me that the situation is as follows. In my study of budget expenditures, I came to the conclusion that a certain part of the pensions of ex-servicemen is paid for out of allocations for defense. If this is in fact so, then it is quite possible that republic budgets show the amounts that they receive for paying pensions—amounts which are comprised both of funds of state social insurance itself and of funds of the Ministry of Defense.[5]

This hypothesis can be verified with a more careful comparison of the figures in columns 2 and 3 of table L-1 with data on the payments of pensions, and with information on changes in the procedures of paying pensions.

Notes

1. *Byudzhet 72,* pp. 117, 181.
2. *Byudzhet 76,* pp. 167–68.
3. Rusin and Eydinova, *Gosudarstvennyy,* 1975, p. 25.
4. Kalitevskaya, et al., *O byudzhetnykh,* 1963, p. 28.
5. It seems that some allocations may be similarly handled by the MVD and the KGB.

Bibliography

Abaturov, A.I., et al., *Ekonomika torgovli: Uchebnik* (The economics of trade: a textbook). Moscow, Ekonomika, 1975.

Aleksandrov, A.M., ed. *Gosudarstvennyy byudzhet SSR: Uchebnik* (The state budget of the USSR: a textbook), second edition. Moscow, Finansy, 1965.

Aleksandrova, E., and Fedorovskaya, E., "Rost blagosostoyaniya trudyashchikhsya i sberezheniya naseleniya" (Growth of the welfare of workers and the savings of the population), *Voprosy Economiki,* No. 10, 1978.

Andreyev, V., and Sviridova, K., "Nekotoryye voprosy ispol'zovaniya kreditnykh resursov" (Some questions of the use of credit resources), *Den'gi i kredit,* No. 11, 1972.

Atlas, M., *Razvitiye gosudarstvennogo banka SSSR* (The development of the USSR State Bank). Moscow, Gosfinizdat, 1958.

Atlas, M.S., "Kredit v sisteme ekonomicheskikh otnosheniy razvitogo sotsializma" (Credit in the system of economic relations of mature socialism), *Den'gi i kredit,* No. 10, 1974.

Atlas, M.S., et al., *Natsional'nyy dokhod v sotsialisticheskom obshchestve* (National income in a socialist socitey). Moscow, Finansy, 1977.

Atlas, Z.V., ed., *Denezhnoye obrashcheniye i kredit SSSR: Uchebnik* (Money circulation and credit in the USSR: a textbook). Moscow, Gosfinizdat, 1957.

Azar, V., and Pletnikova, I., "K voprosu o klassifikatsii i polnoy otsenke uslug v lichnom potreblenii" (On the question of the classification and complete evaluation of services in personal consumption), *Ekonomicheskiye nauki,* No. 11, 1973.

Azarkh, M.R., *Spravochnik po gosudarstvennym dokhodam* (Reference book on state revenues). Moscow, Finansy, 1972.

Barkovskiy, N.D., ed. *Organizatsiya i planirovaniye kredita: Uchebnik* (The organization and planning of credit: a textbook). Moscow, Finansy, 1973.

Barkovskiy, N.D., "Problemy organizatsii denezhnogo oborota" (Problems of the organization of the money turnover), *Den'gi i kredit,* No. 12, 1977.

Batyrev, V., *Denezhnoye obrashcheniye v SSSR* (Money circulation in the USSR). Moscow, Gosfinizdat, 1959.

Batyrev, V.M., *Tovarno-denezhnyye otnosheniya, finansy i kredit v sotsialisticheskom khozyaystve: Voprosy teorii* (Commodity-money relations, finances and credit in a socialist economy: issues of theory). Moscow, Finansy, 1970.

Becker, Abraham S., *Soviet National Income: 1958–1964.* Berkeley, University of California Press, 1969.

Belkin, V., and Ivanter, I., "Finansovyye i vneshneekonomicheskiye svyazi v balanse narodnogo khozyaystva" (Financial and foreign economic ties in the balance of the national economy), *Voprosy Ekonomiki,* No. 4, 1977.

Belobrov, V., "Sovershenstvovat' organizatsiyu priyema steklotary" (Improve the organization of the receipt of glass containers), *Sovetskaya torgovlya,* No. 11, 1975.

Belyavskiy, I., "Sotsial'no-ekonomicheskiye faktory razvitiya roznichnogo tovarooborota" (Socioeconomic factors of the development of the retail trade turnover), *Voprosy ekonomiki,* No. 3, 1978.

Bergson, Abram, *The Real National Income of Soviet Russia since 1928,* The Rand Corporation, 1961.

Birman, A.M., *Ocherki teorii sovetskikh finansov* (Essays on the theory of soviet finance). Moscow, Finansy, 1968.

Birman, A.M., ed. *Finansy Predpriyatii i otrasley narodnogo khozyaystva: Uchebnik* (Finance of enterprises and sectors of the national economy: a textbook), third edition. Moscow, Finansy, 1970.

Birman, A.M., *Ocherki teorii sovetskikh finansov* (Essays on the theory of soviet finance), Vol. 2. Moscow, Finansy, 1972.

Birman, A.M., ed., *Finansy torgovli: Uchebnik* (Finance of trade: a textbook), second edition. Moscow, Ekonomika, 1975.

Bobrovnikov, A.A., *O gosudarstvennom byudzhete RSFSR na 1974 god i ob ispolnenii gosudarstvennogo byudzheta RSFSR za 1972 g. Doklad i zaklyuchitel'noye slovo Ministra finansov RSFSR na shestoy sessii Verkhovnogo Soveta RSFSR vos'mogo sozyva 18 i 19 dekabrya* 1973 g (About the State Budget of the RSFSR for 1974 and the implementation of the budget for 1972. Presentation and Concluding remarks of the Minister of Finance of the RSFSR to the Sixth Session of the Eight Convocation of the Supreme Soviet of the RSFSR, 18 and 19 December 1973). Moscow, Finansy, 1974.

Bogolyubov, K.M., et al., eds. *Spravochnik partiynogo rabotnika* (Manual of a party worker), No. 17. Moscow, Politizdat, 1977.

Buzlyakov, N.I., *Glavnaya zadacha novoy pyatiletki* (The main task of the new five-year plan). Moscow, Mysl', 1971.

Byudzhet 57, see Ministerstvo, *Gosudarstvennyye. Byudzhet 62, Byudzhet 66, Byudzhet 72* and *Byudzhet 76,* see Ministerstvo, *Gosudarstvennyy.*
Cheremisov, F.S., *Resursy prodovol'stvennykh tovarov i ikh ispol'zovaniye* (Resources of foodstuffs and their use). Moscow, Ekonomika, 1975.
Chernov, N.F., "Kadry bankovskoy sistemy" (Personnel of the bank system), *Den'gi i Kredit,* No. 4, 1977.
Chetverikov, P.A., ed., *Sberegatel'nyye kassy SSSR za 50 let* (USSR savings banks during 50 years). Moscow, Finansy, 1972.
CIA (The Central Intelligence Agency), USSR: Gross National Product Accounts, 1970. Washington, D.C., 1975.
CIA, *Estimated Soviet Defense Spending in Rubles, 1970–1975.* Washington, D.C., 1976.
CIA, *Ruble-Dollar Ratios for Construction.* Washington, D.C., 1976.
CIA, *The Soviet State Budget since 1965.* Washington, D.C. December 1977.
CIA, *Soviet Commercial Operations in the West.* Washington, D.C. 1977.
CIA, *USSR: Toward a Reconciliation of Marxist and Western Measures of National Income,* Washington D.C. 1978.
"Dannyye o razvitii Gosudarstvennogo banka SSSR" (Data on the development of the USSR State Bank), *Den'gi i kredit,* No. 9, 1971.
Darkov, G.V. and Maksimov, G.K., *Finansovaya statistika* (Financial statistics). Moscow, Finansy, 1975.
Daynauskas, V.P., "Tseny na oborudovaniye v kapital'nom stroitel'stve" (Prices of equipment in capital construction), *Finansy SSSR,* No. 12, 1978.
Dementsev, V.V., "Finansovyye organy v zavershayushchem godu pyatiletki" (Financial organs in the final year of the Five-Year Plan), *Finansy SSSR,* No. 8, 1975.
Dymshits, I., et al., *Finansy i kredit SSSR: Uchebnik* (Finance and credit of the USSR: a textbook). Moscow, Gosfinizdat, 1956.
Fadeyev, I.I., *O gosudarstvennom byudzhete RSFSR za 1970 i ob ispolnenii gosudarstvennogo byudzheta RSFSR za 1968 god. Doklad i zaklyuchitel'noye slovo Ministra finansov RSFSR na shestoy sesii Verkhovnogo Soveta RSFSR sed'mogo sozyva 23 i 24 dekabrya 1969 goda* (About the State Budget of the RSFSR for 1970 and the implementation of the budget of 1968. Presentation and concluding remarks of the Minister of Finance of the RSFSR to the Sixth Session of the Seventh Convocation of the Supreme Soviet of the RSFSR, December 23 and 24, 1969). Moscow, Finansy, 1970.
Fadeyev, I.I., the same as above for 1973–71. Moscow, Finansy, 1973.
Fedorenko, N., et al, "Parametry upravleniya" (Parameters of management), *Pravda,* 23 March 1978, p. 2.
Fefilov, A., "Vnutrikolkhoznuyu torgovlyu uchityvat' v roznichnom

tovarooborote," (To include intrakolkhoz trade in retail trade turnover), *Sovetskaya Torgovlya,* No. 11, 1975.

Feonova, L.A., et al., *Organizatsiya i tekhnika vneshney torgovli SSSR* (The organization and techniques of USSR foreign trade). Moscow, Mezhdunarodnyye otnosheniya, 1974.

Finansy i sotsialitsticheskoye stroitel'stvo (Finance and socialist construction). Moscow, Finansy, 1957.

Galimon, L.S., *Finansy sel'skogo khozyaystva* (Agricultural finances), second edition. Moscow, Finansy, 1976.

Gallik, Daniel; Jesina, Cestmir; and Rapawy, Stephen, *The Soviet Financial System: Structure, Operation, and Statistics,* U.S. Bureau of the Census, International Population Statistics Reports, Series P-90, No. 23. Washington D.C., 1968.

Garbuzov, V.F., "Finansovaya sistema pered novymi zadachami" (The financial system in face of the new tasks), *Finansy SSSR,* No. 1, 1961.

Garbuzov, V.F., "Uspeshno vypolnit' byudzhet chetvertogo goda semiletki—vazhneyshaya zadacha finansovykh organov" (To successfully fulfill the budget of the fourth year of the Seven-Year Plan is the most important task of financial organs), *Finansy SSSR,* No. 1, 1962.

Garbuzov, V.F., "Resheniya noyabr'skogo Plenuma TsK KPSS i zadachi finansovykh organov" (The decisions of the November CC CPSU Plenum and the tasks of financial organs), *Finansy SSSR,* No. 1, 1963.

Garbuzov, V.F., "Uspeshnoye vypolneniye byudzheta—vazhnyy vklad v osushchestvleniye resheniy dekabr'skogo Plenuma TsK KPSS" (The successful fulfillment of the budget is an important contribution to the implementation of the decisions of the December CC CPSU Plenum), *Finansy SSSR,* No. 1, 1964.

Garbuzov, V.F., "Gosudarstvennyy byudzhet SSSR i zadachi finansovykh organov na 1965 g." (The USSR State Budget and the tasks of financial organs for 1965), *Finansy SSSR,* No. 1, 1965.

Garbuzov, V.F., "Byudzhet pervogo goda novoy pyatiletki" (The budget of the first year of the New Five-Year Plan), *Finansy SSSR,* No. 1, 1966.

Garbuzov, V.F., "Byudzhet yubileynogo goda" (The budget of the Anniversary Year), *Finansy SSSR,* No. 1, 1967.

Garbuzov, V.F., "Uspeshno vypolnit' byudzhet tret'yego, reshayushchego goda pyatiletki" (Successfully fulfill the budget of the third, decisive year of the Five-Year Plan), *Finansy SSSR,* No. 12, 1967.

Garbuzov, V.F., "Byudzhet chetvertogo goda pyatiletki" (The budget

of the fourth year of the Five-Year Plan), *Finansy SSSR*, No. 1, 1969.
Garbuzov, V.F., "Byudzhet zavershayuschego goda pyatiletki" (The budget of the final year of the Five-Year Plan), *Finansy SSSR*, No. 1, 1970.
Garbuzov, V.F., "Byudzhet pervogo goda novoy pyatiletki" (The budget of the first year of the new Five-Year Plan), *Finansy SSSR*, No. 1, 1971.
Garbuzov, V.F., "Gosudarstvennyy byudzhet 1972 goda i zadachi finorganov" (The 1972 State Budget and the tasks of financial organs), *Finansy SSSR*, No. 1, 1972.
Garbuzov, V.F., "Byudzhet reshayushchego goda pyatiletki" (The budget of the decisive year of the Five-Year Plan), *Finansy SSSR*, No. 1, 1973.
Garbuzov, V.F., "Byudzhet chetvertogo goda pyatiletki" (The budget of the fourth year of the Five-Year Plan), *Finansy SSSR*, No. 1, 1974.
Garbuzov, V.F., "Byudzhet zavershayushchego goda pyatiletki" (The budget of the final year of the Five-Year Plan), *Finansy SSSR*, No. 1, 1975.
Garbuzov, V.F., "30-letiye pobedy v Velikoy Otechestvennoy voyne i finansy" (The 30th Anniversary of the victory in the Great Patriotic War and finance), *Finansy SSSR*, No. 5, 1975.
Garbuzov, V.F., "Byudzhet pervogo goda desyatoy pyatiletki" (The budget of the first year of the Tenth Five-Year Plan), *Finansy SSSR*, No. 1, 1976.
Garbuzov, V.F., "Resheniya XXV s'yezda KPSS i zadachi finansovoy sistemy" (The decisions of the 25th CPSU Congress and the tasks of the financial system), *Finansy SSSR*, No. 5, 1976.
Garbuzov, V.F., "Byudzhet vtorogo goda pyatiletki" (The budget of the second year of the Five-Year Plan), *Finansy SSSR*, No. 12, 1976.
Garbuzov, V.F. "Finansovaya politika KPSS" (The financial policy of the CPSU), *Planovoye khozyaystvo*, No. 7, 1977.
Garbuzov, V.F., et al., *Problemy razvitiya sotsialisticheskikh finansov* (Problems of the development of socialist finance). Moscow, Finansy, 1977.
Garbuzov, V.F., "Byudzhet tret'yego goda pyatiletki" (The budget of the third year of the Five-Year Plan), *Finansy SSSR*, No. 1, 1978.
Gerashchenko, V.S., ed. *Denezhnoye obrashcheniye i kredit SSSR: Uchebnik* (Money circulation and credit of the USSR: a textbook). Moscow, Finansy, 1970.
Gerashchenko, V.S., ed., *Operatsionnaya tekhnika i uchet v Gosudarstvennom banke* (Operations technology and accounting at the State Bank). Moscow, Finansy, 1975.

Gnutov, A.P. "Sberkassa segodnya: itogi i zadachi" (The savings banks today: results and tasks), *Finansy SSSR,* No. 12, 1974.

Goloshchapov, V., et al., *Byudzhetnyy uchet* (Budget accounting). Moscow, Gosfinizdat, 1963.

Gosplan (USSR State Planning Commission), *Metodicheskiye ukazaniya k razrabotke gosudarstvennykh planov razvitiya narodnogo khozyaystva SSSR* (Methodological instructions for the drafting of State Plan of USSR national economic development). Moscow, Ekonomika, 1974.

Gostrud (State Committee for Labor and Wages of the USSR Council of Ministers) *Trud i zarabotnaya plata v SSSR* (Labor and wages in the USSR), second edition. Moscow, Ekonomika, 1974.

"Gosudarstvennoye strakhovaniye v SSSR za 30 poslevoyennykh let" (State Insurance in the USSR During the 30 Postwar Years), *Finansy SSSR,* No. 4, 1975.

Gusakov, A.D., *Planirovaniye denezhnogo obrashcheniya v SSSR: Ocherki teorii, istorii i organizatsii* (Planning of the money circulation in the USSR: studies on the theory, history and organization). Moscow, Finansy, 1974.

Gusakov, A.D., and Dymshits, I.A., *Denezhnoye obrashcheniye i kredit SSSR* (Money circulation and credit of the USSR). Moscow, Gosfinizdat, 1951.

Holzman, Franklyn D., *Financial Checks of Soviet Defense Expenditures.* Lexington, Mass., D.C. Heath and Co., 1975.

Ikonnikov, V., *Denezhnoye obrashcheniye i kredit SSSR: Uchebnik* (Money circulation and credit of the USSR: a textbook). Moscow, Gosfinizdat, 1962.

Ivanitskiy, V.I., ed., *Ekonomika sovetskoy torgovli: Uchebnik* (Soviet trade economics: a textbook). Moscow, Ekonomika, 1977.

Ivensen, T., "Voprosy prognozirovaniya denezhnykh sberezheniy naseleniy" (Problems of forecasting the monetary savings of the population), *Ekonomicheskiye nauki,* No. 11, 1973.

Kachalina, L., "Osnovnyye napravleniya mekhanizatsii i ratsionalizatsii upravlencheskogo truda" (The main directions of the mechanization and rationalization of administrative labor), *Planovoye Khozyaystvo,* No. 1, 1976.

Kalitevskaya, A.V., et al., compilers, *O byudzhetnykh pravakh Soyuza SSR, soyuznykh respublik i mestnykh sovetov deputatov trudyashchikhsya* (About the budget rights of the USSR, Union Republics and local Soviets). Moscow, Gosyurizdat, 1963.

Kapelyush, Ya., "Tipichen li Kuchkin?" (Is Kuchkin typical?), *Literaturnaya Gazeta,* 28 June 1978.

Karr, Miriam, "CMEA Debt Review," East-West Markets, Chase World Information Co., New York, 15 May 1975.

Kashin, Yu. I., "Nekotoryye problemy sovershenstvovaniya planirovaniya denezhnogo obrashcheniya" (Some problems of improvement of planning of money circulation), *Den'gi i kredit,* No. 5, 1973.

Kheyfets, S.B., and Zlatkis, B.I., *Sostavleniye i ispol'zovaniye finansovogo plana mestnoy promyshlennosti* (The formulation and utilization of the financial plan of local industry). Moscow, Finansy, 1976.

Khodorovich, M.I., "Dokhody mestnykh byudzhetov ot strakhovykh platezhey" (Revenues of local budgets from insurance payments), *Finansy SSSR,* No. 8, 1975.

Kisman, N., and Slavnyy, I., *Sovetskiye finansisty v pyatoy pyatiletke* (Soviet financial experts during the Fifth Five-Year Plan). Moscow, Gosfinizdat, 1958.

Komarov, V. Ye., and Chernyavskiy, U.G., *Dokhody i potrebleniye naseleniya SSSR* (The income and consumption of the USSR population). Moscow, Nauka, 1973.

Konnik, I.I., *Zakonomernosti vzaimosvyazi tovarnogo i denezhnogo obrashcheniya* (The objective laws of the interrelation of the commodity and money circulation). Moscow, Mysl', 1968.

Koryakin, S.F., *Ekonomika morskogo transporta: Uchebnik* (Maritime fleet transport: a textbook), third edition. Moscow, Transport, 1971.

Kostinsky, Barry L., *Description and Analysis of Soviet Foreign Trade Statistics.* U.S. Department of Commerce, Foreign Demographic Analysis Division, Washington, D.C., 1974.

Kostinsky, Barry L. and Treml, Vladimir G., *Foreign Trade Pricing in the Soviet Union: Exports and Imports in the 1966 Input-Output Table.* U.S. Department of Commerce, Bureau of Economic Analysis, Foreign Economic Report No. 8, Washington, D.C., 1976.

Kosyachenko, G.P., et al., eds., *50 let sovetskikh finasov* (Fifty years of Soviet finance). Moscow, Finansy, 1967.

Kulikov, V.S., "Zadachi organov gosudarstvennogo strakhovaniya SSSR v 1973 g." (The tasks of USSR State insurance organs in 1973), *Finansy SSSR,* No. 4, 1973.

Kurchenko, L., *Balansovyy metod v finansovom planirovanii* (The balance method in financial planning). Moscow, Finansy, 1973.

Ladygin, B.N. and Zotova, N.A., eds., *Sotsialisticheskaya ekonomicheskaya integratsiya: Uchebnoye posobiye* (Socialist economic integration: a textbook). Moscow, Mysl', 1977.

Larionov, K., et al., *Dokhody gosudarstvennogo byudzheta ot sotsialisticheskogo khozyaystva* (Revenues of the state budget from the socialist sector). Moscow, Gosfinizdat, 1954.

Laulan, Yves, ed., *Banking, Money and Credit in Eastern Europe,* Main Findings of Colloquium held 24–26 January 1973, Brussels, 1973.

Lavrov, V.V. and Plotnikov, K.N., *Gosudarstvennyy byudzhet SSSR: Uchebnik* (The USSR State Budget: a textbook). Moscow, Finansy, 1968.

Lavrov, V.V., and Plotnikov, K.N., *Gosudarstvennyy byudzhet SSSR: Uchebnik* (The USSR State Budget: a textbook), second edition. Moscow, Finansy, 1975.

Lavrushin, O.I., *Ekonomicheskaya rol' bankovskogo kredita* (The economic role of bank credit). Moscow, Finansy, 1977.

Levchuk, I.V., *Ssudnyy fond i kredit* (The loan fund and credit). Moscow, Finansy, 1971.

Levchuk, I.V., *Gosbank i intensifikatsiya proizvodstva* (Gosbank and the intensification of production). Moscow, Finansy, 1977.

Liberman, Ya. G., *Gosudarstvennyy byudzhet v novykh usloviyakh khozyaystvovaniya* (The State Budget under the new conditions of management). Moscow, Nauka, 1970.

Makarenko, N.K., compiler, *Sbornik postanovlenii VTsSPS* (Collection of resolutions of the All-Union Trade Union Association), October–November 1975. Moscow, Profizdat, 1976.

Malyshev, I.S., *Vazhneyshiye problemy sotsialisticheskogo vosproizvodstva* The most important problems of socialist reproduction). Moscow, Statistika, 1968.

Marachevskaya, R.A., "O kontrole finorganov za uplatoy v byudzhet podokhodnogo naloga khozorganami obshchestvennykh organizatsiy" (On the control of financial organs over the payment to the budget of income taxes by the economic organs of public organizations), *Finansy SSSR,* No. 1, 1978.

Maslennikov, V.N., "Vypolneniye plana gosudarstvennykh dokhodov—vazhneyshaya zadacha finansovykh organov" (The fulfillment of the plan of state revenues is the most important task of finance organs), *Finansy SSSR,* No. 3, 1976.

Maslennikov, V.N. and Kheyfits, S.B., *Vzaimootnosheniya s byudzhetom predpriyatiy mestnoy promyshlennosti i bytovogo obsluzhivaniya* (Interrelations with the budget of enterprises of local industry and consumer services). Moscow, Finansy, 1971.

Massarygin, F.S., *Finansovaya sistema SSSR* (The USSR financial system). Moscow, Izdatel'stvo Moskovskogo gosudarstvennogo universiteta, 1968.

Massarygin, F.S., *Kreditnaya sistema SSSR* (The USSR credit system). Moscow, Izdatel'stvo Msokovskogo gosudarstvennogo universiteta, 1974.

Mayer, V. "Aktual'nyye problemy povysheniya narodnogo blagosostoyaniya" (Urgent problems of increasing the national well-being), *Voprosy Ekonomiki,* No. 11, 1977.

Melkov, A. Ye., *Kreditnyye resursy Gosudarstvennogo banka SSSR* (Credit resources of the USSR State Bank). Moscow, Finansy, 1969.
Millionshchikov, A., *Nenalogovyye dokhody* (Nontax revenues). Moscow, Finansy, 1967.
Millar, James R., "History and Analysis of Sovet Domestic Bond Policy," *Soviet Studies,* Vol. XXVII, No. 4, October 1975.
Ministerstvo Finansov SSSR, *Gosudarstvennyye byudzhety soyuznykh respublik v pyatoy pyatiletke: Statisticheskiy sbornik* (State Budgets of Union Republics in the Fifth Five-Year Plan: statistical handbook). Moscow, Gosfinizdat, 1957 (designated in short form citation as *Byudzhet* 57).
Ministerstvo Finansov SSSR, *Gosudarstvennyy byudzhet SSSR i byudzhety soyuznykh respublik: Statisticheskyy sbornik* (The USSR State Budget and Budgets of Union Republics: statistical handbook). Moscow, Finansy, 1962, 1966, 1972 and 1976. (A series of statistical handbooks; individual volumes are designated in short form citation by the year of publication—for example, *Byudzhet 62).*
Ministerstvo Vneshney Torgovli, *Tamozhennyy tarif SSSR* (Customs duties of the USSR). Moscow, Vneshtorgizdat, 1971.
Ministerstvo Vneshney Torgovli, *Vneshnyaya torgovlya SSSR v 1975 g.: Statisticheskyy sbornik* (Foreign trade of the USSR in 1975: statistical yearbook). Moscow, Vneshtorgizdat, 1976.
Mochalov, V.V., "O masse deneg, neobkhodimykh dlya khozyaystvennogo oborota" (On the amount of money necessary for the economic turnover), *Den'gi i kredit,* No. 11, 1973.
Mochalov, V.V., "O priroste massy deneg v obrashchenii" (On the increase of the amount of money in circulation), *Den'gi i kredit,* No. 7, 1974.
Motylev, L.A., ed., *Gosudarstvennoye strakhovaniye v SSSR: Uchebnik* (State insurance in the USSR: a textbook). Moscow, Finansy, 1975.
Motylev, L.A., "Udarnym trudom zavershim devyatuyu pyatiletku" (By shock work let us complete the Ninth Five-Year Plan), *Finansy SSSR,* No. 4, 1975.
Motylev, L.A., "Sovershenstvovat' i razvivat' gosudarstvennoye strakhovaniye" (Improve and develop state insurance), *Finansy SSSR,* No. 5, 1976.
Motylev, L.A., "Razvitiye gosudarstvennogo strakhovaniya" (The development of state insurance), *Den'gi i kredit,* No. 2, 1978.
Nikitin, S., "Inostrannyy turizm v desyatoy pyatiletke" (Foreign tourism during the Tenth Five-Year Plan), *Vneshnyaya Torgovlya SSSR,* No. 9, 1976.
Orlov, V.A., *Mezhotraslevyye svyazi torgovli* (Intersectoral ties of trade). Moscow, Ekonomika, 1975.

Orlov, V.M., "Ukrepleniye gosudarstvennoy distsipliny v khozyaystvennoy deyatel'nosti," (Strengthening of state discipline in economic activities), *Sovetskoe Gosudarstvvo i Pravo,* No. 8, 1977.

Pavlov, V.S., ed., *Mestnyye byudzhety SSSR: Statisticheskiy sbornik* (Local budgets of the USSR: a statistical collection). Moscow, Finansy, 1970.

Pchelin, P. Ya., et al., eds. *Gosudarstvennyy bank SSSR v 1971–1975 gg.* (The USSR State Bank in 1971–1975). Moscow, Finansy, 1976.

"Plan devyatoy pyatiletki vypolnen dosrochno" (The plan of the Ninth Five-Year Plan has been fulfilled ahead of time), Finansy SSSR, No. 12, 1976.

Plotnikov, K.N., *Byudzhet sotsialisticheskogo gosudarstva (*Budget of the socialist state). Leningrad, Gosfinizdat, 1978.

Popadyuk, K.N., *Finansy i kredit v raspredelenii natsional'nogo dokhoda* (Finance and credit in the distribution of the national income). Moscow, Finansy, 1973.

Poskonov, A.A., et al., eds., *Kreditno-denezhnaya sistema SSSR: K 50-letiyu Velikoy Oktyabr'skoy sotsialisticheskoy revolyutsii* (The credit and money system of the USSR: On the Fiftieth Anniversary of the Great October Socialist Revolution). Moscow, Finansy, 1967.

Powell, Raymond P., "Monetary Statistics," in Vladimir G. Treml and John P. Hardt (eds.), *Soviet Economic Statistics.* Durham, North Carolina, Duke University Press, 1972.

Reynin, S.N., ed., *Spravochnik po smetnomu delu v stroitel'stve* (*v normakh i tsenakh 1969 g*) Manual on estimating in construction (in the norms and prices of 1969), Vol. II, second edition. Moscow, Stroyizdat, 1974.

Reytman, L.I., *Lichnoye strakhovaniye v SSSR* (Personal insurance in the USSR). Moscow, Finansy, 1969.

Rusin, Z. Kh. and Eydinova, L.L., eds., *Gosudarstvennyy byudzhet SSSR: Uchebnik* (The USSR State Budget: a textbook), third edition. Moscow, Finansy, 1975.

Ryauzov, N.N. and Titel'baum, N.P., *Statistika torgovli: Uchebnik* (Trade statistics: a textbook). Moscow, Statistika, 1976.

Rybin, V.I. and Shrayber, I.I., "Nekotoryye voprosy denezhnogo oborota," (Some problems of the money turnover), *Den'gi i kredit,* No. 12, 1977.

Ryndin, P.V., "Bol'shiye zadachi" (Great tasks), *Den'gi i kredit,* No. 4, 1977.

San'kov, G.V. and Ol'khova, R.G., *Kredit i formirovaniye oborotnykh sredstv* (Credit and the formation of working capital). Moscow, Finansy, 1975.

Schroeder, Gertrude, E., "Regional Differences in Incomes and Levels of Living in the USSR," in V.N. Bandera and Z.L. Melnik, *The Soviet Economy in Regional Perspective,* Praeger, New York, 1973.

Schroeder, Gertrude E. and Severin, Barbara S., "Soviet Consumption and Income Policies in Perspective," in U.S. Congress, Joint Economic Committee, *Soviet Economy in a New Perspective,* Washington, D.C., 1976.

Semenov, V.N., *Rol' finansov i kredita v razvitii sel'skogo khozyaystva* (The role of finance and credit in the development of agriculture). Moscow, Finansy, 1973.

Senchagov, V.K., *Finansy i effektivnost' proizvodstvennykh fondov* (Finance and the efficiency of productive capital). Moscow, Finansy, 1973.

Senchagov, V.K., "Finansovyye metody stimulirovaniya povysheniya effektivnosti kapital'nykh vlozheniy" (Financial methods of stimulating the increase of the effectiveness of capital investments), *Planovoye Khozyaystvo,* No. 6, 1975.

Senchagov, V.K., et al., *Amortizatsionnyy fond v usloviyakh intensifikatsii proizvodstva* (The amortization fund under the conditions of production intensification). Moscow, Finansy, 1975.

Shelikov, S.N., *Spravochnik po finansirovaniyu oborudovaniya,* (Manual of financing of equipment), Moscow, Finansy, 1970.

Shekhovtsev, G.K., *Svodnoye byudzhetnoye planirovaniye* (Consolidated budget planning). Moscow, Finansy, 1976.

Shenger, Yu. Ye., *Ocherki sovetskogo kredita* (Studies on Soviet credit). Moscow, Gosfinizdat, 1961.

Shirkevich, N.A., "Voprosy byudzhetnoy klassifikatsii" (Problems of the budget classification), *Finansy SSSR,* No. 7, 1975.

Shmelev, G.I., "Lichnoye podsobnoye khozyaystvo kak sfera obshchestvennykh interesov pri sotsializme" (The private subsidiary farm as a sphere of public interests under socialism), *Izvestiya AN SSSR,* Seriya ekonomicheskaya, No. 6, 1975.

Shneiderman, I.M., *Statistika uslug,* (Statistics of services to the population), Moscow, Statistika, 1974.

Shubkin, V., "Predely" (The limits), *Novyy Mir,* No. 2, 1978.

Shumakov, A.V., and Zudin, V.S., compilers, *Knizhka partiynogo aktivista* (Book of the Party activist). Moscow, Politizdat, 1974.

Shumakov, A.V., and Zudin, V.S., compilers, *Knizhka partiynogo aktivista* (Book of the Party activist). Moscow, Politizdat, 1976.

Shvarts, G.A., "O roli kredita i banka" (On the role of credit and the bank), *Den'gi i kredit,* No. 12, 1973.

Shvarts, G., *Besnalichnyy oborot i kredit v SSSR,* (Non-cash circulation and credit in the USSR), Moscow, Gosfinizdat, 1963.

Sekretariat SEV, *Statisticheskyy yezhegodnik stran-chlenov Soveta Ekonomicheskoy Vzaimapomoshchy* (Statistical yearbook of member countries of Comecon). Moscow, Statistika, 1974.

Simonenko, G.S., compiler, *Sotsial'noye strakhovaniye v SSSR: Sbornik ofitsial'nykh materialov* (Social insurance in the USSR: collection of official documents), second edition. Moscow, Profizdat, 1976.

Solovov, V.I. "Organizatsiya kreditnogo planirovaniya i problemy yego sovershenstvovaniya" (The organization of credit planning and problems of its improvement), *Den'gi i kredit,* No. 10, 1975.

Solov'yev, Yu. and Shneyderman, I., "Metodologicheskiye problemy ischisleniya obshchego ob'yema uslug" (Methodological problems of calculating the total volume of services), *Vestnik Statistiki,* No. 1, 1978.

"Statisticheskiye materialy" (Statistical materials), *Vestnik Statistiki,* No. 4, 1971.

Sverdlik, Sh. B., "Mezhotraslevoy balans denezhnogo oborota" (Intersectoral balance of the money turnover), in V.P. Suslov, ed., *Nauchno-tekhnicheskiy progress: Modelirovaniye narodnogo khozyaystva* (Scientific and technical progress: Modeling of the national economy). Novosibirsk, Nauka, 1976.

Sveshnikov, M., "Denezhnyy oborot v sotsialisticheskoy ekonomike" (The money turnover in a socialist economy), *Voprosy Ekonomiki,* No. 12, 1974.

Sychev, N.G., *Finansy predpriyatiy i otrasley narodnogo khozyaystva* (The finances of enterprises and sectors of the national economy), second edition. Moscow, Finansy, 1973.

Tarasevich, V. and Leshkevich, V. "Gde cheloveku zhit'..." (Where a man should live) *Literaturnaya Gazeta,* No. 4676, 28 June 1978.

Titarev, M.M., "Resursy kratkosrochnogo kredita" (Resources of short-term credit), *Den'gi i kredit,* No. 11, 1975.

Tkachevskiy, Yu. M., *Sovetskoye ispravitel'no-trudovoye pravo* (Soviet corrective labor law). Moscow, Isdatel'stvo Moskovskogo gosudarstvennogo universiteta, 1971.

Treml, Vladimir G., *Agricultural Subsidies in the Soviet Union.* U.S. Department of Commerce, Foreign Demographic Analysis Division, Washington, D.C., 1978.

Tsapkin, N.V. (Ed.), *Finansy i kredit SSSR,* (Finances and credit in the USSR), Issued by *Vysshaya Partiynaya Shcola,* Moscow, Mysl', 1972.

Tsentral'noye statisticheskoy upravleniye (TsSU) pri Sovete Ministrov SSSR, *Narodnoye khozyaistvo SSSR v 19.. godu: statisticheskiy yezhegodnik* (The national economy of the USSR in 19..: A statistical yearbook). Moscow, Gosstatizdat and Statistika, 1956–1979 (A series of statistical yearbooks for the years 1955–78; individual volumes are designated in short-form citation by the year indicated in the title—for example, *Narkhoz 65*).

TsSU (Tsentral'noye statisticheskoye upravleniye SSSR), *Strana Sovetov za 50 let: Sbornik statisticheskikh materialov* (The land of the Soviets during 50 years: a collection of statistical materials). Moscow, Statistika, 1967.

TsSU (Tsentral'noye statisticheskoye upravleniye SSSR), *Sel'skoye khozyaystvo SSSR: Statisticheskyy sbornik* (Agriculture of the USSR: a statistical handbook). Moscow, Statistika, 1971.

"Ustav banka dlya vneshney torgovli Soyuza Sovetskikh Sotsialisticheskikh respublik" (Chart of the Foreign trade bank of the Union of Soviet Socialist Republics), *Finansy SSSR,* No. 2, 1963.

Vakhrin, P.I., *Formirovaniye osnovnykh fondov kooperativnoy torgovli* (Formation of the fixed capital of cooperative trade). Moscow, Ekonomika, 1974.

Vinokur, R.D. and Volkov, A.M., "Resursy byudzheta i ikh zavisimost' ot stoimostnoy struktury obshchestvennogo produkta" (Resources of the budget and their dependence on the value structure of the social product), *Finansy SSSR,* No. 5, 1976.

Volchikhin, V., compiler, *Spravochnik sekretarya pervichnoy komsomol'skoy organizatsii* (Manual of the secretary of the primary komsomol organization). Moscow, Molodaya gvardiya, 1975.

Volkov, A., "Problemy perspektivnogo planirovaniya finansovykh resursov," (Problems of the long-range planning of financial resources), *Planovoye khozyaystvo,* No. 2, 1975.

Volkov, A.M., *Perspektivnoye planirovaniye finansovkyh resursov* (Long-range planning of financial resources). Moscow, Finansy, 1976.

Voluyskiy, N.M., *Svodnyy finansovyy plan (balans finansovykh resursov i narodnokhozyaystvennyy plan* (The consolidated financial plan (the balance of financial resources and the national economic plan)). Moscow, Finansy, 1970.

Yampol'skiy, M.M., *Resursy kratkosrochnogo kredita* (Resources of short-term credit). Moscow, Finansy, 1974.

Yampol'skiy, M.M., "Resursy kratkosrochnogo kredita i kreditnoye planirovaniye" (Resources of short-term credit and credit planning), *Den'gi i kredit,* No. 11, 1975.

Yevdokimov, V.A., *Kontrol' za ispolneniyem Gosudarstvennogo byudzheta SSSR* (Control over the fulfillment of the USSR State budget). Moscow, Finansy, 1974.

Yevdokimov, V.A., "O klassifikatsii dokhodov i raskhodov Gosudarstvennogo byudzheta SSSR" (On the classification of the revenues and expenditures of the USSR State budget), *Finansy SSSR,* No. 8, 1976.

Zakharov, V.S., "Voprosy analiza denezhnogo oborota" (Problems of the analysis of the money turnover), *Den'gi i kredit,* No. 2, 1976.
Zakharov, V.S., "Rabota po denezhnomu obrashcheniyu: Itogi i zadachi" (Work on the money turnover: Results and tasks), *Finansy SSSR,* No. 4, 1976.
Zaydenvarg, V.A., "Kreditnyy protsess kak tselostnaya sistema" (The credit process as an integral system), *Den'gi i kredit,* No. 2, 1976.
Zaytseva, A., and Moroz, G., "Izucheniye vyborochnym metodom pokupok tovarov organizatsiyami, uchrezhdeniyami i predpriyatiyami v roznichnoy torgovle i na kolkhoznom rynke" (The study by sampling of the purchases of goods by organizations, institutions and enterprises in retail trade and on the kolkhoz market), *Vestnik Statistiki,* No. 5, 1971.
Zhevtyak, P.N., ed., *Finansy predpriyatyy i otrasley narodnogo khozyaystva: Uchebnik* (Finance of enterprises and sectors of the national economy: a textbook), second edition. Moscow, Finansy, 1974.
Zhevtyak, P.N., and Kolesnikov, V.I., *Pribyl' v sotsialisticheskom rasshirennom proizvodstve* (Profit in expanded socialist production). Moscow, Finansy, 1976.
Zhilyakov, V.V., "Poryadok izyatiya v byudzhet nezakonnykh i zavyshennykh assignovanyy po smetam na upravleniye" (Procedure for withdrawing into the budget illegal and overstated estimated allocations for management), *Finansy SSSR,* No. 4, 1979.
Zhurikov, V.N. and Solomakhin, V.N., *Spravochnik po oplate truda v kolkhozakh* (Manual on wages at kolkhozes). Moscow, Kolos, 1973.
Zlobin, I.D., *Finansy SSSR: Uchebnik* (Finances of the USSR; a textbook), second edition, Moscow, Finansy, 1971.
Zlobin, I.D., ed., *Gosudarstvennyy byudzhet SSSR : Uchebnik* (The USSR State budget: a textbook). Moscow, Finansy, 1970 (second edition, 1971).
Zverev, A.G., *Natsional'nyy dokhod i finansy SSSR* (National income and finance of the USSR), second edition. Moscow, 1970.

Index

About the author

Igor Birman was born in Moscow and lived there for 45 years. He received the Soviet equivalent of a Ph.D. in economics from Moscow State Economic Institute in 1960. He worked as a planner and a researcher, taught in various universities and was a special correspondent of *Izvestiya.* He is an author, co-author and editor of 10 books and articles. Among his books are *Optimal Programming* (1968), *Methodology of Optimal Planning* (1971), etc. Some of his books and articles have been translated into German, Polish, Czech and English.

Since his immigration in 1974 in the US he has published a number of articles in *Soviet Studies, The Washington Post, Soviet Jewish Affairs* and many Russian emigre journals and newspapers. He is a co-editor of a new quarterly, *Russia.* This is his first book since he emigrated. Dr. Birman is now finishing a book on Soviet military expenditures.

GPSR Compliance

The European Union's (EU) General Product Safety Regulation (GPSR) is a set of rules that requires consumer products to be safe and our obligations to ensure this.

If you have any concerns about our products, you can contact us on ProductSafety@springernature.com

In case Publisher is established outside the EU, the EU authorized representative is:

Springer Nature Customer Service Center GmbH
Europaplatz 3
69115 Heidelberg, Germany

Batch number: 10830943

Printed by Printforce, the Netherlands